HAND BOOK OF
LEATHER & LEATHER PRODUCTS TECHNOLOGY

HAND BOOK OF
LEATHER & LEATHER PRODUCTS TECHNOLOGY

Written By
EIRI Board Of Consultants & Engineers

ENGINEERS INDIA RESEARCH INSTITUTE
4449, Nai Sarak, Main Road, Delhi - 110 006 (INDIA)
Ph. : 91-11-23918117, 23916431, 23840361, 9312282370
Fax : 91-11-2391 6431, 2391 8117
* E–Mail : eirisidi@bol.net.in
* Website : www.eiriindia.org

Sole Distributor :
India Institute Of Consultants, 4/27 Roop Nagar, Delhi-07

Printed & Published By

ENGINEERS INDIA RESEARCH INSTITUTE

4449, Nai Sarak, Main Road, Delhi - 110 006 (INDIA)
Ph. : 91-11-23918117, 23916431, 23840361, 9312282370
Fax : 91-11-2391 6431, 2391 8117
* E–Mail : eirisidi@bol.net.in
* Website : www.eiriindia.org

Distributed By

Indian Institute Of Consultants (IIC)

ISBN : 81-86732-87-X
Printed in New Delhi (INDIA)

Rs. 850

**Printed & Published by Sudhir Gupta for "Engineers India Research Institute"
4449, Nai Sarak, Main Road, New Delhi-110 006**

Preface

The book **Hand Book of Hand Book of Leather Products Technology** covers almost all the basic and advanced details to setup own Leather unit. The new edition of the book is covering latest methods including Leather Processing, Raw Materials for Leather Processing, Drying and Finishing, Leather Manufacture, Vegetable Tannins, Vegetable Dyes, Preparation of Chrome Liquor, Physical Testing of Leathers, Manufacture of Exotic Leather from Ray Fish, Formaldehyde Free Finishing Recipe for Glazed Kid Leather, Canvas Shoes, Shoe Upper Leather, PVC Footwear, Industrial Hand Gloves, Leather Chappals, Leather Garments, Leather Sandal With P.U. Sole, Leather Travelling Bag, Leather Waist Belt, Manufacturing of Batting Gloves, Shower Proof Garment Leather, Suede Leather, Upholstery Leather, Cricket Ball (Leather), Football (Leather), School Bags, Indian and Overseas Trade Directory of Leather & Leather Products, Chemicals and Machineries

The book has been written for the benefit and to prove an asset and a handy reference guide in the hands of new entrepreneurs and well established industrialists.

Director

ENGINEERS INDIA RESEARCH INSTITUTE

4449, Nai Sarak, Main Road, Delhi - 110 006 (INDIA)

E–Mail : eirisidi@bol.net.in

CONTENTS CUM SUBJECT INDEX

Chapter - 1
Leather Processing

INTRODUCTION

Leather: Braving New Material World: Leather as a commodity has been undergoing major changes in recent years. World trade is competitive. Leather as a material may be unique, but there are several new materials, which are competing with leather for low-end applications. New world of material science is making available for various uses new materials with special properties at a rapid pace. Braving new material world is emerging a challenge for all natural materials. Whereas supply of natural materials like skin and hide cannot expand elastically with the demand, user demand is not likely to wait for any material in short supply. New man made alternatives for natural materials like skin or hide will be found. Prices of commodity products will be influenced by the material commanding the major share of the market. It is only a matter of time before leather may be priced out of law end applications. unless leather sector finds innovative ways of cutting costs and adding unique values to leather.

Leather: Changing Demand Pattern: The major use of leather, fifty years ago, was in manufacture of footwear. In recent times, for too many materials have emerged to supplement leather in footwear applications. The relative importance of non- leather footwear has gained so much that the global trade on non-leather footwear (US $ 30 Billion) exceeds in value the global trade on leather footwear (estimted at US$ 28 billion/year). The use of leather in upholstery is increasing steadily, while the demand for leather based luggage products like suitcases is decreasing. Changes in product mix of leather based commodities are inescapable in a market driven economy.

Customer Driven Changes of Market Economy Models: Customer preferences are undergoing sweeping changes. Leather as a commodity will need to provide added values to the customers. A modern customer values speed and reliability of supply as much as the quality of the product. Customer today is more demanding than ever before. Leather needs to encompass features hitherto unknown in the material. In the web connected world, suppliers of leather and leather products, seem to need to change the way the business is done. Slow and incremental changes can hardly meet the needs of the time changes based on innovations will dominate the future business models of global leather trade. Value for money is emerging the business doctrine. Therefore an attempt has been made to examine some likely changes in leather processing.

DRIVING FACTORS IN MANUFACTURING

Driven by access to materials: In the past, access to raw hides and skins was an advantage in leather processing sector. Various Governments could pass policy decisions against the mobility of indigenous raw hides and skins and restrict the access to raw materials for buyers access to raw materials and processed intermediates to tanners from other countries will become available and necessary. Therefore, protected access to indigenous raw hides and skins is no longer on advantages, unless there is a specific cost benefit. Many small and medium as well as tiny enterprises enjoyed benefits in leather sector because of policy protections and limited mobility of raw hides and skins under changed circumstance, prices of raw hides and skins will reach a global maximum.

Driven by acess to market: Market forces have driven manufacturing of leather and leather products in many countries. Cost leadership nations have commanded prices and created a market for specfic types and quality of products. Meeting an existing and quantified demand has been the model in the segment of market driven manufacturing. In this segment, leather is faced with non-leather materials for price positioning. Brand building in leather products also is influenced strongly by market force dominance rather than clearly spelt out differences in value propositions. In other words, the same product labelled differently seem to command different prices based on the names of labels. Perhaps, this trend will decrease with time.

Driven by Access to Technologies: Global leather trade has not been subject to technology driven manufacturing. Horizontal transfer of technologies in leather sector has been significant in the past. Patent licensing and dealing with IPR poducts has not been common. In the changing directions of business models, technology driven manufacturing and limited access to technologies providing special attributes is likely to become progressively more important. Access to technology may not be as free in Future as is the case now. Value of technology in the recent future may increase significantly.

Innovation Driven Manufacturing: Innovation in manufacturing processes and manufactured products providing to the consumer added value propositions, will certainly emerge the major competing force in the Global leather trade. Innovation driven manufacturing should add considerable value to the raw material and this value addition should be based on tangible and quantifiable parameters expressed in value propositions.

GLOBAL LEATHER PROCESSING PRACTICES: INFLUENCING ISSUES

Linkages to Down Stream Industries: Tanning industry is linked to consumers only through the down stream leather product sectors. The economic viabilities of the down stream industries will determine the strength and scope of tannery sector as well. Since the currently used manufacturing practices in leather product sector employ labour intensive methods, Asia has emerged the major destination for conversion of leather into products. The migration of tanning sector to Asia is partially on account of such linkages to the down stream industries.

External Pressures from Environmental Perspectives: Environmental awareness of societies is different in various social contexts. Compliance to regulations and stringency of legal frame work on environmental issues seem to vary in different social contexts. Therefore, an activity like leather processing is subjected to costs of compliance to environmental norms and regulatory responsibilities. Indications are that leather processing industry will need to meet increasing external pressures and incur additional costs of meetings the environmental perspectives. Paradigm changes are needed in both technologies and mindset in rendering leather processing eco-benign. If leather processing industry were to exit from red category of polluting industries, remarkable decreases in waste discharges and emissions are needed. It is an area of much needed change.

Cost Compulsions: Conserving costs in leather sector will determine soon the global competitiveness of enterprises as well as leather as a commodity. Whereas meat with about 14 times higher realisation than hides of the abattoir level enjoys a global trade of only US $ 16 billion per year whereas global trade on leather and leather products amounts US $ 72 billion per year. With further increases in unit value, volume of leather and leather products will need to decrease. Therefore, there is now a need to seek innovative ways of cutting costs in leather and leather product sectors. If costs are not cut, loss of share of leather in volume market can not be avoided. Leather will have to compete with synthetics for low end products.

CHANGE PARADIGMS IN LEATHER PROCESSING

Atom Efficiencies: Leather processing technologies have evolved with time. There has been many subjective elements which have influenced the evolutionary phase of the development of leather processing technologies. Emission loads of conventional leather processing systems are too large per ton of leather. Atom efficiencies in currently employed leather processing technologies are less than 40%. It is an area suited for considerable improvement with significant cost implications and advantages. Solid waste management systems employed today are not based on optimised atom efficiency models. End-of-pipe treatment methodologies are inefficient with respect to both atom and energy efficiencies. A change paradigm is necessary in this area.

Material Productivity: Productivity of materials including water and raw hides and skins is generally low in tannery sector. Recycling systems are not optimally employed. Change paradigm needs to target 100-200% increases in material productivities in leather processing technologies. This is a needed step, if cost competitiveness is to be gained.

Time and Labour Productivity: Change paradigms need to take recourses of modern advance manufacturing techniques for optimising time and manpower inputs to leather processing. Inventory management and operation research tools are necessary to optimise the productivity quotients in leather processing sector. The presently used methods are too empirical for comfort.

APPROACH PARADIGMS IN LEATHER PROCESSING

Biotechnology for Leather: Towards a Paradigm Shift in Leather Processing: A project has been launched to gain global technology leadership for India through causing paradigm shift in technologies for the manufacture of leather from chemical to bioprocessing. The project focuses on significant reduction of Total Dissolved Solids in treated tannery waste waters by replacing common salt through saltless and ambient preservation of hide/ skin, lime and sulfide free removal of hair and flesh through enzymatic processes and conversion of sulfate in the tannery waste streams to sulfur through the biotechnology routes . Biotechnological recourses through these three measures will enable minimising of environmental risks in leather processing to near zero values.

Knowledge Network Approach: For Biotechnology for Leather: Twelve institutions form the network are Alagappa University, Madurai Kamaraj University, University of Pune, University of Delhi, Agarkar Research Institute, Indian Institute of Science, Spic Science Foundation, Centre for DNA Fingerprinting and Diagnostics, Central Leather Research Institute, Centre for Cellular and Molecular Biology, National Chemical Laboratory and Institute for Microbial technology. The approach is to develop a knowledge network to build strength complementality.

Bio & Ambient Preservation of Skin: In order that ambient preservation of skin without the use of salt or drying is achieved, a concerted effort has been made to identify micro flora responsible for degradation of skin. About 500-600 isolates from a sample of skin could be isolated. These isolates are expected to include also aeroflora. Number of skin micro-flora present seems to vary with different environmental conditions from which the sample is sourced depending on season, type of animal (viz, good/sheep or buffalo/ cattle) and management protocols employed. A more detailed assessment has revealed the presence of more than 130 skin bacteria so far.

Ambient Preservation of Skin/hide: Some degree of success in ambient preservation of skin/hide has been gained through applications of both biocontrol and chemical control approaches.

Gainful results have been obtained so far in the application of some yogurt based strains (like lactobacillus) for ambient preservation of both goat skin and buffalo hide over periods exceeding 3-6 months. Some select organisms, which are capable of controlling the skin degrading bacteria have been recognised (and isolated) for possible applications in bio control systems in ambient preservation of skin. Potentials for bacteriophages have been recognised.

Lead Enzymes for Lime and Sulfide-free Processing of skin/hide: Lead enzymes have been selected and tested for removal of hair and flesh without the aid of lime and sulfide. These lead enzyme samples have been obtained from various sources. Some of the enzymes have shown satisfactory resutls. A possibility for a transition from enzyme assisted to enzymatic dehairing and removal of flesh is strongly indicated.

New Substrate for Assaying Enzyme smaples for Application in Leather Sector: A universal substrate based on a synthetic polypeptide with an internally quenched fluoro phore has been synthesized for screening of enzyme formulations of applications in leather processing. This substrate is being evaluated for its potential in providing a rapid and reliable assay method for enzymes suited for leather processing. This method its based an applications of MALDI-TOF for identifying the cleaving site of an enzyme formulation. Conventional assay methods based on Casein as well as specific substrates are being employed for comparison.

Application of Recombinant DNA Routes for A Lead Enzyme Product: Scale up processes has been done using recombinant DNA technologies & Polymerase Chain Reaction studies. Purification and potentials for cloning of one lead enzyme, which offers potential for dehairing applications, have been carried out. Further work is in progress. A cloned lipase, which is resistant to protease activity (against some enzyme samples) and whose structure is elucidated already, has been recognised. This is being screened for possible applications in leather processing.

Lead Enzyme Products

One sample of protease (which has already been upscaled and standardised) has been selected for dehairing and defleshing applications. Two likely enzyme candidates for upscaling trials have been recognised.

Some Lead products under Commercial Evaluation: Some sample of enzyme isolated from natural sources have afforded promising results in lime and sulfide free removal of hair on both bovine hides and ovine skins.

A public-private partnership has been built for accelerating the pace of commercialisation. This product has been evaluated under commercial scale application conditions with success. Further work is in progress to identify the specific enzyme(s) responsible for removal of hair and clone the enzyme products for global applications.

Concluding Remarks: Some indicative directions of changes in paradigms in leather processing have been examined in this work. It is becoming imperative that changing paradigms should commence from the livestock management, strategic sourcing of raw materials, inventory control pathways, financial management practices, vendor development systems and many other inputs to business processes. Leather processing as a methodology has evolved without taking recourses to scientific principles known to modern sciences and technology practices. The sector cannot hope to co-exist peacefully with the sub optimal output-inputs ratios for long. If the sector does not modernise the mindset and implement strategic changes, the sectori self may be changed by the forces of macro economics and market. Change paradigm in leather processing sector is not likely to be the cherr on top of the ice cream. It will be bread and butter itself. Questions ahead of the sector include as to how manage this change paradigm.

Chapter - 2

Raw Materials For Leather Processing

DETAILED ANALYSIS OF THE CHARACTERISTICS FROM DIFFERENT ORIGINS

The source of raw material for the leather industry is the outer covering of the domesticated animals like Buffalo, Cattle, Goat and Sheep. These are known by the name of hides and skins and are obtained as a bye product of the meat industry. The outer covering of the bigger species of animals like buffalo and cattle are hides and the smaller animals like goat and sheep are called skins. The chemical composition of the hides and skins are protenous is nature and hence they tend to putrefy or decay like any other protein like milk, fish, egg or meat.

Hides and skins begin to decay within two hours after the death/ slaughter of the animal and this is due to bacterial as well as chemical action-Bacteria generally attack the flesh side of hides and skins and multiply rapidly. They emit a fluid which liquifies the hides substance and transforms it into a compound which is soluble in water. The first visible sign of decay is the loosening of the hair and hair coming off which is technically called "hair slip". The curing is the process by which the hides and skins are protected from putrefaction. The putrefaction is rapid in the case of hides and skins specially when the temperature moisture content is high and in the presence of bacteria, enzymes etc. Hence the process of preserving the hides and skins till it reaches the tannery is called curing.

Curing is the process by which the hides/skins are protected from putrefaction by removing the moisture content or by the use of which inhibit the action of bacteria. Common salt offers itself as an ideal and least expensive dehydrating agent and bactericide and hence it is widely used for curing. In places where common salt is expensive or not easily available, dehydration is done by drying in the sunlight to reduce the moisture content or a combination of salt applications and drying. Curing is only a temporary process of preservation. The curing is known generally under the terms of wet salting, dry satting drying indicating the method of temporary preservation adopted. Thus the raw materials are received in the tannery in wet salted, dry salt or dried condition.

Choice of Raw Material : The suitability of hides and skins for preparing different types of leather is determined mainly by their physical characteristics. The difference in the chemcial composition is more quantitative than qualitative.

Vital Role of Selection : Besides the knowledge of the characteristics of the raw hides and skins the tanner should be able to select them properly while purchasing. The conventional methods of selection and grading prevalent in the trade appear to be arbitrary and are often unrealistic. They scarlcey reflect, and much less guarantee, the real quality of the hide or skin with the result that on final analysis, there may hardly exist a price difference between the highest and the lowest grades. From chemical considerations it would appear unlikely that analytical data alone would materially help in arriving at the quality of the hides and skins. An altogether different alternative which lends itself to critical examination will be to select the hides and skins in the limed or picked condition. In this stage the goods may be more realistically assessed with a certain degree of confidence, particularly with reference to grain defects and their ultimate suitability for the desired purpose and end use.

VARIATION IN QUALITY

Indian raw hides and skins can be classified as :

a. Cattle hides e.g., those of cows, oxen, bulls and calves

b. Buffalo hides,

c. Goat skins and

d. Sheep skins.

Each of them is entirely different from one another and the trade is also different. Apart from these variations in their existence, there are great inconsistancies in qualities in the hides and skins of the same genetic type. They can be classified as follows:

1. Basic physical qualities
2. Defects from diseases
3. Defects due to attack by parasites
4. Malpractice and adulteration

5. Biological changes on fallen hides.
6. Bad handling
7. Nail scratches, Thorn marks etc.
8. Bad flaying, trimming, etc.
9. Ineffective curing
10. Bacterial infection
11. Damages due to delay in transport, time and storage

Ante-Mortem Damages : Damages due to parasites such as mites, lice, warble, ticks, larvae from the warble fly, nematodes, worms and other bacteria are caused on the living animals. Ring-worm is caused by a mold like organism which produces circular lessions on the skins breaking down the epidermis causing the hair to fail off and harming the underlying derma, the leather making substance. Foot and mouth disease, hog and cow-pox and warts are produced by an infection of living animals by a specific virus in each case.

Post-Mortem Damages : Since many of the damages are caused on the living animal, the tanner should know about the details which will help him to pick up the best stocks for greater profit. Besides these damages, mechanical damages also occur. Brand marks, wire scratches, poke marks, thorn, healed injuries etc. are some and they can neither be avoided nor be controlled during tanning operations. Improper flaying also leads to heavy damages such as butcher cuts holes, etc. but they can be eliminated by taking proper care while flaying. Curing damages also occur due to the presence of the conjealed blood on the hide or skin when salt which may contain metallic contaminants, is applied. Excessive flesh may slow down the curing process resulting in the putrefication of the proteins. According to Furlong, grain cracks occur while the hides are being sun dried on the ground in hot condition and subsequent folding causes excessive damage.

USE OF PRESERVATIVES

Since the animal skins is composed of proteins, lipids, and carbohydrates, inorganic salts and water, they are liable to be putrefid by external agencies. Hence it calls for proper preservation and storing techniques. The animal skins or hides are also subjected to many damages and have an impact on the quality of the hide or skins. Probably no other damages occuring in the tannery practice cause as much confusion and concern as those caused by diseases and defects,. originally occur in the skin or hides as it is received in the tannery.

CLASSIFICATION

The principal types of hides marketed in India are cattle hides and 'buffs' or buffalo hides. The skins marketed are those of calves (both cow and buffalo) goat and sheep (from adult animals) and kid and lamb skins (from young ones). Skins from snakes, lizards, deer, crocodiles, and wild animals are also articles of exotic value. For processing such exotic skin special permission from wild life authorities will be required. Hides are known in India by various names, such as cow hides, oxen hides, cattle hides, buffs, buffalos hides, etc. In general trade, hides of large and fully grown animals are termed hides : those of under- sized or under-mature are called kips. Generally hides weighing less than 10 kg in the green state and 5 kg in the dry state are classed as kips. However, Indian cow and oxen hides and even those exceeding 5 kgm in weight in the dry state, are known as kips as they have generally a lower weight than those specified for hides in Europe and America.

Details of Classification : Based on the characteristics of the raw hides and skins, they can be classified in detail as follows:

CATTLE

1. Jalandhars
2. Agras
3. Darbhangas
4. Bihars
5. Purnea & Kishenganj
6. Ranchis
7. Bengal, Assam & Orissa hides
8. Madras, Ganjums Nellores, West coasts & Bangalores.
9. Hyderabads
10. Bombay hides
11. Kerala hides

BUFFALO

1. Punjab & Delhi
2. U.P. Hides
3. Bidar Hides
4. Bengal Hides
5. Assam Hides
6. Madhya Pradesh
7. Madras & Andhra pradesh
8. Bombay

GOATS

1. Northern skins (Punjab & Rajputana)
2. U.P. Goats
3. Northern Bihar & Bengal goats
4. Southern goats
5. Hyderabad & Bombay goats

SHEEP

1. Northern sheep
2. Southern sheep

Ref : (Theory and Practice of leather manufacture K.T. Sarkar)

Characteristics of Cow Hides of Different Origin : The cattle hides of the Punjab state are called Jalandhars. They are of large size, big and heavy. Most of them weigh above 10 kgms in wet-salted condition. Out of these good number of them especially from Ferozepur districts have warble holes. The hides are thick and heavy and are mostly obtained from the fallen animals. They lack very much in substance and the texture is very loose and pipy. The general condition of the hides is poor. So they are not suitable for the production of full chrome upper leathers. But these are utilised to produce vegetable tanned football, bag and case leathers. A few per cent of them are vegetable tanned as uppers for slippers for the use by local civilian people. These hides can successfully be used for the production of uppers for Military and Police Upper Boots, upholstery and corrected grain by heavy retanningleathers. The hides from Gurdaspur and Mukerian areas are plumper and heavier than those from any other area in Punjab. It is seen that the Hides from Ferozepur are considerably affected by warbles. Gurdaspur hides are at present free from this defect. Amritsar District cow hides are finer grained than those of Ferozepur or Gurdaspur. Haryana Region (Rohtak, Rewari, Hissar, Karnal, Sangrur, etc.) also produces good hides, but these are processed in that area itself, Kulu and Kangra hides are available in plenty in dried state. But they have extreme damages on the grain by thorn scratches and also develop serious grain cracks caused during transportation. They are usually short, stout and plump. But they very often get damaged in lime as the curing is done mostly by air drying method without proper care by unskilled people. Hides from Nepal and Kashmir, particularly from Srinagar Valley also are available. These are also quite short (particularly those from Nepal), stout and plump, a peculiar characteristic of hides of mountainous regions. These hides too have thorn scratches, holes grains cracks and curing defects. Owing to the ban on cow slaughter, only fallen or dead cow hides are available. Also because of the aged nature of the cattle, most of the hides obtained are quite heavy (mostly aroung 15 kg). Very few light-weight hides suitable for Madras E.I. or chrome tanning are available. The few available ones are not from slaughtered stock and so are not very good. The flaying is done very carelessly by the village flayers, large chunks of meat and fat are left on hides. The curing too is bad.

'AGRAS'

Cow hides from Agra, Kanpur, Lucknow, Bareilly, Rampur, Muradabad, Muzaffar Nagar, Meerut, etc., districts of Uttar Pradesh are termed as 'Agras'. Three ranges of hides are available. Light hides weighing 3 kgm (wet salted), medium weighing 7 to 10 kg. and in the heavies they exist as 10 to 16 kgm, 16 to 20 kgms. The medium hides are of good and uniform substance with narrow bellies, good size and square pattern, and clean grain, fairly free from ticks and warble damages. These hides are perhaps the best available in the country and are suitable for the production of superior chrome leathers. The light hides weighing between 3 to 6 kgms. produce excellent chrome upper leathers of light substance. But their supplies are very limited. Heavy hides of Agra are not suitable for full grain uppers but they are suitable for retanned corrected grain side leathers.

Bihars Cow Hides : Cow hides from Biharsharif, Patna, Monghyr, Bhagalpur, Gangtic Plains etc., are called Bihar hides. Although comparatively inferior to Darbhangas a considerable quantity of them are suitable for chrome and retan upper leathers. A slightly superior quality of hides from the provinces of Bihar obtained are Purnea and Kishenganj hides. Cattle hides from Chota Nagupur are classified as "Ranchis". They are light and vary from medium to very poor selection. The cattle hides from Bihar area can be classified District wise:

Darbhanga : The Darbhanga cow hides are known for their smooth and silky grain and uniform substance and are in great demand by the chrome tanners all over the country. The hides are from young slaughtered animals and hence are of full and uniform substance. This region is very fertile and the climate is good all round the year. The average weight of a cow hide is 10-kgm. yielding leather of about 20 sq.ft. in area. Hides collected from Sitamarhi, Muzaffarpur and Darbhanga are together classified as 'Darbhangas'. What makes Darbhanga hides so precious is the care taken prior to curing and also after curing. Hides are washed after the slaughter and the appearance is retained during the curing process. The grain side is often given a dressing by cleaning and in some cases the hair side is also oiled very lightly. The hides are selected and graded very thoroughly and so it is possible for a tanner to buy exactly what he wants. Hides are graded for quality and also for weight range and so a buyer is not put to much trouble while purchasing a lot pack. The selection and grading is done at 3 to 4 stages and so it is complete in all respects at the time of selling. This is a speciality which explains the tanners' preference for the Darbhanga hides.

Katihar-Kishnganj

In the eastern districts of Bihar, raw hides of a lower weight range 8 kms. and having fairly good substance are obtained but the grain is not so smooth as that of Darbhanga hides. These hides are used for the manufacture of chrome uppers and kips; but the bellies are emptier than in Darbhangas. Vein marks and flay cuts are the common defects in these hides. The curing is done by the merchants after purchase and the time taken for salting after slaughter may be from 24-48 hours. This delay itself may cause considerable deterioration in the quality of hides.

Siwan-Chapra, Purnea Districts : In this area, the hides are of smaller type and of fairly good quality. The hides are like UP. quality hides but have pock and tick marks. The average weight is about 9 kgms. The cattle are mostly of local origin and to a very small extent from Bachur and Haryana cattle.

Patna District : Hides from this area are mostly from local cattle though a very small percentage of Harayana hides are also obtained. These hides are a little bigger and heavier than the other types. The weight range has gone up in the recent years due to ban on cow slaughter, as only the older cattle are slaughtered. The coarser grain and spready nature make these hides unsuitable for fine grained chrome leather. They are rather loose in texture and sometimes show defects due to tick and pock marks. But because of their spready nature they make good raw material for upholstery and also printed case hides. They also yield splits of good areas.

Average weight 10 to 11 kg, giving more than 27 sq.ft. area.

Biharsharif District : Cow hides from this area are very much similar to the Patna in size but have a better grain and are rather lighter. They make fairly good chrome leather with tight grain but the grain is rather coarse and hence appear to be suitable for printed chrome uppers. The average weight is 10 kgms. and generally the hides obtained are mediums. Flay cuts are seen on some of the hides and these are said to be caused by the flaying, done in the early hours of morning.

Gaya District : The hides have a fine grain and are like the Darbhanga's as regards area and weight range. But they are not uniform in substance and the bellies and shanks are very thin tending to produce tinny leather. Hence they are not very much suitable for chrome uppers but make good raw material for vegetable tanned kips etc., weight range is 9 kms. average.

Ranchi District : In this area, thin and small hides are available, the weight range being as low as 7 kgms. Due to the thin substance they are certainly not suitable for chrome upper but can be utilised for producing vegetable tanned leathers. This is a hilly area and only small light weight animals can live. Further down South, in the Chotta Nagpur area which abounds in jungles and hills, still lighter hides of weight range 5 to 6 kgms are obtained. In the trade they are termed as'Samalpurs' and'Raipurs'.

Bengal Hides : West Bengal hides come to the Calcutta market in the wet salted condition. Usually they are from the districts of Howrah, Hooghly, Burdwan and 24 parganas. In fact hides from all places come to the Calcutta market. West Bengal does not produce the hides that are required in that state but the inflow from other places is great. The West Bengal hides contain lot of Butcher cuts due to bad flaying techniques. These are mostly lights, weighing between 3 to 6 kgms. with an average of 5 to 5.5 kgms. A small percentage are from slaughtered stocks. Selected hides are used for chrome tanning and the rest are purchased by the tanners from South India. The light Bengal hides are suitable for tanning into E.I kip of light weight. averaging 2 to 3 kgms.

Cow hides of West Bengal are small and light with thin bellies and shanks. Ticks and pocks marks are predominantly high along with other defects. Permanent wrinkles on the shoulder are also found on a few types of species which are extremely objectionable when they are put to the mineral tanning process. The speciality lies in the fine grain structure of all kinds of species in comparison with those of other provinces. The hides can be classified as follows: Since there is no ban on cow slaughter in West Bengal generally good quality hides are available.

Nagoras : These are not genuine Bengal Cattle. They are from Punjab. The hides are big and stout and yield good substance with a clear grain. But the grains are bigger than those of Bengal hides. Main defects of these hides are warble holes.

Desis : Species of different types of hides of cows, bulls, oxen and calves of West Bengal, Bihar and Uttar Pradesh come under this category.

Hatuas : These are small hides measuring 16 sq.ft. per hide with defects same as mentioned under Desis.

OBSERVATIONS ON THE HIDES FROM WEST BENGAL

Matiabur Howra and Barrackpore Slaughter Hides : They are almost of the same types of Tangra slaughter house hides. Nagoras are few. Flaying defects are of the worst nature.

Assam Hides : Assam hides are mostly smaller in size and more or less similar to East Bengal hides known as'Daccas'. They contain pocks and ticks marks. Orissa cow hides are also smaller in size and ligher in weights. Most of the hides are damaged by branding and infested with ticks. Majority of these hides are converted into E.I kips of inferior quality.

Madras Hides : Principal trade varieties of Madras cows are Ganjams, Nellores West Coasts and Bangalore. 'Ganjams' are from Northern/ Districts of Andhra Pradesh bordering Orissa state. They are light hides of poor quality. They represent one of the better grades. But many of them are obtained from the districts of Western Coast of Kerala South India, viz., Cochin, Ernakulam, Chenganacherry, etc. The hides are small, light weight and are mostly in demand by tanner to produce chrome leathers. Selected ones are used to produce full chrome upper leathers, notably hides from Changanachery and Central Kerala areas. Bangalores are of medium size well grown and plump. They are tanned by local tanners to produce E.I kips of medium and heavy weights. Bangalore kips have a good reputation in the E.I kips trade.

Andhra Hides : Hyderabad produces hides of square shape and fairly good substance and grain pattern. Hides collected from Sholapur district are noted for their square shape and good grain. Hides selected from Adonis and Gulbarga are suitable for full chrome uppers.

Bombay Hides : In this market hides comes from Andhra Pradesh namely from the districts of Circar, Rajamundhry, Vijayawada and Vizianagaram. In the Bombay hides, also include hides from Gujarat. The hides from Northern areas of Bombay State are largely spready in area and are of irregular substance. Some of the hides go for vegetable tanning and only a selected few are suitable from chrome tanning.

Cow Hides from Rajasthan : The production of hides on the basis of cattle population in Rajasthan is very low in comparison to the production of other states. It is estimated that the production is only 4.5% of the cattle population. No slaughtering is done and all hides available are from fallen animals and they are not of good quality. There is no separate market in rural areas. Sales are effected mostly through direct negotiations. Sales takes place from the merchants at Durgapur Marwar, Chittorgarh, Mavli.

Miscellaneous : Focussing on the breeds of the cattle the following observations are made:

Sindhies are available at Sindh area and they are heavier animals. The hides from these are very heavy and quite spready. From Punjab and Haryana we get the Haryana, Sahiwal and Tarparkar breed. These animals are still heavier than the Sindhies. The hides from these animals are very good and heavy but their supply, now is practically nil. "Gir' and 'Kankrerej' breeds are from Sourashtgera Gir hides are very famous for their excellent quality. These hides are rarely available in the Bombay market. From the borders of Mysore and Maharashtra we get 'holligars'. 'Nellores' and'Ongolc' breeds are found in Andhra Pradesh and they give fairly good quality hides. In Madras state the following breeds are available : Kangeyam, Punganur and Umbleachery. The cattle'Punganurs' and 'Umbleacherry'are mainly dairy breeds. The Kangeyam hides is of good quality. In Madras and Bangalore one finds often mixed breeds used mainly for dairy purposes. The commonest of them are 'Jersey', 'Red Dane' 'Gurneseys' etc. and hides from them are of good quality.

Buffalo Hides : In India, buffalo hides play an important role in heavy leather industries and in the footwear industry specially for ladies' and children's footwear and in gents' sandals. Pure vegetable tanning chrome combination tannages and almost all kinds of tannages are imparted to this class of hides and skins for different uses in the respective field.

Classification and Grading : Buffalo hides are more simple for the assessment into grades. Commercially there are two varieties available the 'good' and the 'Rejections'. Female animals are superior to the male animals. They are more plump and have good substance with a finer grain condition and less wrinkles on the shoulder. They are priced well. Dried and dry salted hides are usually disliked by tanners. Wet salted hides are purchased on the weight basis after dusting off a considerable amount of salt.

REGIONAL CLASSIFICATION

Punjab Haryana & Delhi Hides : Slaughtered buffalo hides are practically not available in Punjab. The buffalo hides are from the animal of the dairy type and are quite heavy mostly in the weight range of 30 to 40 kgms. But they are tougher in texture but thinner than the southerns. They are quite spready and thick necked but the substance drops suddenly in bend and butt areas. The bellies are also spongier and quite loose in texture. He buffalo hides show heavy growth wrinkles in the neck area and are spongier than the she buffaloes in the buff and belly areas. Hence, they are 'not preferred by the sole leather tanners, who prefer to buy hides from Uttar Pradesh area. Hides from UP are wider with fairly even substance. The cutting value is more. Punjab buff hides are mostly purchased by the local tanners. They plump very well in lime but do not maintain the substance through the tan liquors unlike those from the South. Buff calves show heavy wrinkles and pebbly grain. They are used by the local tanners, and also sent to Madras for E.I. tanning.

UP. Hides : Bihar hides are heavy weighing 25 to 30 Kgms used to produce sole, belting and harness leathers and cycle saddle leather.

Darbhanga, Muzaffarpur, Champaran Area : Hides from these areas are from Murrah and Desi Buffaloes. Mostly 'She' buff hides are obtained as most of the 'He' buff are sent to Southern Bihar for agricultural work. The hides have a smooth grain and are fairly uniform in substance all over. The uniform thickness and texture make these hides suitable for the manufacture of heavy leather. The average weight of Darbhangas buff hide is above 30 kgm.

Siwan, Chapra, Purnea Area : Buff hides of average weight range of 22 kg. are obtained. The hides, however, have a smooth grain and fairly uniform substance and appear to be good for medium soles etc.

Bhagalpur, Katihar, Kishangung Area : Medium hides and a few heavy hides are obtained from this area, which appear to be suitable for sole leather. They are not greasy and the unfrormity in texture contributes to good yield and strength. The grain is smooth and flat and sole leather made out of these hides is of a fairly good quality. Some heavy hides are also obtained but in 'He' buff hides the grain is rough and neck is thick and hard, as they are used as work animals.

Patna Area : Hides from this area are very greasy and hence likely to produce somewhat spongy leather. The substance is not uniform and the lower angle of weave pattern of fibres make the hides less suitable for the manufacture of heavy leathers. The hides are of medium to heavy range from 25 to 28 kg.

Biharsharif Area : Medium hides and a few heavy hides which are not greasy like the Patnas are found in these parts. The grain is coarser than in Patnas but the necks are spongy and the bellies rather thin. The hides give dark pelt after unhairing and in some places the grain after tanning is "drawn". Growth marks are seen on the 'He' buff hides.

Gaya Area : Hides are generally of medium size 20 to 25 kg. The uniformity in substance is very much marked. The hides particularly of female buff appear to be suitable for picking band leather or similar leather where strength and durability are required. These hides produce leather of smooth grain.

Ranchi Area : Mostly 'He' buff hides are obtained from this area. They are of heavier type having good strength and durability. But the hides usually have prominent growth marks for the obvious reason that the buffaloes are used for agricultural work. But for these defects, they produce leather of uniform substance. Extra heavy hides are available on selection from Darbhanga and Patna and a few 'He' buff hides from Ranchi area. Some of them appear to the quite satisfactory as raw material for picking bands as these hides have a compact fibre texture and uniform thickness.

Bengal Buffaloes : Bengal produces buffalo hides of medium and light weights, but the substance is poor. But a large number of Northern buffaloes are sold as Bengal hides.

3 Goat Skins : Nearly 90% of the goat skins produced in Delhi, Madras, Mysore, Punjab, Kerala and West Bengal are from slaughtered animals. Large numbers of skins are obtained from fallen animals in Bombay, Hyderabad, Madras, Rajasthan and Uttar Pradesh. There is very little variation in goat skin production. But the production is high during certain festivals when the demand for meat increases. There is a marginal increase every year in the availability in the country as a whole.

REGIONAL CLASSIFICATION:

Punjab & Haryana : Goat skins are available in all the districts of Punjab including Kulu and Kangra. They also come from Lahoul and chamba of Himachal Pradesh, Jammu and Kashmir. The goat skins of Amritsar are coarse-grained heavy wooled and quite big. They are mostly good for suede and lining. Selection is poor. The lower Punjab skins are better suited for glaced kid and in further south they are better. The yield a larger area. Goat skins from Chamba are also quite big like the Amritsars but much smoother grain and thinner. The yield in terms of area is much better in goat skins from Chamba than those from Amritsar. Most of the Kashmiri goat skins are available in the Amritsar market, and they come from Jammu and are exceptionally heavy and spready. They are very coarse grained and are often as big as calf skins. Srinagar goat skins are much more hairy and fatty and are slightly smoother grained, but spongier in texture. Kulu and Kangra goat skins are very soft, hairy, spongy, in texture and very narrow in areas. The hairs are white in colour. Because of their pelts characteristics of Kulu and Kangra skins, which have fine grain and good wool are very much priced by the Madras tanners.

Uttar Pradesh : Goat skins from this area are smaller and lighter than Amritsars. Their grain is of medium fineness and the skins can be used for making glaced kid of medium quality.

North Bihar & Bengal : Goat skins of these areas are comparatively small in size yielding about 40-45 sq.ft. of leather per dozen skins. They possess however, very fine grain and are priced all over the world as the finest raw material for superior glaced kid. As regards fineness they can be identified as Muzzafarpur, Daccas, Dinajpurs, Patnas, Calcutta kills, Kustias. In respect of size, Calcutta kills, Kustias, Dacca, Patnas and Muzzaffarpurs are smaller in size. According to the opinion of some glaced kid experts. Daccas are the best goat skins for glaced kid as their grain is fine, substance good and free from warble damage. The skins of Bihar contain warble damages. In summer the damage is more than in winter. Bengal goat skins are free from warble damages. Goat skins from Muzzaffarpur are in great demand and are rated very high in the market. They are superior to the goat skins from nearby districts. As the skins are taken off usually from young goats, which are slaughtered for meat, their quality is, therefore, good. These skins are usually completely black or white in colour, no brown or mixed hair skins are generally found. "Warble holes" known as "Pocca" in vernacular constitute a serious defect noticed in the Muzzaffarpur. It is possible to cover up this defect In the heavy plastered curing, but the defect can be seen on careful inspection of the pack even at the raw stage.

DINAJPURS ETC.

The other varieties of goatskins are (1) Islampurs (Dinajpur), (2) Patnas, (3) Biharsharif, (4) Gayas and (5) Ranchis. The Islampurs are from the Kishanganj area. The curing is done with Khari salt mixed along with earth. The cure is dirty. In size they appear to be more rectangular than the Muzaffarpurs and are in double or mixed colours. The Patnas have longer and coarser hair than Muzaffarpurs and can be easily distinguished by double colours as black and white. The Ranchis and in Gayas are inferior and coarser and are marketed as dry and wet salted stock. These are obtained in combination colours like the Patnas and the cure in case of dried stock is poor.

Deccans : Goat skins from Deccan area are more or less like those of U.P. The skins come from Hydrabad and other districts of Andhra Pradesh. The grain is of medium fineness and the skins are not so fleshy.

Southerns : The goat skins of south and South Eastern part of Madras and Kerala are small, fine grained and suitable for glaced kid. Erode and Thiruchancode goat skins are fine grained and of good quality. Skins which come from Coimbatore, Dindigul, Tricky they are not so fine grained. In Kerala goat skins come from Calicut, Ernakulam and other southern places.

MUMBAIS AND RAJASTHANIES

Goat skins from Mumbai are not fine grained but they are used for making glaced kid by some tanneries. The Kutch type goat skins are from Sourashtra. These skins are larger in size. There are plenty of goat skins available in Rajasthan. In most of the areas goat skins are spongy and coarse grained. Skins from Ajmer district appear to the good. since many of the people in Rajasthan are vegetarians, plenty of goats and sheep are daily sent to the slaughter houses at Bombay and Delhi from Kotah, Rani and Udaipur districts.

Since the sheep and goats are sent out best quality skins are not available in Rajasthan. The Chief centres from where these are sent are Jodhpur, Soni, Pali, Dulser, Palanpur, Abu Road, Rani and Marwar. From Rani station alone doily 2,500 goat and sheep are despatched daily. Next to Ajmer skins, selected skins from other areas are also good. The only place where from some export of goat skins is made is Nazirabad which is a good collection centre. In most areas the skins are spongier and grain coarser. Most of the goat skin available are mainly good for suede leather. Their weight yield is high, the skins having of good substance. A few Madras tannes buy skins from Rajasthan. Selected skins from Naziarabad are good for glace kid but Marwar skins are better for glaced kid.

Sheep Skings : Generally two types of sheep skins are available in India. One is the wool variety or Northern India sheep skin. The other is red hairy type. In hairy variety are mostly seen in Southern State.

Punjab Sheep : Sheep skins are available in all the districts of Punjab Including Kulu and Kangra. They also come from Lahoul, Chamba, Jammu and Kashmir. The sheep skins from Amritsar region are quite big and carry less wool than those from Kulu and Kangra, Chamba and Srinagar. Srinagar sheep skins are extremely large and fatty. Jammu does not have much of sheep skins. Kulu and Kangra sheep are quite small and are very soft and spongy. Afghan sheep skins are also available in the Amritsar market. They are equite spready about 10 sq ft. In area each, and fatty but have many grain defects. They do not make good quality leathers and hence they are sold cheap.

Bihar : In Bihar the sheep population is only about 2% of the total animal population. So only a very few sheep skins are available In Bihar. From the north eastern districts on the indo-Nepal border, white wool hilly sheep skins called 'Makda' are obtained These are white In colour but are poorly cured. The Bihar sheep skins are of medium size, good grain and texture. West Bengal sheep skins are medium and shall sizes with good substance and grain. Sheep skins of Orissa are small but of good substance and grain.

RED HAIR SHEEP OF SOUTHERN INDIA

Sheep skins of Southern India are of good quality, specially the hairy sheep skins which are of good texture producing tight grained leather. The red hair sheep is of best variety. In Madras and Andhra States, Sheep skins are mainly from the southeast coast in the districts of Trichy, Salem, Anantapur, Nellore, Ramanathapuram, Chittore, Coimbatore, Madras, North Arcot, Tirunelveli, Guntur and Cuddapah In Mysore they are mainly come from Bangalore, Kolar, Tumkur, Mysore and Chitaldurg districts.

MUMBAI

In Maharashtra, they come from Mumbai, Satara, Belgaum, Bilaspur and Ahmedpur districts. Mumbai sheep skins are of Gujarat and Rajasthan Origin. They are wooly and do not have a very close and silky grain. But they are very spready. Jaipur, Jodhpur, Pali, Balwar, Nagpur are the principal production centres in Rajasthan. The wool sheep from Bikaner and Jodhpur are well known. They produce good wool and are priced very much. The sheep of other areas do not produce as much or as good wool as those from the above areas. The best sheep are from Bikaner and next to it come from Jaisalmer and Ajmer.

Miscellaneous : Other important sheep skin centres are Delhi, Cochin, Trivendrum, Kolkata, Central Sourashtra, Gokilwad and Surat districts of Sourashtra. There is variation in the production of sheep skins from season to season Production is low in summer and reaches the peak during the monsoon and fall during winter.

1.50 Thus at a glance it is seen that India has got a greater population of cattle and the qualities are comparatively good India's export in the field of processed skins and hides, is increasing. Exports of raw hides and skins and semitanned condition have been restricted almost and eventually exports of finished leathers and leather products have increased and a greater emphasis is on export of finished leathers and leather products. India can compete with the other exporting countries by like China and Pakistan, in the field of tanned goat skin and can retain its monopolystic place with respect to leathers and products from goat skins as buffalo hides.

Increase in raw prices : Because of the mutual competition from the tanners, the raw skin prices have been increasing in alarming proportions. Unless some drastic action is taken into controi the raw price it may become extremely difficult to compete with other exporting countries to offer the Indian Leather at competitive rates. It is also noticed that many raw hides and skins merchants have become tanners, contributing to the increased cost to established tanners.

Recent Development : Because of the heavy demand from the tanners and increasing competition in buying the raw hides and skins, there is considerable mix up of the lots from different regions. It has become almost impossible to differentiate and choose the raw material based on the origin. The quick transporting by lorries by road has made it difficult in to go strictly by the origin. Hence the hides and skins from different places are purchased by the tanners in lots and the sorting and grading is done during the tanning and after finishing. There is also appreciable decline in the vegetable tanning both in rural areas and E.I. tanneries and almost all the materials are converted as finished leathers after chrome and chrome retanning. Even in the export scenario the majority of finished leathers are converted as various leather products and exported and only a minor portion of the finished leathers are exported as such. It is observed that about 800 of the value of exports is through the leather products and only about 20% is realised through the export of finished leather. The development of adequate technical know how, knowledge and development of speciality chemicals have contributed considerably to reduce the difference in characteristics mentioned in detail and have enabled the production of fairly uniform quality of finished leathers and leather products. Final grading will be an indication of the quality of the raw materials purchased.

CURING PROCESSES ADOPTED IN THE TRADE

Introduction : Hide begins to decay within an hour or two after the death of the animal. The decay is due to bacterial as well as chemical action. Bacteria generally attack the flesh side of the hide and multiply rapidly. They emit a fluid which liquifies the hide substance and transforms it into a compound which is easily soluble in water. The first obvious sign of decay is the loosening of the hair folicies technically known as "hairslip". The hide can be protected from putrefaction either by treating with some substance so that the bacteria cannot attack the hide substance, or by removing the moisture from it to such an extent as to inhibit the action of bacteria. This inhibition of the action of bacteria is technically known as "curing".

Types of Cure : The commonly adopted cure for the Indian hides consists of (1) drying and (2) salting. Drying of rawhides and skins is done in the air without application of any curing agent in 2 ways, (a) unframed and (b) on frames. These may be treated with arsenic to prevent the damage through insects, etc - Arsenication curing is generally not practised in India.

Salting : When a salt cure is given, they may be prepared and finished in (a) Wet or (b) dry condition. There is, generally, no difference in the type of cure adopted for kips or buff hides. The local tanners prefer hides in the following order of merit; (1) green, i.e., untreated, straight from the slaughter-house (ii) wet-salted, which remain wet and pliable and can be taken to tanning easily, (iii) dry-salted, as being generally better processed than plain dried hides, (iv) dry-framed and arsenticated and (v) air-dried unframed hides. On the other hand, the suppliers in remote places like Kashmir/Assam who cater to the needs of the tanners in far off places prefer a dry cure—with or without salt for convenience of handling, packing and saving transport cost. The main point, however, is the proficiency with which a cure has been done rather than its type and it is here there is considerable scope exists for improvement in several ways.

DRYING : (a) Unframed Dry Hides (sukties) : Drying the hides in the sun or shade, i.e., evaporating the natural moisture of the tissues stops the process of putrefaction. If properly prepared, these hides can be kept for fairly long period, but the difficulty is in the process of tanning, as they are not easily softened again. The higher the temperature in drying, greater is the difficulty in subsequent soaking and softening. The air-dried stocks become almost as hard as stone and, for that reason, these hides are often called "flint cured". It is seen that this method of curing is the simplest and hardly cost anything. The weight is reduced to and the minimum which also help in saving transport cost. But it does not give good results in selection, grading or tanning. In their preparation, these hides are never washed before drying and after drying and they become crumpled and do not possess the shape which is valued so much by the tanners. They are also improperly trimmed and have flesh, mud and vegetable matter adhering to them. Sukti hides should be kept off from getting damp during storage and transport or otherwise, putrefaction readily sets in. Further, hides produced for marketing in this manner are liable to show defects known as "blisters". Which mean that the drying has been uneven and decay has set in between the inner layer and the outer surfaces of the hides. This is generally detectable only after the hides have undergone soaking at the tannery and, often, as many as 25 per cent, in a lot may reveal this defect. Hence the tanner may not be in a position to weed out such defective hides while buying new stock. Generally, the weight of a sukti hide is about 40 per cent of the green weight of the hides, that is the weight after flaying.

(b) DRY FRAMED HIDES: The method of drying hides by stretching them on suitable frames is easy, inexpensive and requires only a littie extra care to turn out fairly good material. Hides, curedin this way, are considered superior to, and fetch better prices, than, the sukti hides described earlier. The method followed in drying hides on frames is generally identical in all parts of India. Raw green hides are trimmed at the edges and superfluous flesh, dirt dung etc. is removed by scraping. Cow hides may be even washed to remove blood, dung, etc., but buff hides are seldom washed. They are generally wiped with a piece of cloth or a handful of straw. It is said that by washing, the buff hides lose the reddish tinch on the flesh side which is considered a sign of freshness. The hides are then stretched and secured on wooden or bamboo frames by means of strings and are left in the sun for 2 to 5 days until they are properly dried. The frames are always arranged in an incline so that the rays of the midday sun do not stike them vertically. This helps to dry them gradually which is conducive to proper controlling of the curing. Unless the weather is incliment, the frames are kept out in the open during the nights also. Thereafter, the hides are removed from the frames and are folded down the backbone, hair side in. If they are too dry, or, it the folding is done with force, the grain may crack along the backbone, leaving a long scar in the finished leather. They may be further dried for a day or two before packing for transport. The shrinkage between weight and dry-framed weight is the same as in the case of suktis, namely, about 60 per cent of the green weight. Dry hides are immune to bacterial action but they are not exempted from the damages by insects like beetles, on storage. Hence the dried stock are treated with antiseptics and insecticides, like D.D.T., Gammaxene etc. in order to avoid insect damages.

(c) ARSENICATED HIDES : Not generally practised except in the case of known disease affected hides such as poxes, rabies affected dog bites etc. Dry hides, framed or unframed, if not treated with salt of other preservative, are liable to be attacked by insects during storage or transit. The commonest offender is the skin, hide or leather beetle and its grub devours the whole fibre tissue of the hides leaving only the epidermis or the thin outer layer. Largely, in order to prevent the loss from the grub, it is common to treat with mild "poison" specially the dry hides with a solution of sodium arseniate which is highly toxic to such pests. The treatment is given by immersing or dipping each hide for, say, 1 to 2 minutes in a trough containing the weak solution. The hides are subsequently redried in the sun or shade before packing. Hides treated in the above manner are called 'arsenicated". The standard formula is not always followed and the protection may, therefore, not be complete in all cases. The presence of a small amount of poison in the form of arsenate on the hide does not interfere with tanning, but trimmings from such hides can be used only for making glue as it is not advisable to use them for making gelatin. However this is not toxic to the skin while handling.

SALT CURED : As the name suggests, in the curing salt is used as the partial dehydrating and preserving agent. Certain patented preparations have also been tried from time to time in several countries, but salt is so far the best and cheapest material for universal use for curing hides. The curing is based on the same principle, that of rendering the material non-putresible by drawing away part or whole of the natural moisture content of the tissues; and in addition to that, the hide is also subjected to the preservative action of the salt. Salt is not a disinfectant fatal to putrefying bacteria. But, if it is applied before decay has set in, it inhibits the action of bacteria. It is therefore, essential that salting should commence soon after the hide is flayed, but not before the animals body heat is cooled off. In order to get full benefit of the cure, the hide must be clean and free from blood, dirt, etc. before salting. Its efficiency also depends upon the condition of the salt itself, type and quantity used the thoroughness with which it is applied to the hide. Impure or unclean salt results in stains which become perceptible only during tanning.

USE OF IMPURE SALTS : The main merits of these impure salts are their cheapness and availability and the fact that they are readily available. Their use helps to an equivalent measure the conservation of elementary pure salt. Their drawback is the presence of bacteria damaging to the structure of the hides and skins during storage before tanning, due to possible bacterial contamination.

USE OF SAMBHAR SALT : To reduce the cost of salt in industries, which can safely use impure salt, experiments have been conducted at Sambhar. Lake to manufacture and collect salt in two stages, i.e. one of the crop of crystals depositing between densities of 25 to 29 Be' and their other of the slightly impure crop, formin g between 29 Be' to 32 Be'. It is expected that the second crop salt would contain less than 3 per cent sodium carbonate and bicarbonate, and it may be practicable to sell it at a cheaper cost for industrial purposes, such as, for curing of hides and skins. The presence of a slightly high percentage of sodium sulphates in such cheap salts is not likely to prove harmful for this purpose.

KHARI SALT : The Khari salt is inedible and its use for curing hides is perhaps peculiar to India. It is used extensively for curing in the eastern States of Bengal, Assam, parts of the Uttar Pradesh and Bihar. It is generally a combination of sodium sulphate and magnesium sulphate and contains as much as 25 per cent insoluble impurities in the form of earth, etc. For dry salt curing this material is considered to be superior to edible salt, particularly, in the humid regions of Bihar Bengal. However, on account of the large proportion of clay, it provides an excellent scope for those who wish to increase falsely the weight of hides. Sea salt should never be used for curing hides or skins as, in the first place, it is heavily contaminated with organisms which cause "red first place, it contains magnesium chloride which is hygroscopic. The latter helps to retain moisture in the salt leading to easy putrefaction of the same stock.

METHODS OF SALT-CURING : The salt cure is generally carried out by two methods, (a) wet and (b) dry- salting. Pickling and brining the hides are also done but these methods are not popular in India. The details of the two main methods are given below:

(A) WET SALTING : There are several methods by which wet-salting can be carried out but the method commonly adopted in India is that of salting the hides in piles. This is done by spreading them one over the other, flesh side up, on the floor or on wooden frames or on bamboo matting in such a way that the pile is slightly inclined to assist drainage. In this cure also; only the cow hides are washed but the buff hides are generally cleaned with a piece of cloth, straw. After spreading a hide flat, salt (powdered) is rubbed in by hand on the flesh side. Thereafter, another hide is placed over the first, then salted on and the operation is repeated. This continues till the pile consists of 15 to 20 hides. Salt dissolves in the natural moisture and dehydrates the tissues and helps the drainage of fluids from within. Generally, the next day another application of salt is given and a new pile is made, but this time the topmost hide is laid at the bottom and so on. Generally, half the quantity of salt to be applied in full cure is used on the first day, half the quantity on the second day. At times, the operation is completed in two applications only. The hides are ready for despatch in 4 to 5 days. If the wet-salted hides are to be stored for a longer time. They are generally turned over at least twice a week during summer and once a week during winter. If and when moulds develop on stored wet- salted hides, as generally happens during the rainy season, they are cleaned with a piece of gunny. The quantity of salt used varies from 25% to 40% of the green weight of the hides.

STORAGE PERIOD : In wet-salting, the saline liquor permeates the hide which helps to drain off a large proportion of natural moisture and blood. But some saline moisture is still retained and the cured hide remains in a pliable condition. It does not become hard as in the case of dry cures, with or without salt. It is claimed that under favourable conditions, this cure may last for several months but in a warm country like India, it is not advisible to keep wet-salted hides longer than one or two months. The local tanners always prefer the wet-salted hide for their use, because of their ease of soaking unless they are able to get it in the green state which is seldom the case. With the increasing local demands for raw hides, the number of hides cured by this process has also gone up mostly at the cost of dry framed and sukti hides. The wet salted hides are generally preferred not only because of the better curing, but also because they are free from coagulable proteins, which are not required for making leather.

(B) DRY SALTING : The general method practised in Bengal is that the dealers, on receipt of the village hides, fallen or slaughtered, partially salt and keep in semi-dry condition. The Hides are first soaked in salt water for 12 hours or so and then cleaned. These may even be trimmed or fleshed, if necessary. After that, Khari salt in the form of a heavy solution is applied with the help of a brush on the flesh side. They are then left in the sun to dry. At times, the hides may be stretched on frames, but generally, they are spread out on the ground, flesh side up. During the course of the day, two more applications of the salt solution are given. In the evening they are collected from the drying yards and are brought under cover, folded lengthwise flesh side in, and are stacked in piles of 20 to 30 pieces each. In this condition they are left undisturbed for 2 or 3 days after which they are opended out and completely dried. At this stage, 2 or 3 further applications of salt may be given. Thus, by the time the process is finished something like six applications of salt may have been put on the hides. The quantity of salt used may range from 20 to 30 % of the weight of the green hides.

GOAT SKIN CURING : Dry salting method is largely adopted for goat skins in Northern India. Green skins are treated in the initial stages in the same way as that adopted for wet- salting. When the second salting is over, the skins are spread out and a "salt" solution is smeared all over the flesh surface. But however this method is no practised so widely now as was the case some years back. The skins, are ten opened lengthwise and the flesh side exposed to the sun, or suspended on long bamboo poles. Some curers do not open the skins at this stage but do it after drying, as it is claimed that the opening of a dry skin gives a straight and even shape which is difficult to obtain in the wet-condition. The drying on poles is usually complete in one day. Some times, however, it may take a day more. On the following day the skins are placed on the ground in the sun and the sides changed every two or three hours to ensure a thorough drying. They are then ready to be packed for transporting.

SHEEP SKIN CURING: The method of dry-salting sheep skins is essentially the same as that described for goat skins, except for certain minor differences. On the first day sheep skins are salted in exactly the same way as goatskins. The quantity of salt used is, however, small, being about 20 kg for 100 skins. On the second day before re-salting the skins are generally' de-wooled by pulling with a small stick about nine inches long. The rest of the process is the same as that described for goat skins. These are known as "papras" skins and are of thin substance.

ASSAMESE PRACTICS: In Assam, dry-salted skins (mostly goats) are prepared by merchants or their agents from semidried skins which they obtain from small merchants. The partially cured skins are first soaked in water for a few hours then rinsed to remove the adhering blood-clots and dirt and finally suspended from a rope or pole placed horizontally to allow the water to drain. When the skins are still wet, they are brought down and pulled and stretched around to increase the area. The stretched skins are placed in the sun with the flesh side up, and a solution of Khari salt is applied on the exposed surface. The operation is repeated two to four times during the course of the day. Complete drying of the skin usually takes one day, but sometimes it may have to be continued for a day more. Before the skins are dry, they are painted on the flesh side with a suspension of chalk in water slightly acidified with nitric acid. It Is said that this treatment improves the appearance and keeping quality of the skins and retards the deterioration through insect attacks. After this, the skins are dried and stored for future use.

PRACTICE IN OTHER STATES : In West Bengal also, Khari salt is used for preparing dry-salted goat and sheep skins but. instead of using a solution as in Assam, powdered, Khari salt is directly applied on the flesh side of the green skins. The skins are, as usual, kept stretched by nailing them on to wooden boards before the salt is applied. A minimum of two applications on two successive days is necessary before the skins are finally ready. In Bihar, a solution of Khari salt (salt 1 part dissolved in water 5 parts) is dried in the sun. Two to three applications are given on the first day and the drying is allowed to continue for one, two or more days, if necessary. In Chennai, powdered marine salt is used for preparing dry-salted skins. For skins which are known to be afflicted by specific disease like pox, dog bites etc. t, a solution of arsenic is sprinkled on the flesh side before they are allowed to dry completely.

OTHER METHODS OF PRESERVATION

Curing by Pickling : This method is mainly used for dewooled sheep skins exported from New Zealand, Australia and Spain. Pickling preserves skins partly by dehydration and partly because of the low pH obtaining in the system. Generally, sulphuric acid and common salt are used for pickling skins for preservation. Both excess and insufficiency; contain acid or salt are harmful. A pickle liquor should contain 12 - 15 per cent weight/volume of common salt and 1.5 - 2.0 per cent of concentrated sulphuric acid. Excess of acid may produce degradation of collagen and yellowing and less salt may encourage mould growth. Organic acids may however, check mould growth at comparatively higher pH values but produce more damage to collagen fibers. Fungicides like p-nitrophenol 0.1 per cent concentration (wt/volume) or PCMTB and permitted preservatives free of chlorinated phenols prevent mould growth. Before pickling is done for preservation, the skins are given a light liming, unhaired, fleshed, delivered as picked. A method of dry pickling of pelts with a product called Decaltal. N or other non-swelling acid like Naphthaleine Sulphonic acid type has been investigated. Wool from sheep are felmongered by sweating process and preserved by regular salting.

NEVER TECHNIQUES IN CURING

(A) Solvent Dehydration : Dehydration of hide by organic solvents like Acetone etc. or freeze drying etc. has come into existence. Such hides are soaked back very easily. This type of curing exposes more of the substance to be converted as leather. The weight is reduced considerably bringing a reduction in the transport costs. From the tanner's point of view they fecilitate an accurate assortment at this stage. But in this method chemical reactions may take place and even cost more thus involving greater capital, but its advantage is the comparatively easy soaking in tannery.

(B) Curing by Radiation : By the research carried out in BLMRA it is found that the micro-organism can be killed by sterilising the hides with suitable doses or radiation attended by a very small rise in temperature and slight chemical changes occurring in the hide. They are then packed in polythene bags to guard them against reinfestation of organism. But this is not a practicable method and at present it is only of academic interest. Similarly controlled exposure to *'y'* gama radiation imparts good curing.

(C) Curing by Fumigation : Hides are fumigated with ethylene oxide and preserved. Thus sterilised goods are stored in polythene bag, packed and transported.

Red Heat : In India Rock salt Is most suitable than sea salt. Sea salt contain unknown quantities of Potassium, Calcium and Magnesium Salts which serve as nutrients for certain halophilic types of bacteria, particularly the red and violet colour and hide staining varieties. The hygroscopic Magnesium chloride content of sea salt, interferes with dehydration, making it more difficult and result frequently worse preserved hide. Rock salt is usually coarser and does not develop 'Red Heat'. The international council of Tanners have state that the ideal size of grain is 2 to 3 mm cubes, of preferably powdered salt.

Keeping Qualities for Differing Cured Stock

Nature of stock	Moisture content	–	Safe storage period
Green Hides/Skins	60	–	1 or 2 days
Wet Salted Hides/Skins	30 to 40	–	6 to 8 weeks
Dry Salted Hides/Skins	20 to 25	–	9 to 12 wefeks
Dried Hides	10 to 15	–	Over 12 weeks.

Additives used along with Salt. It has been convincingly proved that addition of about 0.5 to 1% of ZnC12 considerably enhances the curing and preservative qualities of salt. Similarly it is possible to preserve the raw materials using a mixture of ZnC12 and parachlormeta cresol or other preservatives free from TCP or PCP.

SOAKING AND LIMING

Objects of Soaking

The first major operation after the stock enters the tannery is soaking. This operation has two purposes: the first to wash from the stock the flesh water-soluble material that might otherwise cause difficulties in later operations, and the second is to cause the fibers to absorb water to restore them to their normal condition. Although the processes are simple, their accomplishment is often fraught with serious difficulties.

Removal of Proteins

Besides the salt used in curing, the water-soluble matter in the raw stock contains soluble proteins from the blood and lymph, some of which are coagulable. The soluble proteins extracted by water are excellent food for bacteria, which multiply rapidly and pose a threat to the stock during the soaking period. The removal of these soluble proteins during soaking is not easy due to the presence of the epidermis, which is not permeable to them, and by layers of adipose tissue on the flesh side, through which they can pass only with difficulty.

Dimensional Changes

During the drying of hides and skins, the fibers suffers a change of shape, as well as of size, depending upon the resistance to shrinkage in any direction, the rate of drying and many other factors. In curing similar changes occur, although they are not clearly so marked as in complete drying.

Soaking of Dry Goat Skins

Dry salted stock is very much more difficult to soak back properly than wet salted stock and the problem is complicated for goat skins because of the fact that the methods employed in drying them differ greatly in different parts of the world. Those that are first cured properly with pure salt and then dried cause very little difficulty and can be soaked back satisfactorily in water. Those that are flint dried require chemicals like caustic soda to aid them in soaking. Some skins are at first treated with impure salts containing alum and other materials that act as mild tanning agents, and the dried; they often cause great difficulties in soaking and subsequently in unhairing.

Percentage Water Uptake

In order to be soaked properly a dired goat skin should take up about 200 per cent of its dry weight of water. In practice, this is rarely attained.

Advantages of Drumming

If an excessive amount of caustic soda or other alkali is added to the soak water, the stock swells too much causing permanent strain that persists even in the finished leather as "wild grain". It is a sound practice to mill the goods in the soaking bath. This mechanical operation causes repeated flexing of stock that separates the fibres. The penetration of water and its uptake are thus facilitated. As a rule, goat skins are not fleshed until after they have been unhaired.

Soaking Heavy Hides

Heavy hides should be soaked for a longer period. Heavy hides that have been well cured may be infected with bacteria throughout their entire thickness. Antiseptics do not penetrate heavy hides very rapidly, and bacteria deeply seated in a hide begin to multiply just as soon as enough salt has been leached out in the first stages of soaking. Improperly cured stock offer a potential danger and it should be passed through the soak bath and into the lime liquors as quickly as possible. Sometimes it is desirable to soak such goods only for overnight in strong brine and then wash to remove the salt. Too much drumming or other mechanical action should be avoided as they cause loose and grainy leather.

SOAKING

Objects of soaking

1. To clean the stock free of the adhering dirt, dung, salt etc.
2. To wet back or to rehydrate the raw stock to almost its original state.
3. To solubilise the soluble proteins and to wash them off.
4. To being back the raw material to its original nature and to make it ready for further processing.

Since the raw materials may differ in their cure, (Varying from fresh green stock to flint dry hides), it will be useful to have a preliminary idea of the various factors that influence the soaking operation. For a good processing of the stock, the soaking should be done as thoroughly as possible so as to condition the stock ready for subsequent liming operation.

Factors affecting the soaking operation

(i) The nature of the raw stock and the type of cure.

(ii) The type of salt used in curing.

(iii) Quality and quantity of water used for soaking.

(iv) Temperature of the soak bath.

(v) Soaking agents used, if any

(vi) pH

(vii) Use of disinfectants or bactericides

(viii) Mechanical agitation.

(ix) Use of wetting agents

(x) Time – A brief indication of the influence of the various factors on soaking is given below:

(i) The nature of the raw stock and the type of cure

Generally cattle hides require a longer time when compared to the skins of the same type of cure.

Fresh or wet salted hides and skins require much less time when compared with dry salted or dry hides.

Dry salted stock takes less time than dry stock.

The case of soaking is in the following order:

Fresh Stock,

Wet Salted Stock,

Dry Salted Stock,

Dry Stock.

Generally the soaking has got to be adjusted according to the type of raw stock- Green and wet salted stock soak back readily in a shorter time, whereas dry salted or dry stock requires greater time and chemicals for proper soaking.

(ii) The type of salt used (if any) in curing

Salts which contain a higher proportion of Mg and Ca Chlorides are advantageous in shortening the time of soaking. That means marine (sea) salt aids in quicker soaking when compared to lake or rock salts which contain Na_2SO_4.

(iii) Quality and quantity of water used for soaking

Generally hard water (containing permanent hardness due to chlorides and sulphates) is advantageous in soaking as this helps to salt out and solubilise the soluble proteins and their removal.

Temporary hardness in water may not influence much, soft water if available in plenty, may also be useful. The quantity of chemicals and bactericides used must be adjusted depending on the quality of water used for soaking.

It is not advisable to use water having high B.O.D. content in soaking as this will help bacterial degradation of the raw stock.

If too little or insufficient quantity of water is used on soaking, there will not be sufficient opportunity for the stock to absorb water freely to the required extent, and hence non-uniform soaking is likely to be the result if too small a quantity of water is used for soaking.

If too much (a very large) quantity of water is used then the concentration of the soaking agents and other chemicals or salt used will not be strong enough to aid proper soaking and to prevent possible bacterial action. Or this will result in wastage of chemicals and make the process more costly.

The following quantity of water may be used as optimum level for different type of stock.

			Water
(i)	Dry or dry salted	–	800 to 1000% on the raw weight.
(ii)	Wet Salted	–	300 to 400% on the Wet salted weight.
(iii)	Fresh or green salted	–	200 to 250% on the raw weight.

(iv) Temperature of the soak bath

Soaking is aided by increase in temperature-but increase in temperature is followed by increase in bacterial action and dissolution of the hide substance.

Too low a temperature below 60°F prolongs the soaking period too much-hence the optimum temperature for soaking can be about 70°F to 80°F. Where the temperature of the soak bath cannot be controlled it is better to control the time of soaking or by, the addition of preservatives, especially when a longer soaking is required.

(v) Soaking agents used, if any

Generally commercial wetting agents or alkallies like NaOH, Na2S, soda ash or lime are used as soaking agents to help quicker and uniform soaking. Sometimes an acid/salt soak is also used. In all such cases the soaking agents used should be in such optimum quantity (in enough quantity) as to aid good soaking and to prevent the bacterial action, without making it too expensive.

The soaking agent used should not be in too high a quantity and concentration as to cause distortion of the fibre structure of the stock. Highly alkaline soak causes swelling, mild acid/salt soak is considered to be advantageous, when used in optimum quantities.

(vi) pH

Generally increasing the pH (to slightly alkaline) by using mild alkallies helps in soaking, but too high a pH or the use of caustic alkali causes permanent distortion of the fibres.

Bacterial action is maximum between the pH range of 5.5 to 8. Hence the pH of the soak bath should be preferably below 5.5. or above 8. But too low pH (below 4.5) or too high pH above 9 are not advisable. That means the pH of the soak bath should be just alkaline about 8.5 or 4.5, and this is about the optimum pH. The alkaline soak bath should be just alkaline (pinkish when tested with pehenolphthalein).

(vii) Use of disinfectants or bactericides

It is advisable to use these, to avoid any possible putrefaction during soaking, especially in tropical countries where the temperature is high. But if the atmospheric temperature is low, below 55°F, this may not necessary. Various disinfectants used in practice are:

(a) Liquid chlorine
(b) Bleaching powder – as to give about 50 to 100 parts per million parts of water.
(c) Sod.hypochloride

(d) Any permissible preservative –available from supplies or para-chloro metacresol

(e) Phenols or chlorinated cresol-

(f) Commercial trade products like 'Preventol' Para Nitrophenol etc.

(viii) Influence of Agitation

Mechanical agitation generally favours quicker soaking but too much agitation is harmful as it will tend to break up the fibres, especially in the earlier stages of soaking. Hence agitation should be done just to the required extent.

Paddle soaking is advisable especially for wet salted and dry salted stock. But in the case of dried raw stock a wet milling in drum towards the last stages of soaking is helpful, using a large float of water and using a drum having low speed 3 or 4 r.p.m.

(ix) Use of wetting agents

Use of commercial wetting agents like sulphated oils, nonionic dispersing agents etc. aids better soaking Teepol, Idet etc. are some of the wetting agents used in practice.

TYPICAL EXAMPLES OF SOAKING PROCEDURE

Type of Raw Stock-Wet Salted

Pit Soaking

1. Weight the stock. Soak in 400% water. Keep for 1 hour in the pit.

2. Give 2 changes of water using 400% water in pit. Keep each time for 1 hour. Mix well each time to wash off dirt. In the case of goat skin out open. Do a rough fleshing or beaming.

3. Give one more change or water and keep for 1/2 hour. Take out and drain. After draining take soaked weight and take to liming.

N.B. In the case of raw stock which has been stored for a long time keep overnight in the pit in the first stage mentioned above, and add lb of lime for every 100 gallons of water.

PADDLE SOAKING

1. Weight the stock. Collect about 300% water on the paddle of suitable size and capacity.
2. Put the stock in paddle. Keep for 1/2 hour. The run the paddle for 1/2 hour. Drain off the water.
3. Collect 300% fresh water. Add the required quantity of soaking agent and bactericide. Run for 10 minutes and then stop the paddle and keep overnight.
4. Next day run the paddle for 1 hour. Take out the stock and drain. Take to liming. If necessary do a rough fleshing.

Type of Stock-Dry (flint dry) hides - Pit cum Drum Soaking

1. Weight the hides.
2. Collect about 800% or 1000% water in pit. Add 3% salt and caustic soda-1/2 lb. per 100 gallons of water. Mix well and put back the stock in this water. If necessary place heavy weights on the hides to keep them immersed. Disinfectants like bleaching powder may also be added at the rate of 1 lb per 100 gallons of water. Keep overnight.
3. Next day, take out and check whether the stock has become wet and pliable. If it has become slightly soft put over a beam and scrape off the flesh side with a blunt knife to open up the wrinkles. Do not use too much force if the hides are tough. Then put back in the same bath. Watch for any putrefaction smell. If so make up a fresh bath by adding bactericide (0.02%)
4. Next day, take out, work on the flesh side over the beam using a blunt unhairing knife.

   If it has become fairly well soaked, put in slow speed drum with 400% water, 1/2 1b. of caustic soda for every 100 gallons of water, and then run the drum for 1 or 2 hours. Take out and drain and take to liming. If it has not become soft continue pit soaking as mentioned above until it becomes well soaked.

N.B. Whenever fresh baths are made take care to add the necessary wetting agents and permitted bactericides.

LIME YARD OPERATIONS

The principal operations which hides and skins have to pass through in the limeyards are (i) Dehairing, (ii) Fleshing, (iii) Cheeking, (iv) Splitting and (v) Scudding. The details of these operations will vary for different types of leathers. However, a general description is given below.

The primary object of the beamhouse operations is to get rid of the hides and skins of these portions that are not required in the finished leather and to put them in proper chemical and physical condition for the subsequent processes. In order to make good leather, this must to done in such a manner so no damage is done to the fibrous portion used in making leather nor to its natural structure. The stock must be put in optimum condition for the tanning operations that follow. In the soaking, dirt and water-soluble materials are removed and restored to natural condition by absorbing water.

EFFECT ON PROTEINS

For making most leathers, the hides and skins must be freed from hair and epidermis and from the glands of the thermostat layer. These structures are made up of proteins called keratin. The fibrous portions to be converted into leather are known as collagen. Both keratin and collagen can be destroyed by strong solutions of acids or alkallies but acids destroy collagen more readily than keratin.

SWEATING

The process involves the subjecting of wet hides and skins to mild putrefaction, which hydrolyses and removes the cells. When cells are removed the hair bulb becomes loose and the hair is loosened and scraped off with ease. This hair loosening by putrefaction is similar to the hair slip observed in hides and skin cured by salting or by drying has been unduly delayed, or in wet salted hides which have been stored for a long time.

SWEATING CHAMBERS

This process is carried out in the sweating chambers whose temperature is kept at above 20°C, and the air is maintained at a high relative humidity. The hides and skins are hung up in these chambers from overhead rafters. Owing to the comparatively high temperature of the chambers the bacterial action takes place in about 48 hours after the good have been hung up, & the hair is found to be loosened. The stock is then removed from the chambers and the hair or wool is scraped off. A good deal of ammonia and amines are evolved in the sweating chambers which assist hair loosening.

IMPORTANCE OF TEMPERATURE AND HUMIDITY

The temperature and humidity of the sweating chambers have to be carefully controlled. Even by controlling temperature and humidity uniform results cannot be guaranteed and damage to the hides and skins cannot always be prevented. On account of these reasons 'Sweating' process has been abandoned in most countries. The only application of sweating' at the present time is de-wooling sheep skins where wool is more valuable than the pelt. After removal off wool the skins are generally hung from beams in a closed room in which the air is kept warm and humid. During the process a considerable quantity of ammonia and amines are evolved and these assist in unhairing action. Just as soon as the hairs slip easily, the skins are removed from the sweating chamber and dumped into saturated lime solution, the lime solution serves to check further bacterial action and causes the skins to swell. The skins upon coming from the sweat chamber are in a flaccid and slimy condition.

USE OF LIME

In many countries all over the world, lime was, solely employed for unhairing, but later as a result of scientific and technological advances, the usage of other "sharpening agents" was introduced. Lime was used extensively due to the fact that it inevitably causes no loss of substance and weight. It is not dangerous in use, and excess of lime does not cause damage due to its limited solubility.

SOURCE OF LIME

The source of lime is chalk or limestone which consists of calcium carbonate ($CaCo_3$). Many limestones contain large quantities of magnesium, iron and alumina and are deposited in the form of clay. The presence of nagnesia and clay is injurious not only by lowering the quantity of available lime but also making it difficult to slake. The iron may get fixed on the grain as iron oxide and cause stains. Quick lime (CaO), when treated with water combines with the evolution of heat and converted into its hydrate i.e. Ca $(OH)_2$. This is very rapid and easy when the lime is porous. When it is over heated the tanner loses most of the available lime. Exact amount of water and good temperature will ccelerate the slacking of lime. Unlike other substance, the solubility of lime in water diminishes as the temperature is raised.

ACTION OF LIME

The action of the lime on the hide is both chemical and physical. The cells off the epidermis swell up and soften the grain layer and the hair bulbs are loosened. The hairs are scraped off with a blunt knife. The hides swell and plump and at the same time, the connecting substance off the fibre is dissolved and they become split up and finally dissolved. As it gives firmness the tanner takes a good deal of advantage while fleshing hides and skins. Lime also assists tanning by splitting up the fibre into its individual fibrils and thus exposing a greater surface to the action of tan liquors. This is advantageous for the leather in the later stages of tanning. In the case of sole leather the hide must be plumped to get weight and firmness. Another advantages of lime is that it acts on the fat and soapnifies them making them easily soluble. If these fats are not released from the hides permanently, then during the subsequent processes they will combine with strong acids, and cause grease spots on the finished leather or darken the colour.

CUSTOMARY LIMING PROCEDURE

The usual method of liming is simply to pile the hides flat one at a time in a milky solution of lime in suitable pits, taking care that each hide is completely immersed. Once a day at least, the hides are drawn out, the liquor well agitated to make the undissolved lime to dissolve and again the goods are piled one over the other and well immersed in the liquor. Since the exact quantity of lime which could be dissolved is unknown and excess added is only a waste and not injurious. Only the lime in solution acts on the hide and always to maintain the unifon concentration, an excess of lime is added. Where hides are suspended in lime water, which is constantly circulated and kept to its full strength by agitation, the unhairing is quicker than still laying in lime. Mechanical agitators are also in use to agitate the undissolved lime settled at the bottom of the pits to make them soluble, Skins are frequently limed in paddles or pits.

QUANTITY OF LIME USED

The quantity of lime used by tanners for different hides and skins is variable, according to the effect which is desired to produce. The strength of commercial lime varies from above 80 and goes down to 30% of available calcium oxide. A perfectly fresh milk of lime is much more rapid in action than one which has been used. This is partially due to the fact that some bacterial action takes place in an old lime and ammonia is formed, which assists unhairing in addition to the effect of lime itself. The lime in old liquors remains in suspension for a much longer time and is more evenly distributed.

USE OF OLD LIMES

An old lime is charged with ammonia and other products, which act on the skin. Lime has considerable antiseptic power and a new lime is practically sterile, but very old limes especially in hot weather, often contain large number of active bacteria. Their excessive presence is always an indication that putrefaction is going on. If their number is in excess, the leather from such lime liquors will be loose, and dull-grained and in extreme cases the hides may be totally destroyed. Old lime liquors unhair much more readily and have a greater softening effect than new ones. For firmer leathers the old limes must be kept within the narrow limits. In the case of finer leathers the qualities are achieved by adding sharpening agents to the lime. On dried hides, which are difficult to soften and have great likes are useful. Very old lime liquors containing an excess of ammonia and lime sometimes in hot weather cause swelling of the goods, with a destruction of the fibrous structure. Such skins produce leathers of inferior quality.

NEW KNOWLEDGE IN LIMING

In the old liquors ammonia helps in unhairing while in using the fresh liquors, bacteria plays a major role. Thus in the olden days only lime was used as the sole unhairing agent. The properties of certain chemicals were studied and they were put to use as good sharpening agents, for accelerating the unhairing process, reducing the time, labour, costs etc. Following are some of the chemicals which are used in leather industry as sharpening agents in the unhairing operation.

SODIUM AND POTASSIUM HYDRATES

In recent times, the use of caustic soda is recommended as a substitute for lime. Though its action is very similar to lime its solubility is greater and more powerful than lime and a solution of same strength as a lime solution is almost immediately exhausted, and also a stronger solution is dangerous to the hides. It has more antiseptic in action than lime and does not readily unhair without the bacterial aid. It also swells more readily and violently and it is difficult to keep the grain smooth and free from wrinkles. When caustic soda is used, it is easily washed completely unlike the lime. In the production of soft grained leathers, caustic soda is not used.

SODIUM SULPHIDE

It is very soluble in water. In a 2-3% strength sulphide liquors, hides unhair rapidly. A 30-40% solution of sodium sulphide is thickened with lime made as paste and applied on the flesh side of the stock. These goods are piled for a few hours after which time the hair is reduced to a puipy paste. The same effect is produced by drawing the hides carefully through a similar solution without lime. Skins and lighter hides are best unhaired by painting the mixture on the flesh side, when it will loosen the hair or wool in a few hours without destroying it.

Good samples of sodium sulphide are of yellow colour and contain 28.32% off dry sodium sulphide, which readily deliquesce on exposure o Fused sodium sulphide can now be obtained which contains nearly twice as much actual sulphide (up to 60%) as the crystal form. The dark green colour in many samples is due to the presence of iron sulphide. A good quality of sulphide should have a yellow colour.

MECHANISM OF UNHAIRING WITH SODIUM SULPHIDE

Sodium sulphide in water forms sodium sulphydrate and caustic soda. The sulf-hydrate causes a rapid loosening of hair while caustic soda causes vigorous plumping of the fibres and saponifies the natural grease. Since excessive plumping will damage the hides, the quantity of sulphide should be within the limits. Generally 1 to 5% is used, depending on the raw material. Addition of common salt makes the grain smoother and aids removal of soap and a high concentration of if checks excess plumping.

SODIUM SULPHYDRATE: NaHS

This is produced when sodium sulphide is dissolved in water. It can also be produced by passing hydrogen sulphide into lime solution or by the reaction of sodium sulphide on lime solutions. It is crystallised, soluble in water and on steaming it becomes hydrated sulphydrate. Sodium hydrosulphide has no swelling action like caustic soda, and in the presence of lime acts as an excellent unharing agent. As it does not swell the hide and the grain will be smoother. Hence it is regarded as a better sharpener for unhairing operation, than sodium sulphide particular for fine grained leather. Sodium hydrosulphide in its pure form has not yet been introduced in use in many tanneries.

ARSENIC SULPHIDE

There are two varieties of Arsenic sulphides red and yellow. The chemical formula of the former is As_2S_2 and the latter As_2S_3. Though both can be used for unhairing the red variety is mostly preferred by the tanners. This is not being used now to any extent because of the poisonous character of Arsenic.

REASONS FOR USE OF ARSENIC SULPHIDE

The use of arsenic sulphide mixed with lime as depilant is of very old origin and it still being practised by some tanners on account of the results it produces, especially in the case of fine grained leather. Red arsenic is insoluble in water and usually it was added to quick lime while the lime is being slaked. During slaking, the mixture is well stirred. The heat generated converts the red arsenic into calcium hydrosulphide which makes the hair loosening. This is added to the lime pits containing lime, liquors. Arsenic sulphide is used to unhair goat and sheepskin to make fain grain leather such as glaced kid, glove kid, etc. It can also be used for fine box calf. With the introduction of more modern methods of unhairing, use of arsenic sulphide has become limited. Instead of adding the lime and arsenic sulphide paste to lime liquors the paste is also sometimes used for painting on flesh said off the skins. The painted skins are piled flesh to flesh till the hair becomes loose to be easily scraped off. The unhaired stocks are limed either in straight lime liquor or in lime liquors sharp ended with arsenic, to open up the skin texture and to soaponify the natural grease. The disadvantage of using arsenic sulphide is its toxicity.

MISCELLANEOUS CHEMICALS (SODIUM CYANIDE) (Rarely used)

This possesses unhairing action and it is reported that it is generally used for sharpening lime by some tanners though it is highly poisonous. Similarly hypo, thioglycolic acid, etc. also possess the unhairing action and they are used in conjunction with lime. But since they are extremely costly, they are not used in actual practice. After a careful study of the sweating process it was found that amines also possess the unhairing action and they were introduced an commercial scale, Dimethylamine is twice as strong as the monomethyl. Its usage is introduced in U.S.A. where it is commercially manufactured. Like arsenic sulphide dimethyl amine does not produce any swelling and the grain is smooth.

ENZYME UNHAIRING

It was found hair can be loosened, and depletion can be accomplished under widely different conditions by enzymes from many diverse biological sources. Animal proteases (pancreation), microbial enzymes were first employed, but enzymes of vegetable origin or secreted by moulds and bacteria are found effective and put into use.

ADVANTAGES OF THE ABOVE METHODS

Hair and wool can be obtained without any chemical damage and, therefore, their quality is better than when using chemical methods. This methods of the depilation process, (differing from the liming process) leads to cleaner effluent which otherwise is contaminated by the dissolved proteins resulting from the pulping of the hair. Nevertheless it is not sufficient to make these enzymes act on hides and skins in a weak alkaline pH range, but it is necessary to prepare the substrate itself, i.e. the animal skin, in an appropriate manner. This is done by alkaline pretreatment.

OTHER TYPES

Easier and safer to handle are methods of hair loosening in which a pretreatment of the hides with alkali is not necessary. Proteases of micro-organisms such as fungi and bacteria are suitable. The hair loosening action of the proteases is based on the fact that these hydrolyse the plasma proteins of the mucous layer. By this hydrolysis the link between the epithlial layer and the epidermis is loosened and the hair can be removed easily. For the loosening of the hair it is sufficient to use only proteases, and no other enzymes need be present.

ENZYME FOR DEWOOLING

Along with hair and epidermis the so-called scud is, also removed when working by hand or by the machine. With hides that are not enzymatically treated but limed with lime and sodium sulphide this is possible only after the bating when the pelt becomes fallen again. Enzymatic unhairing yields very clean and 'scud free' pelts. The enzymes for the enzymatic hair loosening must be applied to the fleshy layer in sufficient quantity. The enzymes diffuse more easily through the flesh side. When sheep skins are dewooled, the powdered enzyme is sprinkled on the flesh side. For now hides or goat skins enzyme treatment may be done in the drum or the paddle.

ROLE OF MECHANICAL ACTION IN UNHAIRING

The unbairing of hides and skins on the machine costs less labour. But unhairing the hides by drumming is still cheaper. With the lattice door on and the water fed continuously, the hair is removed and the most of it is washed out of the drum. Considerably more quantity of hair remains on the hides when unhairing is done by machine;'The remaining hair must be pulped in the subsequent liming process with lime and sodium sulphide. The expenditure of chemicals is much lower than when liming according to the traditional process. It must be taken into consideration that alkaline swelling is important for the handle add the fullness of the leather, especially for the manufacture of upper leathers. As for sole leathers, it is possible to obtain good marketable products even without alkaline swelling, which are distinguished by higher abrasion resistance and lower water absorption. Unfortunately, here too, we find the inconvenience of short hair though it does not impair the wear resistance of the leather sole, Therefore, the aim is to obtain an absolutely clean unhairing of 100% in order to produce a leather which has satisfactory fullness of feel and handle.

OXIDATIVE UNHAIRING

The latest method of unhairing adopted in most of the Western Countries is the oxidative unhairing. It is claimed to save a lot of time, production cost and labour. Yet another advantage claimed is that it gives an extremely clean and white pelt. But it calls for greater care and supervision in chrome tannage, especially while basifying. Other problems associated with this is the pungent odour and its prohibitive cost.

NEW ADVANTAGE IN OXIDATIVE UNHAIRING

Since 1964, hides have been unhaired with chlorine dioxide ($C1O_2$) using Impropel CO (Hoechst), which breaks the disulfide bond of Keratin. Hair is dissolved in the drum and if pre-fleshed hides are used the entire process from soaking to tanning can be done in the same drum in 30-35 hours. The drum should run at 6 r.p.m. and generate a little heat, so the temperature is maintained between 28° and 38°C during hair loosening. This takes 20 hours.

EFFECTS OF OXIDATIVE UNHAIRING

The hide fat is soaponified and the fatty acids are chlorinated and they are easily emulsified by the free chlorine that is present. Only the amino acid is attacked, and there is no decomposition of collagen. Prolonged treatment with chlorine dioxide ($C1O_2$) therefore, does no harm; however leather characteristics cannot be modified by changing the sharpness of the" lime as could be done by the old process. The entire operation is carried out in the near acidic range. The hide does not swell In this process, neck wrinkles, veins, and loose grain are much less prominent. The free chlorine is taken up in 15-20 hours by the collagen and has a tanning action, which produces a tight grain. This, method is good for cattle hides and calf skins but it is best to pre-unhair sheep and goat skins with enzymes.

Short hair and fat can then be removed and the skin loosened by the oxidative process. Skins must be depickled before vegetable tanning. Keratin· sulfonic acid gives a clear of slightly turbid solution in water and is biologically broken down so that no treatment in needed before discharge of the waste water to the sewer.

OTHER ADVANTAGES

The oxidative method of loosening hair or wool with chlorine dioxide (Impropel CO, Hoechst) is good for sheep skins because it does not swell the skin, removes fat and scud easily, and bleaches the skin. Wool would be destroyed by the chlorine dioxide so it should first be removed by shearing, painting or enzymes, by usual methods. Spongy parts of the skin are made much firmer by this method; also skins with 15-20% fat are almost fat-free after treatment. Leather from sheep skins unhaired with chlorine dioxide had greater tensile, tear and burst strength, and greater stretch. The skins are dyed better. Goat skins can also be unhaired with chlorine dioxide but unless the hair is removed first much more chemical will have to be used to decompose all the hair. This process cannot be used for glove leather because the skin structure is not loosened enough.

Fleshing, Cheeking, Splitting, Rounding Fleshing

Some flesh adheres to the hides and skins after liming. The flesh which swells in the lime liquor should be scraped off at this stage. This may be done on the fleshing beam (the same as the unhairing beam) and cutting off the flesh with a sharp knife. This operation is called hand fleshing which is a skilled work. Only the flesh has to be cut out without cutting similar to unhairing machines with the difference that the helical-spiral blades of the fleshing knife cylinder are sharp and not blunt as in the case of the unhairing machine. The limed fleshing obtained are used for making glue and is an important tannery by-product.

Cheeking

The neck of some cow hides or buff calf skins is thick and to make it of even thickness the neck is split. This is done by a neck splitting of checking machine. Instead of using a separate machine for splitting the neck, a band knife splitting machine fitted with an adjustment for splitting the neck can be used.

Splitting (Lime splitting)

Cow hides and thick calf skins are split after fleshing and checking. The splitting is generally done by the band-knife splitting machine. The thickness of the pelt can be adjusted as desired, by lime splitting. Splitting produces valuable splits as the by-products which are subsequently tanned and finished into suede splits of split linings.

Rounding

Heavy hide meant for making sole, belting and picking band leather are rounded after fleshing the limes hides. Roundings means cutting a hide into but, shoulder and bellies. Butts are tanned for sole, belting and picking band leather as the but is the most substantial part of a hide and produces sole, belting and picking band leather of the most suitable quality. The shoulder and bellies are suitable for making inferior varieties of leather. The shoulder and bellies are called 'Offals'. The offal and butt are separately tanned and finished. Occasionally for very heavy hides, the butt is divided into two parts each of which is called a 'Bend'. For some kinds of leather the shoulder is not cut off from the butt. The shoulder and butt together form a Back. When this back is divided into two halves each half is called a 'Half back' From here the stocks are moved to further pretanning operations, namely, Deliming, Bating and Pickling.

Actual Liming Process

The use of lime by the tanner is a very happy choice because lime has got a very limited solubility in water and slight excess does not cause damage the skin while the use of materials like caustic soda, soda ash etc. have appreciable solubility and even if there is a slight decrease or and increase in quantity will make appreciable difference in concentration.

1. The solubility of lime at the room temp, is roughly 5 kg/500 litres. The saturated solution of lime is very easy to make.
2. The Ca ion has only half the swelling as that of Na ion. If we prepare solutions of equal pH of NaoH and $Ca(OH)_2$, the swelling of hide in NaOH will be double that in lime.
3. The ready availability and cheapness of the material makes lime the most useful material.
4. This method is fool proof, and gives the same result in many hands.Other materials like NaOH or KOH at the same pH will result in coarsen the grain considerably, weaken the fibers, hydrolyse hide substance in a very short time and make the leather weak. Lime also attacks the hide substance gradually changing the protein, it also breaks down the structure slowly, and lime hydrolysis (breaking down of collagen into simpler substances, is a slow process but accelerates with temperature) Temperatures above 22°C are not very conducive for the operation of liming, Beyond 30°C the acceleration is more pronounced and above 30°C the digestion of hide substance becomes very prominent.

Object of liming

1. To remove materials from hide which cannot be converted into leather and this means the removal of,halr, epidermal layers cells, pigments and the decomposition products, and the adipose tissue.
2. To open up (prepare) the hide for the subsequent tanning operations suitably.

   The liming is so done as to effect a proper opening up of the fibers so that not only the penetration of the tanning material cans be effected, but also that the best results can be achieved and that is the reason, for so many liming methods that are in practice.
3. To partially soaponify the greases and fats. This is not quite correct in the case of Indian hides. The Ca soap that is formed is insoluble in water, unlike, Na. soap).
4. To remove some of the interfibrillary proteins. The important part of the liming is that the swelling and opening up of the fibre structure together with the loosening of the epidermal layer and adipose tissue and hence this operation is to be carefully watched and controlled.

The swelling is greatest in the belly, lesser in the bend, and least in the butt portion. Along the crop section the swelling is greater in the grain, lesser near the adipose tissue, and least in the middle larger.

Belly > Bend > Butt

(fibers are in the tighest owen state in butt)

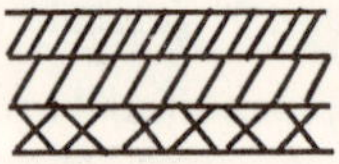

Grain > F2 > F1.

The fibers are weakest at the junction of G, F1, if the grain is too high, these weak fibers get broken, and the grain is bound to be loose. This is seen by the hair slip, formation and that is the reason why chrome tanners do not select hides having hair slip, since they want a tight grain.

In liming procedure the greater is the liming, the greater is the weaking of the above fibers, and greater is the possibility of having loose grain.

Effect of Temperature in Liming

a. Lower Temperatures: Greater solubility greater pH hence greater swelling. High Temperature lesser solubility. Lesser solubility therefore lesser pH therefore lesser swelling.

$$Ca\,(OH)_2 = Ca \times (OH)_2$$

As OH ion increases: H ion will decrease pH will increase.

Therefore swelling increases at lower Temperature. Though there is slightly less swelling because of the lesser solubility of lime, In higher temperature, the advantage in certain cases is more than off set by increased hydrolysis of the hide due to high temp. Hence it is best to choose a lesser Temperature always. But in India we cannot have a cool temperature of the lime solution, hence to avoid loose grain, the limining time should be reduced as far as possible, when the fibers are just opened up hence, (The limining should be controlled carefully).

Having known the basic action of line, it should be possible for the tanner, to adjust the manner of liming, according to the characteristics required for the final leather. If a greater opening up, is desired the tightness of grain (brake), can be sacrifed and a longer limining can be given. Where a tight grain is very essential and a firm character is desired then the limining time should be reduced as far as possible. In some cases of leather where high angle of weave, is desired as in sole leather where as in some leather firmness is desired with a light degree of opening up. This can be manipulated by using the right quantity of new or old lime liquor. The addition of small quantities of agents like soda ash caustic soda may be used. Where a leather of great softness is required old limes may be employed as they contain appreciable quantities of Ca ions and also some bacteria along with hydrolised amines. Artificially mellow liquors can be prepared by adding appropriate quantities of NH4Cl to lime liquor. In presence of $CaCl_2$ tends to make the pelt must whiter in color, than straight lime. For the very same lime if water having more of permanent hardness is employed, the pelt comes out much better and is definitely advantageous where white leather have to be obtained. Presence of $CaC1_2$ induces a liotropic effect and definitely loosens the break of final leather, but the leather comes out free of scud and unusually clean and white.

Sodium Sulphide: is available bath in crystalline and fuse form. Crystalline type is only 30 to 33% purity. Fused type is more commonly used and contains 60 to 62% Na_2S. The rest of it are all polysulphides, Fe,Na_2SO_4, and $Na_22S_2O_3$ etc. The sulphide is very reactive chemically, and should not be exposed to atmospheric Co_2.

The sodium sulphide has a tendency to react with line, producing 4 moles of NaOH for each mole of Na_2S used. When it is dissolved in water, hydrolysed into NaOH and NaHS

$$Na_2S + H_2O - NaSH + NaOH$$

$$2\,NaSH\,Ca(OH)_2 = 2NaOH + Ca(HS)_2$$

When NaSH reacts with Ca(OH)2, it producer.

For every 100 kgs of Na_2S, used when it is actually used in lime it produces 160 kgs. of Sod. hydroxide. It means that for each kg of Na_2S used 1.23 kgs. of hydroxide is produced. Because of the excessive production of NaOH, pelts limed with a mixture of lime and sulphide tends to give a high course grain, as well as pipy grain, particularly on the cow hides. This excess of alkalinity should be controlled, if a leather of tight grainaw fine break is to be obtained.

1. Sulphide can be applied as a paint along with lime and this paste is applied on the flesh side and the hides are piled for overnight or 24 hrs. The hair is loosened and it can be straight away removed. The concentration that is used sulphide varies from 5 to 10% (10% is more widely used).

(a) Shortening the time of unhairing or sharpening of unhairing action, depends on the rate of percolation of this mixture through the flesh side on to the grain side. The concentration of the sulphide paint is very high and it can do considerable harm particularly if the time of contact is prolonged and temp is high. But sulphide, where used in large volume of water as in pit it will produce much more swelling as against the painted stock. Even though the quantities, may be the same still the fact that more H_2O is available in the pit system increases swelling much more than there painted stock. The viscosity the Na_2S solution, can be artificially thickened as a slurry by adding china clay etc, instead of lime.

2. There is another method of dipping the hides in the paint with tongs (of 22 Be) of dilute strength, and then piled. This dipping methods is more suitable for hides than in the case of skins. The paint is further diluted in dipping method enable the unhairing to be done quickly, within 12 hours. (or even overnight.) can be used a more dilute solution of sulphide. for paints percentage of Na_2S is varies from 1 1/2 to 2% on the green salted weight.

3. Sodium sulphide can also be applied in the pits and in this case the quantity of Na_2S is used is between. 4 to 1%. If high % of Na_2S issued in pits, swelling is more and hair is more weakened as expected. Where we use pit system, as is done in the case of E.I. tanned leathers, belting, etc, Where sulphide is acting as a Sharpening agent for unhairing and When the hair is to be recovered and hair can be sold this pit liming method is used. When the % of sulphide increases beyond 6% on the weightt of hide with 400% float then the hair is weakened in the pit system where the hair is a byproduct and can be sold the percentage of Na_2S is not allowed to go beyond this limit of 0.6% are used by several vegetable tanners and they help in the removal of hair more easily and the hair is not also damaged. Sodium sulphide in long-contact, in dilute solutions of Na_2S are more destructive, disorganizes the structure of the hide, produces loose grain than the strong solutions of sulphide which are capable of giving tight texture, and tight grained leather. (The presence of small quantity of Fe, as impurity becomes significant in vegetable tanning of E.I. tanned leathers, as results in darker shade. Hence they use only a dilute solution of sulphide)

4. It can also be done in paddles, with the same float and same quantity off Na_2S. The advantage is that (1) the greater uniformity of the product, because of its agitation possible. Too much agitation is also harmful and if the lime contains gritty particles. Then the grains is actually scratched with the rough surfaces, and this is harmful to the hides. (2) Another defect in paddle is towards end of the day of unhairing the hair from the looser portions like belly etc. tend to mat or clog together. Which is definitely disadvantageous. Hence towards the end of unhairing the paddling should be done only once a day and for not more than 5 minutes. During the start of the limining, agitation is three times a day and five minutes. Paddlign is more uniform product than in pit system, unless the hides are suspended.

5. Drum Liming: Liming can be done in drum, but the float has to be the

same as in a paddle, or otherwise agitation will be too severe, for limining. Fibers are broken up and rinkled grain is likely to result. At best the limining drum should have not more than one or 2 R.P.M. and also the height or (diameter) should be lesser and the length is to be more. If drum liming is done, it can run only for 5 minutes an hour It is always better to minimize the agitation The quantity of float should be such that the water is very nearly equal to the axle.

The very dilute solutions results in slower unhairing, and lesser plumpness. But higher concentration result in quicker unhairing, but it is likely to lead to swelling, yield loose grain. But in painting system we get quicker unhairing with out the danger of obtaining the looseness of the grain.

In drum limining, we can avoid the use of lime. Sulphide con; is 1% solution and for a float 400%, quantity of sulphide can be 4% to 5%

Quantities of Na_2S to be used

For goat skins-for glaze kid = 2 to 3% on the wet salted weight Suede etc.

For Cow-hides = 1 1/2 to 2%

Buffalo = 1 1/2 to 2%

Sheep skins = 2 to 3%

On the weight of hides.

1. Sulphide Paint

Stock: Washed, soaked, Drained goat skins.

Weight :

Green salted weight	–	1000 kgs.
Glaze-Kid	–	1000 skins.
Heavy skins	–	800 skins.

Work on the flesh side. Remove flesh pile. flesh up.

Make up paint-as:

Line: 150 kgs. of slaked shell line or (140% CaO)

250 kgs. of line paste slaked line. (25% CaO)

Dissolve sulphide 25 kgs. of sulphide + 50 Kgs. or 50 kgs. of hot water-

Add to lime powder, add water to bring the Bee 25; (1) Mix well.

(2) Put in a wooden tub.

(3) Take a long stemmed brush or mop. or burlap-dip in paint. apply on flesh side.

Fold along the back borne	:	
Pile in an empty pit	:	Goat skins are
Close well	:	more tough.

Next day unhair.

II. Sheep skins

Stock: Washed, soaked, Drained Sheep skins out Green Salted weight 1000 kgs.

No: of skins – 600 Nos.

(Sheep skins are not washed because they will be containing a lot of hair)

All proportions are the same, and the qty. of sulphide may be increased to 40 kgs. and qty of (lime-can be increased to 400 kgs. (lime store slaked)-Shell lime 250 kgs. strength 25 B.

(a) Where the hair is to be recovered

Apply the paint on the flesh side and pile it in the manner of flesh side touches the other skins flesh side, and make it as a pad and (so that no grain side is to touching the other skins flesh side), smaller (area) skins are kept to the level. Pile to grain from large to smaller skins up-Wait for a 8 hours and after, wipe out the hair simply by a brush.

(b) Where lime alone is used as a paint

200 kgs. of shell lime (400 kgs of Limestone slaked concentration 40 Be. Apply it on the flesh sides, and & i) fold it along the back bone (2) turn the head down and fold to the flesh side (3) Then turn the back side (see and fold. Keep these folded skins in some small warm-chamber, or in narrow trenches and keep it.

In fact the time-required will be greater (longer) depending on temp (12 to 24 kgs) in this case.

It is better to hang it in hooks or ropes.

It should be unhaired, as soon as the hairs easily come out.

Sheep Skins: It is used only in the-Case of glove leather, book binding leather etc, liming etc.

III. Cow hides: For chrome upper leather stock = 1000 kgs. of washed, drained soaked-weight.

Green fleshing is done on the flesh side on beam to Remove any loose flesh. Then make Make up paint at:-

Line – 50 kgs. of shell slaked lime, or 120 kgs. of slaked lime.

Na_2S: 15 kgs. of sulphide, water = 25 to 30 kgs.. Make it as a point: concentration 22 Be to 25 Be.

Apply on the flesh side; and then pile up (flesh to flesh). If we pile it gets heated, change the pile in between and keep it for 24 hrs.

After 24 hrs. it is unhaired, and washed.

IV. Buffalo hide:-

Lime: – 100 kgs. of lime. (shell lime)

Na_2S: -- 10 Kgs.

Water = Be concentration = 20 Be.

Dip this solution, the hides and the pile it (need not be flesh to flesh), as such leave it for 24 hrs.

After 24 hrs. unhalring and the wash.

In Indian climate, Na_2S (weight lime) will lead too much of alkallinity. Hence to avoid this defect, we can use a small amount NH_4C1 or $(NH_4)_2$ SO_2 and neutralise the excess alkallity.

If we use (NH4)2 SO 4 about 50% of the weight of sulphide should be used. If we use NH_4C1 about 40% of the weight of sulphide should be used:

This is the amount, assuming that the NH4C1 and $(NH4)2SO_4$ is 100% pure. Dissolve the ammonium salt and then mix the sulphide solution with lime and then apply.

The Best temperature that is found for obtaining the best type of leather Is to 25^0 following the above procedure.

Even if there is any excess of (NH4)SO4 is present which has not been reached, it can be adjusted or rectified by giving a lesser time of bating. The bating should be adjusted so as to get the best feel, and it will have to be gained by experience.

(a) The excess of alkallinity can also be destroyed, by using small amount of acid.

(b) If we add acid direct to Na_2S then H_2S will be liberated.

(c) If we add acid to the lime, Na_2S mixture (contains-$Ca(OH)_2$, NaOH).

But in practice we can add about 1/7 th on the weight of Na_2S, sulphuric acid 1/7 on the weight Na_2S, of H_2SO4, dilute it weli and then add to neutralize the excess of alkalinity.

The unharing action or release of scud is affected by this practice. Hence only 1/10th of the theoretical quantity is used

The reason for the addition for the smaller quantity of H_2SO4, then the theoretical quantity required, is due to the fact the $Ca(SH)_2$ that is formed, helps to take care to suppress the excess swelling

For hard natured stock like (dry and dry salted stock) soda ash can be ed, about 1/4%, to get a more opening up; (depending upon the type of opening up that is desired)

Acid Addition: Dilute the acid, add the acid, gently stiring well each time to ensure that these are well mixed.

Paint is applied, or piled (flesh to flesh), folded, kept in a closed narrow room, and take out. Next day unhair them, them put in 400% water adding a small quantity of lime then the unhaired skins are thrown in it, mix well, the skins are quickly taken out, add the diluted acid with spitting, put pack the skins and then after 1 hr. again take out and then put back and leave.

For Glaze kid, the skins can remain the pits for 5 or 6 days, handling twice daily.

Bi Sulphide: (Hydrosulphide)

NaH S is also sold as 70% Flakes; or as 40% solution (solution) and are marked.

NaH S markedly differs from Na_2S. Its solubility in alcohol differs; and either we can separate a mixture of Na_2S and NaH S by using alcohol and either.

NaH S is taken up readily by either and Na_2S is not taken up.

Very bright yellow crystals are obtained. But the main draw back is it is hygroscopic and easily attacked by C02. It is more susceptible for oxidation.

NaH S is very useful for Glase Kid, and for chrome leather Manufacture.

Analysis and properties of NaHS

We can use a combination of Na_2S and NaHS. It will give a more swelling (2:1 properties of Na_2S:NaHS) or even 1:1 depending on the extent of swelling desired.

If it is available in commercial scale, it is enough if we use 60% of NaHS, on the weight of Na_2S weight suggested.

Barium Sulphide: Ba S

Barium Sulphide is a mild depilating agent and there is no problem due to the excess of alkallity, and hence there is no excess swelling; It can be readily used if it is readily available in commercial scale. It is still to be explored as an unharing agent in leather industry.

CaSH Calcium Hydrosulphide: It can be readily prepared by passing (merely) H_2S through Ca(OH)2 or lime solution.

MgHS: Mg is easily available in nature throughout MgHS can easily be prepared by passing H_2S through MgOH solution:

Arsenic Sulphide: AS_2S_2 ; AS_2S_3

Has got tendency to oxidise quicker formerly old tanners used to mix AS_2S_2 along with Quick lime and Slake it along with quick lime CaS is also formed and no excess alkallity is produced. This was formerly used specially for Glaci Kids (in Germany) and other fine quality (fancy leathers)].

Alternately this can also be used along with lime solution separately after slaking. It is sold as 65% Arsenic sulphide.

III. ENZYME UNHAIRING

In this case, these enzymes were marketed in India (By Fenner and Co., calcutta) as "Epilol", This enzyme requires, that the skin must be pre treated with NaOH in paddle as a quarter % solution on the volume. Run paddle in this NaOH solution (5 minutes 3 times each day). Next day take out, pile; wash and then it is made ready for bating.

Bate paddle is maintained at a temp of 35° F, and the Epilol is added 1 to 2% on the weight of hide depending on the weight of (nature of stock). 400% water [It is essential and the skins should be washed to bring the pH to 8 to 8.5] Skins are entered, paddled it for one day, running for 10 minutes and stopped.

Next day morning paddled for 2 hrs. and then unhair, wash subsequently and taken for further liming if required. The skins may be left in 5% lime & water in pit of paddle for about 2 days for ensure proper swelling. Then they are taken for fleshing. After fleshing, deliming can be done. No bating is necessary in this case which itself is an advantage.

N.B.: This enzyme does not work, if the stock is not pretreated with NaOH (1/4% solution) in paddle.

Advantage: There is no excess of swelling and grain is also tight.

IV. Amine Unhairing: (American Method)

Monomethyl or Dimethyl amine: Monomethyl amine is less active than Dimethyl amine. Dimethyl amine is more widely used as Ca Dimethyl amine sulphate) $(CH_3)_2$ NH H_2SO4

Dimethyl amine

Disadvantages:

1. It will easily evaporate, and giving a foul odor.

Advantages:

1. Fine grain is obtained.
2. No swelling.
3. Even a slight excess is used it does no harm. Maximum has been suggested at 3% usually only 0.4 to 0.6% is commercially used in combination.

If it is to be used alone usually 1.5 to 2%

It can be used, where we want to produce a perfect white leather, without the danger of obtaining any stains.

Disadvantages:

1. As it is highly volatile, padding time should be-cut short.
2. It is expensive.
3. Controversial experiences are reported and opinions still differ. It can be combined along with either Na_2S or NaHS or other materials.

It is sold as a liquid.

V. Amide Unhairing: Diacyndiamide

This has also an mild unhairing agent.

This can be used along with other agent like NaHS, $Ca(OH)_2$. It is sold under the name "Chem. X" by Chemtan Company of U.S. The quantity used is only 0.4% and Na_2S is be used along with it 0.6% only.

6. Using of Ca 50_3; Na_2 SO_3; $Na_2S_20_4$ (Hydro sulphide) A mixture of allll these are sold as an unharing agent " called all "Hydras". It is readily available.

   Advantage: This can be used alone or along, with lime and particularly suited for white leather Manufacture."

Quantity that can be used ranged from 0.2 to 0.6%

No excess swelling.

The hair removed is not damaged at all, and unhairing is more quick.Time required will be about 2 days. Skins become perfectly white, due to excellent bleaching action.

No danger due to stains; and scud can be removed very easily.

Approximate Compositions of Hydras

$CaSo_3$	– 50	:	
Na_2So_3	– 10	:	Proportion
$Na_2S_2o_4$	– 40	:	

Even if a slight excess is used, then is no damage to hair or grain.

Soda ash upto 0.2% on the weight of hide can be added, if more opening up is desired.

(5) Particularly in the manufacture of suedes, it is not necessary to add soda ash.

The container should be kept fully closed tight.

UNHAIRING PROCESS - PIT LIMING PROCESS

For a straight lime - unhairing if it is goat skin it will take about 8 days.

" Cow hides " 10 days. ; " Buffalo " 10 days.

For Goat & Sheep skins: Usually after the 1st day of liming, and in the second day they will take out of the pit, put back, and handle it on 3rd day and 4th day; upto 5th day skins are put rapidly one by one and scattered (goat & sheep), with stirring the lime. On the 5th day & 6th days skins are spread on and 7th day, no handling is done.

If it is winter season, they will handle upto 7th day, no handling on 8th day and unhaired on 9th day (one extra day is allowed.)

Skins are handled with more care, and attention because they are delicate and are very costly.

Cows & Buffs: Second day (take out & put back well spread out) 3rd day-rapidly put all these after taking a 4th & 5th, 6th day simply take out & put back for the first three days, for all skins & hides. Skin is taken by the hand drawn through the lime and then left with the head facing the corner and butt facing the center of the pit. From the 4th (4 & 5 & 6th day). in the case :of cow- hides &Buffs hides, they are taken out by hand put back and thrown into the lime pit, spreading all ever the pit. From the 7th and 8th day, each day they are spread out. On 9th they do not handle and on 10th day they are unhaired. In winter season, one day more is allowed.

Sometimes if the water is very hard, and if the lime is very poor in quality (below 18% Cao-slaked lime) it should not be used. If the permanent hardness is 25 degree it should not be used. If it is below 7 degree permanent hardness, it can be used. Above 7 degree permant hardness it will lead to difficulties on unhairing.

Permanent Hardness can be rectified by using soda ash before adding lime.

2. So far as the lime sulphide paint, unhairing is usually done on the 2nd day.

It is done in pits (Lime sulphide) solution, it can be unhaired either on the 3rd day or on 6th day or in between depending on the quantity of sulphide used.

If it is glazed Kid-2nd day unhairing (by painting method). For box & Willow sides-the unhairing can be done on the same day or on the second day (depending at the time at which the paint is applied. There is another process for willow sides, in which unhairing is done on 3rd day).

If 1% sulphide, is used on the wet salted weight of hide. Unhairing can be done only on the 5th day. If we still cut down the % of sulphide, it can be done only on the 6th or 7th day without short hairs.

In drum liming, if we want to pulp out the hair 2% concentration sulphide should be used.

Actual Operation of Unhairing

1. By hand: The direction of the knife should not be is opposite direction to the hair growth.

Goat skins have a tougher grain and sheep skins have a tender grain, Push out the hair, in the direction of hair growth, gently without damaging the grain by applying a small pressure.

N.B. In the case of skins, it is necessary to make a bed of the skins before unharing. This is the procedure is adopted for goat and sheep.

In the case of sheep skins, the hair is removed very carefully applying only a very mild pressure.

For goat skins, a slightly higher pressure can be applied.

For cows, calf, and sheep unharing should be done very carefully, by applying only a mild pressure, where the knives are used, the edges should be carefully sharpened. In any case all Knives should be checked.

Improvement

We can use a rubber bed 3/4th inch. over the beam, in the nature of a-cushion-It should not be too soft nor it should be too hard. Then the beams would not be damaged or-cut.

Unhairing by Machine : Can be done in the same manner as in fleshing Machines. But different in make.

In the case of unhairing machine, they use a bladed cylinders in which the the Blades are made up of brass or stainless steel and the blades are put in a helical manner the pitch of which is 34" ie. Helical blades are fixed right handed and left handed converging from both sides(Converging to the center or diverging from the center)

Blades are being fixed, by means of plug of long thick wires or (rod like) (made up of brass copper or steel) The object of having this type of fixing is to replace the blades when it is worn out. It is not welded.

The R.P.M. of the cylinder is 1400 (Directly driven by Motor)

Object is to put (apply more horse power-There is actually a rubber rolls Diacyndi of medium softness to support the hides and these rubber rolls are slightly softer than those used on fleshing machine. There is a top grip roll which holds or the leather and feeds the skins. All these grip rolls are corrugated (or groved) and that gives the grip to prevent the marks on the skins, Burlap (sack jute) is wound on the roll to prevent the grip marks speed of the grip roll in 100'/Min., production rate is 100'/Min., speed of the cylinder is 1400 R.P.

Blades Position is Rubber bed Dia-8"

There is one defect. Top grip roll-6" dia only.

(1) Thinner areas can be easily worked out by hand than by machine. To make the machine more effective rayons type of bolster rolls have been proposed and used. Another type is pneumatic type of cylinder. Air is pumped in inside the shell of the bolster bed (like a motor car) and it takes up thick and thin areas equally well. In these cases adjustment of main parts should be carefully done.

(i) Position (distance) between the blade cylinder and the bolster roll. The cylinder can be moved backward or forward. A separate handle is provided, at both ends of the machine gets adjusted (advance or receded) to the same extent.

Disadvantages: In the case of sides, (right and left) individual adjustment of the position of the cylinder on the both side is preferable. In this-case greater precision and care is necessary.

(ii) The rubber roll itself can be brought forwards or backwards.

(iii) Top grip roll can be raised or lowered.

(iv) Pressure variation is also possible, if heavy spring are fixed or provided on the bloster roll and top grip. Hence too much pressure application is not possible. Variation on the springs on the top of grip roll and on the both the ends of the rubber roll is possible.

(v) **Clutch System:** Great care is to be taken about the clutch system. The clutch system is of friction clutch system-The clearance roll distance between the rubber roll and blade is usually 7"

Another friction shoe type clutch is also used (as in Motor car)

Nowadays, hydraulic systems are being used. (All hydraulic equipments). (initial cost is high, replacements are easy) In this system no-clutch is necessary.

In the third method, pnuematic system can also be used.

Amide Unhairing

Diacyndiamide has a mild unhairing action

$$H_2N - CN\ H_2 - N - C = N$$

$$CN - NH_2\ N = C - N - H_2$$

This is normally used along with other agents like NaHs + Ca/OH_2 etc. It is sold under the name "Chem-X" by Chemtan Company in U.S. The quantity used is only 0.4% and Na_2S is used along with it.

LIMING

Liming is an important and critical process in leather making, and hence will have to be carefully done depending on the type of leather required to be produced. It is generally believed the final properties of the leather are influenced to the maximum extent in the lime yard and hence it is said that 'Leather is made in the lime yard'.

Factors influencing the Liming Process

(a) The type and nature of the stock.

(b) The type of leathers required to be produced.

(c) The quantity and quality of lime.

(d) The addition of sharpening agents.

(e) The quantity and quality of water.

(f) Temperature.

(g) Agitation.

A brief analysis of the influence of these factors is given below:

(a) The type and nature of stock: The liming process has got to be adjusted suitably for different types of raw materials like cattle, goat and sheep skins. The degree of soaking which -the material has undergone earlier will also have to be taken into consideration while liming. Hence the quantity of different chemicals used, the type of liming, and the period of liming etc. Will' have to be carefully adjusted depending on the raw material and the type of leathers desired to be produced.

(b) The type of leathers required to be produced: The process of liming decides the properties of the leather finally produced. It can be adjusted suitably either to produce a hard and tough leather, or to produce a soft and silky leather like chamois or glove leather. Hence the liming process has got to be done depending on the type of leathers desired.

(c) The quality and quantity of lime: Lime has got only a limited solubility in water and even if a slight excess is used it will not cause much harm in straight liming system. But in the case of a combination system involving the use of sharpeners like sodium sulphide, the proportion of lime to other chemicals will have appreciable influence in the unhairing process.

Slaked lime $Ca(OH)_2$ is generally used for liming. The quality of the available lime CaO content and the composition will vary depending on the source of lime. Presence of MgO Magnesium oxide tends to coarsen the grain of the final leather. Hence it will be better to know the actual available lime CaO content, the composition, and the source of lime, before one actually uses it for processing. The quantity of lime and other chemicals can then be suitably adjusted to produce the desired type of leather.

(d) The addition of sharpening agents: Sharpening agents are added to quicken the unhairing process and to shorten the period of liming. The sharpening agents commonly used are Sodium sulphide, Sodium hydrosulphide (NaHS), amines and similar chemicals. They generally act on the S – S (disulphide) linkage of the hair protein keratin and cause quicker loosening of the hair. It also usually increases the alkalinity. The quantity of such sharpening agents and the period of liming will depend on the type of leather produced. Generally skins and hides which contain too much hair will require a larger quantity of Na_2S, than the hides which contain lesser hair density. If a large quantity of sharpening agent is used the period of liming can be considerably reduced.

(e) The quantity and quality of water: Generally it is advisable to use soft water for liming. But hard water does not cause any, appreciable harm in liming except-that it may cause some wastage of lime or other alkalies which arc consumed in softening the hardness. But too much of permanent, hardness, especially due to chlorides produces a thin and flat leather. Temporary hardness does not have much influence in liming.

Quantity: Too small a quantity or insufficient quantity of water causes uneven liming whereas too large or excess of water will consume more chemicals to make up the required concentration, thus making the process expensive. Pit liming requires a larger quantity of water, the paddle liming requires a lesser quantity and the drum liming requires still lesser quantity. Usually the water required for different liming methods for different raw materials are calculated on the soaked weight or sometimes on the raw weight basis.

(f) Temperature: The solubility of lime decreases with increasing temperature of the bath, but the solubility of other chemicals used in liming increases with temperature. Generally the liming process and unhairing are quickened with increase in temperature. But too high a temperature in liming bath is not advisable as it will cause hide degradation and loss of hide of the protein. Too low a temperature slows down the liming operation.

(g) Agitation: Mechanical agitation in drums or paddles will help in quicker liming. But it is also attendant with possible rupture of the fibre structure. Hence too much agitation is to be avoided for obtaining satisfactory results. Usually for liming only drums of low speed below 4 r.p.m, are used. In the case of paddles, care should be taken to avoid overloading of the paddle and there should be a good liquor to goods ratio (about 2.5 : 2) to obtain satisfactory results.

TYPES OF LIMING

(a) Pit Liming: This is a popular method used for almost all types of leathers. The goods may be limed in pits either using only lime (called straight liming) or in a combination of lime with sharpening agents like sodium sulphide. Whenever pit liming is adopted, it will be advisable to handle the hides once or twice daily and stir the liquor to obtain uniform liming results.

In straight liming process in pit, lime is used in sufficient quantity in water, and the unhairing action is caused by the alkalinity. In such a system the unhairing action takes place in a shorter time in summer and slightly longer time in winter. The addition of old lime liquor (once or twice used) will also help in quickening the unhairing, because of the presence of dissolved proteins.

Two pits system: In this system, first the unhairing is caused by a pit liming process which uses a predominantly used, lime liquor (sometimes containing sodium sulphide). After unhairing, the goods are put in another pit which contains fresh lime liquor (sometimes containing an additional alkali-like caustic soda or soda ash). The second pit serves to open up and plump the hide structure.

Three pit system: In this method, the goods pass through three liming baths known as old, medium and new time liquors.

The old lime liquor is one in which more than two lots of goods have been passed through and this contains a large bacterial concentration. This causes quicker unhairing action, and dissolution of the interfbrillary proteins, and ultimately contributes to softness and pliability of the final leather. The goods are first placed in this old lime liquor and kept handled until the unhairing action is noticed.

The medium lime liquor is one in which one lot has passed through and it contains some bacterial concentration and some alkalinity. In this pit the opening up of the fibre structure is continued and partial plumping of the hides takes place. There is some amount of soaponification of the fat taking place in this pit. Scudding is rendered easy for the hides coming out from the medium lime pits.

In the new lime pit, the fresh lime alkalinity swells and plumps the collagen fibres. It has good soaponifying action. This will contribute to a higher weight yield of the leather on vegetable tanning.

(b) Paste Liming (Paint liming) method: Calf, goat and sheep skins unhaired by this method, especially with a view to saving the hair and wool which is a valuable by-product. A calculated quantity of sodium sulphide is dissolved in hot water, and slaked lime is added and mixed to form a paste of thick soupy consistency. This paste is applied on the flesh side of the soaked skin with a brush or mop. The painted skins are folded or piled flesh to flesh and kept covered with gunny sacks for 6 hours or overnight. Next day, the unhairing is done and further liming is done in pit or paddle to continue the liming operation and to open up and swell the fibre structure. This method is generally practiced for calf skin upper leathersand for fine grained leathers from goat and sheep skins.

(c) Paddle Liming: Paddle liming is generally used for shortening the liming duration. Usually sodium sulphide and lime are dissolved in paddle with about 200 to 250% of water on the weight of goods and the paddle is run for definite periods to effect unhairing. Care should be taken to avoid overloading the paddle as it will lead to non-uniform liming. After unhairing, further liming can also be done in paddle using fresh lime and other alkalies. The object of this system is to shorten the duration of liming.

(d) Drum Liming: This is practised in large production units, specialising in upper and crust leathers. The required quantity of lime sulphide is taken and added to the slow speed drum containing 100

200% water. The speed of the drum used for liming should not be ore than 3 or 4 r.p.m. as higher speeds cause too much strain and rupture of the fibre structure because of the alkalinity and agitation effect. After about 3 or 4 hours, the unhairing is caused and the whole hair is pulped and can be washed out by washing with large quantities of water. Further liming if necessary can be carried out in pit or drum using the lime.

The main advantage of this method is the drastic reduction of the liming period.

(e) Other methods: Felmongering, sweating and enzyme methods. These are based on partial bacterial degradation of the epidermal system using enzymes in the correct humid and hot chambers or pits. Mostly these methods are not very popular in commercial tanneries.

Precautions in Liming Process

(1) Always use the correct and calculated quantities of chemicals and lime depending on the raw material and the type of leathers desired to be produced Follow the liming most suited to the type of stock and the leather required to be produced.

(2) Periodic inspection and care is necessary to avoid over-liming.

(3) Do not expose the surfaces of the limed hides or skins to the atmosphere for longer periods, as these tend to absorb CO_2 from the atmosphere and form calcium carbonate ($CaCO_3$) which causes coarseness and brittleness of the hide. Such patches on hides are known as 'lime blasts'.

(4) Avoid using drums of high speed for liming.

(5) Detailed liming recipes are given under different processing details. After unhairing the hides and skins are generally given a further liming using straight lime (sometimes with an addition of caustic alkali) to plump up the structure and to loosen the adipose or flesh layer, so as to make it easy for fleshing. Fleshing may be done normally by hand or by machine. After fleshing the stock is generally known by the name 'pelt'. They are weighed, subsequently washed, scudded before taking to deliming.

Reliming

After unhairing reliming is to be done. It is optional and has to be adjusted as per the leather that is desired to be made. It is necessary for specific E.I. leather. Duration varies from 3 to 7 days. 3 days in the case of goat, 4 days for sheep, 5 days for cows 7 days for buffs.

Reliming is an important operation in E.I. and on it depends the final colour yield etc. If we prolong the days, we get a looser grains, duller grain, but greater weights, hence greater yield.

Objects of Reliming

It can give greater plumpiness than regular liming because only new lime is used. A little addition of caustic soda or soda ash can also be given.

The same degree of swelling is not obtained in the unhairing bath lime as swelling constricts the hair follicles and contracts and the hair is not easily released. When the unhairing becomes difficult short hairs are noticed. Hence in the first liming only a mellow or old lime is used as there will be less swelling and easy unhairing.

1. If there is greater plumpiness we get a greater yield due to the greater fixation of tannins. This plumpiness is given to maintain the greater thickness, in the reliming operations so as to get greater fixation of vegetable tannins.
2. If the opening up of the fibres is too much, then the colour and feel will be darkened and hard. So these two qualities must be balanced skilled depending upon whether we want greater yield or we want better colour or finer feel. These two tendencies are contradictory and hence have to be balanced depending upon the type of leather desired.

There is a difference (variation) in plumping from pelt to pelt and has to be balanced.

Quantity of lime

By addition of more of lime, more swelling will not be achieved as the solubility of lime is limited. For 100 skins about 2 buckets i.e. about 15 to 20 kgs only is use about 4 to 6% lime on the weight of skins. Quality of lime also affects the leather.

In E.I. tanning fleshing is usually done only after the reliming. If we add salt to this lime solutions, skins swell, if more caustic alkally is added (Na_2CO_3 or caustic soda), the colour also becomes fine which is desirable, and but also makes the grain coarse. The addition of this alkali will also remove the grease, and leather is dry and pliable it will affect the apperance and hence not pleasing and which is undesirable as the grain becomes prominent.

Fleshing

Fleshing is done either by hand or by machine. If it is hand fleshing each hide is put over the beam and worked on the flesh side. There is no need to make a pile in this case on the sufficiently long limed hide, flesh comes out easily where the liming is not long enough hand fleshing is difficult. That explains why for chrome leather machine fleshing is practised. If it is over (very long) limed, it cannot be machine fleshed due to stiffness of the hide and hence will result in cuts. For E.I. leather machine fleshing is not done for hides. But for goat and sheep it can be used.

Fleshing machine is very similar to unhairing machine and fleshing knife is easily distinguished and it has a convex and concave side. Convex side should be outside when doing fleshing. Knife should be frequenyly ground on a piece of porcelain and must be not cut the leather. If there is cut, it will be considered as a defect. Where the hides are not stiff enough the hides will be pulled out of the lime in evening, and immersed in cold water and remain overnight and then taken for fleshing on next day, This is specially good for hides. For machine fleshing for goat and sheep this is not very essential. Machine fleshing is not done if the hides have been long limed and if it is done it will cut the leather. For sides it is better and machine should be used with very great care. Hand fleshed sole leathers are better than machine fleshed sole leather. Handwork is limited because it is very slow and liable to get cuts with skilled and unskilled workers. Hand fleshing require high skill and labour Cost is very high in the case of goat and sheep. In the case of hides even skilled men cause cuts and machine can be used.

Machine Capacity, H.P.

Fleshing machine for goat and sheep -72" (6') working width. H.P.0 required for goat and sheep i.e. 10 to 15 H.P. for hides for chrome leather H.P. required is 20 to 25 H.P. for whole hide fleshing machine 9 ft to 10 ft of 2700 mm to 3000 mm working width for sides 6' (72") capacity of a hours machine with a good workmen is 2000 skins, for sides 500 side per day for very light sides750 sides per day .

Rounding

Rounding is an operation carried out in heavy leather lime yards to separate the offals (thin portions of bellys and shanks, shoulder head etc.) which are spongy and then and cannot make as firm a leather as the Butts. Bellys and offals are tanned separately and are made into cheaper varieties of leather while the body is taken for costly leathers sole, belting and industrial leathers. Many of the industrial leathers will have a value only if they have a particular thickness. So the thinner portion have to be cut out because it is not sufficiently thick and also they are spongy.

The best way to mark the positions, is to make it by feeling the thickness by hand; from back bone to the belly side.

For Indian buff-hides, the back bone area is comparatively less in thickness than the other back portion and hence has to be removed.

The hide is placed on a table, sufficiently raised (to 3 1/2' high) and well illuminated on a large table. Hide to be rounded is placed on the table examined where the exact place where the belly starts. A cut is made along the line where the belly starts. Similarly the shoulder is cut off. Hide is then folded along the back bone, belly and other thin areas are also cut off in a similar manner, knife used is a butchers knife and it should be made straight edged.

Shoulder should always be kept as double shoulder, it should be weighed, bend should be weighed and belly should be weigh separately.

Since the butt records the yield of the valuable part of leather percentage of leather yield of each lot as butt should be of great importance. Also the subsequent leather obtained also depends very much on the amount of butts. For working out the final yield these figures are necessary. It is difficult to asses which should be the figure because it depends on the quality of the stock. Butt about 50 to 70%; Bellys may be 20 to 40%, shoulders 10% head may be or may not be taken.

ROUNDING

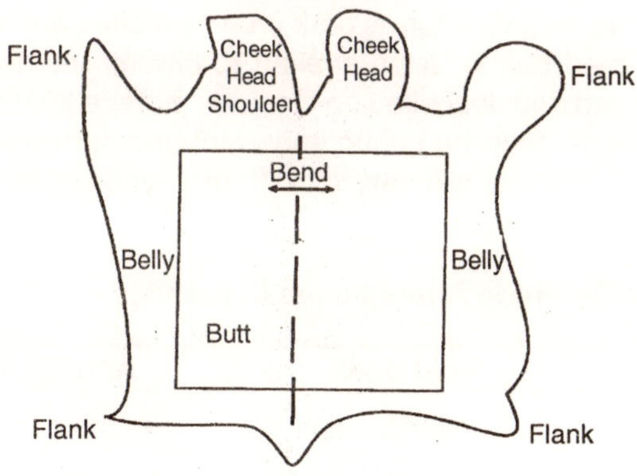

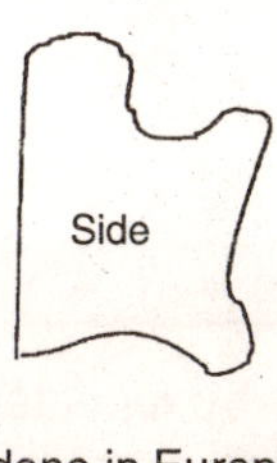

Rounding operation is mostly done in European stock and rarely done on Indian buffalo hide. However it can be done on buffs also as in picking bands etc.

These results are to recorded permanently for it gives the % yield of each lot.

In this rounding shop itself one can assess the raw stock, and the quality of purchase.

Indian hides are not rounded for sole leather. But for specific industrial leather purposes the hides can be rounded. Rounding is usually done after fleshing. In industrial leathers this rounding is absolutely necessary because here the suitability and durability is important.

DELIMING, BATING, PUERING & DRENCHING DELIMING

Objects of Deliming

The pelts after fleshing are in a plumped condition and are full of lime and the pH is high (above 12). But before they are taken for tanning, it is necessary to free them from lime, reduce the plumping and to lower the pH nearer to the tanning range. This process is known as deliming and it is usually done by treating the limed pelt with some mild acids or acid salts.

If deliming is not done, and if the limed pelts are treated with vegetable tan liquors, the tannins combine with lime and produce Calcium tannate on the grain, which on oxidation forms dark brown patches and cracks on the surface. If the limed pelt is taken straight to chrome tanning liquor; the chrome will be fixed and deposited on the outer surface leaving the interior undertanned. Hence deliming is and important and necessary operation. But the extent of deliming will vary for different types of leathers having different desirable properties.

Some Common Deliming Agents used In practice.

Acids	Acid Salts	Ammonium Salts
Boric Acid	Sodium bisulphite	Ammonium Sulphate
Acetic Acid	Sodium bisulphite	Ammonium Sulphate
Formic Acid		
Hydrochloric Acid		
Sulphuric Acid		
Naphthalene Sulphoric Acid.		

Deliming can also be done by repeated or continuous washing by water, but this takes longer and requires more efforts because of the limited solubility in water. Strong acids like Sulphuric or Hydrochloric are economical, but are risky to use as they are likely to swell and produce leather which crack if they are not used with care. Hence mild acids or acid salts or Ammonium Salts are generally used.

If sulphuric Acid is used for deliming it produces $CaSO_4$, which has only limited solubility. Hence this is used only for hard and tough leathers. Other acids listed above form soluble Calcium Salts, which can easily oved by washing.

$$2\ HX + Ca\ (OH)_2 - Ca\ X_2 + 2\ H_20$$

acid soluble lime salt.

$Ca\ X_2$ being soluble is washed and removed from the pelt.

Method of Deliming

The fleshed pelts after weighing are washed first in soft water repeatedly to remove the surface lime. Then they are treated with the deliming agent (about 0.5 to 3.00 of Ammonium Salts, depending on the types of leathers produced) in a pit, paddle or drum, until the lime is removed to the equired extent.

The deliming is tested by adding phenolphthalein indicator on the out section of the pelt. Complete absence of pink colour formation indicates complete deliming. In partially delimed hides, pink colour will be formed in the inner layers of the cut section. Usually one or two scuddings are done during or after deliming.

Extent of deliming

In conventional 'sole' leather tannage only partial deliming is done, and a thin layer of limed layer is kept in the middle layer, so as to avoid any putrefactory damage likely to occur during the long and slow tannage.

Generally speaking in slow tannage and for harder types of leathers, it is advisable to keep a thin layer of lime in the middle, but in the case of soft and flexible types of leather complete deliming is necessary.

The pH of the pelt after deliming is usually about 8.0 but in the case of skins and hides which are to be bated the pH is kept around 8.5 to 9, which is about the optimum pH for bating.

Some Equations of deliming

(i) $Ca(OH)_2 +$	H_2SO4	$CaSO_4 + 2\ H_20$
	Sulphuric acid	Calcium sulphate
(ii) $3\ Ca(OH)_2 +$	$2H_3\ BO_3$	$Ca_3\ (B0_3)_2 + 6\ H_2\ 0$
	Boric acid	Calcium borate (soluble)

(iii) $Ca(OH)_2$ +	$2CH_3COOH$	$Ca(CH_3COO_2) + 2H_20$
	Acetic acid	Calcium acetate (soluble)
(iv) $Ca(OH)_2$ +	$2NH_4C1$	$CaC1_2 + 2NH_3 + 2H_20$
	Ammonium chloride	Cal.Chloride (soluble)
(v) $Ca(OH)_2$ +	$(NH4)_2 S04$	$CaSO_4 + 2H_3 + 2H_20$
	Ammonium sulphate	Ca. Sulphate

Need for Deliming : Although lime in many respects is a most useful and satisfactory means of loosening hair, it is necessary that it should be completely removed, at least from the grain surface. If it is not done so, its action on tannins is most injurious and is often harmful in tanning. For soft leathers the skins should be brought from a swollen to a soft and flacid condition. Hence the process of removing the lime is termed as Deliming. These processes can be reviewed from the earlier stages modern method based on the scientific and technological aspects.

Old Practices : In the olden days the deliming was done completely in plain water either in pits, or in running water. But as time passed on and due to the introduction of chemicals, equipments of mechanical type etc., the older methods were slowly replaced. The availability of many chemicals their reactive properties and then effect on hides and skins were studied and subsequently adopted in many 'processes. Thus Deliming was done with chemicals instead` of simply by water.

Effect of Mere Washing : Mere washing is never thoroughly effective, and a much more efficient method is to suspend the hides in the case of sole and belting leathers to which smaller portions of mild acid areadded till the lime is nearly but not fully neutralised. But the chemical problem is not so simple as it appears. Any excess quantity of strong acid will swell the pelt which will prove to be more dangerous in tanning than in lime, making dark coloured and brittle or tender leather. Acids of extremely weak nature capable of forming soluble lime salts and obtainable at low cost are used. On the other hand a salt of weak base which will replace lime and would not damage the pelt also may be alright. But with certain precautions and in special cases stronger acids can be used successfully.

Some Chemical Deliming Agents : Acetic, formic and lactic acids are safer than Sulphuric acid but, are costlier than Sulphuric acid. Sulphuric acid is commonly used heavy leathers, because of the low cost Mineral acids are used with great care and they should perfectly free from iron and all the equipments used must also be free from Iron. Ordinary sodium bisulphite has the disadvantage of leaving practically the whole of the lime in the form of Calcium sulphite, in the hide. Hence it is not suitable for sole leathers. Boric acid also has been extensively used now as a deliming agent. It also gives a better colour when employed for sole leather. Even after bating it is used to remove the free lime if any present. In those cases it acts as a drench. Boric acid has considerable influence in preventing drawn grain and gives light colour. Borax has also been used as a deliming agent. Repeatedly because of its ability for frequent regeneration as boric acid, by the addition of acid. Ammonium chloride is used with advantage for deliming chrome leathers. These ammonium salts are best suited Lactic acid had come largely into use as a deliming agent recently. If it is used in excess it tends to plump and swell the leather. In many cases, it may be substituted for the bran drench with advantage and is much more rapid and less dangerous in hot weather, but the effect is not identical in all respects.

Deliming agents

The deliming agents usually used are 1. Ammonium Chloride 2. Ammoalum Sulphate 3. Boric acid 4. Acetic acid. 5. Formic acid 6. Lactic acid. Also mineral acids like HCl and H_2SO_4 can be used under certain conditions. Now in addition to this is CO_2 which forms a very mild acid can also be used. One can also use Ammonium carbonate or Ammonium bicarbonate etc. Even Sodium bicarbonate can be used where we want to deposit $CaCO_3$. Also there are many other materials like oxidation products of petroleum products. These are cyclic carboxylic acids which have been developed in Germany. (Paraffin oxidation products) sold by Bohime Fatle Cheme, Germany. There are supposed to give greater filling capacity of the leather. These materials which have got the sequstering capacity (ca. complex forming capacity) so that Ca is actually removed and one such agent Werscine" by Versine Company, U.S.A. That actually involves the removal of Ca. straight away. Sodium meta phosphate can also remove the Ca by sequesteing capacity but it is fixed in pickling. Now it is for the tanner to choose the particular agents. It is easy to calculate the quantity of various deliming agents necessary to remove 1 kg. of CaO in terms of quantity and also money.

Cost of Acids to remove 1 kg. of lime. Cost per kg of lime (as CaO).

1. Ammonium Chloride produces an alkaline reaction, produces Cad_2 and pulls down very much the skin, and NH_4OH is also alkaline. NH_4C1 is used wherever a well let out leather is desired as for gloves, garments etc. Glacekids are also bated or delimed with NH4C1 so as to get the let out and smooth feel, it is not used for deliming chrome side leather because the lack of solidity and tightness of the NH_4C1 delimed leathers. Glacekids bated wit NH_4Cl show a much fallen leather than $(NH4)_2SO_4$ and hence preferred on glace kids. It is not quite cheap as $(NH4)_2SO_4$ Therefore where there is a specific advantage exists, only in such cases NH4C1 is being used.

2. Ammonium Sulphate is used much in deliming and bating of side uppers calf skins etc. This $(NH_4)_2SO_4$ deposits $CaSO_4$ which is deposited in the skin and improves the temper of the leathers. The grain is not so smooth as that of NH_4Cl. $(NH_4)_2S0_4$ is also used in the case of goat skins, such as crushed kid etc. where too much let out feel and smoothness of grain is not so important Goat suedes.

   The coarse grain feel is due to the momentary appearance of $CaSO_4$ on the grain where as $CaC1_2$ is soluble in water. The smoothness is obtained by bating. If there is an excess of $CaSO_4$ on the leather then bating will be affected and the final leather will be very grainy. It is quite cheap. Quantity of $(NH_4)_2$ SO_4 required for re 1 kg. of CaO is = 2.4

3. **Boric acid:** It is a weak inorganic acid, very mild in action. Boric acid is obtainable as pure and does not swell the skin even if added a little more. It is a safe material. Ca borate that is being formed is much more soluble and it is easily removed from the leather. But because it is an acid the grain is much cleaner after deliming acid. If the hide or skin has initially has lime blast, boric acid cannot remove the lime blast. Because it is not an alkally it can be expected to produce a fine colour of leather in vegetable tanning, than any other.

   It's cost is high and is always expensive and produces a softy waxy feel (characteristic feel). If we use boric acid in large quantity the solubilised Ca as Calcium borate will try to act on the hide substance. Causing a loose grain, but if used in mild quantity, boric acid produces a smooth, clear grain leather, it is mild inorganic acid, in many places a short rinse in boric acid is given before taking to the bark tanning. For chrome leather, this need not be used for it is to be pickled. For vegetable tanned leather, it is used at the end or for stepwise deliming. We can also used boric acid for acidifying sole leather tanning yards.

4. CO_2 (H_2CO_3): The idea of using CO_2 is not actually new and has been suggested for a long time. CO_2 reacts with caustic lime forming $CaCO_3$ which can further be converted into $Ca(HCO_3)$ CO_2 can directly be bubbled from the cylinder into the deliming bath and any excess does not cause any harm. This CO_2 can best form a solution of pH 4.5 and not less. Hence there is no danger of swelling of skins due to excessive use. Though initially CO_2 causes a rough feel to the grain of the leather, it does not persist. CO_2 deliming is claimed to give a tight leather, particularly in the flanks and no Ca is said to exist in the final leather and atleast one glacekid manufacturer in U.S.A. is using CO_2 for deliming. CO_2 is used as the dry ice which is available in plenty and quite cheap. Dry ice is held in cylinders from which CO_2 is delivered

through. Pipe passing through a pressure gauge and hot water can (to heat the CO_2) and let into the deliming bath, through a 1/2" pipe (perforated) at the bottom of the paddle. CO_2 is added in 2 or 3 instalments with frequent checking with Thymol or Bromo Thymol blue (pH 8 to 9.6) (pH 6 to 7.6).

5. Bisulphite [$Na(HSO_3)$]

It is acidic and can be split up into Na_2SO_3 and fo $CaSO_3$, gives a sort of bleaching effect of the grain in addition of deliming H_2SO_3 reacts with lime forming $CaSO_3$. Na_2SO_3 also reacts with lime forming CaSO producing $CaSO_3$ and NaOH.

This is used in sole leather yard because the grain is bleached by SO_2. NaOH form does not allow the skin to loose it thickness. Sides remain plump after removal of lime and also get bleached. So this will suit Leather intended for sole, are surface delimed in a strong solution of $NaHSO_3$.

Time is shortened of the concentration is more. (If we can use SO_2 if available the surface deliming a more, but destroys leathers quickly. $NaHSO_3$. is only a salt of H_2SO_3.and too much falling down of the skin, and is used more is sole leather tannage. Commercial strength of $NaHSO_3$ is 64 to 65%. It gradually looses SO_2 and hence is kept quite closed. $NaHSO_3$ can be added in the soak also, because it gives resistance to bacterial action danger. ($NaHSO_3 + Na_2SO_3$ is also used in sulphite ion of extrácts.)

6. **Inorganic acids:** HCl is very powerful acid and can be used for deliming because it acts on $Ca(OH_2)$ forming $Cacl_2 + H_20$.

This $CaCl_2$ formation gives a smoothness of grain, but it rapidly attacks the hides substance. The deliming takes place very rapidly because the product formed is completely water soluble. The disadvantage is the leather is very much pulled down and plumpiness is lost, leather becomes flat without temper. If the concentration of the bath is high (If pH is below 3.5) then the swelling of the outer layers happens and if the temperature is also high then considerable damage will result by acid hydrolysis. The leather looses its value and the structure will be destroyed, and therefore it has to be used with great care and in small instalments after diluting. Acid should be added only after diluting to 1 to 2 of water.

2. H_2SO_4 as a deliming agent, is not advisable because of the rapid break down of the hide substance at increased temperature. And also being a strong acid producing insoluble $CaSO_4$, it is not favoured as a

deliming agent. But in practice appreciable amount of deliming really takes place by using H_2SO_4 in pickling stage where leathers of lime content are pickled with H_2SO_4 and salt, the real deliming is taking place with H_2SO_4. In such cases the temperature of the bath should be controlled and preferably not exceeding 80 F. Taking very great care that temperature is below 80°F. We can used H_2SO_4 for deliming after diluting to 10 times, and when deliming takes place at 70°F and the acid is added gradually.

It is used, where the skins have been limed in waters of high hardness particularly temperature, the formation of $CaCO_3$ is inevitably on the grain. Such leathers cannot be easily bated. So to remove the skin of the $CaCO_3$. such leathers are rapidly passed through. H_2SO_4 solution. Kept at a pH of 3 to 3.5 and the skins are first rinsed to remove this CaC03 and then taken to the bating bath. This same treatment can be given to leathers to be vegetable tanned; to remove either lime blast or water stains.

Lime blast can be formed by exposing the limed skin to the atmosphere. It is caused by atmosphere CO_2 on the lime. On the surface of the pelt, or it may caused by the water stains. The presence of lime blast is objected because of the fact, that such leathers cannot be dyed and finished subsequently, satisfactorily and result in patchy appearance.

Organic acid

Oxalic acid is moderately strong, it can cause swelling and hence should be carefully used. It is also very good bleaching agent and therefore very much used for bleaching vegetable than leathers and before the delimed leathers go into the vegetable tanning. A rise in oxalic acid before they go to vegetable tanning considerably helps in getting a light coloured and uniform product. It also removes Fe stains.

Oxalic acid acids reacts with $Ca(OH)_2$ forming Ca oxalate which is insoluble, as white dense precipitate.

It is expensive. But is always used wherever vegetable tanning is done. Oxalic acid is used in the last wash, before taking to vegetable tanning i.e. 1/2 kg for 100 of skin to be washed. (1/2 kg of oxalic in 800 litres of water).

Lactic acid we can use this to get a very smooth effect on skins and skins treated with lactic acid get a slippery feel. It is very weak but gives very smooth grain so glace kid tanners prefer to give a rinse with lactic acid. The Ca lactate formed is easily soluble in water, and hence skin loose their smooth feel. But lactic acid is very expensive and hence can be used where the increased cost will be justified.

The cost is too high and the quantity to be used is only 1/2 a per cent on the weight of skins. It is also used as a dip for belting and sole leathers.

Formic Acid

It is one of the strongest of organic acids and also expensive. The deliming is very rapid and Ca formate that is formed is soluble in water,and leather falls rapidly. But being an organic acid it is not having attendant danger of swelling too much or increase in the ash content of the leather. The presence of Ca formate in the skin increases the chances of rapid chrome penetration; upto a certain extent this masks the tannage which will be advantageous. The use of organic acids in deliming bas to be viewed in the light of the formation of the masking salts which may be carried over to the chrome tanning leather from the deliming bath via pickling. Whenever we use organic acids they should be taken Into consideration, because of the salts like Ca formate or Na formate is a masking salt.

Acetic Acid

It is a weak organic acid forming Ca acetate by reacting with $Ca(OH)_2$. Ca acetate is water soluble. It also rapidly brings down the hides and skins because it is a very weak acid, it can be safely used for deliming purposes and the quantitative used is 1/2 to 1% on the weight of the skins.

2.2 Kgs of acetic acid per 1 kg of CaO cost is also high. Because the strength is only 60% the actual quantity used 3.5 kg per 1 kg of CaO. This is about double the quantity of NH_4C1 required to remove the 1 kg CaO. Hence the cost is also high. Hence the total cost will be several times that of using NH_4Cl or $(NH_4)_2SO_4$. Hence this acid can be used only in small quantities towards the end, particularly for vegetable tanning where acidic grain is specially advantageous.

Immediately after the fleshing, the leathers must be washed to remove the surface time. This washing may be done either in paddle or in drum or in vats. And if it is in a dum, it should have perforations or it should be fitted with slat slotted door.

Some Uncommon Deliming Agents : Materials like Zinc Sulphate Alum, Phosphates, Oxalates etc. are also other deliming agents. Several adds of the aromatic series and oxidation products of petroleum, hydrocarbons etc. have been used from time to time and these are recommended as deliming agents. Aromatic acids also act as powerful antiseptics.

BATING

Objects of Bating

(1) To clean the grain surface free from dirt scoud etc. and make it smooth and fine.
(2) To open up the fibre structure by enzyme action.
(3) To remove the coagulable and interfibrillary proteins.
(4) To facilitate easy scudding.

Bating action can be considered in two aspects (i) It continues and completes the deliming action by chemical action (ii) It opens up the fibre structure and removes interfibrillary protein by the action of enzymes like Tryspin, Pancreatin etc. Usually commercial bates contain the enzymes in a medium of inert material like flour and a chemcial deliming agent like Ammonium Sulphate or Chloride. In olden days originally 'Pigeon dung' which contains active enzymes was used for bating. Later 'Dog dung' was used and this process was known by the name puering, but with the advent of commercial bates, the conventional dung bates have become less important.

Testing of Bated Pelts

A well bated skin should have the following characteristics:

(1) The grain surface should be smooth, slippery and silky in feel.
(2) The skin should retain the thumb impression when pressed by the thumb and after removal of the pressure.
(3) The skin should be fallen and flaccid.
(4) The flesh should become tender and can be easily scrapped off.
(5) The skin should be permeable to air, tested by pressing the trapped air bag to allow air to pass through the grain.

Factors influencing the bating

(1) The type and nature of the pelt.
(2) The type of leather required to be produced.
(3) The nature of the bate and its concentration.
(4) Temperature of the bate bath.
(5) pH of the pelt and bath.
(6) Time.

A brief indication of the influence of these factors are given below.

(1) and
(2) **The types and nature of the Pelt**

The degree and extent of bating procedure for different types of pelts will vary for different types of leathers. Usually calf and cow hides for upper leather will receive a milder bating when compared to goat skins. Goa and sheep skins for garment and glove leathers will require more drastic bating in order to make them more soft and stretchy. Hence the degree of bating will have to adjusted suitably to the required extent depending on the types of leathers required to the produced and the nature of the pelt under processing.

3. The nature of the bate and its concentration

In the trade many types of bates with varying concentration of active enzymes are marketed and hence while choosing the material and quantity of the bate great care is essential.

If the bate used is of high enzyme concentration lower quantities will be sufficient, and if it is of lower concentration, a larger quantity will be required. Hence a thorough knowledge of the nature of the bate is essential.

The quantity of the-bate required for bating will also depend on the nature of the pelt and the type of leathers desired to be produced. Higher the quantity of bate used, quicker will be the bating action, but it is attendant with greater risk, specially during the summer season or when the temperature of the bath is higher. Lower the quantity of bate used, slower will be the bating action.

Temperature

Since bating is essentially an enzyme action this is very much influenced by the temperature. Higher the temperature, more drastic and faster the bating, but it is more risky and is likely to damage the pelt by bacterial action-Lower the temperature, more slower is the bating action and less will be the efficiency of bating. Hence the optimum temperature has to be maintained during the bating. Usually for bating a temperature around 35° C to 39° is considered to be the optimum for bating. (Body temperature)

pH of the Pelt and Bath

The ideal pH for bating is about 8.3 to 8.5. Too high a pH above 8.5 will not make the pelt to become fallen and flaccid, and too low a pH below. 7.5 will not contribute to proper opening up. Hence for obtaining satisfactory results the pH of the pelt should be about 8.5.

Time

Since bating is an enzyme action great care is necessary in controlling the duration of bating. Too long a bating will make the pelt very tinny and flat and finally even lead to putrefaction, but too short a bating will not give satisfactory bating. Hence a close watch and periodic inspection of the pelts during bating is very essential. The time of bating has got to be determined by the conditions of the pelt during bating and not by any fixed schedule of time. In commercial tanneries the bating is done in dosed paddles and the bate specialist periodically inspects the lots and removes the bated pelts as and when they are satisfactorily bated.

Method of Bating

Bating may be done in drum, paddle or pit. For light skins like sheep and goat it is advisable to bate in a paddle with a covering hood to maintain the temperature. About 200% warm water at about 35°C is taken in drum or paddle and the required quantity of bate (about 1%) is added and the drum or paddle is run for about 3 to 5 hours. Periodic inspection of the pelt is done to check the progress of bating, and as the skins get bated they are removed to the warm water washing bath. Later they are taken for scudding and pickling.

In the case of overnight bating the pelts are kept in cold water bath to which 1/2 the quantity of the bate is added and mixed well. The pelts are allowed to remain overnight. The bating action starts and slowly progresses. Next day sufficient quantity of hot water is added, or the temperature is slowly raised by passing steam through until the bath temperature is about 35°C. Then mechanical agitation is continued until a satisfactory bating is obtained.

Usually the quantity off normal bate required for gout and sheep skins is about 1% on the pelt weight, for making glace kid and garment leathers. In the calf skins and cow hides for upper leather, the quantity of normal bate required is only about 0.4 to 0.6% on the pelt weight. But in the case of concentrated or extra strong bates the quantity required will only be about 1/ 10th of the quantity indicated earlier.

Drenching

This was practised in olden days and this operation means treatment of the pelt with a mild acid (usually organic acid) sometime prior to pickling. Conventional drenching is done by using fermented wheat bran solution, which contains organic acids formed during the fermentation.

Conventional drenching process

This process has the following function:

(i) It clenses the pelt by mechanical action to produce a white pelt.

(ii) It separates the fibres by penetration of the gases formed during fermentation.

(iii) In continues and completes the deliming and brings down the pH of the pelt, nearer to pickling.

In recent years, the conventional drenching processes have become less important and are replaced by weak organic acid rinsing of the pelt.

The drenching may also be done in paddle, drum or vat. The skins after drenching will become very soft and pliable and the surface become very clean and silky. In modern tanning practices this drenching process not adopted in trade.

Puering : Originally puering consisted of handling or steeping the goods in a weak fermented infusion of pigeon or dog dung for a time usually extending for some days and is applied to the heavier classes of dressing leather. Puering is similar process applied to the finer and lighter skins such as glove and glaced kids and moroccos, where dog-dung is substituted for that of birds. Since the mixture is used in a warm condition the process is generally over in few hours. Drenching is occasionally used as a substitute for Bating or Puering. Drenching always cleans the skins, slightly plumps them and completes the removal of lime from them before they are taken for tanning. All these methods are fermentive processes and their effect is not equal to chemical one in removing lime but they are also of bacterial. They act on the cementing substance of the hide fibres than producing a softening effect along with a reduction in the hide substance. In the manufacture of softer leather, therefore, this effect is much desired; but in other cases such as in heavy leathers like harness and strap leather etc. this effect is not required. Nowadays puering and drenching are not practised and it is of only theoretical interest.

Early Bating Agents : Both bating and Puering are of bacterial action. If there is no control over the process, then the entire stock will be ruined. The chemical action is the removal of lime. In olden days only the dog dung and pigeon dung, were being used to get the required softness as in the case of light leathers. Subsequently many chemicals were introduced in the tanning industry. Ammonium chloride was used as a bate. Later bating liquor consisting of Ammonium Chloride and sodium bisulphite, along with sulphuric acid was used. French Calf leathers were produced in England just by repeated soaking in cold water and working on the beams. Warm water then replaced cold water. Salicylic acid from phenols found use as a bate. Similarly many coal-tar products were used as hates, but they are no more in usage. In India the used babul bark liquor is much used as a bate after fermenting the 'infusion'. From this, Gallic acid was used as deliming agent but it gave dark oxidation products with lime.

Synthetic Bate : D. Ottoo Rohm then synthesised the Synthetic bate which is, called 'oropon'. Rohm also believed that enzymes are most essential for bating and, instead of culture, an infusion of animal pancreas was used as the source for enzymes. The enzymes are activated by ammonium salts. The animal pancreas contain Trypsin and in admixture with Ammonium salts, Oropon was manufactured. Recently Microbial based enzyme bates and unhairing agents are also produced.

Trade Products : All the bates whose active constituents are proteolytic and lipatic enzymes are generally called enzymes bates. Several such Synthetic bates based on Pancrease or Microbial enzymes are on the market now, and are used by tanners.

Degree Bating : The mildness or intensiveness of bating depends upon the type of hides and skins and the condition in which they were received in the tannery (i.e. wet or dry salted or dried). It also depends on the way they were limed and the characteristics dasired in the final leather. Bating can be made mild by reducing the temperature, duration and concentration of the bate liquor and it can be made intensive by reversing the above conditions. Dry hides and skins require more intensive bating than green and wet slated ones. The grains of goat skins vary from hard to soft according to the regions of their production. Thus Indian goat skins produced in the north and known as 'Amritsars' are hard grained whereas the goatskins known as 'Daccas' and 'Muzzaffarpoes' are soft grained. Similarly, the goat skins known as 'caoe goats' are hard grained than South American goat skins. The hard-grained goat skins have to be bated more intensively than the soft grained ones. Skins which have been sulphide limed are to be bated more intensively than those which have been limed in straight lime liquor. Similarly, long limed pelts require less bating than short limed ones.

Bating Process : Bating may be done either in a paddle or in a drum. For light skin such as sheep, goat, calf and light kips it is advisable to bate in a paddle because in a paddle the skins move gently and the progress of bating can be closely watched than if bating is done in a drum. Heavy hides for harness, belting etc. can be bated in drum because it is difficult to keep them in motion in a paddle as they tend to settle down at the bottom of the paddle. For bating in a paddle 300-400 per cent and in a drum 200-300 per cent and water (on pelt weight) is used.

Type of Paddle Used : The bating paddle is usually provided with a lid in order that it may be covered during bating to prevent cooling of the bate liquor and also to prevent escaping of ammonia which is formed as the reaction proceeds between the salts of ammonia and the alkali present in the pelt.

Need for Adjustments : Unhaired, fleshed and scudded pelts are washed in 2 or 3 changes of water in a drum or running water in drum or paddle. The washed pelts are now ready for bating. The actual procedure of bating is adjusted for different types of hides and skins and depending the properties of final leather desired. Manufacturers of Synthetic bates usually prescribe procedures of bating and tanners take their prescribed processes as basis for their work and modify them by working experience so as to get desirable properties in the finished leather.

Bating Pelts for Vegetable Tannage : This is optional and should have an elastic grain, and which must moreover be light coloured and spotless in order that it may be used either in natural colour or dyed into level and light shades. This is achieved by bating with enzyme bate. The bating material makes it possible to shorten the liming period to the necessary extent with a view to get a tough and elastic leather. The fine grain and good feel can be obtained in a better and surer way by bating with a suitable bate. For making vegetable tanned kips addition of deliming agents during bating is important because the pelts must be brought to the first liquors in a completely delimed condition. An addition of 0.3-0.5% of sodium bisulphate for deliming is often advantageons in maintaining paler colour in the finished leather.

Conditions of Bating : Bating is done with a view to obtain a Silkly grain on the pelt and also to remove the scud and to produce a supple leather. In gloving leather bating is necessary to get the "run" and stretchiness and Suppleness in the case of clothing leather. There is also a claim that bating tends to produce a tight leather. From Indian point of view it is to remove the scud and to have a clean pelt, (Particularly in the Goat skins) concentration, time and the pH are the important factors to be controlled. The bating process is judged by Slipperiness of the grain, scud release test, Thumb impression, air-porosity test, and the release of the flesh.

Main Enzyme Used in India : Pancreatin is the (Tryptic) enzyme used for bating in India, and this is obtained from cattle Pancreas. Recently Microbial enzymes bates have been manufactured and used successfully and are available on commercial scale. Animal pancreas can be obtained from organised slaughter houses. In Rajasthan and Punjab area the rural tanners do deliming and bating with **"Sada"**–fermented flesh flour etc. Here, there is no proper chemical control. This produces a slippery grain and is a very risky method. By complete deliming and bating, a soft leather is obtained and if half delimed and then bated – a firm leather is produced.

ACID Wash : After bating an acid wash is given to the pelts to bring the pH to 5 (Lactic or Acetic 1/4-12%). This gives a smooth soft leather particularly for Glaced kid or calf skin. Butric acid can also be used.

DRENCHING: Occasionally drenching is done. Drenching is a treatment with fermented bran. Drenching has cleansing action carbon-dioxide is evolved and some organic acids are produced due to fermentation. Carbondioxide itself is a good deliming agent. Usually wheat bran is used. It is soaked in water and fermented for three or four days. The whole bath starts frothing. Sometimes, the pelt is put in this and allowed to ferment. This is known as rising drench. This will give very good results. This can be a dangerous method when the temperature is high and the goods may be permanently damaged.

Still Drench : The goods are put in the paddle with drench and drenched for 3-4 days. It is very useful in the case of finer leather like Gloving etc. The acid wash after bating is actually a substitute for Drenching. This drenching process is not done in practice now and is only of historical importance.

Scudding : After bating, the Scudding can be done manually, or mechanically or in a drum with a very little float, almost in a dry condition. Scudding this way removes all the scud and for better results the pelts can pass through the scudding machine. At this some oxidative unhairing agents can also be used to remove the black and salt stain in wool sheep, buff calf etc. Sodium chlorite with a weak acid is used, Generally lactic acid or Glycollic acid is used. By this treatment salt stains are also removed and grading can go up appreciably.

Pickling : Pickling is the process where animal skins are treated with salt and acid and conditioning them for the subsequent tannage. As the process can also be used for the preservation of pelts, has become of increased importance from its use as a preparation for mineral tanning.

Basic Principle : The general method is to swell the pelt with an acid and then treating it with a strong solution of common salt. The pelt becomes very flat and thin and is converted into a sort of white leather. If placed in water it at once swells. The earlier method of pickling was to swell the skins in sulphuric acid much diluted and then to bring them down in strong salt solution. But it is now universal to add salt to the pickling solution itself to control excessive swelling. A suitable strength for the rinsing solution itself will control excessive swelling. A suitable strength for the rinsing solution is about 80 gins. of common salt and 7.5 gums. of sulphuric acid per litre. A much weaker solution of acid is sufficient for adequate pickling and a more satisfactory pelt results. The acid is taken up by the pelt but it is necessary to add salt occasionally. After paddling or drumming in the pickle bath for a few hours, they are left in the same liquor for some hours in saturated brine with advantage. Skins may be effectively pickled in with very much smaller quantities of acid and salt, but they are more liable to suffer from mildew. Pickled skins should not be brought into contact with water. The water dilutes the brine and acid acts on the pelt causing an excessive swelling.

USE of Organic Salts : In the place of mineral acids, organic acids such as formic acid, acetic acid, etc., can be used with great advantage in the subsequent tannage. Formic acid has strong germicidal properties in itself These organic acids can also be used in small quantities along with the mineral acid. For such pickle liquors, either sodium or calcium formate or formic acid in the pickle system is introduced. Several methods of pickling are introduced which do not involve the use of acids. Several acids which do not swell the pelt and do no harm to them such as Napthalene Sulfonic acids. etc. are put into usage recently. But these are more expensive.

This can be done in one bath with,

Sulphuric acid	2%	
Salt	20%	on the pelt weight
Water	200%	

Paddled or drummed, the goods can be left inside the drum for equilibrium pickle.

Dry Pickle : The pickled goods are exported in a dry condition, which saves considerable amount of cost in freight charges. The dry weight will be 1/3 rd of what it would be otherwise. In dry pickling the goods are packed in a dry condition. During drying the salt comes out and rupture the fibre structure. Once it is dried it is not easy to wet back. But the Spanish people actually export in a dry condition. They depickle the pelt with hypo, dry and export them. Even here there is the possibility of salt rupture. Working on these lines, a product has been put on the market which contain sulphophthalic acid and cationic wetting agent. The sulphothalic acid is a non-swelling acid. While using this minimum amount of salt (2%) is used. They are dried in shade and they wet back in 5 to 10 minutes. This is good for suede and other flesh side finished leathers. For fine grain leathers this may not be useful.

Depickling : Skins pickled with acids still retain enough acid to cause excessive swelling and to produce cracky and rotten leather if vegetable tanned. To prevent this usually, they are given a treatment with sufficient salt. When it is desired to give a normal tannage without salt the pelt must be first depickled. The acid must be neutralised or moved. This is done in any weak alkaline solution but with great care. When pickling is used as a preparation to chrome tannage, the object is not for preservation. If a heavily pickled pelt is put into a neutral dichromate solution it will be depickled by action of dichromate, sufficient chromic acid is liberated to chrome the skin. For the chrome tanning pickling is also often useful, in enabling a more basic liquor to be used at the outset without precipitation or case hardening the skin, or over-tanning the outside. Pickling can be done to achieve two purposes. One to preserve pelt for exports and the other is to prepare the pelt for chrome tanning.

DETAILED OBSERVATION OF BATING

A bated leather should first show the effect of enzyme when the pelt is examined.

1. A particular flaccid appearance and feel.
2. The whole skin will be capable of folding on itself in a small place like a palm.
3. The slippery grain. A particular soft feel. All are these in addition to the continuation deliming action such as
   a. each removal of short hair and scud
   b. capable of retaining the thumb impression
   c. porosity to pass the air through.

OBJECT OF BATING

1. To remove the grainy appearance of the grain and make it smooth.
2. To remove the pigment, hair roots, grease and scud off the grain layer, so that a leather of clear grain may be produced.
3. A particular softness and feel may be imparted to the leather.
4. To remove the elastic stretch that is common in upper leather and to impart a plastic stretch as in glove leather and in general structure of leather improves in the bating. Glove leathers are bated for a longer time than upper. A garment leather is given a little less bating than glove leathers. These bates not only digest the elastic fibres of the grain layer, but also hydrolysis the grease.

CONDITIONS OF BATING

1. This reaction is enzymative and chemical. It is highly specific that temperature should be 90°F to 100°F. Bating at lower temperatures is more slow. If the bating temperature is high the bacterial activity is more. This clashes with the fact mentioned before that a limed stock will hydrolise more at high temperature. It may be mentioned that the above that lime hydrolysis is more pronounced above 85°F leathers containing appreciable amount of lime, should first be bated at 85°F and temperature should be gradually increased to 95°F depending on the activity desired temperature may be adjusted. But activity falls off above 110°F and is very harmful.
2. **pH :** The pH should be preferably between 8.2 to 8.3 i.e. when bating activity is at its peak. Some times bating can also be done at a pH of 7.5 if necessary. A high pH 5.3, combined with high temperature of 95°F will loosen the break and therefore some prefer to bate at 7.5 pH

and 85°F. Thus the temperature and pH must be varied to suit particular type of leather and the extent of bating desired. A temperature of 95°F and pH 5.3 should not be considered as rigid and unflexible. Changes must be made to suit particular leather and the enzymatic activity desired. Certain leathers have to be treated drastically rapidly. Cow hides for upper bating is mildly done and therefore high temperature and alkaline pH are harmful. Goat skins are hard natured like dry salted skin of Dried origin must be bated drastically. Glove leathers must be bated for a long time and drastic moderate bating is necessary for garments. Upholstery etc. have to be bated differently.

3. **Where to Bate :** Paddle batting is commonly used. Closed paddle is preferable because of darkness and ammonia released will be confined and pH will remain constant. Closed paddles are preferred also because of the darkness, and abitutes to keep warm to encourage bacterial activity. Bating can also be done is drums where a drastic bating is necessary because it can be done at high pH and temperature can be maintained constant. More mechanical action and hence rapid bating. Bating for glove, garments, clothing etc. can be done in drums.

Scudding : At this stage some oxidative unhairing agents can also be used to remove the black scud and salt stains in wool sheep, buff calf etc. Sodium chlorite with weak acid may be used for better results or Generally lactic acid or Glycollic acid can also be used. By this treatment salt stains are also removed and grading can go up appreciably.

Pickling for Preservation & Export : This can be done in two bath or in one bath. In the first bath for every 100 kg. of bated pelt 2 kg. of sulphuric acid (sp. gr. 1.84) 30 kg. of salt and 120 liters of water are used. In the second bath a saturated solution of salt is used. The pelts treated in the first bath are drummed or paddled here, for a few hours until the pelts fall adequately, the pelts are kept in the bath and in the next day they are drained off. They are then packed in containers after treating with a suitable preservative/antiseptic for export. A layer of salt is spread over the top of the container. Care should be taken to use only permitted preservatives free from PCP.

This can be done in one bath with,

Sulhuric acid	2%
Salt	20% on the pelt weight
Water	200%

Paddled or drummed, the goods can be left inside the drum for equilibrium pickle.

DRY PICKLE

By dry pickle, it is not meant the pickling is done in dry condition or reduced float. But the pickled goods are exported in a dry condition, which saves considerable amount of cost in freight charges. The dry weight will be one third of what it would be otherwise. In dry pickling the goods are packed in a dry condition. During drying the salt comes out and rupture the fibre structure. Once it is dried it is not easy to wet back. But the Spanish people actually export in a dry condition. They depickle the pelt with hypo, dry and export them. Even here, there is the possibility of salt rupture. Working on these, a product has been put on the market which contain sulphophthalic acid and cationic wetting agent. The sulphothalic acid is a non-swelling acid. While using this minimum amount of salt (2%) is used. They are dried in shade and they wet back in 5 to 10 minutes. This is good for suede and other flesh side finished leathers. For fine grain leathers this may not be useful.

DEPICKLING

Skins pickled with acids still retain enough acid to cause excessive swelling and to produce rotten leather if vegetable tanned. To prevent this usually, they are given a treatment with sufficient salt. When it is desired to give a normal tannage without salt the pelt must be first depickled. The acid must be neutralised or removed. This is done in any weak alkaline solution but with great care. When pickling is used as a preparation to Chrome tannage, the object is not for preservation. If a heavily pickled pelt is put into a neutral dichromate solution it will be depickled by action of dichromate, sufficient chromic acid is liberated to chrome the skin. For the basic process pickling is also often useful, in obtain a more basic liquor to be used at the outset with-out precipitation or case hardening the skin, or over-tanning the outside. Pickling can be done to achieve two purposes. One to preserve pelt for exports and the other is to prepare the pelt for chrome tanning.

For vegetable tanned leathers a mild pickling followed by depickling or pretanning with syntan helps to obtain a good and uniform colour and smooth grain. For certain industrial leathers like picking band leathers, a heavy and strong pickling followed by thorough depickling with hypo, results in a mild deposition of sulphur in inter space imparting a sulphur tutnage and also acts as a solid lubricant.

PICKLING

Pickling is the process of treating the pelts with a solution of acid and salt to bring them to an acidic condition. The delimed and bated pelts have a pH of about 8, and by pickling the pH is brought down to a pH of about 2 to 3.5 depending on the amount of acid used.

Pickling has two main objects in leather manufacture :

(i) Conditioning the pelt ready for tanning-specially in chrome tanning.

(ii) Preservation of the pelt for a longer time prior to tanning.

In the first case the pelts are given a mild pickling and in the second case the pelts are given a heavier pickling. Higher the pH value of the pelt in the pickle bath, greater is the tendency for the chrome tanning salts to fix on the grain.

Functions of Acid in Pickle

When a delimed or bated pelt is put in a pickle bath, the following reactions take place :

(i) A part of the acid neutralises the free alkali.

(ii) A part of the acid decomposes and neutralises the bound alkali in the pelt- i.e. alkali collagenate.

(iii) A part of the acid combines with the pelt chemically,

(iv) A part of the acid is physically or mechanically held in the interspaces of the pelt structure.

By combined action of all these factors the pH is lowered to about 2.0 to 3.5 depending on the quantity of acid.

Functions of Salt in Pickling

When a pelt is placed in acidic solution it starts swelling, specially in the absence of salt. But in the presence of salt (neutral salt) the tendency of swelling is arrested. The salt supresses the swelling action, because of its dehydrating action, thus counteracting the action of acid for swelling. Hence the quantity of salt used will have to be adjusted depending on the quantity of acid used in pickling.

Usually in pickling about 6 to 10% of salt is used for a float of 100% water and an acid concentration of 1 to 1.5% on pelt weight. Lesser quantities of salt may not be adequate to suppress the swelling and may cause damage to the pelt, but too high quantities of salt will lead to a very thin and flat leather in chrome tanning. Also, too high a concentration of in pickle will cause precipitation of tannins specially in vege tanning bath.

Common Systems of Pickle Bath

Usually for pickling sulphuric acid/common salt system is practised,but in special cases a combination of sulphuric acid/organic acid and salt is also used. Sometimes Hydrochloric acid-Salt System may also be used. In many cases Formic acid is often used either alone or in combination with

Sulphuric acid. This helps to obtain a smoother grain and a lighter coloured leather. Also many tanneries prefer to use Sodium sulphate (Glaubers Salt) for pickling. It is also possible to use a buffer salt in pickling. Buffer salts (like Sodium formate) have a very good influence in imparting grain tightness and extra fullness to the final leather, but all these are more expensive. But the most common practice is to use a Sulphuric acid-Common Salt system for pickling because of its lower cost.

Sometimes about 2 to 3% of Potash alum or chrome alum is added in the pickle bath, specially while processing thin and empty raw stock, for obtaining greater fullness and smoother grain. Potash alum salts help to partially fix the grain layer prior to actual tanning- Similarly non-swelling acids like Sulphophthalic acid or naphthalene Suiphonic acid etc., may also be used for obtaining greater fullness and grain smoothness.

Types of Pickle

By altering the pickle with reference to pH in particular, it is possible to change the characteristic properties of skins to be vegetable tanned. The lower the pH the better the colour and fixation and higher the pH the greater the fullness and penetration of tans. Pickling is done to a certain pH so as to carry out the chrome tanning. Otherwise if the pH is high the chrome will be precipitated and no tanning is done. Generally 3 types of pickles can be used as follows :

	Light Pickle	Medium Pickle	Heavy Pickle
pH	Greater than 3.5	3-3.5	Less than 2.5
Character,	Coarse grain and the leather will have good substance.	Reasonably good grain. Substance will be better.	Smooth grain and the leather is tinny and empty.
Acid H_2SO_4	0.75 –1.00%	1–1.25%	1.5–2.0%
Salt NaCl	6 – 8%	8%	12 – 15%
Water	80-100%	80-100%	80-100%

The less the acid the greater the substance and coarser the grain. The more the acid the smoother is the grain and empty is the leather. The deposition of fine particles of Sulphur, by depickling with hypo, inside the fibres in the Heavy and Industrial leathers, act as a fine solid lubricant and a mild sulphur tanning takes place and hence a good amount of acid is given in the pickling of these leathers.

Equilibrium Pickle

If the goods are left in the same pickle bath overnight, then the pickling is known as equilibrium pickle. Here the pH of the pelt and the pH of the bath are brought to the same level. By doing so, a uniform tannage is obtained. When pickling is done for 1-2 hours and the cross section is checked, pH will be different at various layers. If it is so, the goods are plumped in Chrome tanning and a firm leather is obtained. In the case of equilibrium pickle a flat smooth leather is obtained.

Varieties of Pickle based on Ingredients

Dry Pickle

Working on this, Germany has introduced a commercial product called **'DECALTAN'**. The goods are drummed for 1-2 hours. Decaltan contains 2-3% Sulfophthalic acid and 0.1-2% cationic wetting agent. The Sulphophthalic acid is a non-swelling acid. While using picaltan a minimum amount of salt 2%) is used. They are dried in shade and they wet back in 5 to 10 minutes. This is good for suede and other flesh side finished leathers. For good grain leathers this cannot be used.

Varieties of Pickling can be as follows:

Common

1% to 1.5% H_2SO_4

6 – 8% Salt Most commonly used prior to chrome tanning

75 – 100%

2% Hydrochloric acid

6 – 8% Salt It produced a fine grain and soft leather.

75 – 100% Water

1% H_2SO_4 This gives firm and full leather.

3 – 4% Na_2SO_4 (Sod. Sulphate)

1% H_2SO_4

2 – 3% Aluminium Sulphate

$(A1_2(SO_4)H_2o$ Gives finer grain and full leather

4% Salt

75 – 100% Water.

0.5% H_2SO_4

2 – 3% Chrome alum
4% Salt
75 – 100% Water

This gives finest grain and this is mostly favoured.

Masked Pickle

0.5% Sulphuric Acid
1% Formic Acid
6 – 8% Salt
75 – 100% Water.

Gives fine grain and the Chrome tanning is much favoured.

Instead of formic acid other organic or non-swelling acids can be used. Sometimes syntans are also used and the grain is protected.

0.5% H_2SO_4
2% Auxiliary Syntan
4 – 6% Salt
100% Water

The pelt is treated in this for 1 hour and chrome tanning is done. This is done for gloving, clothing and white leathers.

Another commercial product known as Calgon (polymeric meta phosphate) finds application in pickling.

2 – 3% Calgon
1.5 - 2.0% H_2SO_4
70% Water

Specially used for thin empty pelts.

The pH should be 2 – 2.5. Calgon has got tanning action also. No swelling takes place, and the pelt will be clean opaque and white in appearance and free from stains. In vegetable tanning, after calgon treatment the pelt can be straightway taken to a strong liquor. (60°B.K.)

Since Sulphuric acid is cheaper than Hydrochloric acid, it is mostly used pickling. No salt is needed and hence this is a salt free system.

De-Pickling

The object of de-pickling is to reduce the excess acidity of the pickled pelt and this is specially done for heavy industrial and textile leathers like pickling band, chrome belting etc. Usually de-pickling is done using hypo (8 to 15% Sodium thiosulphate) in a very short float of (20 to 40%) depending on the degree of depickling desired. De-pickling not only reduces the harmful acidity by replacing the strong acid by a weaker Sulphurous acid, but also deposits fine particles of Sulphur which imparts a mild Sulphur tannage and acts as a solid lubricant. It also raises the pH of the pelt above 3.5. Such a mild Sulphur pre-tannage also helps in imparting a greater strength and solidity to industrial leather. This may also be done for some leathers meant for vegetable tannage. De-pickling may also be done using others salts like Sodium bisulphite and mild alkalies like Soda bicarb, or with mild pre-tanning Syntans. Further details on this may be found in details of processing different types of leathers.

TANNING

Tanning is the main process by which the putrefiable nature of the hides and skins is changed and the permanent resistance to bacterial action is imparted, or in other words the main object of tanning is to convert the putrefiable raw hides and skins into a substance known as leather, which does not putrefy, dries out soft and does not swell when wetted back Substance which impart such characteristics to the raw pelt are called tanning agents.

Tanning Agents

The following tanning agents have been found to be successful in producing satisfactory commercial leather.

1. Vegetable tanning substances containing tannins.
2. Mineral ranning substances like aluminium, chrome and zircoium.
3. Oils containing large amounts of unsaturated groups like fish oil, cod oil etc.
4. Formaldehyde, Glutaraldehyde etc.
5. Synthetic tanning agents or syntans.

Tanning processes have been developed making use of these tanning agents for producing commercial leather, and these are known as follows:

1. Alum tanning process.
2. Chrome tanning process.
3. Vegetable tanning process.
4. Oil tanning process.
5. Formaldehyde tanning process.
6. Tanning with syntans, zirconium etc.

Apart from individual tanning processes based on the above, several combination tanning processes are also adopted in the trade, by making use of more than one tanning agent, to impart several desirable properties, characteristic of each tanning agent used.

Typical examples of such combination tanning processes are :

1. Semi-chrome process-First vegetable tanning followed by chrome tanning. (for garment, suede leather etc.)
2. Chrome Retain process-First chrome tanning followed by vegetable tanning. (for upper leather)
3. Formaldehyde and oil tanning-First formaldehyde followed by oil tanning, (For chamois leather).

Similarly many such combinations are possible for producing different types of leathers.

Olden Methods Practised

Alum Tanning

Tanning with alum is the oldest known inorganic tannage. It was known as alum tawing and was used for tanning of skins and also glove leather. After the discovery of chrome tannage the importance of this tannage has diminished. At present, these are used to a small extent for hair on tannage and in combination tannages. Alum tanning consists in druming the pelt with the following, or this can also be applied as a thick paste on the flesh side, with less water, and this method is know as Alum 'Tawing'.

Potash alum	6 – 8 kg.
Sodium chloride	1 – 2 kg.
Yolk of egg (yellow)	8.15 kg.
Flour	8 – 12 kg.
Water	50 – 60 litres.

The skins are then dried without washing. This operation combines both tanning and fat liquoring. The main disadvantage of this tannage is that this does not resist hydrolysis and the shrinkage temperature is very much lower than the other known tannages- Potash alum and aluminium sulphate are normally used for tanning purposes. These should be free from iron because iron will produce patches in the latter stage. Solutions of aluminium sulphate have an acidic reaction as the salt hydrolysis in water forming the basic oxides and sulphuric acid. Aluminium salts are easily hydrolised, on hydrolysis form $A1_203$, which is easily precipitated. Hence Alum tanning salts produce a less permanent tanned leather. Sometimes because of the salt used in tanning, it absorbs water from the atmosphere, and it is observed small droplets are formed similar to sweat. The salt also causes salt spucing. Recently pre-basified basic Aluminium chlorides and sulphate tanning agents have been produced on a commercial scale and these are considered to have better stability and tanning characteristics.

There is an obvious difference between the hydrolytic behaviour of aluminium salts and chrome salts, and this difference is attributed to the fact that the aluminium atom is unable to complex firmly with sulphate ions. Further comparative studies on aluminium and chrome salt solutions have shown that the aluminium salt does not olate and oxolate to the same extent as chrome salts. Hence the inferiority of aluminium as compared to chrome.

Some typical Alum tanning recipes are given below:

1. For Kid Skins on Pelt Weight.

Potash Alum	–	5%
Salt	–	3%
Egg yolk or its substitute	–	10%
White Flour	–	8%
Water	–	45%

. For White Tanning of Sheep Skins on Pelt Weight.

Potash Alum	–	10%
Salt	–	5%
Egg Yolk or its substitute	–	5%
White Flour	–	6%
Water	–	40%

3. Tawing Paste for Fun Skins.

Potash Alum	–	10 Parts.
Salt	–	5 parts.
Egg Yolk or its substitute	–	5 parts.
White Flour	–	12 parts
Water	–	40 parts

Preparation of the Alum Tawing Paste

1. Flour is stirred well and mixed with one fourth of its weight of water at ordinary temperature.
2. Alum and salt are dissolved in one fourth of their weight of hot water. Then the water is cooled by adding another one fourth of the water, to about 50° C.

3. Egg Yolk or its substitute is stirred in cold water at 25°C to 27°C to a soupy consistency.
4. Add the flour and water solution to the alum salt solution and mix well. Then add the egg yolk water mixture slowly, stirring well. Stir and mix the whole mixture and now it is ready for use in tanning.

Note:

1. In alum tanning-specially by using the tawing paste, the paste is uniformly applied on the flesh side, repeatedly, and allowed to dry slowly. During drying, the skins are repeatedly staked over a knee staker until the pelts become very soft on drying.
2. It is not advisable to wash the skins after alum tanning in pit or drum, as this is likely to strip the alum, and make the leather thin and hard.
3. Usually thicker skins require a larger quantity of the tawing paste or mixture and take a longer time for tanning.
4. It is necessary to check the completion of alum tanning by drying out a cut piece. The cut piece should dry out soft or should become soft on staking without leaving any 'Glossy' layer in the middle. If such a glossy layer is noticed, the tanning should be continued.
5. Repeated staking of the tanned skins is very necessary to make the leather soft.

VEGETABLE TANNING

Vegetable tanning is one of the earliest tannages known to mankind. The classical meaning of vegetable tanning is that the previously conditioned pelt is treated with an aqueous infusion of tree barks, pods, fruits or roots,by which process the pelt is made imputrecible. The active chemical component which is capable of combining with the protein 'collagen' to convert into an imputrecible material called 'leather' is known as the Tannin'. These tannins are usually water soluble and easily extracted from the bark, roots, pods, leaves or fruits.

In olden days only the fresh infusions of barks etc., were used for tanning, but in modern times concentrated solid extracts and spray dried tanning powders, almost moisture free, are available on the market.

Occurrence of Tannins

Tannins are chemical substances for the conversion of hide or skin into leather, and they occur widely in the plant kingdom. Although almost every plant or tree contains tannins to some extent, higher plants and trees like oak, wattle, babul, chestnut, sumac, quebracho, myrobolams, avaram, konnan etc. contain more tannins. There are tannin bearing plants in both tropical and non-tropical climates, but a large number of tannin bearing plants are found in tropical countries. The tannins may occur predominantly either in the barks, roots, pods, leaves or in the fruits depending upon the specific plant or tree.

The tannin content in the plant material may vary and is influenced by the climate, soil, season, age of the plant and many other factors.

Classification of Vegetable Tanning Materials

Vegetable tannins are divided chemically into two main groups, namely pyrogallol and catechol groups. They are also known as hydrolisable and condensed tannins respectively.

Pyrogallol or hydrolisable tannins usually give yellow to tan brown colour, contain high acidity, and contains more sugary matter. On keeping these tend to hydrolisc and deposit insoluble matter (usually ellagic and chebulinic acid) on the surface of the leather as yellowish-white patches. These are also known as bloom. Penetration of pyrogallol tannins is also relatively slow. Because of these reasons, these are considered to be inferior in tanning action. Among the pyrogallol tannins 'sumac' leaves contain a high amount of neutral-buffer salts and this is considered to be a good tanning material. Typical example is myrobolam nuts.

Catechol tannins usually are more reddish-brown, contain low acidity, sugary matter and salt. These readily penetrate and combine with the pelt, usually give a higher weight yield of leather. On exposure they become darker and reddish in colour. They do not readily hydrolise or deposit bloom on the leather.

Principle of Vegetable Tanning Process

The previously conditioned pelt is treated with an infusion of barks in water, along with the bark. The tannins ooze out slowly in the solution, and the oozed out tannins are gradually absorbed and combine chemically with the hide substance, converting into leather. This is the basic principle of the olden method of contact tannage.

Later on, previously extracted tannins in the form of concentrated tanning solution, block and spray dried extracts are made and used for tanning with the main idea of reducing the tanning time, and quickening the rate of tanning.

Leaching

Mellow or heavy tannages are developed for sole leather in the place of oak bark tannages. In these cases, liquors of higher strengths are used. This is achieved by leaching the tannins with cold and hot water respectively. This technique of leaching the tannins cuts short the tanning time and gives rise to a better yield and hence it is found to be cheaper. In the heavy tannages, bleaching is resorted to obtain a fine good colour. This bleaching technique later led to the manufacture of solid extracts. To get solid extracts, most of the tannin is extracted with water and the leach liquor thus obtained is settled, concentrated and evaporated. The following are the few types of solid extracts available in the market to-day.

(i) Quebracho, (ii) Wattle, (iii) Myrobolam,(iv) Cutch and (v) Gambier, etc. These extracts contain in them: (i) moisture (ii) fraction of insolubles and (iii) tannins which are soluble. For example the quebracho solid extract contains 18 to 20% water, 5 to 8% insolubics and 63 to 64% tannin. The advantages of solid extracts over the barks, woods, etc. are as follows:

(i) In the case of solid extracts tannin content on weight basis is higher whereas in the case of barks the tannin content on weight basis is low. The extract poses less problems in its transport from one place to another.

(ii) In the case of barks, they are to be soaked at least a couple of days prior to the tanning. This difficulty does not arise with the extracts, as it can be dissolved readily.

(iii) Lastly barks are likely to be adulterated with mud, etc. and the adulteration of solid extracts is not that common.

(iv) The tan content in barks may vary in each lot of purchase and it may be difficult to determine the exact tan content. But in extract it is supplied in standard strength. Thus solid extracts have many advantages over the barks, wood, etc. Similar to solid extracts there are some tanning materials which are marketed in the form of liquid also. Now tannin extracts are available with standard quality specification.

Dark colour of Solid Extracts

Tannins get easily oxidised and become darker in colour on heating and concentration, but in the making of solid extracts, one difficulty was experienced. While making solid extract the strong liquor obtained by leaching was dried under a partial vacuum and at high temperature, and the tannin stayed in this condition for a fairly long period of time. During this lengthy evaporation period, there was always a certain amount of darkening of colour, due to oxidisation of the tans. But later concentrated products were introduced in the market overcoming these difficulties by suitable bleaching, and the use of solid extracts has become very popular. The next stage is to prepare a product with less moisture to reduce loss of tannins. Consequently spray drying is introduced.

Spray Drying of Extracts

By this process the long and time consuming evaporation in the manufacture of solid extracts is shortened. In this process a highly concentrated liquid is sprayed in a tall highly heated chamber called a spray drier through which the fine droplets pass through a spinning atomizer. These droplets lose the moisture while falling through the chambers in the hot air, giving rise to a very fine powder with only about 5 – 6% of moisture and the very high tannin content. Now it is obvious that the moisture content is reduced to 1/3 of that of the solid extract which means a greater ease in handling etc. In short the advantage with the spray dried extracts can be listed as follows:

(a) General ease of handling.

(b) Ease of accurate measurement of quantity.

(c) Clean bags no loss of extract by adhesion to the bags as in the case of solid extracts.

(d) No spillage or waste due to leaky bags.

(e) Ease and rapidity of dissolving in drums or in paddles even in the cold.

(f) More tan content per ton.

(g) Less freight per ton unit.

Apart from all these basic advantages, the spray dried extracts are also much lighter in colour. The tanning characteristics are basically the same.

Different Vegetable Tanning Materials

During the past few years more and more types of vegetable materials have been made available in the spray dried form. Some of the important tanning materials and their characteristics are given below.

Quebracho

Quebracho tannin comes from the wood of trees in South America and Southern Paraguay and Brazil. Most of the tannin is extracted in South America by leaching, the leach liquor is settled, evaporated and shipped as solid extract. During the past few years, a spray dried product has also been made available. The extract is generally in two forms -(1) ordinary or untreated and (2) clarified or treated.

1. The ordinary quebracho contains about 5 – 8% insolubles which will settle down when diluted. It gives a reddish coloured leather and it becomes more dark on exposure.

2. The sulphited quebracho extract is digested hot with 3 to 6% sodium sulphite or sodium bisulphite. This treatment reduces the insolubles to less than 1 % and these are of a much lighter colour and less sticky in nature. This is done to speed up the rate of penetration and to get a pink coloured leather.

Wattle

This tannin comes from the bark of the tree. First found in Australia, but now grown in South and East Africa. The tannin is leached and shipped as solid extract and also in spray dried form. Treatment of the extracts with small amounts of metabisulphite or hydrosulphite bleaches the colour greatly. In fact by bleaching with hydrosulphite an almost white leather and can be produced.

Several types of wattle extracts containing 66% tans are marketed and this is one of the most used tanning materials all over the world. It is the most popular tanning material known to tanners.

Myrobalan

This is obtained from the fruit of a type of tree found in India. This fruit is dried, leached and made available in the extract and spray dried forms This can even be modified and used as a self tanning agent in the spray dried form. There are products of modified myrobalan extracts in use as self-tanning material. Freshly leached myrobalan gives a fine yellow colour on the surface, and also imparts greater resistance to oxidation on wattle tanned leathers. Because of these reasons myrobalan liquor is used as a topping material in the famous East Indian tanned leathers. Also myrob liquor or myrob powder is mixed with wattle or other catechol tanning materials in sole leather tanning to obtain a more lights; coloured leather.

Avaram Bark (Turwar)

The botanical name is Cassia auriculata. In Madras and in other parts of South India it is known as 'Avaram' (Turwar in Bombay). The bark is obtained from a shrub which grows in plenty in Hyderabed and Mysore. It Is also available in Rajasthan and Gujarat States, where it is known as Aval. The bark is marketed in small chips which are soft and brittle. There are three grades available to the South Indian tanners. Thick barks are usually used for tanning' kip hides. Medium and thin barks are used for calf, goat and sheep skins. Avaram bark contains on an average 16 – 18% tannin. It is a catechol tan and produces an exceedingly light colour on leather. Penetration is fairly quick. It gives a golden yellow colour, a mellow tannage and hence is considered to be the ideal material for the old conventional E.I. tanning.

Babul Bark

The botanical name is Acacia Arabica. Babul bark is obtained in the northern part of India and Sudan. In Sudan, the Babul pods contain a high percentages of tannins, which give light coloured leather. Babul bark contains on an average 12% tannin. Sudanese Babul pods are reported to contain as high as 30 to 50% tans. The tannins in Babul belong to the mixed tanning group in which the catechol tannins predominate. A major proportion of vegetable tanned leathers in India is tanned using Babul bark, especially in the rural areas.

Konnan Bark

The botanical name is Cassia fistula. Konnam bark is obtained from another South Indian tree and is used by the traditional tanners of East India tanned kips and skins. The average tan content is 11 – 14%. It gives a fight colour and good filling.

Goran Bark

The botanical name is Ceriops Roxburghiana. It belongs to the Mangrove species. Barks of all mangrove plants have a highly coloured tannin. As such goran also produces a red coloured leathers. However, tannin content of goran is fairly high (26 – 36%) and can be regarded as a potential source of tanning which can be utilized. Now specific treatment methods have been developed to make the colour lighter.

Chestnut

The botanical name is 'Castanea vesoa' which grows in France, Italy, Spain and Switzerland. In the United States the most important source is the wood of the American tree, Castanea dentata. The tannin occurs to a great extent in the wood of older trees, particularly the heartwood. Chestnut is a pyrogallol tannin and is used principally for heavy leather tanning, such as sole, belting, etc. It has a high tannin fixation value and produces a firm and a plumpy leather.

Because of its higher acid content, chestnut is not used alone for tanning. In the manufacture of brown picking band leather chestnut is a valuable additive in blends with quebracho. It produces leather with a yellowish-brown colour with somewhat greyish cast.

Gambier

It is obtained from the leaves and twigs of the shrub 'Nauclea gambier native to East Indies. The twigs and leaves are treated in boiling water to prepare an infusion which is later concentrated and thickened with starch. Plantation gambler is scientifically manufactured extract and has the maximum tannin content. Gambier is reputed for its low acidity and high salt content and is therefore an exceptionally mellow tannin.

Special Qualities of Gambier

It produces fast-to-light leathers of enormous strength. Owing to its low acidity and high salt content, gambler tanned leather has smooth grain and mellow handle. Gambier tanned leather is able to take up fat readily and is also able to retain it remarkably well. For these reasons it is not only an ideal tanning material for retanning chrome or vegetable tanned leather but has been traditionally employed by the carriers and tanners of textile and mechanical leathers. Gambier belongs to the catechol group of tannin and yields a light- buff coloured tannage which, however, discolours rapidly on exposure to light. It can also be used as a mordant in chrome upper leather.

Bleached Extracts

These bleached extracts are such extracts which are digested or treated with bleaching agents like sodium bisulphite, sodium sulphite etc. They are generally known as sulphited extracts. In this process the amount of insolubles is reduced to a lower degree and converted into one of rapidly penetrative type. By this bleaching, better colour is achieved. Normally, during the evaporation to make solid extracts there is always a danger of oxidation of the tannin taking place resulting in a darker colour. In fact it is possible to make a pale leather by using bleached wattle extract (Kenmosa GS Powder) instead of the normal wattle extract which normally gives a pink coloured leather. In vegetable tanning the colour being an important factor, the bleached extracts have gained very much importance.

PRACTICAL CONSIDERATIONS IN VEGETABLE TANNING

Some Important Characteristics of Vegetable Tanning Materials

(1) Tan content.
(2) Non-tan content.
(3) T/NT Ratio.
(4) Acidity.
(5) Salt content.
(6) Add/Salt content.
(7) pH.
(8) Colour.
(9) Astringency.

1. Tan Content

By definition tannins are those chemical constituents which chemically combine with hide protein converting them into leather. But in actual tanning along with the tannins, some non-tans, are also physically absorbed by the pelt.

Different tanning materials have different amount of tannins, present in them. For effecting good tanning the tanning, content in the substance should be fairly high along with the other related substances. Usually the barks used for tanning contain about 12 to 30% Tans in them. In the case of extracts it is fairly high. Too low tan content, below 10% will not be economical to use, and too high tans will make the tan liquor highly astringent and sometimes make the leather surface harsh. Hence for best tanning there should be an optimum tannins to non-tannins ratio.

2. Non-Tans

Non-tans are also important and useful materials in tanning. These are usually salts of weak acids, or low molecular weight tannin constituents, sugar or starch material etc. These are usually absorbed by the pelt alongwith the tannins. The general word non-tans is a vague term, and strictly speaking there is no clear Demarkeation between the terms tans and non-tans. Non-tans usually mellows down the reaction of tannins, by first penetrating into the hides and subsequently get partially displaced by the more powerful tans. These non-tans impart the mellowness in leather In actual tanning.

3. T/NT Ratio

For good tanning the T/N.T. ratio should be within the optimum limits of 15 to 1.7. Too high proportion of tans will make the leather harsh, and surface cracky, whereas too much non-tans will make the leather spongy and empty.

4. Acidity

Since tanning materials are organic substances containing phenolic 'OH' groups they exhibit different degree of acidity depending on their pyrogallol or catechol nature. Usually pyrogallol tannins are more acidic, when compared to catechol tannins. Phrogallol tannins are also easily hydrolised forming weak organic acids. Too high acidity will make the liquors too astringent, and will not help optimum tannage. Too low acidity will not help obtaining good yield. Hence usually in tanning two or more tanning materials are blended to achieve optimum effect in tanning.

5. Salt Content

Usually vegetable tannins also contain some salts of weak organic acids, which act as a buffer salt, and these generally help in controlling the acidity and regulating the tanning. These salts are essential components in vegetable tanning. Too high a salt content, and too low salt content are not desirable.

6. Acid/Salt Ratio

Each tanning material has its own characteristic acid/salt ratio, and has its specific tanning properties. For optimum tanning properties, usually tanners blend two or more tanning materials to adjust the correct acid/salt ratio. This can also be referred to as 'buffer index'.

7. pH.

Tanning materials in their acqueous infusion have characteris pH values. Usually pyrogallol tannins exhibit a lower pH value, as compared to catechol tanning materials which have a higher pH. The pH value of any tanning material will depend on its acid, and acid salt content in it. The pH value of a tan liquor will have its own effect in tanning. Greater the pH value, slightly darker is the colour, faster the rate of penetration and lesser is the fixation in the pelt. But if the pH is lowered, the colour becomes lighter, the rate of penetration becomes slow, but the fixation is high. Hence in actual vegetable tanning, the pH value of the tan in liquor in the early stages is kept high around pH5, and then in the later stages of tanning the pH is gradually lowered to about 3.8 to obtain greater fixation and yield.

9. Astringency

Astringency is a term usually associated with vegetable tanning material and is usually specific for different tanning materials. It depends on various other factors like T/N.T. ratio, acid/salt content, buffer index etc. Astringency is the characteristic which usually indicates the power of drawing together of the fibre structure specially on the grain, and is also related to dehydrating capacity of the tanning material from the pelt. Very high astringency in tanning materials is not desirable as it will lead to drawn grain, and too low astringency will not effect proper tannage. Hence in vegetable tanning usually more than one tanning material is blended for the best results.

FACTORS INFLUENCING TANNING

1. The nature of the pelt.
2. The type of leathers required to be processed.
3. The nature of the tanning materials used in tanning.
4. The concentration or quantity of the tan BK° strength.
5. pH.
6. Agitation.
7. Temperature.
8. Time.

1. The Nature of the Pelt : Different kinds of pelt, and their preconditioning will have their own effect on the tannage. Usually cattle hides require greater quantity of tannins, when compared to the skins. Similarly in a well delimed or pretreated pelt the tanning is done more easily and faster when compared to a partially delimed or improperly pretreated pelt. Hence for obtaining good vegetable tanning, the quantity of the tanning materials used, and the method of its treatment will have to be adjusted to suit the particular nature and condition of the pelt.

2. The Nature of Leathers required to be produced: Usually sole and other heavy leathers will require a heavier tannage, when compared to the lining or other semi-tanned leathers. Hence the quantity of the vegetable tanning materials, tanning duration etc. will have to be adjusted carefully depending on the type of leathers desired.

3. The Nature of the Tanning Materials Used: Each vegetable tanning material, or extract, used for tanning will have its own characteristics like T/N.T. ratio, Acid/Salt ratio, pH etc. Hence these will have to be carefully chosen to obtain optimum results. Usually in practice, more than one tanning material is blended (mixed together) to obtain sfactory results.

Usually solid extracts, powder or liquid extracts are used and these will be used in smaller quantities as they are of high concentration. When barks, leaves or crushed fruits are used, these will be in larger quantities.

4. Concentration: Higher the concentration (as High BK strength) greater is the rate of penetration and fixation, lower the concentration, slower is the rate of penetration and fixation. But too high a concentration in the early stages of tannages, will make the grain drawn, and will lead to case hardening. Hence in actual tanning it is started at a lower BK° strength is and as the tanning proceeds the BK° strength is gradually raised, finally ending up the tannage at high concentration.

5. pH: pH has a remarkable influence in tannage, Usually a higher pH around 5, the rate of penetration is fast, but the fixation is low. As the pH is lowered the penetration becomes slower but the fixation becomes higher. Hence in actual tanning, it is started at a comparatively high pH of 5, and as the tanning proceeds it is gradually reduced to about 3.8 or 3.9. finally ending up at a pH of about 3.7 or so. Hence in tanning it is necessary to have a good control of the pH also.

6. Agitation: Mechanical agitation favours quicker tannage. Hence drum tanning or paddle tanning is much faster than pit tannage. But too much agitation, especially in the paddle will lead to greater oxidation of the tannins leading to darker colour. In drum tanning, if the speed of the drum is too fast, if too high concentrations are used in the beginning without proper pretreatment, a drawn grain will be produced. Hence for vegetable tanning in drums only drums of slow speed or 3 or 4 r.p.m. are used and the pelts are properly pre-treated.

7. Temperature: Generally higher temperature favours quicker penetration and greater fixation. But too high a temperature above 85°or 90°F will lead to greater oxidation of the tannins and darkening of the colour. But too low temperature will slow down the tannage and lower the fixation. Hence in traditional sole leather tannage, the tanned hides are kept in 'dusters' where considerable heat is developed in the pile of leathers in pit.

8. Time: It may be generally said that with increasing time there is greater fixation, but the modern trend is to achieve the optimum tannage in the shortest time, to achieve maximum economy. Hence the tannage processes are suitably adjusted to have the tanning done in as short a time as possible.

With a proper appreciation and understanding of the above influencing factors, and the characteristics of the tanning materials used, it is possible to achieve optimum results in vegetable tanning.

CHROME TANNING

The process of tanning hides and skins with basic chromium salt (Sulphate) is known as chrome tanning.

Chromium belongs to a group of elements having as trivalent and has a valency of three, and a secondary valency of six. A typical salt of trivalent chrome is Cr_2O_3. Chromium can also form poly nuclear complexes.

Principle of the Preparation of Chrome Tanning Salt

Generally di-chromates of Potassium and Sodium are also oxidising agents and are reduced to chromic salts by the organic and inorganic reducing agents. In this reduction the hexavalent acidic chromium is changed into trivalent basic chromium. This is the basic principle of the preparation of basic Chromium Sulphate for tanning. Chromium in the acidic hexavalent state has no tanning power, but in the reduced basic trivalent state exhibit good tanning characteristics.

Mechanism and Concept of BASICITY

Normally the dichromate on treatment with acid (Sulphuric or Hydrochloric) produces chromic acid or its chromic salts, and on Hydrolisis they yield extremely acidic solutions in water. When a portion of the acid formed by this hydrolisis is neutralised, then the residual basic salts start exhibiting tanning properties. Thus the tanning properties increase in proportion to the amount of neutralised acid, or with the amount of reducing or basifying agent added. Thus it will be possible to have one, two or all the three acid radicals replaced by the hydroxyl (OH) groups, which will be corresponding to 33% and 66% and 100% basicity. But highly basic liquors will be precipitated.

Hence in actual tanning liquors of low 33% basicity are used to start with and subsequently basified to effect the tanning action. Basicity concept is an indication of the extent of the (OH) groups attached to the Chrome in the trivalent state. Because of the predominant acidic charge of the complex, these are mainly anionic in action.

But there are methods for preparing with specific properties desired. Ready made Basic Chromium Sulphate extracts are available commercially which are generally used.

PREPARATION OF CHROME LIQUORS

Conventional Method

Usually for preparing an approximately 33% basic chromium sulphate liquor, the following procedure is adopted.

(1) Sodium dichromate	–	100 parts.
(2) Sulphuric Acid (1.84 sp. gr)	–	95 parts.
(3) Molasses	–	35 parts.
Water	–	Sufficient Quantity.

100 parts of Sodium dichromate is dissolved in 2 to 3 times its weight of water. To this the concentrated sulphuric acid is added.

The molasses, diluted to pouring consistency is slowly added with stirring. Initially the reaction appears slow, but with gradual additions, intense heat is developed with the evolution of fumes and the liquor appears to boil and come up. Vigorous stirring and controlled addition will be necessary while preparing chrome liquor. Usually the chrome liquors required for tanning are prepared a few days in advance prior to actual use.

Testing for Reduction

(1) Dilute the chrome liquor in a large volume of water in a while enamel or porcelain dish. The edges of the liquor surface in contact with the white surface should be bluish-green and should not show any yellow tint.

(2) Dilute the chrome liquor, dip a white filter paper. The boundary of the liquor on the filter paper should not be yellowish, but it should be green.

Chemical Test

Take a few ccs of the chrome liquor in a test tube and dilute. Add a few ccs of ammonia liquor and heat well. The chrome will become turbid and appear to precipitate. Then filter the above. Examine the filtrate. It should be colourless like water and should not be yellow at all.

A further confirmatory test can be done by adding a drop of starch solution and Pot. Iodide. It should not show any blue tint.

If the prepared liquor answers these tests, then it shows the reduction is complete. If it does not satisfy these tests, further reduction can be achieved by adding a small quantity of Sodium bisulphite, Glucose. or hypo, until a satisfactory reduction is achieved.

Other Reducing Agents Commonly Used

Inorganic	Organic
Sulphur di-oxide SO_2	Glucose.
Sodium Sulphite Na_2SO_3	Cane Sugar.
Sodium bi-sulphite NaH $S0_3$	Molasses.
Hypo-Sod. thio Sulphate $Na_2\ S_20_3$	Glycerine.
	Saw dust
	Starch Flour
	Leather shavings

Usually organically reduced Cr liquors help to produce a leather of increased fullness, with uniform chrome fixation throughout the cross section of the pelt, whereas inorganically reduced liquors produced comparatively flatter leather.

After preparing the chrome liquor, it can be analysed for Cr_2O_3 content and the basicity, so that it can be used as a standard chrome liquor for chrome tanning and for calculating the exact quantity required tannage.

Conventional Practice of Chrome Tanning Procedure

The exact method of chrome tanning for different types of chrome leathers will vary depending on the properties of final leather. However, a general outline of the process is given below:

Procedure

The Cr tanning may be done either in the pickle bath or in separate bath. In the case of chrome tanning in a fresh bath about 2 to 3% of salt is added to the drum containing about 80 to 100% water based on the pelt weight. The drum is run for about 2 minutes to allow the salt to dissolve. (This salt added Will prevent the swelling of the pickled pelt when placed in the tanning drum). The pickled pelt is loaded in this drum and it is run for 5 minutes.

Later chrome liquor containing about 4.5 to 5% weight of di-chromate equivalent, at about 33% basicity is added in 3 instalments of 20 to 30 minutes interval. Later the drum is run continuously for about 4 to 6 hours (in case of thick pelts) until the complete penetration of the pelt by chrome is noticed (as tested by cutting a piece and examining the cross section). The pH of the tanning bath may be about 2.5 to 3 at this stage.

Later the pH of the bath is slowly raised by a process known as basification, by adding about 1 to 1.5% of a mild alkali like soda bicarb, or borax or hypo etc., slowly as a solution to bring the final pH of the bath and leather to about 3.7 to 3.9. Later the drum is run for 1 hour to fix the chrome.

When the pH is low, below 3, the chrome liquor has good penetrating power, but the extent of chemical combining or fixation is low. But when the pH is raised to above 3.5, the rate of penetration is slow, but the fixation is high. Because of this principle the chrome tanning is usually started at a low pH to ensure quick and complete penetration, and later the pH is slowly raised by basification to a higher pH around 3.8, to obtain good fixation and tannage.

Note:

1. The quantity of basifying agent, will depend on the extent of the pickling,

whether the tanning is done in the pickle bath or fresh bath. If the amount of acid used in pickle is high or if the tanning is done in pickle bath, then greater quantity of basifying agent will be required. If the degree of pickling is low, or if the tanning is done in a fresh bath, then the quantity of basifying agent required will be less.

2. Usually the basifying agent is a mild alkali and is dissolved as a 10% solution and added slowly to the tanning bath in 3 or more instalments at 20 to 30 minute intervals. If a strong alkali is used or if the rate of addition of the basifying agent is too rapid, then there is the possibility of the grain becoming harsher or coarser because of the greater fixation on the grain side. For best results, the fixation of chrome should be as uniform as possible throughout thickness of pelt.

3. After chrome tanning, the tanned pelts are taken out from the bath and piled on a wooden horse and kept for ageing for at least 2 to 3 days. This will allow greater fixation by stabilisation of the chrome complex and ensure a more uniform distribution of chrome.

4. The tanned leather is tested for its stability by conducting boiling test or observing the shrinkage temperature. A well-tanned chrome pelt should stand at least 2 to 3 minutes boiling without undergoing any dimensional changes, or it should have a shrinkage temperature of over 100°C, when tested with a shrinkage temperature apparatus.

Usually tanners cut a small rectangular piece of the chrome tanned leather in wet stage, mark its outline clearly on paper and later put the piece in boiling water and allow to boil for 2 or 3 minutes. Then the piece is taken out, cooled and verified regarding its shape and size by placing it on the originally marked outline. If it exactly coincides with the outline, it shows the tanning and basification is right. If it shows a shrinkage, it denotes it requires some more basification or some more chrome is required in the tanning.

The above is brief and general method of chrome tanning, but in practice this may vary in detail for different types of leathers. With increased knowledge and latest developments in technology, many variations and novel methods of chrome tanning procedure have been introduced in the trade.

FACTORS INFLUENCING CHROME TANNING

1. The condition and nature of the pelt.
2. The type of leathers required to be produced.
3. Concentration of the chrome and basicity, the type of chrome extract and liquor.

4. pH
5. Time.
6. Temperature.
7. Agitation.
8. Float
9. The nature and quantity of the basifying agent used and the method of its addition.

1. The Condition and Nature of the Pelt

For chrome tanning, the pelt should be well pickled prior to the tannage.If the pickling is uniform a more uniform distribution of chrome can be expected and the penetration of chrome will be much faster. If on the other hand if the pickling is not uniform (if the inner layers of the pelt slightly less acidic there will be greater fixation at the centre, and lesser on the outer layers and the tannage may become slower).

In the case of very heavy and compact textured hides, sometimes greater quantity of chrome may be required, and it may take a longer time for tannage etc. When compared to a thin and less compact textured hide. Similarly the goat and sheep skins will be tanned in much lesser time than the cattle hides.

2. The Type of Leathers Required to be Produced

The quantity of chrome and extent of chrome tannage will have to be adjusted to suit the type of leathers required to be produced. For example the upper and industrial leathers require a more thorough chrome tannage, when compared to the glove or garment leathers which may require a more mellow tannage to impart more softness, stretch and flexibility. Hence it is very necessary to adjust the chrome tannage bearing in mind the properties of the final leather desired.

3. Concentration of Cr_2O_3, Basicity and Type of Chrome Liquor

Generally speaking higher concentration helps to get greater fixation, but may become more expensive. It may also make the grain more coarse. It may add to the effluent load.

Similarly lower the concentration of chrome, less will be the fixation, and it imparts a more mellow tannage. But too low a concentration will not impart sufficient stability, and will not give enough shrinkage temperature. Because of these reasons optimum quantity of chrome will have to be used for chrome tanning, depending on the type of leather desired.

Usually lower the basicity, less the fixation, but the penetration may be faster. Higher the basicity, greater is the fixation, but slower will be the penetration. Hence in actual chrome tanning, chrome liquor of low basicity about 33% basicity is used in the beginning, and after penetration it is raised by adding the alkali for further basification. Or in some cases, the later additions of chrome liquor are done with 40% and 50% basicity chrome liquor.

Type of Chrome Liquors: Usually for chrome tanning, the normal chrome liquor as mentioned earlier is used. But in special cases a masked chrome liquor containing large amount of organic acid salts are used along with the chrome liquor. In such cases, it enables the pH to be raised to a much higher level, ensures a more uniform distribution, and greater fixation of chrome. Usually the leathers produced are more soft, plumper and have greater substance. While using such liquor great care is Also needed to adjust the tannage to suit the final properties of the leathers desired.

Readymade Basic Chromium Sulphate extract powders are available. These usually contain about 25 to 26% of its weight of Cr_2O_3 content (i.e. is about 50% of its weight of di-chromate), and have a basicity of about 33%). In normal chrome tanning about 8 to 10 per cent on pelt weight of this powder extract is used, instead of the prepared liquor. The extract is dissolved in 2 or 3 times its weight of hot or cold water and is added in drum, in 3 instalments to the tanning bath. In special cases as in dry tannage, the extract may also be added in one feed in the powder stage in a very short float.

4. pH

Lower the pH of the pickled pelt and the tanning, greater is the rate of penetration, but the fixation of chrome is lower. But higher the pH of the tanning bath, slower is the rate of penetration, but the fixation of chrome is higher. Hence the chrome tanning is commenced at a lower pH and after complete penetration, the pH is gradually raised to higher pH by the addition of mild alkali.

5. Time

With increasing time, there is a greater increase in penetration and fixation. Too short a time in chrome tanning will not ensure adequate tannage, whereas too prolonged a time will cause delay in processing. But it is better to allow a few days of ageing, after tanning, to ensure proper stabilisation of chrome complex and its relation with the hide protein.

6. Temperature

Generally higher temperature favours a greater chrome fixation, but is attendant with a risk of uneven tannage, specially when the quantity of chrome used is less. Similarly too low a temperature slows down the rate of chrome tanning. Also higher temperature will mean more expensive process in the cost of heating and hot water. Normal chrome tanning is done at room temperature.

7. Agitation

Mechanical agitation helps in quicker tannage and even distribution of chrome. Because of this chrome tanning is usually done in paddle or drum with a good speed of rotation (i.e. about 10 to 12 r.p.m.) For the same reason, drum or paddle tannage is much quicker than the chrome tanning in vat or pits.

8. Float

The quantity of water used in chrome tanning is also important. Too large a float will require a greater quantity of Cr, for the same degree of fixation. This will also lead to dilution of chrome complex and to higher basicity.

To small a quantity will not ensure even distribution of chrome, there may be greater fixation on the surface. Hence it is always better to use optimum quantity of water as float (say about 80 to 120%) in drum during chrome tanning.

9. Nature and Quantity of Basifying Agent Used

Usually mild alkalies like soda bicarb., borax, hypo, bisulphite or sulphate is used for basification. But if strong alkalies are used, this will lead to greater fixation of chrome, coarseness of the grain and uneven tannage. Similarly if too high quantities of the basifying agent is used, or if they are added too quickly this will also lead to, uneven fixation, and coarseness of grain. Hence the quantity and type of basifying agent used should be carefully chosen to ensure proper tannage.

10. Presence of Neutral Salt

Too much of neutral salt like Soda chloride or Sod. Sulphate are not desirable, as this will make a thinner and flatter leather, and, will hinder the chrome tannage. But if no, or too little a salt is used specially in fresh bath Cr tanning, it may cause plumping of the pelt, and will give an empty tannage. Hence only the optimum quantity of neutral salt about 2 to 3% on pelt weight is used.

If too much salt is used, it will lead to salt spue and spoil the appearance the final leather.

On a careful consideration of these factors, it becomes clear that it is essential to use optimum quantities of the various chemicals in proper conditions, with great care.

Ready made chrome tanning salts are available in the dry powder form which contains roughly about 25% its wt as Cr_2O_3 content are normally 33% basicity.

NEWER DEVELOPMENTS IN CHROME TANNING

1. **Dry or Floatless Chrome Tanning:** In this the dry extract powder or very concentrated chrome liquor is added to the pickled pelt in drum without float or in a very short float. The chrome extract being almost anoinic, as it immediately dissolves, slowly changes cationic in charge. In the anionic stages it has very little affinity for the pelt and hence quickly penetrates into the interior. Later when the charge changes to cationic, the fixation and reaction takes place with the pelt, thus effecting the tannage. The entire quantity of the chrome powder is added in one feed in the beginning itself. By this method the penetration is much quicker, and after the penetration, the bath is slowly diluted and the float is increased by addition of water, when the real tanning and fixation takes place.

Dry Chrome Tannage the following advantages are claimed

1. Smoother grain.
2. Better bellies and flanks.
3. Greater weight.
4. More uniform chrome distribution.
5. Considerable saving of time.
6. More efficient chrome uptake.
7. Light blue colour, good for pastel shade dyeing and finishing.

The main factors influencing dry tannage are dilution, time and temperature. For good tannage the pelt should be gradually diluted with slightly increasing temperature.

2. **Self Basifying Chrome Extract or Self Basifying System of Tannage:** Recently spray-dried chrome tanning extract powders with high amount of sulphate masking agent and containing inert self-basifying agent like Calcium Carbonate/formate are introduced in the trade. The special advantages claimed for such products are it eliminates cumbersome basifying procedure, ensures adequate and

uniform tannage and requires less careful control. That means-it not only relieves the botheration of controlled additions of alkali for basification at regular intervals, but also allows the tanner to continue the tanning outside normal working hours in the tannery.

Double bath chrome tanning was practised in olden days, for making conventional processing of glace kid. The essential feature of the process is the bated pelts (goat skins) are first treated in the first bath containing dichromate and Hydro-chloric acid. The chromic acid in this bath penetrates thoroughly. After a preliminary setting and piling, the pelts are treated in a separate second bath containing hypo and hydro-chloric acid added in controlled intervals. In the second bath, the reduction and basification takes place effecting the tannage.

The main advantages claimed for this double bath process are (1) very fine smooth grain, uniform chrome fixation, soft and full leather, but it involves lots of labour, time and cost.

Double bath chrome tanning process has become obsolete and is only of historical information there are restrictions stipulating that the leathers should not have Cr_6.hexavalent chrome.

OIL TANNING PROCESS

Many oils and fats (which are having unsaturated carbon linkages) are found to have tanning properties. One of the important leathers made by oil tanning is Chamois leather, which is very soft, silky and is. of a cream yellow colour.

The oil tanning is based on the oxidation of cod or fish oil, because these oils have numerous unsaturated bonds, i.e. all the valencies of the constituent carbon atoms are not satisfied. These unsaturated free fatty acids combine with oxygen to form oxidised form of fatty acid aldehydes and peroxides which effect the tanning action on the pelt.

For oil tanning, delimed pelts (with or without a pretreatment with formaldehyde) are treated with fish or cod oil and are exposed to air in an enclosed chamber, which is humid and hot at about 50°C and are allowed to get oxidised slowly. Gradually the oxidation of the oil takes place forming acronaldehyde and crotonaldehyde which impart the tanning action. Side by side some peroxides are also formed contributing to the tanning action.

Finally after a period of one to two weeks of oxidation, the excess oil and residual products are washed off by repeated washing with alkali and soap; later the leather is dried, and buffed. This produces a soft, silky, yellowish leather.

Characteristics of the Oil

1. Usually fish or cod oil contains about 18 to 20 carbon atoms and contains about 6 to 8 unsaturated double C = C bonds.
2. The oil used should have high iodine value about 120 to 180, low acid value below 5, and sufficient degree of unsaturation for subsequent oxidation. It should also be free from proteinous sediments in the bottom of the barrel containers.
3. It should not be rancid.
4. Blown-fish oil (oxygen bubbled) fish oil is preferable for actual usage.

Characteristics of Oil Tanned Leathers

1. The shrinkage temperature is rather low i.e. 70°C.
2. The leather wets back easily and dries out repeatedly without becoming hard, or it retains softness even after repeated washing and drying.
3. It has characteristic yellow colour, and has an aldehydic smell.

PRINCIPLE OF OIL TANNING FOR CHAMOIS LEATHER

1. The pelt is prepared suitably to open and plump up the structure by a good liming and later delimed well. In many cases the grain is shaved off after a preliminary formaldehyde tanning.
2. The pelt is treated with about 25 to 30% of its weight of cod or fish oil and drummed well for 6 to 8 hours, to break open the fibre structure and to allow the oil to penetrate inside and to combine well.
3. On application of oil, a water in oil emulsion is formed, and slowly the water content in the pelt is reduced. The oil penetrates into the pelt.
4. After oil application, the pelts are hung up in a hot and humid chamber. During this period auto-oxidation of the oil takes place and a typical aldehydic odour is noticed. This reaction is also an exothermic reaction, when a considerable heat is generated.
5. The period of oxidation is about 2 to 3 weeks, forming various oxidation products. The end point of the reaction or completion of the tannage is determined by the characteristic yellow colour, stopping of the heat generated and water uptake.
6. Subsequently the excess uncombined oil and other oxidation products are removed by washing in water, using some alkali (like soda ash) hot water and soap etc. Washing should be complete without having any greasy spots.

7. On drying after washing, the leather dries out soft and can be repeatedly washed and dried retaining the softness.

LATER DEVELOPMENTS IN OIL TANNING

Of late synthetic oil tanning agents have been developed based on sulpho chlorinated mineral turpentine or other mineral oils. These are specially processed to have the desired degree of unsaturation having the capacity to combine with the pelt and to get subsequently oxidised to effect the tanning of the pelt. Synthetic oil products tanning other products marketed by different firms under various brand names.

The washing after tanning can be done with soda and/or hypo. The period of oxidation is found to be less than natural fish oil. The leather obtained is comparatively more white in colour. Many tanners use a blend of this synthetic oil and natural cod or fish oil for oil tanning. During tanning about 15% of Synthetic oil like Immergan and 2.5% of Soda Ash is used, to counteract the harmful acidity that may be formed made. But in the course of time, and based on experience, it is found that the strength of this synthetic oil tanned leather is lower than the natural oil tanned leather.

FORMALDEHYDE TANNING

Formaldehyde is a useful and mild tanning agent, and is adopted on a commercial scale as a pretanning agent, for chamois leather tanning, or as an individual tanning agent in the manufacturer of picker saver leathers. If the formaldehyde tanning is done properly it imparts a mild, soft and flexible type of leather.

Principle of Formaldehyde Tanning

In the case of chamois leathers tanning, formaldehyde is used as a pretanning agent, and the outline of the process is as follows:

1. Well limed goat or sheep skins are delimed using boric acid or any other non-ammonium salt.
2. The delimed and washed pelt is treated with about 3 to 4% of commercial formalin in about 50 to 70% float of water in drum. The drum is run for about 4 hours, and subsequently the pH of the bath is raised to about 8 using the addition of soda ash and the drum is run for 2 hours. During this time, the fixation of formaldehyde and tannage takes place. Later the pelts are horsed up and sammed and the grain layer is removed by splitting or shaving.
3. Subsequently oil tanning is done, using about 25 to 30% of fish oil as detailed in the oil tanning process, the drum is run for about 6 hours. Later the skins are hooked in a hot room and oxidised for a period of 2

to 3 weeks. After oxidation the skins are washed repeatedly in water and soda ash, until the skins become non-greasy.

4. After drying, the skins are staked, trimmed and buffed on both sides to make a soft velvety nap. The tanned leathers will appear very soft and creamish- yellow in colour.

These leathers can be used for petrol filtration to remove the trapped moisture, and can also be used for polishing jewels, silverware etc.

Formaldehyde Tanning for Picker Saver Leathers

1. Heavy and thick cattle hides are chosen and given a good liming with straight lime and caustic soda to give a plump and thick pelt.

2. After unhairing and fleshing, the pelts are washed with boric acid or non- ammonium based deliming agent. Complete deliming is necessary.

3. After washing, the pelts are treated in drum in 50% water, using 5 to 6% formaldehyde. The drum is run for about 8 hours, and later the pH is raised to about 8 by the addition of soda ash. Then the drum is run for about 2 to 3 hours.

   The excess formaldehyde is washed off, if necessary using about 0.5% ammonium salt, until no more formaldehyde smell is noticed.

4. After the tannage, the pelts are nailed flat on boards and dried after drying they are cut to the required size of strap.

5. The straps are steeped in a mixture of Glycerine and water (40:60) for a few hours, taken out and dried. A top dressing of french chalk or china clay can be applied to improve the appearance.

Important Points to Remember in Formaldehyde Tanning

1. The liming should be done well to open up the structure and to obtain a thick pelt.

2. The deliming should be complete. It is not advisable to use ammonium salts as deliming agent, as any remaining ammonium salt will combine with formaldehyde, giving difficulties. If the deliming is not complete, a cracky grained leather is likely to be produced.

3. The formaldehyde used should be about 40% strength and should be sufficient in quantity about 4 to 6% on pelt weight.

4. After initial drumming in a bath of about 5 hours in formaldehyde the pH of the tanning bath should be raised to about 7.5 to 8%, using soda ash or any other alkali. Then only fixation and tannage will take place. The penetration is good when the pH is low and the fixation takes

place at the higher pH.

5. After tanning, it is better to wash off the excess formalin, using a mild ammonium salt washing.

6. The formaldehyde tanning is mostly practised as a pretanning process prior to oil tanning for chamois leathers. It is also used for pretanning prior to vegetable or chrome tanning using about 0.5 to 0.75% formaldehyde for chrome upper leathers, in special cases.

Recently other aldehydes like Glutaraldehyde, dialdehyde, starch etc. have also been used for tanning, to impart certain desirable properties like sweat resistance, greater filling etc. Crotonaldehyde and acronaldehyde etc. formed during oxidation of unsaturated oils, are the other aldehyde tanning agents as found in the oil tanning of chamois leather.

SYNTHETIC TANNINGS

Use of Syntans

(a) **Pretanning:** Nowadays it has become a practice to pretan the pelt with some syntans and then to tan them rapidly with a highly concentrated tanning liquor. The principle behind this approach is that the outer surfaces of the pelt is given a mild tannage, so as to make it possible to use a higher strength of tan liquor for tannage, without overloading the grain and without the danger of case hardening.

(b) **Bleaching Syntans:** There are certain types of syntans which can be used for bleaching vegetable tanned leather. Leathers tanned with darker colour tannins can be treated with such bleaching syntans and these produce a lighter colour. These are generally more acidic in pH and functions as a partial stripping and bleaching agent.

(c) **Combination Syntans:** These are a different type of syntans, which can be used for retanning of chrome leather, and these can be used as a substitute or additive to vegetable tannin for retanning chrome leathers in the manufacture of chrome upper leather. These are known as replacement or combination syntans.

Syntans may be defined as any high molecular organic compound containing reactive groups, or mixtures of such compounds, capable of converting animal skins into leather. They may differ from natural vegetable tanning materials in chemical structure. They are usually highly soluble in water having similar of dissimilar tanning units having varying degrees of combining properties with the reactive groups of hides and skins.

Classification of Syntans

The syntans in general can be classified into three distinct groups:

(a) Auxiliary syntans.

(b) Combination syntans.

(c) Replacement syntans.

(a) Auxiliary syntans: These are sulpho acid type, and for reaction with the pelt depend on the strong sulphonic $S0_3H$ acid group. They are more acidic and show low pH. These are generally used for pretanning and also for bleaching purposes. These are generally low molecular weight products and are mostly based on phenols, cresols etc.

Properties: These accelerate the vegetable tanning, enables better utilisation of vegetables tans, prevents mould growth in tan liquors, effects a bleaching action on vegetable leathers, increases the fat absorption and the tensile strength of the leathers. Its limitation is * the uptake is only low and cannot be considered as a substitute for vegetable tannis.

(b) Combination Syntans: The syntans under this group give good buffering action, possess weak acid groups similar to vegetable tannins, and the molecular weight is higher. These can partially replace natural vegetable tannin and also exhibit the advantageous qualities of auxiliary syntans. For reaction with the pelt, they depend mainly on the weak acidic 'OH' phenolic groups, and to a limited extent on the strong acid group.

They are less acidic in pH (around 5) and structually they closely approach vegetable tannins and exhibit predominen the characteristics of phenolic 'OH' groups.

Properties: Good filling and weight giving properties, can be used in combination with vegetable tans, have bigger molecular weight, usually unstable in presence of salts and can be used for replacing up to 25% of the natural vegetable tannins consumed.

(c) Replacement Syntans: These are usually weakly acidic and are sensitive to acid and salt. They can replace vegetable tannins in part of completely, at all tanning conditions and give a good degree of tannage to leather. These consist of a dispersion of highly condensed high molecular compounds in a suitable medium. The tanning action mainly depends on the phenolic groups for reaction with collagen.

They are still less acidic, high molecular weight and depend on the phenolic 'OH' groups for tanning power.

Properties: These can be used as a substitute for natural vegetable tannins, and can be used in high proportions instead of vegetable tannins.These are least stable to acids and salts.

In the trade, these syntans are marketed by different firms under different brand names, having specific purposes in tanning. Hence before using these trade syntans the full characteristics of the particular syntan will have to be studied carefully before using for a specific purpose. By a careful choice of the right type of syntans in optimum quantity and desirable property can be imparted to the leather. Further details on the use of syntans can be obtained from the suppliers for specific purposes.

Zirconium Tannage

In recent years zirconium tannage has been developed for making white leathers, white sports goods and flexible soles. In view of the availability of large quantities of zircon sand in India is found possible to prepare a suitable tanning agent from zircon.

Zirconium Tanning: Zirconium tanning is done at a low pH of about 2 and gradually raising the pH in presence of a masking salt like citrate, acetate etc. The leather exhibits a good filling effect contributing to fullness and can be used for speciality leathers like sports goods, hockey and cricket balls. Zirconium tanned leather has good scuff resistance and strength. The quantity of zirconium tanning varies from 20 to 30% on pelt weight in different processes and type leathers desired. The penetration is rather. slow and time consuming. Hence a combination of chromium and zirconium tannage is found to be very useful for leather with thick substance, like hockey or cricket ball.

Some important mechanical operations after tanning

For several types of leathers, the final thickness are strictly to be obtained and this is normally done after the main tanning. The tanned leathers are kept piled in wet stage for about 48 hours for allowing the equilibrium to be attained for ideal results. Then they are conditioned to the required moisture content to make them suitable for certain mechanical operations to achieve the desired thickness.

This conditioning of the leathers is known by the term **"sammying"** – which aims at retaining certain moisture content say about 40% to 45% of its weight. This is done by partial drying to reduce moisture content, either by open drying or by mechanical means using a sammying machine. It should be ensured that uniform moisture content is just enough to make them suitable for further mechanical operations to obtain the required thickness. Various types of sammying machine are available and one should choose the machine depending on the materials processed and the final leather desired. After sammying the leathers are further processed in machines to obtain the correct thickness uniformly throughout the leather.

This is achieved by using mechanical means, using splitting and or the shaving machines. In the case of cattle hides and buffalo hide or side leathers, initially the tanned leathers are split to obtain roughly uniform thickness and then finally shaved using a shaving machine. The working width and the type of machine have to be chosen carefully according to the type of raw materials processed and the final leathers desired. For example, for upholstery leathers, where a wide width or whole hide are to be obtained, a wider working width will be required and where only skins are processed a smaller working width will be sufficient. Similar the machines may be simply mechanical or hydraulic. The cost of the machines may vary widely depending on various factors. These machine operations have to be carefully done as these are important factor. Usually the splitting is done in the splitting machine, keeping a slightly higher thickness uniformly through out the side/ hide. Then they are carefully inspected and taken for shaving - shaving is done later to obtain the uniform thinckness desired and checked with the thickness gauge for uniformity.

A detailed description of these machines are beyond the present scope of this review. But it has to be emphasised here that these are very critical operations, and hence great care is required to obtain the correct thickness uniformly, avoiding any cuts or holes or any machanical chatter marks. Usually very skilled operators are employed, and it is very vital to maintain the machines carefully, to obtain the leathers without cuts or damages at this stage.

After these mechanical operations, inspection and assortment, the leathers are taken for further processing, like washing neutralisation, retanning, dyeing and fat liquoring which all come under the category of post tanning wet operations.

POST TANNING OPERATIONS – NEUTRALISATION

The operation of neutralising is done after the shaving and is intended to remove the free acid in the hide as well as part of the combined acid. It is well known that a chrome leather does not reach equilibrium immediately after tanning. The chrome complex goes on changing liberating more and more acid, some of the acid-is also fixed with the basic protein group. So the acid coming from the chrome complex in addition to the acids held by the protein if allowed to remain in the hide will cause acid hydrolysis of the skin protein leading ultimately to grain crackiness and tearing up of leather. Unneutralised leather will be having sufficient acid and Hence do not give satisfactory results in usage. High acidity will cause poor tear resistance, poor overall strength of leather and grain crackiness. Such leather if worn as shoe uppers will not serve long particularly in humid atmosphere and will have to be very quickly replaced. If the neutral salts are present in the leather **salt spues** occur, Salt spue is due to the neutral salts present in the hide which com up to the surface as a fine deposit. This will come up repeatedly even after frequent wiping. "Salt spueing" is particularly found when temperature and humidity undergo changes rapidly. Such leathers are very unattractive and cause pinching on the toes of the wearer if used for shoes. To avoid to the harmful effect of the acidity and neutral salt present, the leathers must be neutralised and washed. The finishing operation also will be considerably affected adversely if the leather is not neutralised.

The object of neutralising is not to remove totally all the acidity present in the hide, but only to remove the harmful acidity. By harmful acidity it is meant that the pH of the leather is below 3.3. Since chrome complex does not reach equilibrium quickly it is necessary to take the pH of the leather a little over this value (3.3) so that even if a little more of acid if produced after some time no harmful effect will be observed. The leather usually has a pH of about 3.5 pH at the time it comes to neutralisation though the pH might have been 4 to 4.1 at the time of taking the hide out of the chrome bath. This is due to chrome complex becoming more basic and liberating more acid with the consequential lowering the pH of the hide.

In general it is often seen that the alkallies like bicarbonate, borax, ammonium bicarbonate, hypo, mixture of ammonium chloride and sodium bicarbonate, etc. are used as neutralising agent. Usually 1 to 2% of these material are added for neutralising chrome uppers in two or more instalments in 200% of water on the shaved weight of neutral salts stock.

The extent of neutralisation will depend on the type of leather desired. In case of upper leather where temper is required, the neutralisation may be partial and where softness is required as in glove leather the neutralisation should be complete. If neutralisation is carried out to a greater extent in upper leather, it may, cause looseness of grain and, if and neutralisation is not sufficient it may cause hardness and crackiness in upper leather. In the case of chrome retan upper, complete neutralisation may be required, in order to prevent the crackiness of leather due to oxidation of vegetable tannins on storage. In the case of glove leather, if neutralisation is not sufficient it may not only affect the run characteristics, but also may cause harshness of the product and will cause tearing. Similarly in each type of leather the neutralisation should be carried out to the optimum extent, depending on the nature of the raw material, type of tannage and the final leather desired. Hence the importance of neutralisation, choice of the neutralising agent and the extent of neutralisation, etc. cannot be over emphasised.

It is not proposed to give receipies for processing different types of leathers, as they may vary depending on the chemicals and auxiliaries used, only the basic principles of different operations are discussed to have better understanding of the basis of different stages of leather processing.

In actual process of neutralisation, it is essential to choose the correct neutralising agent, according to the ultimate characteristics of the leathers desired and carry out the extent of neutralisation to the appropriate degree. The extent of neutralisation can be checked by cutting the wet leather and examining the cross section by using the indicator solution, particularly the colour produced. Normally the common indicators used for checking neutralisation are Bromocresol purple or Bromocresol green.

While processing, it is very essential to add the neutralising agent as a dissolved solution, gradually over a period of time or in three or four instalments to ensure the grain smoothness and other characteristics–Any sudden addition of neutralising solution is likely to cause violent fluctuations in pH on or around the surface of the leather and this is likely to damage the surface characteristics. As far as possible a gradual and continuous addition as a thin strem of neutralising solution is ideal to obtain grain smoothness, and to avoid harsh grain and pipeyness.

Combination Tannages

Each type of tannage gives its own characteristic properties to the leathers tanned with it. Vegetable tannages impart a greater filling up, chrome tannage gives a greater hydrothermal stability, strength and better physical properties, formaldehyde and oil tannages give greater water absorption and easy wetting properties – Alum tannages has comparatively less stability, easy wettability and is partially reversible.

In order to ensure the desirable properties in leather and to take advantage of the characteristics for different tannages, it has been found possible to adopt the combination of more than one type of tanning materials. By a judicious blending of more than one compatible tannage in appropriate proportion it is possible to obtain all the desirable properties. Typical examples of such combination tannage are (1) Semichrome tannage-initial vegetable tannage followed by chrome tannage, (2) Chrome-retanning-initial chrome tanning followed by vegetable tanning, (3) Formaldelyde-oil combination tannage, (4) Alum-formalydeyde tannage, (5) Sulphur-oil and vegetable tannage, etc., (6) Chrome Syntan-Vegetable tanning, (7) Aluminium-Chrome tannages.

In the semichrome tannage, the high 'water absorption, and lowerstrength properties of vegetable tannage are altered by a subsequent tanning with chrome to reduce water absorption and improve the strength and other physical properties. Similarly the characteristic lack of filling ability of chrome tanning is overcome by imparting a vegetable syntan retanning. Apart from this object, this combination also enables easy snuffing and scuffing properties of the grain surface like – correction of minor defects, easy printing or embossing etc. Similarly the very high water absorption properties of formaldehyde tannages are suitably followed by a combination tanning with oil tanning to produce chamois leather with a ready water absorption and wetting and drying properties. Yet another typical combinations is the sulphur-oil – and vegetable tanning which is adopted for a high strength property of picking band and other industrial leathers. The interfibrillary sulphur deposition formed during the pickling and hypo depickling, acts as a solid lubricant, and the oil tannage and vegetable retanning adding to the physical strength properties. Alum-formaldehyde, Alum-zirconium Alum-chrome, chrome zirconium combination tannages are adopted for various kinds of utility leathers, sports goods or other industrial leathers. Thus by adopting a careful blendings of different combination tannage it is possible to obtain the desired properties such as highly stretching glove leather, to no-stretch foot ball leather, washable chamois leather, garment leathers, shoes upper, water proof sole leathers, various types of industrial leathers etc. for different end uses. This will depend on the type of raw material, the details of processing adopted, desirable properties of final tanned leather. The post tanning operations and the finishing techniques are suitably modified. But it can be safely said that in combination tannages ultimate leathers have a predominant tendency to reflect the characteristics of the initial tannage given with slight modification of the same by the subsequent tannage imparted. Great care and attention is essential in choosing the right combination of tannages and other process details to obtain the desirable properties. It has almost become a practice to adopt the combinations of more than one tannage in modern leather processing. Many combination tannages can be worked out to get the desirable and advantageous properties climinating or reducing the draw backs of any particular tannage.

Mordanting & Dyeing

USE OF MORDANTS

Usually neutralised leathers after washing are mordanted. This mordanting is done with a view not so much to increase the affinity of the leather for acid and direct dyes, but to dampen the affinity. A cationic chrome tanned leather has very good affinity for acid and direct dyes. With so much affinity for anionic dyes (acid and direct dyes only) the chrome leather might tend to fix too much dye in certain local areas in preference to other areas. In order to develop uniform shade or what is called "levelness" in dyeing, mordants are used. The function of the mordant is to dampen any local over-affinity for the dye and to produce uniform fixation of the dye all over the area. The function of the mordant in chrome leather is not the same as the usual mordant function as in textile dyeing. A chrome leather, does not have good affinity for basic dyes. In such cases, vegetable retanning of the chrome leather or mordanting with a vegetable tanning will increase the affinity of leather for basic dyes.

METALLIC MORDANTS: When dyeing vegetable tanned leathers it is well known that these have very high affinity for basic dyes. Basic dyes are also preferred by vegetable tanners. So when dyeing vegetable tanned leather with basic dyes, the loosely combined vegetable tan goes out into the dyeing bath and causes patchiness of dyeing. The loose tannins must be insolubilised within the hide itself so that it cannot do any harm, when using basic dyes. The agent, that is used for the purpose is also called a mordant. Metallic mordant is used for this purpose. Since these metallic mordants themselves cause coloration, they should be used with care so that the shades produced by them may not adversely affect the shade that is to be produced by the basic dyes.

OTHER MORDANTS: Acid dyes themselves on chrome leather or on vegetable leather act as a mordant for subsequent basic dyeing. Basic dyes are mordant for acid and direct dyes and for certain dyes called chrome mordant dyes, dichromate is a mordant. Even on chrome leather the dichromate combines with dye and in turn fixes on to the leather. Vegetable tannins, also act as good mordanting agents on aluminium tanned leather for basic dyes. But these produce much coarseness of grain on the Alumtanned leathers, which is not desirable particularly gloves. Certain synthetic tanning materials based on phenols have been synthesised called as mordanting syntans. Syntans have replaced vegetable tannins as mordants in glove leather manufacture as syntans unlike the vegetable tannins, do not affect the grain and feel of glove leather. Oil tanned leathers, have no affinity for usual dyes except the sulphur dyes. Sulphur dyes are much used in the textile industry but not used in leather dyeing. They are not soluble in water, but dissolved in Sodium Sulphide solutions. Oil tanned leather can stand alkalies unlike vegetable or chrome leathers. Therefore these dyes can be used for oil tanned leathers.

DYEING FORMALDEHYDE LEATHERS: Formaldehyde tanned leather have very poor affinity for any dye. If they have to be dyed, they should be given a retannage with chrome or vegetable tannin. Certain leather tanned with some of the synthetic resins or polymers have poor affinity for dyes. They have to be mordanted with chrome or vegetable tannin for rich shades or the tannage with these resins should be done after dyeing. These polymers are generally used for greater fullness, tighter bellies and flanks, and for producing a close nap, etc.

Mordants for Chrome Leathers : Materials which are used as Mordants for chrome leather are usually vegetable tannins, vegetable dyes etc. The chrome leathers are usually treated with tanning materials of low astringency. Materials which are astringent will cause coarseness and brittle grain and therefore should not be used. Materials that are commonly used for modanting are gambier, chestnut, quebracho, etc., gambier being mostly used. The treatment with vegetable tanning materials increases the plumpness, feel, tightens up the grain, increases gloss and lustre in the finish, gives level dyeing, and also modifies the base colour, to suit the subsequent dyes. Material like gambier, slightly changes the shade to brown, so that it is beneficial to subsequent dyeing. Sumac and wattle are also used for getting fawn and beige shades. They change the chrome base colour.

Vegetable Dyes : There are also other materials, that are called mordants like Haematin (logwood), fustic, Sausage orange, Hypernic, Saffron wood, Quercetin, Beech wood, etc., – which do not have tannins but have colouring material and these colours can be modified with metallic strikers to produce a variety of shades, either alone or in combination. The metallic strikers used with these are Alum, Potassium Tatanium, Oxalate, Tartar emetic, Stannic Chloride, Copper Sulphate, Ferrous Sulphate, etc. Each one of these materials can produce interesting shades with the individual wood dyes. Further combinations of these agents can be made to produce light brown, dark colours, medium colours, chocolate colours, black, etc., They considerably reduce the amount of coal tar dyes needed to produce shades, and therefore are economical in producing a variety of shades with a minimum quantity of expensive coal tar dyes. The many variations of brown are produced with gambier, fustic, sausage orange, hypernic in combination with potassium titanium oxalate (P.T.O.), etc. sausage orange is used for greenish yellow shades and hypernic for Maroon shades. For lighter browns, Gambier, fustic with P.T.O. must be used. Thus any number of combinations are possible.

Dyeing : After mordanting, the leathers are usually dyed. In olden days dyeing used to be mainly done with coal – tar dyes. In many cases coal-tar dyes are offered in a wide variety of shades of guaranteed uniform quality, from lot to lot. The types of dyes, which are actually used for leather are somewhat limited in variety, owing to the fact that leather cannot treated in strongly alkaline baths. The use of vat and sulphur dyes is ruled out. A lot of developments have taken place in the dyes, including the ban on the use of 22 arylamine based dyes which are considered harmful to the user. However a broad based classification is as follows. Detailed information can be obtained from the suppliers of dyes and special reference books on dyes and only permitted dyes are to be used.

Types of Dyes : 1. Acid dyes, 2. Direct dyes. 3. Chrome mordant dyes, 4. Basic dyes.

ACID DYES: Acid dyes are the sodium salts for dyes. In dyeing the dye has to be generated from its sodium salt by the addition of acid. Acid dyes are not acidic in reaction, as may be misunderstood, but they require acid for the liberation of the dye. The full shade is produced on the liberation of the dye from the dye salt. The exact quantity of acid required for each dye varies, depending on its molecular structure. Acid dyes have good affinity towards chrome leather. They have reduced affinity for vegetable leather. On semi – chrome or retanned leathers it is in between the two. The shades produced by the dyes are not only dependent on the total quantity of chrome fixed on the leather but also dependent on the nature of the chrome comlex. It is often seen that in a lot of mixed chrome leather, tanned to different pH values but having the same chrome content, the same dye produces different shades thereby indicating the effect of the nature of the complex.

Basic Dyes : The basic dyes on the other hand contain groups to make them soluble in water. They are converted into hydrochlorides or sulphates. They have a strong cationic effect whereas the acid and direct dyes carry negative charges on the dye molecule.

Direct Dyes : As the name itself indicates a direct dye candy directly without a mordant. Some direct dyes are used in leather dyeing. Direct dyes are very similar to the acid dyes in property. So far as chrome leather is concerned, they penetrate a little less fast and develop more deep shades on the surface. They have much bigger molecular size than acid dyes, in general. They have little or no affinity for vegetable tenned leathers. Therefore they are not be used on vegetable tanned leather. They have poor affinity for semi-chrome or retan leathers.

Chrome Mordant Dyes : These dyes require the use of bichromate as a mordant, for dyeing: The chrome- mordant dyes, which are used along with dichromate on leather, produce much levelling effect and are most light fast than the other dyes. Of late chrome mordant dyes have been prepared with the chrome molecule built into the dye structure itself, and these are called "premetallised dyestuffs". These can be applied on leather, in the neutral condition itself, and it is not necessary to lower the pH value of the dyebath. Great levelness and considerable fastness to light are achieved by using these types of dyes.

TESTING OF DYES: Very often it is required to know whether a particular dye is acid, basic, direct etc., Basic dye can be easily tested. It is precipitated out either by treatment with bicarbonate or tannic acid or by addition of a known acid dye. The acid and direct dyes cannot be easily separated among themselves. The only test which can easily be applied is the direct dyeing test. Direct dyes will dye cotton directly, whereas acid dyes will not dye cotton without a mordant.

FASTNESS AND OTHER PROPERTIES: Dyes in general do no have absolute light fastness, whereas pigments particularly the earthern or mineral types have very good light fastness. Certain dyes however are formulated specially to achieve greater light fastness. Basic dyes have poor light fastness. Certain important properties of dyes must be taken into consideration before they are chosen for use on particular leather.

Chapter - 3
Drying And Finishing

Drying of Leather : Leather is dried under natural conditions in drying lofts or dried in heated chambers under controlled humidity as a continuous operation using the counter current hot air flow, or used to be dried also under tension on glass plates with a film of paste.

Different Condition for Different Methods: The conditions existing in each case are different and the resulting products also vary.

Where production speed is not very important and where a softer type of leather is required, drying lofts may be used under natural drying conditions. Continuous toggle driers are used in large establishments producing side leathers and kid skins. Conveyor driers are employed for drying wet seasoned or pigmented and sprayed leathers. Tunnel dryers are employed in side leathers and other skins processing where pasted products are not required. The equipment naturally varies widely. The manner of drying and rate of drying are all different because the materials kept into the dryers are also different in moisture content.

Paste-Drying : The paste drying was first practised in U.S.A. and though patents were obtained using the principle as early as 1910, the commercial application of the patent came along only during the later part of 1940. The moist, well set leather is pasted on a smooth surface-glass or porcelain-and is dried under controlled temperature and humidity in a hot chamber. That is principle of the pasting unit. The leather dries to a very smooth surface and is taken off the plate after 3–4 hours when it is perfectly dry. The advantages of the paste drying is that a very smooth well laid out leather is obtained, in a shorter time. The leather is much improved in appearance. The area also increases to an extent of about 10.0%. Paste drying, after all, is drying under very well set condition. A thorough setting effect is obtained and the resultant leather is really good, provided all the conditions and factors have been carefully, controlled and maintained.

Need For Control of Conditions : The conditions of drying must be well controlled or otherwise a loose, pipy grained and broken-fibred leathers will be produced. Also, other factors like liaming, tanning, fatliquoring, the quantity and quality of distribution of oil, the ingredients of the paste, the amount of plasticiser in the paste, the drying temperature and the humidities are all important which must be maintained at the optimum conditions.

Pasting-Unit : A pasting unit usually consists of 4 separate zones or sections wherein the temperature and humidities of air are different.

This is done with a view to obtain a very uniform and even drying of the leather without affecting desirable and the good qualities of leather. Neither slow drying nor the quick drying will be produce a good leather. Inside the drier, a chain conveyor slowly takes the boards from the inlet to the outlet very gradually and can be operated mechanically or pneumatically, outside the drying unit the plates travel through the spraying booth and then back into the drying unit. An automatic chain conveyor is provided which drags each plate gently into the unit.

Duration of Drying : The duration of drying is dependent on the leather and the operation conditions. The speed of the automatic chain conveyor may be set to any convenient rate. Generally the time of drying is about 4 or 5 hours. The biggest unit has in general about 250 plates.

Drying Chamber : The drying is constructed out of non-conducting insulating materials. An air space between two layers of non-conducting materials will give good thermal insulation. Felt, Hair, paper, wood are all good insulating materials. Inside the chamber a number of fans are provided to circulate the air well. The object is to avoid any empty spots or pockets of air. Such empty pockets of air affect the drying rate. These fans produce a lot of turbulance which also increase the rate of heat-transfer.

Factors Involved in Drying : The initial moisture content of leather, the final moisture content desired, the temperature and humidity under which the leather is to be dried, the air velocity, the quantity of exhaust, the proportion of drying unit-air to be mixed with the outside air, the rate of transfer of heat, the capacity and horse power of the fans, the exhaust fan capacity, the location of fans, the ducts for distributing air, the construction of the plates, chamber must all be calculated, designed and then properly executed. It is very exacting and very interesting job.

Application of Paste : The sides are usually stripped away after drying at the exit end. The movement of the plates through the wash booth is done by a small motor rotating two rubber wheels which gently push forward the plates one after another. The plates go one after another down a mid inclined plane. As the plates,travel, the prepared paste is applied by spray gun on the plate. On both sides of the plate the paste is applied. For each side there is a pressure vessel in which the paste is contained. The paste is applied by means of a special nozzle. To facilitate this work, the gun and the tank are placed near the worker. The gum is suspended from above. And is sprayed continuously. The rate of spraying should be at the same rate throughout the day till the shift ends. Each operator does about 250 sides for one shift. Generally one side of the frame of the one big side is pasted. If it is a small side two sides are pasted. The average area is about 25 sq. feet in area.

Pasting and Drying : The spraying of the paste over the side is placed over the glass frame and then worked over with a sticker from the middle towards the backbone and then forwards. After setting well and removing the wrinkles, the setting is done downwards starting from the backbone. Care is taken to see that there are no air pockets between the paste and the side. Those areas which cannot be properly accommodated on the glass are trimmed. Some loser portions of the hide are cut away and a perfectly well laid out leather is obtained. The entire work has to be done within a short time. The frames leaving after the pasting is done are taken into the dryer by a conveyor chain. When once inside the dryer another conveyor chain takes over and slowly takes the plates to the end of the dryer at the controlled and pressed time. The actual time naturally varies, but on the average, it is about 4 hours.

Pasting Formulation and Other Conditions : There have been many difficulties before the pasting could be made a success. Though many of the factors are not known, the variables are too many and each and every tanner has to do his own experiments to strike a balance between his liming, tanning, fatliquoring oiling off in the grain, the viscosity, solid- content and plasticisers of his paste, thickness of the sides etc. There is no fixed paste formulation. If the viscosity of the paste is too low, too much paste will sink into the grain of the leather and leather will crack in the grain. There will not be sufficient bonding strength of the paste to the board and the leather will fall away from the plates during drying. There should be sufficient oil present in the grain layer and in the paste. The addition of plasticises to the paste lowers the bond strength between the plate and the leather. Since, the film strength on the grain should be oiled well and the plate should be thoroughly washed if satisfactory results are to be obtained. It is clear therefore that a paste that gives sufficient bond strength in the case of a thin dry surface leather will not work with a greasy, heavy leather, though the same might be products of the same tannery. For a thin leather, to support weight, against gravity, a low viscosity film need be sufficient. For heavy leather with a greasy surface where bonds are difficult to form, requires a paste with more viscosity and solid content.

Ingredients for Paste : The paste is generally made up in the Tapioca tannery. Tapioca starch which is available in India is a good base for the paste. Wheat flour is also added to this and cooked well with sulphonated oils to plasticise the film formed. This plasticizer may be adjusted for each type of leather. Thus in the same tannery there are 3 to 4 different pastes are used for pasting depending on the substance. The viscosity is related to solid content. Nowadays materials like carboxy methyl cellulose and hydroxy ethyl cellulose are available which are used to increase viscosity without increasing the solid content.

Rate of Drying : The rate of drying affects the leather quality. Too rapid drying will cause case hardening and it is undesirable. The removal of moisture must be done gradually. The free moisture is first removed in the initial zones. The chemically bound water is removed considerably in the final leather. If high temperatures and too low relative humidity is employed at the end, the leather looses much of its feel, and there is considerable shrinkage in leather. The removal of the last quantities of water is done rather slowly. The migration of moisture is dependent upon tanning, nature of the hide, amount of oil etc. Too temperatures and the employment of very high air velocities are not necessary or advisable.

Paste drying is not used or practised in recent times because of the complications mentioned earlier.

Typical Conditions of Temperature and Humidity : The drying is started at a fairly high humidity as that the moisture may gradually be removed in a five section dryer. The initial temperature may be adjusted to say 130°F and the air introduced at the bottom may be 15°F higher than the temperature in at the top. The relative humidity my be gradually increased in the subsequent section by increasing the wet bulb temperatures and if possible the dry bulb temperatures. For a dryer, having an initial temperature of say 130°F, the following plan may be successfully worked out.

	1 hour dry at 130°F and 15% relative humidity
Next :	1 hour dry at 130°F and 30% relative humidity
Next :	1 hour dry at 130°F and 38% relative humidity
Next :	1 hour dry at 130°F and 50% relative humidity

alternatively:

First:	1/2 hour dry at 150°F and 35% relative humidity
Next :	1 hour dry at 146°F and 38% relative humidity
Next :	1 hour dry at 145°F and 42% relative humidity
Next :	1 hour dry at 143°F and 46% relative humidity
Next :	1 hour dry at 140°F and 50% relative humidity

Interpreting the Condition : In the first example humidity is different in the drying unit (i.e.) quantity of water (in kgs.) per kgs. of dry air. In the second case, the absolute humidity is kept the same throughout and the rate of drying is kept lower as the drying takes place more and more. The reason for keeping the humidity (absolute) constant is that in the zonal system, some air always goes from one zone to another and in order to avoid violent fluctuations in the controls, the air has been kept practically at constant humidity by controlling instrument which can be more easily done. The first one can be used where only one zone exists (i.e.) in small units where more than one zone does not exist. It is not always necessary to use only the above temperature and humidity but certain principles have to be born in mind. The final leather, if it remains at comparatively low temperatures and high humidities tend to absorb appreciable moisture and hence the final temperature and humidity should be such that the leather does not retain more than say 10-12% moisture. Chemical engineering books have the graphs between the percentages of water held by organic fibrous materials under different humidities and temperatures. Some tanners do not heat the air more than 130°F. The initial drying is done at 130°F and 30% humidity and finally it is finished at 115°F and 50% humidity and still maintain more or less uniform humidity. The exact final temperature depends on the particular leather being dried and the characteristics desired.

Location of Exhausts : It is well known that the moisture carrying capacity of the air is increased by increasing the dry bulk temperature for a fixed wet bulb temperature. The exhaust fan is provided to remove the saturated or nearly saturated air out of the system since air when it is at that wet bulb temperature cannot remove the moisture. Really when the hot air first hits the moist leather the air is cooled down very nearly to its wet bulb temperature depending, on the length or time of contact and other conditions. The moist air usually being heavy stays down and the fresh air is sucked in at the bottom, reheated and discharged at the top. The exhaust should always suck from the bottom, the moist air. The same air is never recycled alone but is mixed with fresh air which further lowers the humidity of the heated air by adjusting the damper on the exhaust duct.

This explains in brief the paste drying unit and the paste drying of leather.

A More Economical Units : Recently a U.S firm has introduced a new unit which uses the principle of drying by conduction rather than by convection as in the case of the pasting unit detailed above. Since it is not a circulation of air, the fans and heating coils and humidity controls are eliminated. There is no big railings elaborate fittings and space occupation system, but only a series of smooth plates on which the leather is pasted as before. The plates are hollow and contain hot water kept at a constant temperature by thermostatic mechanism. Since the expensive fans, heating coils, humidity controls and other devices have been eliminated the cost of the unit is much less. The drying is very much quicker and results are said to be equal the results with other conventional systems. This is specially developed for small tanneries and is not intended to replace the earlier model units which are essential for big production. The other principles of the paste and oiling of the grain will hold good here also.

Other Dryers : The methods of leather drying other than the pasting are:

1. hanginng on stationary hooks or poles
2. tacking on boards
3. hanging on hooks or poles in continuous tunnel dryers
4. toggling out in frames in cabinet or tunnel dryers
5. laying flat on a wire conveyor in tunnel dryers or overhead rails/shafts.

There are toggle dryers which are manufactured using two types of air circulation. The air is applied on leather in jets and then it will result fast drying. As is to be expected, drying by this type will not be suitable on vegetable tanned leathers, though on chrome leathers, it may be not too drastic. Another type of dryer of the same class is where the air flows parallel to and in between the frames. The air covers the entire leather surface. The drying is more uniform and speedy. This dryer is used on chrome and vegetable tanned leather and the fast air flow makes the drying quick.

Vaccum Drying : Vaccum drying is becoming increasingly popular of late for full grain and for aniline leathers.

The grain-break and feel in vacuum drying are better, and the leathers are not much stretched as in paste drying. The surface of the leather is also smooth but it may give less area compared to paste drier. Drying is done in two stages. It is not necessary to samm or set the leathers. In the first phase the leather is dried to a moisture content of about 30-35% which is sufficient for staking operation. After staking in the second phase complete drying is done when a fine tight grained leathers are obtained because of the ironing effect of plating.

Some of the difficulties experienced in this method of drying are the formation of stains due to unfixed dyes and fatliquoring agents which are brought to the top of the grain surface during vacuum drying specially when the fixing or exhaustion is not done properly. For efficient drying under this method these operations should be done carefully to fix them well.

Finishing : The finishing of leather consists in the appli film-forming materials to the grain to provide abrasion and stain-resistance and to enhance aesthetic appeal. Finishing is the final operation in leather manufacture before they are sent to the market and as such it is of considerable importance. The finishing department in a tannery is the area where an alert and creative mind adds the final touches to enhance the natural beauty of the product in addition to increasing the serviceability. It is here that many imaginative effects are produced by varied applications of colouring matter compounded with different film-forming materials.

Different Methods : Pigment-finishing is practised to upgrade the skins of coarser grain wherein covering of the defects is aimed at Aniline-finishing is applied to those leathers possessing superior grain characteristics; the skins generally receive light applications of transparent coating materials containing subtle amounts of colouring matter (liquid dyes). Many variations in finishing are employed each one producing their characteristic effects on the finished leather. Various finishing materials are now abundantly produced by the chemical industry. Both aqueous and solvent-type finishes are used in leather-finishing.

Pigment-Finishing : The pigment finishes have the advantage of covering the stains and defects and presenting a uniform colour over the whole area of the skin or side. This advantage is being made use of increasingly as more and more of grain snuffed sides and corrected grained leathers are produced. Even though the normal supplies of components and dyestuffs are available, ready to apply finishing compounds are increasingly used.

Different Shades in Finishing

White : The pigments normally used in leather finishes are as follows: Titanimum oxide (both Anatase and Rutile types) which is marketed in 4 different grades viz.,

1.98-99% 2.78%

3.50% 4.30%

The first grade is perfectly white and is called Rutile'. The other grades undergo changes in colour on long storage. The other minerals like white pigments are used alone or in combination with others are Barium Sulphate, Aluminium oxide, zinc oxide, white lead etc., which undergo discolouration or yellowing gradually on storage or use.

Black : (Carbone Black, bone black, iron oxide).

The carbon black pigment is obtained by incomplete combustion of natural gas from petroleum wells. Bone black has got poorer staining power as compared to carbon black. This pigment is obtained by charring degreased bones and contains about 40-70% of mineral matter. The iron oxide-black, has a poorer mass and is used in leather finishes mixed with carbon black. Other common black pigments used are based on vegetable blacks aniline black, cobalt oxide black and black lakes based on Phosphotungstic acid.

Yellow : Lead Chromate, Cadmium sulphide, sclenide, iron oxide. Lead chromates is obtained by adding dichromate to lead salt solution. The colour of the compounds depends on the concentration of the reactants, the pH etc. Cadmium sulphide is prepared by passing H_2S through Cadmium salt solution the intensity of the yellow shade depends on the pH conditions. Natural iron oxide is dirty yellow. The synthetic oxide is prepared by precipitation of $FeSO_4$ by Na_2CO_3 of better quality. Organic yellows possess brilliancy and are better than mineral yellows.

Orange : Lead Chromate.

Brown : Iron Oxide.

Blue : Ultramarine blue, Phthalocyanine blue, iron blue etc. The ultramarine blue is prepared by heating in a furnace a mixture of Kaolin, Sulphur, Carbon and Sodium Carbonate and Silicon dioxide. The pigment ground in oil is used in finishing patent leather, using linseed oil, lead perroxide for conversion into an alkyde polymer.

Green : Chrome green pigment is cheap and is resistant to acids and alkalies. They possess good fastness to light, good opacity and high density.

Red : Cadmium sulphide - selenide: organic lakes and toners. Chrome red, a basic lead chromate, mixed with cadmium and selenium sulphides, is also used as pigments.

Selection Of A Pigment :

The factors that are taken into consideration in the selection of a pigment are that they should have:

1. good light fastness,
2. good covering power and
3. resistance to acids and alkalies and
4. stability to heat.

The pigments should not

1. be soluble in water or oil medium,
2. change with atmospheric conditions,
3. interfere with other pigments with which it is mixed, and
4. bleed in subsequent coats.

Pigment Dispersions : Most of the tanners now purchase the pigment dispersions from companies who are specialised in the manufacture of pigments and other finishing auxiliaries. The pigments are dispersed in a medium using some kind of mill which does the work of breaking up the pigment agglomerates into fine particles. Various kinds of mills such as ball-mills edge runners, roll mills and pebble mills and a variety of equipments are employed. The pigments for the finishing seasons are prepared dispersed in casein solution, containing sulphated castor oil or (T.R.O) as plasticiser and suspending agents which are compatible with the other components. The pigments are dispersed to give as small a particle size as possible to cover the maximum area and hence the maximum surface area and hence the maximum covering in the form of thin film, the dispersions must not show setting, particularly setting to a hard,gelly mass which is difficult or impossible to stir back into suspension.

Aniline Finishing : This type of finishing is applied to leathers with superior grain characteristics and the coatings given are transparent as a result of which all of the inherent beauty of the grain shows through. The dyes are the only colouring materials employed in full aniline finishing. The higher the ratio of dye to pigment, the greater will be aniline effect or aesthetic appeal produced by the finished leather. The aniline finished leathers are in demand for high quality footwear. The leather is given a level dyeing with suitable dyes and finished with organic pigments mixed with suitable protein binder and may subsequently be plated or friction-glazed in glazing machine. Special topping with tinted lacquers may be employed to bring up special effects on top to make the leathers more appealing and distinctive from the synthetic substitutes. Semi anilines are those containing greater proportion of pigments than dyes, and are usually applied for leather with fairly good grain characteristis.

Binders: Proteins (particularly casein), waxes such as carnauba wax, bees wax etc. and natural resins such as shellac are widely used as the constituents of binders. In addition to natural binders such as casein synthetic acrylic resin binders are available in which hydrophylic groups are introduced.

Casein : The casein should be free from mineral acid and fatty matter.It is soluble in Borax, Ammonia and other similar alkalies. The viscosity of casein solution is dependent on many factors. A solution of casein in Borax has got greater viscosity than in Ammonia. Too high a temperature of water during the preparation of the casein solution tends to hydrolyse the casein and the viscosity of the final solution is affected. Casein is sensitive to formaldehye as well and gets precipitated as a gel by the addition of formalin.

Shellac: Shellac is a natural resinous excretion of the lac insects. It is deposited on the twigs of "Kusurut" trees in Northern India. These twigs of the tree are converted into shellac resin.

Other Materials : Other materials which deserve mention here are milk glue, gelatin egg albumin, blood albumin, plasticizers, gum tragacanth, linseed, muscilage, irish moss, agar-gar alginates, methyl cellulose, carboxy methyl cellulose, cellulose esters, Hydroxy ethyl cellulose, polyacrylates, and preservatives like lemongrass oil, citronella oil paranitrophenol/ nitrobenzene etc.

Resin-Finishing: Certain types of synthetic resins have occupied dominant position in the resin finishing of leathers and this is attributed to the special properties of these resins making them well suited for the purpose. A suitable synthetic resin has to possess softness and extensibility since it must be able to stretch with the leather without cracking. The resins which are presently used in the bulk of resin finishing are acrylic resins, methacrylic resins, methacrylates, and synthetic methyl rubbers'BUNA' based on butadiene. They are prepared by emulsion polymerisation. Polymers made from the acrylic acid esters possess a high degree of stretch and this is one of the reasons Why theybecome very popular for use in leather finishing.

Acrylics : For the same ester group a methacrylic resin is very much harder than an acrylic resin. Poly Methyl methacrylate is more regid than the poly methyl acrylate. The poly (methyl acrylate) has the same degree of softness as poly n-butyl methacrylate. Different degrees of softness and flexibility are obtained by choosing from a wide range of single monomers and copolymers of two or more monomers.

Synthetic Rubbers : Synthetic rubbers based on butadiene are also used to a considerable extent in the field of leather finishing. Butadiene, when polymerised gives a very soft resinous material; but on copolymerisation with suitable monomers resins with the required degree of softness and stretch could be obtained.

Scope For Use : The resin dispersions are normally used in conjunction with other finishing auxiliaries, such as protein solution as emulsions, pigment dispersions, thickness and levelling agents. The attainment of good surface filling is largely due to the fact that the resin are aqueous dispersing agents. The resin dispersion deposits a highly dear transparent, continuous and tough film as soon as the water phase is absorbed by the leather. The film has greater adhesion to the surface particularly to snuffed grain or open-grained leathers like splits. A continuous elastic film of the resin is formed on the surface pores of the leather. The film has high refractive index. Resin-finishing is a simpler and best suited for finishing poor quality hides and for corrected or snuffed grain leathers.

Non-Aqueous Leather Finishing System : The nonaqueous finishes employed at present are based on nitro cellulose lacquers,vinyl resins and plyurethanes. The leather obtained with this type of finishes, are remarkably fast to wet-rubbing and has colour fastness. Previously the urethanes were supplied as a two component system, butyrate recently single component systems are made available.

Lacquer Finishing : The system is composed generally of cellulose nitrate (called nitro-cellulose) plasticizers, solvents and diluents, other ester of cellulose such as cellulose acetate cellulose acetate bu etc. can also used Cellulose nitrate is used to a great extent.

Cellulose Nitrate : The cellulose nitrate is prepared by reacting cellulose (cotton linters, wood pupal etc.) with a mixture of nitric and sulphuric acids under carefully controlled conditions. A product with a nitrogen-content around 12% is desirable. A higher nitrogen-content reduces the solubility and a lower figure associated with greater solubility precludes its use in coating.

Plasticisers : The plasticisers in the nitro-cellulose finishing system are condensation polymers built up by the reaction of polybasic acids with poly-hydric alcohols. These polymers are superior to the conventional plasticisers such as Tricresyl phosphate, Dibutyl phthalate and castor oil, the polymers keep the finish flexible for longer periods of ageing.

Solvents : The solvents used in N.C. finishing compositions are esters, alcohols and ketones, such as ethyl acetate, butyl acetate, butanols acetone, methyl ethyl ketone etc. The alcohols such as ethyl alcohol and butanol form the auxiliary solvents and many other Hydrocarbons can be used as diluents.

Coloured lacquers : Coloured lacquers are produced by incorporating either dyes or dispersed pigments in the clear lacquers containing the components mentioned above; the pigments are dispersed in lacquer medium. Dullening agents such as silica and metallic soaps are added wherever a subdued gloss or matted effect is desired.

Vinyl And Other Finishes : Vinyl resin finishing systems are prepared with polyvinyl chloride resins or copolymers of poly vinylchloride and poly vinylacetate. The vinyl resins give tough films with a rather low degree of extensibility. Polyurethane finishes are widely used in patent leather finishing. This type of finishing differs from other types of solvent finishes in that it is a reaction lacquer with low shelf life. The components of the finish are mixed shortly before application when the film- forming material is produced. The polyurethanes are also used in surface impreganation of side leathers to improve break and scuff resistance, similar to low molecular weight acrylic resin solutions.

Equipment : In the conventional seasoning machine, the finish is pumped into a trough where it is picked up by a rotating felted roll. A rotary brush transfers the finish from this roll and deposits it on the leather which passes beneath on a bolster. Mechanised swabs apply the coating material onto the grain and smoothens it.

Curtain Coater : In the curtain-coating machine a heavy coat of finish is deposited on the leather. The finish is pumped into a reservoir placed above the coveyor that transports the leathers. The finish is allowed to flow down as a thin unbroken film/sheet through a narrow slit the bottom of the reservoir.

Automatic Spray Equipment : Rotary spraying machines consist of several spray guns mounted on a unit which revolves continuously over the leathers moving on conveyors. Electronic devices such magic eyes or sensors are nowadays available which help spraying the season only on the leather surface thereby effecting considerable saving of spraying mixtures. The automatic spray unit is attached a long conveyor to heated tunnel driers, in which the conveyor belts travel - By the time the leather on the conveyor reaches the end through of the tunnel, the leathers are dried. This continuous and automatic spraying and drying unit is very popular and is most commonly need in larger products visits.

Hand Spray : When the productions is not very large or where the investment capacity is limited, special spray booths are needed and the spraying is done using a spray gun which has a small storage for the finishing season, which is sprayed through the nozzle with the help of compressed air. Before the spray is used, one or two coats of pigment season is applied manually by hand swabing or with a brush or velvet pad. Then the leathers are dried, after fixing.

After complete drying the protein season finished leathers are glazed in friction glazing machine or fine smooth finished roller machine. In the case of resin finished leathers are given a hot plating in a hydraulic press either with a smooth plate or printed depending on the degree of grain defects to be masked.

After this the finished leathers are measured using a pin wheel measuring machine or electronic area measuring machine. Finally they are inspected assorted and graded as per the requirements of the buyers.

It may be noted that in the case of leathers with large or appreciable grain blemishes, which cannot be corrected or marked, a film transfer finishing technique is adopted using a fancy pattern transfer film with adhesive at the top side of the leather over which the transfer paper is laid evenly without air bubbles/patches and pressed using a suitable plate in hydraulic press or roller mechanism. For more attractive appearance a golden or silver finish paper is used or papers with different metallic shades and pearly appearance are also commonly used to improve aesthetic appearance.

The tedious process of leather manufacturing can be summed up as eternal vigilance is the price of leather. This means a very careful approach at every stage is vital for obtaining the best results and value for the finished leathers.

Leather Made Out Of Different Raw Materials

The earlier chapters have dealt with the constitution of raw hides and skins available in India, their properties and how they are made into leather. In fact modern leather making is an art based on scientific knowledge and it is believed that there is nothing like leather. The types of leather made out of various raw materials are listed below:

Type Of Leathers

A. From Buffalo Hides

1. Sole
2. Belting
3. Harness
4. Saddlery
5. Hydraulic leather
6. Picking Band
7. Picker Saver
8. Raw hide pickers
9. Tanned pickers
10. Shrunken grain leather
11. Bag tanned sole leather
12. Kattai
13. Bunwar leather
14. Upholstery Leathers
15. Upper Leathers (printed)

Articles And Products Out Of The Above Leathers

1. Cut soles
2. Shoe bottom
3. Insoles
4. Industrial belts

5. Saddles
6. Conductor Bags
7. Ram Rings – U types
8. Ram Rings – V types
9. Link belts
10. Round belts
11. Washers
12. Foot valve leathers
13. Picking Band straps
14. 4 B Pickers
15. 29 B Pickers
16. Pickers saver straps
17. Washes of various types
18. Waist belts
19. Chappal straps
20. Document cases
21. Saleman bags
22. Brief cases
23. Hand bags
24. Purses
25. Transistor cases
26. File folders
27. Dust shields for railway wagon wheel axles
28. Ladies' Shoe upper
29. Upholstery leather
30. Upper for 'Casuals' footwear

b. From Cattle Hides

As in the case of buffalo hides, following is the various types of leathers and products made from cow hides.

1. E.I. Cow calf·
2. E.I. Tanned kips

3. Bag tanned leathers
4. Full chrome upper
5. Chrome retan
6. Nubuck leather
7. Case hides
8. Oil seal leather
9. Roller skins from chrome tanned calf
10. Semi alum upholstery
11. Semi chrome upper
12. Lining leathers
13. Football leather
14. Volley ball
15. Hockey ball
16. Cricket ball leathers

Products Out Of The Above Leathers

1. Shoe uppers
2. Straps
3. Purses
4. Document cases
5. Brief bags
6. File holders
7. Suit cases
8. Upholstery
9. Fancy articles
10. Pouches
11. Linings
12. Oil seals
13. Washers of various types
14. Textile spinning mill aprons
15. Conductor bags

16. Sitting pouches
17. Travel bags
18. Santiniketan type articles
19. Holding strips in buses
20. Bellows for vestibuled train carriages
21. Miner's boot
22. Mittens
23. Skieng boots
24. Mountaineering boots
25. Air travel cases

C. From Goat Skin

1. Pickled goat skins
2. Blue chorme goat skins
3. E.I. Goat skins
4. Glazed kid
5. Shrunken kid / Suede upper leathers
6. Chrome crust and mordanted crust from wet salted goat skins
7. Lining Leather
8. Grain garment leather
9. Suede garment leather
10. Morocco leather
11. Chamois leather
12. Gold and silver kid
13. Parchment leather
14. Fancy finished/printed leathers.

D. From Sheep Skins

1. E.I. Tanned sheep skins
2. Glove leather
3. Blue chrome sheep
4. Lining leathers
5. Diaphragm leather

6. Roller skins
7. Semi chrome garment leather/suede garment leather
8. White shuttle cock leather
9. Full chrome garment leathers/suede garment leather
10. Fancy or exotic type finished leathers.

PRODUCTS

1. Shoe upper linings
2. Diaphragm from Gasometer
3. Garments
4. Gloves
5. Fancy finished articles
6. Watch straps
7. Camera case
8. Shuttlecock
9. Spectacle cases
10. Wallets
11. Ladies Hand bags

E. Products From Crocodile Skins

For Exotic sources for which prior permission is to be obtained from wild life authorities etc. as many of these items are banned for using for making leather goods like fancy leather goods, ladies hand bags,watch straps, men's shoes etc.

F. Products From Reptile Skins (Articles)

Waist belts, ladies hand bags, watch straps, wallets, purses.

G. Products From Finished Lizard Skins

Wallets

Hand bags

Purses

Watch straps

Musical instruments

H. Newer Sources of Leathers

Frog skins

Bandicoot skins - Tails

Horse hides

Camel hides

Pig skins

Ostrich wings.

An overview of the various stages of processing starting from sourcing of raw materials to finishing have been furnished on the basis of the principles of leather manufacture, in a very simple and understandable manner which can be followed by floor level technician. It is to be mentioned here that a deliberate and special effort has been made to avoid complicated equation's and formulae which intertwined with the fundamentals of leather processing. As far as possible even the names of chemicals processing stage are given in commercial form and not as chemical formula. This should be considered only as a formal introduction to the intricacies of leather process and by no means a detailed dissertation.

Regarding details of processing various types of leathers, it will be a multiplication of the multitudes of formulae appeared in detail in various papers literature and as recommended by many chemical manufacture and suppliers. It will be a futile exercise to give detailed recipies mentioning particular branded chemicals, as it can be construed as an conceiled canvassing or promotion of sales efforts. Hence a general basis of processing certain important types of leather will be furnished for reference as a general guidance. It is re-emphasised here, that no formulation of the details of the processing is universally applicable or acceptable and hence these should be adhered/amended to suit the local conditions and as per the by as requirement to meet the changinng fashions and market requirements.

It is also to be mentioned here that leather processing involves approximately nine branches or disciplines of science and innumerable interplay of engineering and technology and hence the, task, becomes more complicated to explain and interpret all the details of processing. However based on the past experience of many tanners spread all over the country and many nations typical examples of some processes are provided. It is realised that there is scope for improvement at every stage of this attempt and the author will be grateful for suggestions observation and more so of criticisms in this attempts. It is also accepted that there have been lapses in editing, proof reading and corrections which are obvious, and for every attempt will be made to reduce the occurrence such lapses-mistakes-Readers valuable views and suggestions invited before the gigantic task of detailed dissertation is attempted.

Leather making till the mid fifties was considered to be an art as it was mainly dependent an human skill judgement and discretion. With the earnest attempt of the scientists to understand the intricacies of the processing of leather, began the scientific interpretation of the processing, later it reduced the complications of involving so many variable factors which make it beyond the possibility of eliminating the human element/skill/judgement totally in leather processing assessment, quality control and grading. Even after many achievements and startling discoveries of the science in leather processing, it has not been possible to defy the influence human judgement and skill, and continues to be considered as a blend of technology and skilled art. It gets confirmed by the failure of the attempts to totally automising or mechanising the processing of leather. At best it could be considered as the scientific interpretation of leather processing and not an evolution of technology based on scientific knowledge. Opinions may differ, but everybody with a basic knowledge will admit that the theory only explains the reactions taking place and not vice versa. It is with this background it is said that just because one is able to write a possible/probable reactions formula on paper, it need not necessarily take place in actual practice. Never the less attempts are continuing and should continue to rationalise the processing techniques eliminating the human factor to the maximum possible extent. A complete solution to this solution is eluding the concerted efforts as on date and still continues to be a blend of science, technology and still in certain areas like assessment, grading, etc.

Special Note

A Typical model of a process control chart is indicated for regular production in commercial tannery. This should be considered as indicative only and not exhaustive and can be modified as per the production details. The advantages of following such a system are it enables quality control and standardisation of regular production, greater uniformity, to trace the mistakes of any, and fixing responsibility for Inspection and quality control at every stage. Such a system if adopted will help in getting ISO certification easily. Disadvantages are it is laborious, time consuming and requires strict adherence of lot system without mixing up. The initial assortment in raw/pelt stage and the final sorting and grading is approximately in agreement it will indicate as the. correctness of otherwise of the source of purchase, cost, and reliability. Finally it enables the easy costing of the leathers continuous monitoring as per the frequent change in the cost of various chemicals. Many conflicting opinions have been expressed for and against this system, because of the difficulties mentioned. But from an objective view it will be necessary and advantageous for regular production units to rectify mistakes if any before it is too late.

SPECIAL INSTRUCTIONS IF ANY

Soaking to TANNING	
TANNAGE	
SPLIT	
SHAVE	
RETANNAGE	
DYEING	
FAT LIQUOR	
DRY NORMAL PASTE VACUUM	
ANY OTHERS	

Typical Model of a Process Control Chart

Lot no. *Pieces* *Weights m/kg* *Bale No. (Source)* *Lime Loss/Gain*	*Material* *Grade* *Raw* *Supplier* *Sides/Skins*	*Date* *Soaked Weight* *Pelt Weight* *Shaved Weight*		*Lot No.* *Date*

PROCESS

Day	Day	%	Chemicals	From	To	pH	Temp o.d.	Minutes	Remarks
			Soaking Fresh water - 1st day Wetting Agent used (Name) Sodium Sulphate if used Preservative Any other chem. used if any						Date Lot No. Packed Date - Lot No. Inspect Sort. Observations

SAME SOAK - 2ND DAY

			Green flesh - 3rd day Wettifng Agent Sodium Sulphide Preservative Liming Drum Water - Time Running Lime - Time Running Sulphide - Time Running						Lot No: Condition Date - Lot No. Observ. Defects/ Damages if any Indication

			Unhair - Relime Lime Any other chemical used Flesh Pelt weight - (Note)							
DELIMING AND BATING										
			Washing - 1st day Washing - 2nd if done Water Ammonium Sulphate (Deliming used agents) Bate-used-Note-Temperature Scudding Washing Scudding							Lot Date Pelt Weight Condition/Observation Machine Unhair/detail - Scud Fleshing machine Manual Indicator Test
						PICKLING				
			Water - 50% (Half) Salt Acid - Run Time if added Masking Agent (if used) Calcium Formate (if used)							Date - Lot No. Obervation Inspection Report
						CHROME TANNING				
			Water: % Run Salt if fresh bath Chrome Extract/Solution Run							Date: Lot No.: Observations Indicator used-remains

Date		Day			Lot No.		Remarks/Observations							
Process/Retannin	Pcs.		Kgms.		Machine Used	Remarks	Date	Pcs.	Pass. No	Opr. sig.	Pcs	Pass No.	Opr. sig.	Sup. sig.
Rechroming Water	%	From	To	pH	To Machine-oper. Dept. To M/C Department									
Chrome Ext./Run used					Saw									
Sod. Bicarbonate " Wash Bicarbonate "					SET									
Neutralisation	%	Water-Temp. 0°C			SPLIT									
Sedium carbonate quality used					SHAVE SAM-Pressure	N o t e shaved weight								
Name of Syntan if used - Quantity					SET Pressure									
Sod. Bicarbonate "					Vac. Dry-Moisture>Stake									
Washing Veg. Ext. "					Dry-Hang/Paste/vac.									
Dyening Dyes used					Store in crust. stage									
Quantity-Run					Condition									
Fixing-Acid used Qty.					Stake									

Fat Liquors used						Vacuum Dry.									
i. Actl. % Quantity						Toggle-Buffing									
ii.						To Finishing-Date									
iii.															
Formic Acid-Run Exhaustion qty. used															
Pres. used if any															

NO. OF LOT

NO. OF PIECES

ASSORTMENT FOR FINISHING

Aniline/Semi Aniline/Print or Platr/Suede Shade

Date	Materials used	Method of application	Spray		Shade Specify	Remarks if any
	Pigments	Hand Swabing Curtain Coat it	Rotary Machine	Hand Spray		
	Binders-Protein Resin					
	Plasticiser/Fixing					
	Lacquer/Laq Emulsion					
	Plate/Print					
	Measurement/Assortment					

General Remarks

Store/Handed over to Ware House

Date :

Lot No.

No. of pieces Grade 1 2 3 4

Area ....

RECENT DEVELOPMENTS AND CONCEPTS

FOR SOLVING EFFLUENT PROBLEMS

PROCESS MODIFICATION TO REDUCE POLLUTION LOAD AND VOLUME OF EFFLUENT BY CLEANER TECHNOLOGY

(1) SALT LESS OR LESS SALT INCURING

(2) LIME LESS OR LESS LIME IN LIMING

(3) AMMONIUM SALT - FREE DELIMING

(4) BETTER CHROME EXHAUSTION
OR REUSE OF CHROMIUM YARD
CHROME VI FREE TANNING SALT

(5) USE OF ONLY PERMITTED DYES & PRESERVATIVES

(6) BETTER EXHAUSTION OF DYES AND FATLIQUORS

(7) FIXING WITHOUT USING FORMALDEHYDE

(8) RECYCLING OF WATER/REDUCED USEAGE OF VOL. OF WATER

(9) FILTRATION OF EFFLUENT THROUGH PEBBLE, SAND AND ACTIVATED CHARCOAL CARBON BED/FOR REMOVING ODOUR, COLOUR AND STINK

END OF THE PIPE TREATMENT TECHNIQUES

SEE EFFLUENT TREATMENT FLOW SHEETS

BASIS OF CLEANER PROCESSING TECHNOLOGY

Environmentally Friendly Chemicals For Leather Processing

A. IDENTIFICATION OF PROBLEM AREAS

(1) CURING : SALT AND PRESERVATIVES USED

(2) LIMING : SODIUM SULPHIDE CAUSTIC ALKALINITY

(3) TANNING : NON BIODEGRADABLE MATERIALS NEUTRAL SALTS

(4) CHROME TANNING: (HEXAVALENT CHROME)
CHROME IN EFFLUENTS
BAN ON THE USE OF 22 TYPES ARYL
AMINE BASED DYES

(5) DYES : BENZIDINE BASED DYES-NOT ALLOWED
UNABSORBED DYE - COLORED EFFLUENTS

(6) FAT LIQUORS : RANCID SMELL AND FAT SPUES

(7) FINISHING : RESINS : RESIDUAL SMELL.
SOLVENTS : FIRE AND HEALTH HAZARD.
FORMALDEHYDE : PUNGENT ODOUR
AMMONIA: PUNGENT ODOUR

(8) SOLVENTS : ODOUR AND FIRE HAZARD

B. ALLIED AREAS : RELATED ASPECTS

(1) HIGH VOLUME OF WATER USED AND EFFLUENTS

(2) BYE PRODUCTS : FLESHINGS, TRIMMINGS,
SHAVINGS, BUFFING DUST

(3) BULK VOLUME: SOLID SLUDGE ACCUMULATION
AFTER EFFLUENT TREATMENT USED LIME.

APPROACHES TO SOLVE THE PROBLEM AREAS

POSSIBLE REMEDIAL MEASURES

1. CURING: SALTLESS CURING - USE OF BIOCIDES
FREEZING – PRESENTLY OF
THEORETICAL INTEREST

NITROGENOUS PRESERVATION
TANNERY PROCESS – REMOVAL OF
SALTING BY DUSTING - PRESOAKING TO
REMOVE SALT – SEGREGATION OF SOAK
LIQUOR EVAPORATION – RECOVERY OF SALT
USE OF ONLY PERMITTED PRESERVATIVES
LIKE BUSAN 30-TCMTB. LUNACID-AP ETC.
IN PROCESSING. FROM SOAKING, WET
BLUE STAGE AND FAT LIQUORING. ALL STAGES.

2. SOAKING: REDUCED VOLUME OF WATER USED – COUNTER CURRENT SYSTEM FOR SUCCESSIVE LOTS USE OF PERMITTED PRESERVATIVES FOR SOAKING

3. LIMING: SODIUM SULPHIDE – NOT ONLY PRODUCES HIGH ALKALINITY BUT ALSO PRODUCES HYDROGEN SULPHIDE-ABNOXIOUS ODOUR LIME USED - BULK VOLUME SOLID SLUDGE AFTER USE – PROBLEM OF DISPOSAL

ALTERNATIVE METHODS

(1) ENZYMATIC UNHAIRING – DEVELOPMENT OF CLARIZYME. AT COMPARATIVELY LOW COST PROCESSING METHOD – STANDARDISED FOR SKINS BEING DEVELOPED FOR HIDES.

NEUTRAL SALT BUILDUP

(1) THE CAUSTIC ALKALINITY PRODUCED IN LIME YARD AND THE HIGH ACIDITY COMING OUT FROM PICKLE BATH WILL ENABLE MUTUAL PRECIPITATION AS NEUTRAL SALT

(2) INORGANIC SALT BUILDUP – IN THE WASHINGS, DELIMING, NEUTRALISATION ARE THE MAIN SOURCES -USE OF CARBON-DIOXIDE FOR DELIMING HAS ENABLED THE REDUCTION OF THE SAME.

(4) CHROME TANNING

IN NORMAL CHROME TANNING AS PRACTISED ABSORBS ONLY 70% OF THE CHROME TANNING SALT USED LEAVING ABOUT 30% OF THE UNABSORBED CHROME SALT IN THE EFFLUENTS. THIS CAUSES DIFFICULTY IN DISPOSAL – ALSO CONSIDERED TOXIC. THIS COULD BE TACKLED BY

(a) USE OF HIGH EXHAUST MATERIALS IN CHROME TANNING –

(b) MODIFICATION OF CHROME TANNING SALT FOR BETTER EXHAUSTION

(c) USE OF LESS CHROME OR CHROMELESS TANNING PROCESS – USE OF ALUTAN ALCHROTAN

(d) RECOVERY AND REUSE OF EXHAUST CHROME IN PROCESSING ELIMINATING THE FLOW OF CHROME IN EFFLUENTS.

(e) USE OF HIGH SPEED CHROME PENETRATOR MACHINE – ENABLES BETTER ABSORPTION OF CHROME PRACTICALLY LEAVING NO CHROME IN THE EXHAUST

(5) DYES: USE OF OPTIMUM QUANTITY OF PERMITTED DYES.

USE OF INSTANT DYEING TECHNIQUES

AND SPECIALITY DYES.

(6) FAT LIQUORS: USE OF FATLIQUORS CONTAINING NATURAL VEGETABLE OR ANIMAL SOURCES CAUSES NOT ONLY RANCID ODOUR BUT ALSO FAT SPUES. USE OF SYNTHETIC FAT LIQUORS ENABLES THE REDUCTION OF FREE FAT ACCUMALION – ODOUR AND FAT SPUE.

(7) FINISHING: SOLVENTS – LACQUERS USED DURING FINISHING POSE FIRE HAZARD APART FROM TOXIC EFFECT ON PERSONS RECENT STRESS HAS BEEN ON THE USE OF WATER BASED FINISHES OR EMULSIONS WITH LESS SOLVENTS. FORMALDEHYDE FREE FIXING.

B. ALLIED ASPECTS

(1) HIGH VOLUME OF WATER USED IN PROCESSING LEADS TO LARGE VOLUME OF EFFLUENTS

CAN BE TACKLED/REDUCED BY

(1) LESS FLOAT/FLOAT LESS TANNING TECHNIQUES WHEREEVER POSSIBLE.

(2) USE SPECIAL EQUIPMENTS: LIKE HIDE PROCESSORS – HIGH SPEED PENETRATORS – ETC.

(3) SPECIAL TECHNIQUES LIKE COUNTER-CURRENT FLOW TO ECONOMISE USE OF WATER.

(2) BYE PRODUCTS:

FLESHINGS-TRIMMINGS-FOR GLUE MAKING

SHAVING - BUFFING DUST - LEATHER BOARD MAKING

(2) BULK VOLUME SOLID WASTES

(1) USED LIME AS FILLERS

(2) USE OF SOLID SLUDGE FROM TANNERIES FOR LIGHT WEIGHT BRICK MAKING - ROAD FILLING, LEVELLING OF SURFACES, PITS, ETC.

EFFLUENT COLLECTION, TREATMENT & DISPOSAL

Characteristics of the Effluents

The tanneries generate liquid waste from operations like soaking, liming, unhairing and fleshing, deliming and bating, pickling, tanning (chrome or vegetable), dyeing and fatliquoring. The quantity of effluent discharged amounts to about 30 litres per Kg of hides / skins processed. In case finishing units the quantity will be about 50 litres per Kg of raw material.

Characteristics of the effluents generated at different operations are as given in Table below:

Table

Typical Analysis of Tannery Effluents

S1. No.	*Characteristics*	*Source of Effluents*					
		Soaking	*Liming*	*Deliming*	*Vege-table tanning*	*Chrome tanning*	*Comp osite (incl. washings)*
1.	Volume, ltrs/ 100 kg. hide or skin tanned	480	470	320	360	430	—
2.	ph: Minimum	7.7	9.9	2.4	5.1	2.6	7.6
	Maximum	13.2	13.2	10.1	6.7	3.2	12.2
	Average	9.3	12.7	8.0	5.8	2.9	9.5
3.	Total Solids mg/1						
	Minimum	11250	16200	1410	8250	8300	11920
	Maximum	54800	79660	15550	55560	74800	31000
	Average	21200	48400	5870	31800	11550	20000
4.	Suspended solids mg/1						
	Minimum	145	1.235	220	585	260	1280
	Maximum	5080	23290	4450	9960	705	6080
	Average	2590	10330	1390	3510	480	3170
5.	BOD (5 days, 37 Deg.C), mg/1)						
	Minimum	260	4400	500	6000	—	2800
	Maximum	7500	24000	3500	31200	—	14800
	Average	1610	10000	1520	19290	1000	7000

Characteristics of the effluents generated at different operations are as given in Table below:

Ways & Means to reduce the volume and intensity of Tannery effluents

The tanneries can reduce quantity of effluent through economical use and reuse of water as well as by the following methods:

- Good house keeping
- Process Modification
- Reuse of fairly clearer fractions of the waste
- Recycle after partial or complete treatments

Good house keeping invariably brings better results. Avoiding spillages leaks, carrying out the process in a regulated manner can bring in considerable reduction in waste volume.

Process modifications, such as use of paddles and drums for soaking operations instead of the conventional pits, batch washing operations etc. considerably cut down the volume of the waste Water.

Waste waters arising out of the washing after bating, pickling and neutralising, which are fairly clean are reused for operations such as washing the hides and skins after soaking, liming and also for floor washing.

In the unhairing process, the usage of sulphides is to be reduced by using chemicals such as 'amines' and the sulphide free lime liquor is reused and can be used treating the chrome effluent.

Further, segregation of the fraction contributing the major pollution load and treating it separately is also adopted. In the case of tannery wastes, the salt laden soak waste is highly pollutional in character due to excessive chloride. The soak waste is segregated from the main stream and evaporated in solar evaporation basins. If the salt applied to a hide a preservative is taken as 45% of the total weight, about 1/3rd binds itself the to the hide, half can be brushed or dusted and the balance of 1/6th drains off during preservation. The salt bound on the hide find its way in the effluent from the soaking operation. But often the dusted salt also gains in the effluent. Hence, proper thorough dusting and collection of the dusted salt and preventing it from gaining access alongwith the effluent, reduces the salt content of the waste.

Waste reduction in case of vegetable tanning is achieved by the use of drums, giving higher fixation of tannage, allowing lesser quantity of tannis in the effluent. Use of syntans also contributes towards increased fixation of tannins.

In case of chrome tanning process, a reduced concentration of the chromium is achieved by:

- Improving the fixation of chrome
- Reuse of chrome liquor and
- Precipitation of chromium from the chrome liquor with an alkali and redissolving and reusing the chrome precipitate.

Increasing the fixation of chrome is achieved through a number of ways like:

a) Decreasing the acidity of the pickling operation and increasing the basification after the tanning process.

b) Reducing quantity of neutral salts present during the process of chrome tanning and the tanning liquor.

c) Reduction in chrome dosage.

d) Increase of temperature at the end of tanning process and duration of tanning.

However, the quality of the tanned leather desired is sometimes a constraint in adopting the above methods. The maximum practicable fixation achieved can be considered as 85%.

Another method of waste reduction is use of chrome liquor for pickling operations. In this case, the chrome liquor has to be acidified by adding the pickle acid to the liquor. But constant analysis of the spent chrome liquor has to be carried out. Accumulation of sulphate ions entering with the pickle acid and the chrome tanning agent may take place. Increased sulphate concentration may make the leather stiff and this can be avoided with the use of little or no sulphuric acid or by the precipitation of the liquor with calcium before use.

Treatment of Waste from Tanneries

The treatment of tannery wastes is broadly classified as:

a) Segregation

b) Primary Treatment

c) Secondary Treatment

a) Segregation

The salt laden soak waste and the pickle liquor is segregated, neutralised to pH 7.0, screened and evaporated in solar vapouration basin.

In case of chrome tanning industry, the spent chrome tan liquor is segregated and mixed with lime liquor to precipitate the chrome to be disposed separately. Reuse of spent chrome is also possible by precipitation and treatment to get basic chromium sulphate or by reuse of spent liquor in the initial tanning stages.

b) Primary Treatment

The waste from tannery may contain coarser impurities, hence it is screened to remove these impurities before further treatment. To even out the flow of effluent, an equalisation tank of 24 hours capacity is provided, which also serves as a setting tank for removal of suspended impurities. After this the dissolved toxic impurities are further chemically treated, coagulated, floculated and separated through sand-bed filters. The filtered liquor is now ready for biological treatment.

c) Secondary Treatment

For secondary biological treatment of the settled waste, the following methods are adopted either individually or in combination.

a) Anaerobic Lagoon

b) Aerated Lagoon

c) Oxidation ditch

a) Anaerobic Lagoon

This is used where sufficient land is available for providing the treatment unit and disposal. This effluent after treatment is disposed on land for irrigation after satisfying the condition as per IS 3307: 1977.

b) Aerated Lagoon

The tanneries which have sufficient land for treatment but do not have the land for disposal of the treated effluent, use combination of treatments such as anaerobic lagoon or oxidation ditch. The effluent is dispassed into any water course after satisfying the condition laid down in IS2 490 Part I to III.

e) Oxidation Ditch

The tanneries which do not have enough land for providing treatment as well as disposal of treated effluent, can go for aerated lagoon followed by oxidation ditch. The treated effluent is disposed into in land surface water after satisfying IS 2490.

Major Problems Involved in Treatment of Tanning Wastes

- High amount of Total Dissolved solids (TDS) due to high TDS content of raw water.
- Chlorides content in treated effluents do not confirm to the standards even after segregation due to common salt and sodium sulphate.
- Toxicity of effluents not well established.

Selection of Suitable Treatment Technology

This is based on the following factors:

i) Location & topography of tanneries
ii) Availability of Land
iii) Final mode of treated effluent discharge
iv) Operational and Maintenance cost
v) Regulation of pollution control boards and local bodies.

Future Outlook

The system of common effluent treatment must be introduced for the group of tanneries in one locality which will ensure efficient operations, maintenance and protection against pollution at considerable reduced costs. However, these common treatment plants will take care of the secondary treatment as mentioned earlier. No common treatment plant can undertake to do the primary and secondary treatment for all the tanners because of volume of suspended matter and the quality differs greatly from tanner to tanner.

Whenever tanneries are isolated it is advisable to separate the effluent at each stage of operation and plan the disposal independently so as to reduce the complexity.

SOLID WASTE UTILISATION

The various solid wastes generating in tanneries are Hair, Wools, Fleshings, raw and crust trimmings, splits, chrome shavings & sludge, buffing dust etc.

These solid wastes have economic value and are used in manufactured of variety of products. Some of the solid wastes are exported and generate valuable foreign exchange. The usage of different solid wastes is as under:

a) Goat Hair

The current production of goat hair is estimated at 19.2 million pounds worth Rs. 152 Lakhs. In India the annual growth rate of population of goats was 2.7% between 1961 to 1982. The goat population for the year 1990-91 is estimated at 115.9 million heads.

The goat hair is used for brushes, mixing with felt and packing in furniture item. The keratin protein is recovered and bleached and is utilised for industrial purposes.

b) Sheep Wool

The sheep population in India in 1990-91 is estimated 51.5 million heads. The annual growth rate between 1961 and1982 was 0.9%. The current production of wool is estimated at 87.5 million pounds worth Rs.19.7 crore. This wool finds application in manufacture of carpets, blankets, rugs etc. Indian wool finds increasing demand in export markets of the USA, USSR & other countries.

c) Fleshing & Raw Trimmings

These are used as a basis for fat rendering and in the manufacture of glue ad gelatin.

d) Crust Trimmings

These are used for the manufacture of leather board after defibering.

e) Vegetable Tanned Splits

These are used for the manufacture of leather board and as a substitute for insole leathers for shoes. Thicker splits are utilised for P.U. laminated leather for shoe uppers, bags etc.

f) Vegetable Tanned Leather Waste

This has fertilising properties and is used as a source of Nitrogen.

g) Lime Sludge

This is used as a filler material in road construction.

h) Split Waste

This is used for manufacturing ginning washers. Thicker splits are dyed into shoe suede upper or used for P.U. liminate upper or bag leather.

i) Chrome Shavings

This is used for the manufacture of leather board & manure. The protein from shavings is also recovered after dechroming and is used for industrial purposes or for making special syntans.

j) Buffing Dust

This is used as a fertiliser and as flooring material.

ECONOMY OF WATER AND CHEMICALS AND ENERGY EFFICIENCY

Technology in Water Management

a) The analysis of the Indian tanning industry reveals the alarming fact that water is one input which is consumed in the largest quantity. There is hardly any consideration of rationalising the use of water.

b) The water consumption by the tanning segment is the greatest. The high consumption stages being, all the wet operations. The tendency to use larger floates and absence of any recycling of liquors results into higher water consumption.

c) The finishing sector uses relatively lower quantum of water (for rechroming, retanning, dyeing, fatliquoring and spray finishing.)

d) Apart from the increasing scarecity and cost of water, the high consumption also leads to high effluent volumes.

e) These effluents without treatment have polluted the natural underground resources of tanners themselves. Many tannery areas are now using water having upto 5000 ppm hardness.

f) It has also been observed that absence of any treatment facility for softening the raw water often results affects the action and requirement of chemicals.

Economy of Chemical Utilisation

a) In general the consumption of chemicals in the Indian tanning industry is at a considerably higher level. There is a tendency to use excessive quantity of chemicals at every stage than what is absorbed during the processes. There is hardly any attempt towards process optimisation to reduce the quantity of chemicals by recycling and recovery of chemicals at each stage. There is no attempt to effectively exhaust and utilise used chemicals in the process itself.

b) This fact leads to the higher cost of chemicals in the production of leather (18 to 25 per cent) as compared to the European tanneries (12 to 15 per cent).

c) Most of the chemicals being non-bio-degradable, the higher consumption, of chemicals also leads to higher concentration of toxic chemicals in the tannery exhaust (salt, sulphide, lime, chrome, dyes and fatliquors). This naturally has led to the effluent treatment problems like, high capital cost of installation of treatment plants, difficulties associated in minimising the levels of toxicity (BOD and COD) to the stringent standards prescribed by the Pollution Control Authorities, and the detrimental effect on the environment through discharge of such effluents.

Energy

a) The tanning utilises maximum energy in running of drums and machines, in heating of water and drying processes. The trend towards modernisation has involved the use of various continuousl/semi-continuous machines which consume higher energy as compared to batch mode of operations.

b) Energy is estimated to contribute about 8 to 16 per cent and is the third largest component of production cost.

c) However, no attempt has been made to set the norm for energy consumption (specific energy consumption at various stages).

d) The lack of efficient energy management is acutely felt in view of the chronic shortages of power and quality of product experienced in the major leather producing states.

Chapter - 4
Leather Manufacture

Introduction

For organising any industry the following factors are considered to be important.

Men

Materials and

Money

These are known as the three important "M"s. This only emphasises the need for organising the Financial resources, effectively utilise all the available materials, by properly mobilising the skilled man power at various levels.

Recently two more aspects are also considered as important:

Management and

Marketing

These aspects are vital for making the enterprise more financially viable and technically sound.

These are general concepts as applicable to all the industry. In the case of the leather industry also, these factors are equally important. Hence a vital study of these aspects are considered essential for making the units successful.

Special Features of the Leather Industry

The Leather industry is essentially based on raw materials which are obtained as a bye product of the meat industry. Hence the industry has practically no control over the cost or quality of the raw material which will be dependant on the ever fluctuating price and demand of the meat industry. In addition, the raw material is highly heterogeneous in nature. Each hide or skin vary in structure and chemical compositions. Quality from one another, and species to species and within the skin itself. Hence, technically it poses a greater challenge to the technologists. As is true of any natural raw materials, for processing leather efficiently the technologists should have a clear understanding and appreciation of various branches of physical and chemical services and engineering aspects as the leather processing involves chemical and physical reactions and utilisation of a number of machines.

Apart from processing complications, the marketing of leather is a skilled job, as this is considered to be an international commodity. Therefore the type of leather selection and grading and the cost aspects are dictated by international changes in demand pattern and competition from various countries. As such, it will be seen for successfully organising a leather industry, one has to have a thorough appreciation of all these aspects.

Leather forms the raw material for a number of leather product industries like footwear, leather goods, garments, travelware, sports goods, etc. For organising these leather products industries, a more careful and systematic method of approach will be required as these industries deal with more value added products requiring greater; technical, management and marketing skills.

Technical Feasibility appraisal and Project Reports

Before one starts any industry, it is necessary to make a careful study of the various technical aspects to be evaluated as to whether the proposed unit will be technically and economically viable as a commercial venture. This -involves initially analysing the availability (if the raw material specially from the point of view of quality and quantity, the cost of the same and the various chemicals and auxiliaries used in processing skilled labour resources required at various levels and infrastructures required. The possibility of marketing the product in the existing marketing conditions is very essential making realistic appraisal of the possible future trends, both in the national and international scene.

When the preliminary feasibility studies indicate positive result, it becomes necessary to prepare a detailed project report in order to make an assessment of the financial requirement for providing all the infra-structural facilities for the proposed project.

The Project Report highlights the following aspects:

Financial Aspects

1. Fixed Capital

1. Cost of the Land required for its procurement, registration and development cost, etc.
2. Cost of the buildings including the space required for the processing like factory sheds, administrative offices, including other allied infrastructure like workshop shed, sanitary, plumbing and effluent treatment plant, etc. This will also include common labour welfare amenities like rest rooms, toilets, quarters for essential staff etc.
3. Cost of Plant & Machinery. The project report will also give a detailed list of all the machines required, Source of procurement, detailed specifications and the approximate cost of the same. This will also include essential spares etc. This may also include any specific machines required specially for the effluent treatment boilers, transformer for power, pumps, Motors, workshop infrastructure etc.

The cost of land, Buildings, Plant & Machinery form the basic core of the fixed capital requirements.

II. Working Capital Requirements

The working capital requirements will indicate not only the cost of all the raw materials, chemicals, power, water, steam, fuels and other resources for processing, but also the direct cost of inputs that goes into production, like the cost of labour and supervision, works manager, etc. The cost inputs of all these factors for a specific period of time of processing will be worked out.

III. Overheads

Indirect overheads like interest on borrowings, fixed statutory commitment charges, for indirect off ice overheads, one time, investment like project preparation cost, contingencies, expenditure in connection with the promotion of the projects, etc., will also be indicated in the project.

IV. Profitability

The Project report will also indicate the annual cost of production, expected sales realisation, break even point, gross profit, after deduction of taxes, cash flow statements showing the cash inflow (source of funds) and out flow (utilisation of funds) details of a period of ten years giving the details of the amount of the schedule of repayments, taxes, depreciation, etc.

From the financial angle these are the most important aspects, which are essential for raising the necessary funds, specially from financial Institution.

Technical aspects

Technical aspects will make a critical assessment of the availability and suitability of raw material to ensure a continuous production, appraisal of the quality of the raw material, product-mix in keeping with the marketing potential assessment, a minimum viable level of production capacity of the plant, etc. The technical aspects will also identify all the essential machines needed for the specific and products, consumption of chemicals per day, both in quantity and costwise, cost of maintenance of machines, source of supply, the cost and quality.

Other aspects like the quantity of water, power, steam, fuel, personnel required at various levels like unskilled, skilled, machine operators, supervisors, yard and works managers, quality control laboratories, etc., will all be indicated together with the approximate cost. The technical report will also furnish detailed drawings about the plant layout, location of machines, worksheds and various infrastructures.

Cost of the Project will be indicated as follows:

1.	Fixed Capital Cost of Land		
	Buildings Plant & Machineries	A	
	Margin Money for working capital	B	
	Projection promotion cost Contingencies,		
	Project Engineering, Consultancy, etc.	C	
		A + B + C	Project cost
			E

Margin money for the working capital will include :

1.	Raw Materials	–	15 days
2.	Chemicals Cost	–	1 month
3.	Utilities (1 Month)	–	1 month
4.	Labour & Supervision	–	1 month
5.	Stock-Work in progress	–	15 days
6.	Stock in credit-sale	–	1 month
			D

Since the financial Institution like Banks, etc. is likely to finance upto 75% of D, the margin money required to be provided by the project is worked out as only 25% of D. This is indicated as B-above.

If the cost of the project is worked out as E, the industrial financing institutions are likely to finance the projects according to the debt to equity ratio for each industry. Generally for the leather industry this is likely to be 2 to 2.5: 1.

Debt finances by institution – 66% of E

Promoters and entrepreneurs sale – 34% of E

When a duly prepared project report is correctly appraised by the financial institute, the finance is arranged, the actual implementation of the project is taken up. Usually for a well planned project, the actual implementation of the proposal could be carried out in a period of 12 to 18 months time.

In the case of small scale industries, considerable time could be saved by occupying sheds in industrial estates, where most of the common infra-structural facilities will be available and the project capital cost could also be reduced by occupying readily built factory sheds on rental basis, the financial institutions will also extend concessional credits on liberal loans.

For actuals implementation of the project, the following are the important aspects :

Factors which influence the section of site for the project :

(i) Availability of Raw Materials

(ii) Availability of Chemicals

(iii) Water-Quantity and Quality

(iv) Labour

(v) Power

(vi) Transport

(vii) Proximity to marketing area

(viii) Governmental incentives/policies

(ix) Ease of treatment/disposal of effluents possibilities of joining C E T plants (Common effluent treatment)

(x) Agglomeration-Ten for forming groups of specialised nature

II. Selection of personnel/training

Since the leather industry is a highly skilled personnel oriented industry it is very essential to select the proper persons for the specific jobs and train them specially in the operation of latest machineries.

III. Purchase of raw materials

The most important aspect in the leather processing industry is the purchase of raw material of the high quality at reasonable price. It requires a special skill and personal judgement on the part of the management. Since the raw material contributes to nearly 60% of the cost of production, any mistake committed at this stage, cannot be off set at any other stage.

Break up of the cost of products

Cost of Raw Material – 60

Cost of Chemicals – 25

Cost of Labour & Supervision – 6 to 8%

Direct overheads like steam power maintenance, etc. – 8 to 9%

IV. Need for quality control and Standards

For ensuring a steady market for the products it is very essential to have a built-in system of quality control at the stages of processing by having a process control laboratory with all the modem facilities. The quality control lab should not only analyse, test and assess all the chemicals and auxiliaries purchased before using them in processing but also draw samples at various stages of processing, control pH & analyse all the aspects. The finished leathers produced should also be subjected to chemical analysis and physical testing for maintenance of quality standards as per standard specification.

V. Quality assessement of Grading of Leathers

a) Final grading/quality assessment and selection of leathers are all being carried out by visual assessment only in commercial tanneries. As such it is very essential to have skilled personnel for carrying out the job. Any mistake of wrong grading and assessment is likely to effect, adversely the profitability of the whole unit.

b) Yet another aspect is the accuracy in measurement, reducing the wastages in trimming, etc. If the measurement is not properly done either it may result in losses due to undermeasurement or to claims from buyers if it is overmeasured.

VI. Utilisation of Bye-Products

The leather industry produces a number of bye products like fleshings, trimmings hair etc., which could be profitably utilised/sold for making other saleable material which can add to the profitability.

VII. Effluent Treatment–A Social Obligation

The expenditure on effluent treatment is a small portion, though the initial cost of establishment of the treatment plant may be high. This should be considered as in integral part of the cost inputs, contributing to the cost structure. Though this may make a small cut in profits, this is to be considered as a social obligation of the factory to provide pollution free environment society. Without this statutory obligation the very existence of unit will be in jeopardy.

VIII. Management & Marketing

Since the leather industry is highly subjective and dependent on persons, the management will have to be always alert to keep pace with the changes in marketing conditions both in purchase and sales. In an ever increasing potential for market demand for leathers, marketing of leather will have to be done carefully to obtain the best possible price for various items of products. A clear monitoring of the purchase apparisal of proportions of the product-mix.

As originally envisaged with the actual achievements, practically realised is very essential. Any imbalanced increase in the proportion of the low value items of product or a continuous reduction in the proportion of high value products should be viewed seriously and corrective measures implemented in time.

IX. Need for quality control and standards

Some useful hints for successful Management of Leather processing Unit.

1. There should be adequate stock of the required raw materials to ensure a contineous production. Over stocking of raw material will lead to excess blocking of the capital, whereas inadequate stock may lead to break in production.
2. There should be adequate quantity of the required chemicals and auxiliaries for enabling continued production. Imported chemicals may have to be stocked for a longer period whereas indegenous chemicals may be stocked for a shorter period only. In other words there should be an efficient inventory control in the stores department.
3. The purchase of raw material, its quality and cost aspects will have to be strictly monitored.
4. There should be constant vigil and supervision in the production yard to ensure control and supervision of the machine operators for accuracy and precision.

5. There should be a continuous system of preventive maintenance of machines to prevent break down of machine leading to disruption in production.
6. The skilled workers and machine operators have to be properly trained in the operation of modern machines.
7. Great care is required in the assortment of the leather in various stages like wet blue in the crust stage to divert the leather for proper items of the product-mix.
8. Care should be taken to prevent excessive trimmings leading to loss in area of the finished leathers.
9. The final assortment and grading of leathers will have to be very carefully done by experts.
10. Great care is essential in the measurement of the final leathers.
11. There should be a system of proper feed back regarding the changing pattern in market demand, to streamline the production as per the requirements of the market.
12. The top management should have an effective system of monitoring the purchase strategy and the production output according to the marketing strategy planned.
13. Involvement of professional experts to management and marketing is essential.
14. Effluent treatment and disposal will have to be effectively monitored to prevent the pollution of the environment.
15. Management of the personnel including the labour force is very essential to ensure a smooth running of the factories.
16. Adequate attention should be paid to provide protection from all hazards like fire, electrical short circuits, chemical fumes, etc., as the processing involves use of inflammable and many other hazardous chemicals/ materials.
17. It will be useful to have a tie up with the product sector to plan the production as per the requirement of the product specifications.
18. Planning of the lay out of the machineries will have to be done on modern steamlined forward motion, avoiding unnecessary wastage of time and movements.
19. The local statutory provisions like factory and labour laws will have to be strictly followed.

20. Adequate ventilation and lighting arrangements will have to be made to provide a healthy and conducive atmosphere for the work force ensuring prevention of accidents.

There should be constant monitoring of the cost of production, individual cost of raw materials, chemicals used and cost of all other infrastructural production inputs. Periodic review of the cost of production and revision of sales prices according to the market conditions is a vital necessity.

Chapter - 5
Vegetable Tannins

The earliest reported use of plant materials containing polyphenols was al hides/skins into leather. The polyphenols constitue distinctive and unique category of higher plant metabolites and from an important class of Non-Wood Forest Produce (NWFP). Their uniqueness lies not only in their relatively large molecular size to suitably orient into collagen matrix but also in their non-involvement in metabolic pathways providing energy for growth and reproduction. These natural tannins considered to be one of the most important group of higher plant-defensive secondary metabolites i.e. they are not involved in metabolic pathways providing energy for growth and reproduction.

Vegetable tannage is probably the oldest of all tannages. Variety of leathers such as sole, belting, kattai and bunwar, saddlery, upholstery, lining, luggage, sports goods, book binding, etc. are produced employing vegetable tannages. The world famous East India tanning process of south India (popularly known as EI tanning) was based on avaram *(Cassia auriculata)* bark, konnam (*Cassia fistula*) bark and myrobalan (*terminalia chebula*) nuts. Currently wattle or mimosa (*Acacia mearnsii*) bark is used predominantly in place of avaram and konnam. The EI leather processed are further processed into different types of finished leathers such as glaze kid, suedes, box and willow, gloving, clothing, lining, etc. The leather that are grouped under East India Leathers are shown in Table - 5.1

Table - 5.1
EI Finished leathers

Raw material	*Type of Tanning*	*Finished Leathers*
EI Cow Hides	Veg. tanned	Linings, upholstery, case and fancy leathers; sports goods and curried uppers
Raw material	*Type of Tanning*	*Finished Leathers*
	Combination	Plain and printed shoe uppers, semi-chrome upholstery
EI Buff Hides	Veg. tanned	Cheap retanned soles, luggage splits, cheap shoe upper splits
	Combination	Printed leathers
EI Cow Calf	Combination	Fancy bookbinding, linings, printed
	Veg. tanned	leathers, pocket books
EI Buff Calf	Veg. tanned	Printed leathers for several uses
EI Sheep	Veg. tanned	Linings, fancy, bookbinding, roller skin, hat and printed leathers
	Semi-chrome	Glove, garment, velvets and gasometer leathers
EI Goat skins	Veg. tanned	Fancy, morocco, lining and printed leathers
	Semi-chrome	Suede, glazed kid, garment leathers

This list is indicative and not exhaustive

Vegetable tanning of hides hides and skins renders the finished leathers suitable for conversion into consumer articles of natural elegance and touch. The emitted effluents are biodegradable.

Vegetable tannins were used in the leather industry as raw plant materials from ancient times till the middle of 19th century. From then on, the tanning extracts, first introduced into the leather industry during 1860 – 1870, are used as solid (block) extracts or spray dried powders. Of the total vegetable tannins produced in the world, 90% are consumed by the leather industry and the rest by others. Of this, 65-70% are used by the heavy leather industry and the rest by the light leather industry. Vegetable tannage of light and heavy leathers require 18-20% and 25-30% tannins respectively. This clearly indicates that the demand for vegetable tanning materials is directly linked with the demand for heavy leathers of which sole leather is the major one which inturn depends on the popularity of leather as a soling material.

However with the recent awareness regarding the use of ecofriendly materials in leather process industries, the demand is slowly growing for vegetable tanning materials which are considered to be one of the environmentally safe products used in the leather industry causing minimum pollution/effluent problems.

The term **"Tan"** is said to be derived from the Celtic word for oak and the word **"Tannin"** was first introduced by Seguin in 1796 to denote the water extractable matter in certain plant tissues capable of converting animal hide/skin into leather. The vegetable tannins are watersoluble polyphenolic compounds having molecular weight in the range of 500-3000 daltons. The low molecular weight compounds are too small for effective cross-linking and high molecular weight counterparts are either insoluble or too large for cross-linking with polypeptide chains. These tannins, besides participating in the usual phenolic reactions, can impart special properties like ability to precipitate alkaloids, proteins, etc. Since no single constituent of any tanning material with definite molecular weight and structure can be identified as responsible for the (characteristic) tanning properties of that particular plant material, the term **"Tannin extract"** is used to define the aggregate action of these polyphenolic compounds. Aqueous tannin solutions or infusions known in the trade as **"Tan liquors"** are colloidal in nature with a wide range of particle size.

The natural phenolic esters such as those of p-coumeric acid and caffeic acid which are invariably mono – and bis – esters of polyols and esters of o – and p– hydroxy benzoic and protocatechuic acids are less frequently encountered in nature. However esters of gallic acid ranging from simple mono esters like glucogallin to the complex polygalloylated esters (Gallotannins) occur more readily in nature. The polygalloylated glucose esters along with proanthocyanidins together constitute the vegetable tannins of commercial and technical importance.

Based on their chemical structures, these vegetable tannins are classified into two types:

(i) **Hydrolysable** *(pyrogallol) tannins:* These are esters of phenol carboxylic acids like gallic acid *(gallo tannins)* and hexahydroxy diphenic, nanohydroxy triphenic, gallagic, chebulic, terchebulic acids *(ellagi tannins)*. They have the characteristic property of undergoing hydrolysis to form "sludge/bloom".

Popular tanning materials like sumach *(Rhus coriaria, Rhus typhina)* leaves, dhawa *(Anogeissus latifolia)* leaves, myrobalan (Terminalia chebula) nuts, chestnut *(Castania sativa)* wood, valonia *(Quercus aegilops)* acorn cups and beards, etc. belong to this type of tannins.

(ii) **Condensed** *(catechol or flavonoid)* tannins: Condensed proanthocyanidins based on C15 flavonoids and are polyhydroxy flavan 3 0 l – dimers/trimers/and other oligomers. They undergo progressive over polymerization/oxidative degradation leading to the formation of "Tannin Reds/Phlobaphenes".

Commercially most important tanning materials like quebracho

(Schinopsis lorentzii), wattle *(Acacia mearnsii)*, avaram *(Cassia auriculata)*, babul *(Acacia arabica)*, Konnam *(Cassia fistula)*, Karada *(Cleistanthus collinus)* etc. belong to this group.

Table - 5.2 highlights the differences between them.

Table - 5.2

HYDROLYSABLE AND CONDENSED TANNINS

Hydrolysable	*Condensed*
Produce "Sludge"/" Bloom"	Yield "Phlobaphenes"/"Tannin Reds" on Standing
Less Astringent	Highly Astringent
Well buffered	Poorly buffered
Small molecules	Large molecules
Loss of tannins on storage is more	Loss of tannins on storage is less
Leather is lighter in colour	Leather tends to red on exposure to light

From leather manufacturing point of view, the condensed tannins are more important as compared to hydrolysable type of the total vegetable tannins consumed by the leather industry 65-70% are condensed type and the rest belong to hydrolysable type. In addition to the above, tannins based on stilbenes have been reported.

The identification of gallo –, ellagi – and condensed tannins is done by two-dimensional paper chromatography employing Whatman No. 1 paper and the solvent systems: (1a) 6% acetic acid (VN) in the first way followed by (1 b) n-butanol-acetic acid-water (4:1:5, VN, upper phase) in the second way and/or (2a) 6% acetic acid (VN) in the first way followed by (2b) sec-butanol-acetic acid-water (14:1:5, VN) in the second way using the respective spray reagents like (i) potassium iodate, which reveals the galloyl esters (gallo tannins) as red to pink spots and gallic acid as orange-red, on white background, (ii) nitrous acid spray which relveals the ellagi tannins (hexahydroxydiphenoyl esters) by the immediate formation of rose-red spots which change rapidly through green, brown and purple to indigo-blue (5-10 min.), (III) NSSC sprays for ellagi tannins which are revealed by yellow and pink, orange, brown colours, (iv) base mixture for characterizing ellagi tannins which are revealed by different colours changing through grey and tan shades to yellow- orange or brown-orange, within 3-20 min., (v) vanillinhydrochloric acid spray for condensed tannins which are revealed by purplish red spots developed after spraying and warming, (vi) picric acid spray for catechins (condensed tannins), after 30 sec. stable red spots being obtained and (vii) ferric chloride- potassium ferricyanide spray for phenolics which are revealed as prussian blue spots on white background.

Eventhough a few tanning materials have been mentioned in the literature as belonging to mixed type, strictly speaking they do not belong to the mixed type, since the tannin constituents of both condensed and hydrolysable types are not present in one and the same part of the plant material. However there are several plant materials containing hydrolysable tannins in one part and condensed type in the other part of the same plant material. Also there are plant materials which contain the tanning constituents of one type along with the low molecular weight compounds/monomers/ precursors etc. of the other type present together in the same part of the plant material. As stated earlier, these cannot be strictly classified under mixed type. In any plant material, the different parts contain tannins of either type.

The vegetable tannins are present in all parts of the flora in concentrations varying from traces to as high as 30-35%.

Traces to small quantities of proanthocyanidin dimers (low molecular weight condensed tannins)	Apple, Strawberries, Blackberries, Coffee, Tea, etc.
Ellagitannin constituents	Clove buds in traces
Reasonably good quantities	Babul (15%), Arecanuts (20%), Cashew testa (25%), Tamarind seed testa (25%)
Large amounts	Wattle (30-35%), Myrobalan (30-35%), etc.

Though the vegetable tannins are present in different parts of the plant, only those parts which contain tannins in large quantities are is used commercially. This is subject to meeting the commercial requirement of colour and yield of leather.

Bark:	Wattle, Babul, Avaram, Konnam, Sal, Arjuna
Wood:	Quebracho, Oak, Chestnut
Heartwood:	Cutch
Leaf:	Sumach, Dhawa
Pods:	Dividivi, Babul
Nuts:	Myrobalan, Ghatbor

Root (Tubers):	Canaigre
Galls:	Chinese, Turkish
Acorn cups & Beards:	Valonia
Seeds:	Sal seeds
Husk (testa):	Cashew husk, Tamarind husk
Buds:	Clove buds
Rind:	Pomegranate
Pod Shells:	Babul Pods

However, from practical tanning view point these raw plant materials can be classified into three broad types:

1. Barks/woods – where the tree is felled for bark/wood for tannin extraction, the quantity and quality of tannins depend on the age of the tree eg. mimosa - 7-8 years, babul 6-7 years, avaram 5 years etc.
2. Seasonal materials like leaves/nuts/pods including galls - their quality and quantity depends on the appropriate season and proper methods of collection, drying, storage etc.
3. By-products of other industries such as cashew testa, tamarind seed testa, deoiled sal seeds etc.

The exact role played by tannins in the plant material is not yet clearly understood. They are supposed to function as:

(i) protective agents due to their astringency,

(ii) toxic agents being phenolic and

(iii) resistant to frost in temperate zones.

The vegetable tannins together with the precursors, low molecular weight compounds and monomers have several properties which are useful to our day-to- day life. These include:

(i) Medicinal properties

(a) The triphala chumam, consisting of a mixture of myrobalan, beheda and amla nuts (all ellagi tannins) is a good ayurvedic medicine,

(b) Gum-paint preparations used in the inflammation and soreness of the gums contain gallotannic acid (gallo tannin, tannic acid) to an extent of 25-30% and

(c) The cardiovascular tonic crataegutt, tincture cratagus are based on the dimeric proanthocyanidins of *Cratagus oxycantha*.

Recent studies on the toxicity of vegetable tannins towards human skin have clearly shown that human beings are not allergic to tannins of babul, wattle and myrobalan.

(ii) Other properties

(a) Taste properties through reactions with the salivery proteins and the glycoproteins present in the mouth.

(b) Palatability of many fruits that occur on ripening are associated with the concomitant changes in the nature and concentration of tannins present in them.

c) Ability to precipitate proteins.

d) Undesirable darkening due to the formation of higher polymeric quinones by the enzymatic dehydrogenation of polyphenols.

Criteria for material selection

A number of parameters have to be considered before selecting any plant material for tanning/retanning purpose.

These include:

(i) Sustained availability,

(ii) Nature of tannins and their molecular weight

(iii) Colour

(iv) Yield of leathers

Skins – minimum 25-30% yield

Hides – minimum 40% yield

(v) Tannin/Non-tannin (T/NT) ratio (see Figure 1).

(vi) Astringency which controls tanning power, rate of penetration, and buffering capacity of the salts present,

(vii) Proneness to oxidation

(viii) Acid/salt content

The leaching efficiency cannot be improved by extracting more water soluble matter since it will increase nontannins, adversely affect T/NT ratio and thereby making the product unsuitable for the given end use. Further if the T/NT ratio is less than 1, the extract cannot theoretically contain more than 50% tannins, the other 50% being nontannins. In actual pratcice since some tannins are lost during manufacturing process and there is always a proportion of moisture in the extract, the tanning percentage in the final extract will be less than 50%. Therefore to get an extract with more tannins (>60%), it would be preferable to have a T/NT ratio of more than 2.

In addition, the nontannins also effect the quality of leathers as evidenced by the physical properties of leathers. The non-tannins include phenolics like low molecular weight compounds/ monomers/other compounds biogenetically related to tannins and non-phenolics compounds – all other plant products.

Eventhough nontannin constituents do not directly contribute to the tanning process, their effect is more pronounced on the physical properties of leathers. Non-phenolic compounds generally contribute towards properties like fullness, feel, colour, etc. Hence, care should be taken that more nontannins are not extracted. Of course the acid/salt ratio is very important' from tanning point of view.

Fig.1: T/NT RATIO OF TANNIN BEARING PLANT MATERIALS

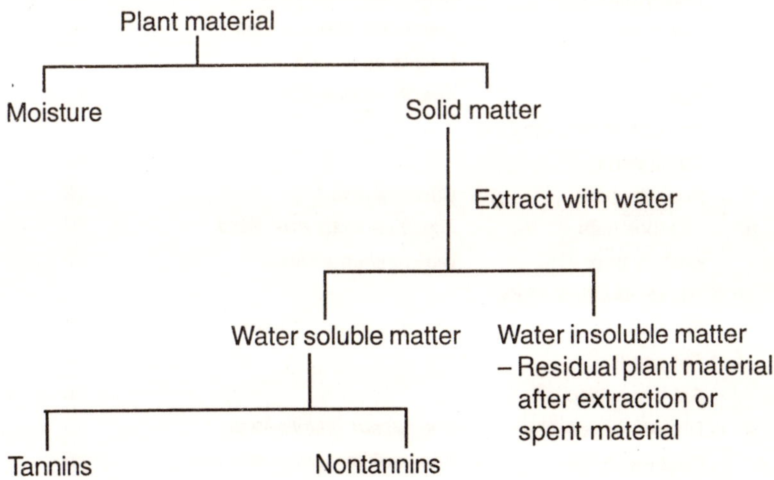

T/NT ratio	>1	High astringency Rapid penetration Good tanning action Useful for self tanning
	<1	Low astringency mellow tanning action Useful for retanning

While comparing the different tanning materials for their tanning characteristics, the following properties should be considered:

(i) Nature of tannins, their particle size/molecular weight, character of its acidity, proneness to oxidation and behaviour at elevated temperatures,

(ii) Buffering capacity of the salts present,

(iii) Acid/salt content and ratio.

Considering these factors, about 15 tanning materials have been identified (Table - 5.3) which are popularly used, in the leather industry either as raw plant materials or in the form of solid extracts or spray dried powders with minimum 60% tannin content (on dry basis).

Table - 5.3

Popular Tanning Materials of India

			Tans %	*Non-tans* %
1.	Wattle bark	*Acacia mearnsii DeWilld*	35	10
2.	Myrobalan nuts	*Terminalia chebula Retz*	35	15
3.	Avaram bark	*Cassia auriculata Linn*	16	8
4.	Babul bark	*Acacia nilotica (Linn)*	13	11
	Del syn. A. arabica Linn			
	Babul pods		18	28
5.	Konnam bark	*Cassia fistula Linn*	12	10
6.	Ghatbor nuts	*Zizyphus xylopyrus Willd*	10	15
7.	Karada bark	*Cleistanthus collinus*	20	12
	(Roxb) Benth & Hook			
8.	Sal bark	*Shorea robusta Gaertn*	8	8
	Sal seeds		7	11
	Sal seeds-deoiled		10	14
9.	Dhawa leaves	*Anogeissus latifolia Wall*	15	15
10.	Cashew testa	*Anacardium occidentale Linn*	25	10
11.	Tamarind seed testa	*Tamarindus indica Linn*	20	10
12.	Arjun/Kahua bark *(Roxb) Wight & Arn*	*Terminalia arjuna*	16	8
13.	Cutch extract *Willd*	*Acacia catechu (LInn)*	55	35

Indian Tanning Materials and their potential

Globally about 4 lakh tons of vegetable tannin extracts consisting of quebracho, mimosa and chestnut and to a little extent valonia are supposed to be produced and consumed. Of this nearly 80% production is accounted for by China, CIS and India.

Indian domestic requirement is estimated as 75,000 tons of vegetable tannin extracts. With an increase in demand for more eco-friendly tannages, the demand is likely to increase. As against this, current Indian production capacity is of the order of 9000 tons of wattle extract any, 8000 tons of other extracts like cashew testa, myrobalan etc. About 15,000 tons of wattle extract is being imported annually. The balance of 45000 tons, has to be partly met from locally available materials and the rest through additional imports.

Although the tropical and sub-tropical climatic conditions prevailing in India support rich flora of tanning materials, not all the popular vegetable tanning materials that are available in the country meet the required quality and quantities (Table - 5.4).

Table - 5.4

Availability/Potential Of Tanning Materials in India

S. No.	*Plant Materials*	*Places of Availability*	*Quantity*	*Potential*
1.	Wattle Bark	Tamil Nadu, Karnataka, Uttar Pradesh, Western Ghats Region	42,000 tons (Green bark with 50% moisture) in Tamil Nadu	76,000 tons
2.	Myrobalan Nuts	Madhya Pradesh, Andhra Pradesh, Orissa, Karnataka, Tamil Nadu, Punjab, Himachal Pradesh	50,000 tons estimated	5-10 lakhs tons
3.	Babul Bark	Tamil Nadu, Andhra Pradesh, Gujarat, Karnataka, Orissa, Bihar, Punjab, Himachal Pradesh	1.0 Lakhs tons	NA
4.	Avaram Bark	Tamil Nadu, Andhra Pradesh, Karnataka, Rajasthan	3,000 tons in Tamil Nadu	7,500 tons in Tamil Nadu other places not known
5.	Cashew Testa	Kerala, Tamil Nadu, Andhra Pradesh,	5,000 tons (Kerala & TN put together) Other places to be estimated	15,000 tons in T.N alone, other places to be estimated
6.	Konnam	Tamil Nadu, Andhra Pradesh	NA	NA

NA : Not Available

Even those available in sufficiently large quantities are associated with some inherent deficiencies as mentioned below:

(i) Hydrolysis of tannins to form sugars – fermentation, mould growth, stinking smell, formation of sludge/bloom and loss of tannins in the case of hydrolysable tannins like myrobalan nuts, dividivi pods, sal seeds, etc.

(ii) Progressive polymerization and oxidation leading to an increase in insolubles, formation of phlobaphenes/tannin reds, decrease in tannin content, poor penetration, yielding darker colour leathers in the case of condensed tannins like babul, cutch, karada, etc.

(iii) Extraction difficulties due to the formation of gums and mucilages in the case of ghatbor, swelling of the material eg. tamarind seed testa.

(iv) In the case of timber species like sal, arjun (kahua), the bark could be collected only at the time of felling the tree for timber by which time the tannins in the bark might have been highly over polymerized resulting in the defects mentioned in (ii).

Such deficiencies limit the use of these plant materials in the leather industry. For better, fuller, proper and effective utilisation, they require modifications by physical and chemical methods. The most effective method is to blend them with other tanning materials for the counteraction of the deficiencies of one material with the advantages of other materials. Treatment/ mixing with syntans and chemicals is another effective method of modification.

In this context it is worth understanding the reasons for the fuller utilization of valonea/chestnut, though both belong to hydrolysable type and are likely to be associated with the deficiencies common to hydrolysable tannins as mentioned in (i). The tannin constituents in myrobalan nuts, sal seeds, dividivi pods and valonea acorn cups/chestnut wood clearly reveal that structurally the tannins of myrobalan nuts, sal seeds, dividivi pods etc. are all based on O-glycosides which are likely to undergo hydrolysis during extraction/tanning process whereas the tannins of valonea/chestnut are based on C-glycosides which do not undergo hydrolysis during extraction/tanne, other ning process thereby making the tannins of valonea/chestnut most useful for self-tanning.

Tannin Extracts

From ancient times till the middle of 19th century, vegetable tanning was done employing tannin extracts prepared by the tanner *insitu* from raw plant materials which are in the form of barks, wood, fruits, leaves etc.

Insitu extraction process has certain specific advantages viz, low cost technology and simple method of extraction. It is amenable for adoption at village level as the tannin bearing plants can be collected from nearby forest areas. However, this method has inherent disadvantages like:

(i) high cost of transportation of raw plant materials particularly those containing less than 10-15% tannins to those distant places where tanneries are located,

(ii) low efficiency of extraction leading to dilute liquors,

(iii) energy intensive evaporation process needed for obtaining concentrated extracts; further this facility is not available with most of the rural tanners,

(iv) large space required for storage of raw stock and liquor,

(v) loss of tannins, formation of insolubles and fermentation products, generation of dark coloured compounds etc. during storage of such liquid extracts,

(vi) high cost of procurement and storage of raw tanning materials some of which are seasonal; loss of tannin during storage.

Manufacture and marketing of liquid extracts has certain disadvantages. Due to their sensitive nature, they need care during storage and transportation, particularly in the case of tanneries which are located in distant places and are connected by roads which are in bad condition. Side reactions like hydrolysis leading to the formation of sludge/bloom, fermentation, loss of tannins, over polymerization leading to the formation of phlobaphenes/tannin reds, increase in insolubles etc. are likely to take place during the transport of liquid extracts thereby making the extract useless for self tanning/retanning.

As a result of these disadvantages, the possibility of producing solid tannin extracts from raw materials was explored during 1860-1870 when solid quebracho extract (moisture content 18%) was first introduced into the leather industry in Argentina. Since then, solid extract manufacture has gained importance. The current trend is to manufacture spray dried powder extract with a moisture content of 5-6%. Recent trend is to manufacture extract in the forms of granules to avoid dust pollution and thereby avoiding the occupational health hazards.

The advantages of solid/spray dried extracts are:

(i) Tanning with extracts takes less time,

(ii) Very easy to get concentrated tanning liquors of any strength, thus leading to a quicker and heavier tannage,

(iii) Consistency in quality, more so in the case of seasonal materials,

(iv) An extract can be tailored to get a specific product by suitably blending the different materials and

(v) Transportation costs and storage space are less.

However, the possibility of adulteration exists which can be checked rather easily at raw material stage.

The wide range of vegetable tannin extracts that are now available to the tanners offers many potential benefits to them for producing leathers of highest quality.

The present day vegetable tannin extract manufacturers have made significant strides in making vegetable tannages more cost-effective and application-specific by developing specialised formulations. Probably the most important step in this direction has been the development of spray dried powdered extracts which have now largely replaced solid extracts. The primary objective of their introduction is to reduce their transportation costs and to facilitate fast and easier application at the tannery level. Another advantage is that the spray dired extracts do not need to be dissolved prior to their introduction into the tannage. This development has became particularly important for its easy adoption to drum tanning operations. The spray dried extracts could be loaded directly into drums to produce concentrated liquors which are required in rapid tannage systems. Technically, it is much more convenient to load powdered extracts into a retanning drum than a viscous tanning extract solution.

It is well established that the vegetable tanning extracts contain phenolic molecules of varying sizes, many of them comparatively large, and it is their physical and chemical characteristics which determine the overall rate of penetration of the tannins into the structure of the hides and skins. Clearly, a reduction in the average size of tannin molecules in the tan liquors would accelerate the rate of penetration. The use of chemical treatment to enhance the solubility characteristics of solid vegetable tanning extracts was another development of far reaching significance to quebracho and chest nut extracts. In more recent times, vegetable tannin extract manufacturers have started marketing chemically modified extracts which are appropriately designed to achieve specific effects on the leather.

A recent development in the field of extracts is the introduction into the market a range of extracts which produce different coloured leather otherwise known as tanning-cum-dyeing agents under the group multipurpose products. The tanning and colouring processes proceed simultaneously with the added advantage of much better colour fixation. For several years, the vegetable tanners have been spending considerable time and money to produce and supply leathers of different colours and this development provides a solution to this long-standing problem. Where large quantities are used for retannage, coloured extracts allow a substantial reduction in the quantity of dyestuff required during the subsequent dyeing process. However, the limitations in the range of colours available and their intensity should be kept in mind while using such multipurpose extracts. It may also be noted that such multipurpose auxiliaries will have one main purpose with additional advantages of the secondary properties, in the present case, the tanning-cum-dyeing extract having the main properties of tanning with additional advantages of colouring properties.

The wide range of vegetable tannin extracts that are now available to the tanners offers many potential benefits to the tanners for producing leathers of highest quality.

Manufacture of Tannin Extracts

Traditionally the tannins are extracted with water as solvent in open vats at moderate temperature. However, water used for extraction (leaching) should not contain iron and should be soft.

Generally plant materials are extracted with the main idea of extraction of:

1. A single constituent - the process is essentially meant for the extraction of that particular compound eg., Caffeine from tea.
2. A group of structurally related compounds which are extracted and used either as such or after isolation of the required active component from that mixture. The process involves the extraction of such mixture, eg., cinchona alkaloids.
3. Natural formulations consisting of mixture of a group of structurally identical compounds along with biogenetically related compounds and other plant products. This method, essentially involves the extraction of complex mixtures of natural plant products having a specific/Potential application, e.g., tannins.

As already mentioned, there is no single constituent identified as responsible for the tanning properties of the plant material concerned. The commercial vegetable tannin extracts or "tan liquors" as they are popularly known in the leather industry are mixtures of polyphenolic compounds with a definite T/NT ratio, astringency etc., along with other plant products.

The main unit operations and processes involved in tanning extract manufacture are shown in Figure 2.

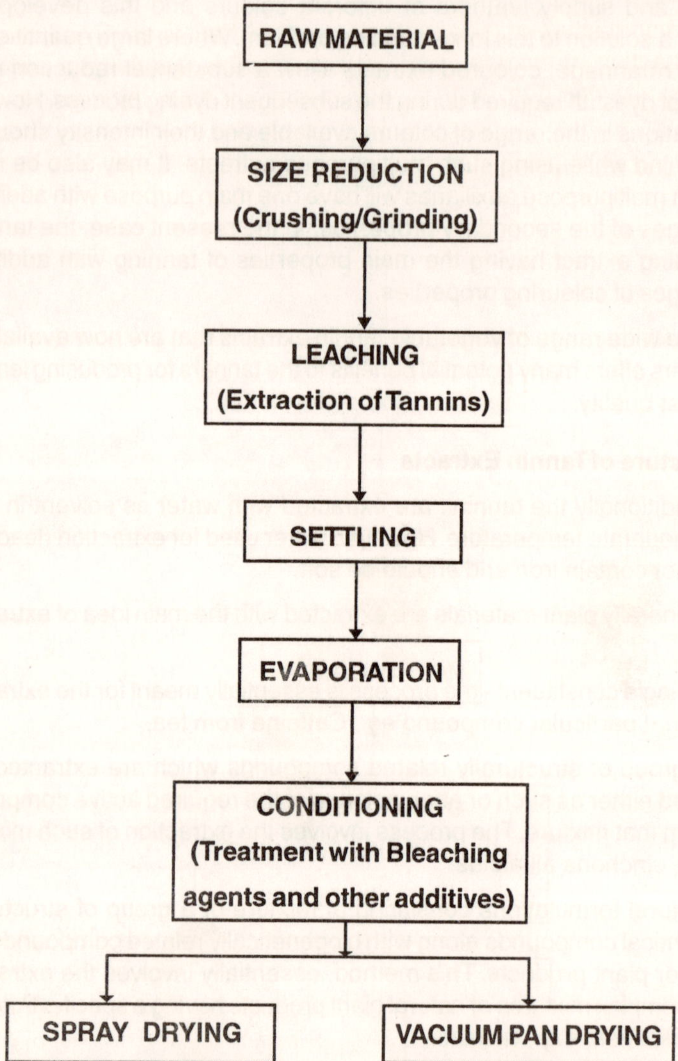

FIGURE 2

PROCESS BLOCK DIAGRAM FOR THE MANUFACTURE OF VEGETABLE TANNIN EXTRACTS

The manufacture of the vegetable tannin extract is essentially based on the extraction of tannins from the tanning materials using a suitable solvent, usually water, followed by concentration and spray drying to get powder or solidification to get solid (block) extract. The following steps are involved in the process:

(i) Selection of raw materials,

(ii) Size reduction – crushing and grinding,

(iii) Leaching (extraction of tannings),

(iv) Settling,

(v) Filtration,

(vi) Concentration (evaporation),

(vii) Bleaching,

(viii) Dryng – Solid (Block) extracts
– Spray dried powder and

(ix) Packing.

Selection of the raw materials

Selection of the raw materials is made on the basis of the different criteria like tan/non-tannin content and good colour etc. mentioned earlier. The raw materials should be free from fungal/insect attack or rotting and should be fresh as far as possible.

Generally the raw tanning materials used for the tanning as well as extract manufacture can be classified into three types:

1. Barks/woods – where the tree is felled for bark/wood for tannin extraction, the quantity and quality of tannins depend on the age of the tree eg. mimosa – 7-8 years, babul 6-7 years, avaram 5 years etc.
2. Seasoinal materials like leaves/nuts/pods including galls – their quality and quantity depends on the appropriate season and proper methods of collection, drying, storage etc.
3. By-products of other industries – in this type of raw materials there is no possibility to assess the quality and the material has to be accepted as such eg. cashew testa, tamarind seed testa, deoiled sal seeds etc.

Size reduction (Crushing/Grinding)

Barks of like wattle, babul are disintegrated into small size (5-15 mm long) and nuts like myrobalan are crushed to 1-10 mm. The size reduction helps in better leaching of water solubles.

Technically there are several advantages of employing small particle size for achieving high extraction efficiency. However, from pressure drop, grinding energy and product purification cost points of view, too fine grinding is not favoured. Further, for fine powders may lead to an increase in insoluble content in the final extract. Hence a particle size range of 5-15 mm is, therefore, favoured from overall extraction plant cost.

Leaching (Extraction of Tannins)

The extraction of the tannins from the physically disintegrated plant material is by solid-liquid extraction, generally by the following processes:

(i) Open vat extraction,

(ii) Rotary system,

(iii) Pressure autoclaves,

(iv) Open vat with Archimedean screw,

(v) Vacuum extraction (Nance process) and

(vi) Gas lift agitation method.

Whichever process is employed, it is essential that the temperature of extraction be kept as low as possible, and the liquors are not over exposed to the atmosphere, to avoid oxidation. Iron contamination should be avoided. As already mentioned, since there is no single constituent of any tanning material with any definite structure and molecular weight that is identified as responsible for tanning action of that particular plant material, the term "tannin extract" is used to define these polyphenolic compounds. As such the manufacturing process involved the aqueous extraction of the mixture of polyphenolic compounds and not a single constituent. Any effort to get more water soluble extract in order to improve extraction efficiency, care should be taken to see that water soluble non-tannin constituents which will effect the T/NT ratio and quality of the product are not extracted. Accordingly care has to be taken in optimising the different parameters like time, temperature, the selection of materials of construction, quality of process water etc. Brief description of the different processes is given below.

Open Vat Extraction

One of the most commonly used methods of extraction is by means of open vats connected in a series.

The vat system runs up water or liquor from a previous vat to the next vat to a few inches above the false bottom, when the bark is added together with water. Heating is carried out by means of perforated steam coil, which at the same time imparts a certain amount of agitation. It must be remembered, however, that the water of condensation dilutes the liquor, which means extra cost needed for evaporation. In operating such system consisting of a series of vats of leachers, each charge of water passes through the whole series, so that at the end of the process a fairly concentrated liquor is obtained.

As the raw (plant) material moves through the series of extraction before being almost spent, the temperature of extraction is increased to about 100°C in the last stage wherein the fresh water is used for extraction. Early extractions are done at a lower temperature, since the somewhat strong liquor comes in contact with fresh bark. The difficulty soluble material extracted at higher temperature gradually precipitates out and is filtered in the plant material bed.

A golden rule for open vat extraction is to extract the major part of the tannin at as low a temperature as possible so as to avoid thermal decomposition and darkening in colour of the liquor. For charging the material on a large scale, the general practice is to use conveyors which are of the Archimedean screw type of belt conveyer with a throw-off. For discharging extracted plant material it is found more convenient to use suitable doors made of gun metal on the sides of the vat or circular doors at the bottom of the vat. This will permit the spent material to drop into trucks or on to some form of conveyer by which it is taken for disposal or to the boiler house for use as fuel.

Rotary System of Extraction

In this method, a series of drums are used as extraction vessels, and by the continual agitation brought about by rotation, a very satisfactory extraction is achieved. They are operated in exactly the same way as a series of vats, i.e., the liquor passing from one drum to the other and the bark remaining in the drum, receiving multiple extractions. Although not in very large use, this method of extraction is said to give very good results.

Autoclaving

The material is extracted under pressure by the autoclaving process. This process generally yields a larger extract than ordinary open vat extraction. At the same time a certain amount of tannin is reported to be lost. It is not clearly established as to whether the loss of tannin is due to enhanced pressure or temperature or due to the extraction of more nontannins. It is generally accepted, that pressure extraction yields a higher amount of extract than is obtained by the open leach method, but the product is darker in colour and contains a higher proportion of non-tannin substances.

Open Vat with Archimedean Screw

This consists of a long wooden trough, in which is fixed copper and brass Archimedean screws. The bark is fed in at one end and carried forward by the screws. Water admitted from the other end of the trough flows in counter-current manner. When extracted, the bark falls into a hopper and is carried away by elevators. Clogging is reported to be the main drawback of this system. Otherwise, this method is known to give excellent extraction results with many materials. Careful observance of time and regulation of the quantity of leaching water are of great importance in order to achieve maximum extraction.

Vacuum Leaching (Nance Process)

The extraction of tanning materials under reduced pressure is the underlying principle of the Nance process. It is expected that in vacuum extraction practically no decomposition or discoloration takes place. The method offers certain advantages like high extraction efficiency and light coloured product. It is reported that the extraction of tannins was carried out at low temperatures and 75% of the total tannin was extracted in three changes of water.

Gas Lift Agitation Process

This process of extraction has the advantage of effectively handling of very finely ground material with out encountering clogging in the leachers earlier.

Though there are several alternative processes available for tannin extraction, commercially multistage counter-current batch extraction in open vats has received favour throughout the world in view of its simplicity.

In this connection whatever be the method of extraction adopted it Is worth mentioning that during the course of increasing extraction efficiency, more of the unwanted non-tannins should not be extracted thereby resulting in a product with less T/NT ratio (< 1), less astrigency etc.

Settling and Filtration

The liquor withdrawn from the leaching battery is collected in a settling tank and is allowed to settle down for about 4-6 hours to separate the insolubles and any foreign matter and sent for filtration. Gravity filter is more ideal to filter the leach liquor which is filtered using a filter cloth of 10 micron.

Concentration (Evaporation)

The filtered liquor which contains generally 9-10% solids is further concentrated to 35-40% in a suitable evaporator. Multiple effect evaporators generally triple effect evaporator is recommended for commercial use because of steam economy and suitability of carrying evaporation under vacuum, as the annins are heat sensitive.

Bleaching

The manufacture of tannin extract is basically a physical process involving unit operations like leaching (extraction), evaporation (concentration) and drying. The only unit process involved is bleaching the extracted tannin liquor to get a lighter coloured product.

Bleaching is generally carried out by treating the concentrated liquor with sodium bisulfite, sodium sulphite and sodium hydrosulfite for 4 hr followed by oxalic acid for 1 hr (In case the liquors are to be left overnight for more than 10 hours, addition of suitable PCP-free preservative is suggested).

Solid Extract

Solid extract is produced from the concentrated liquor with 35-40% solids by further evaporation carried out in a vacuum pan, stirred until a very viscous liquid containing about 85% solids is obtained. The slurry so obtained is run into wooden blocks and left as such for settling into solid extract with about 15% moisture.

Powder Extract

The liquor containing 35-40% solids is spray dried to get the powder extract with 4-6% moisture.

Recently granulated powders are introduced to avoid, dust pollution and occupational health hazards due to the fine nature of spray dried powders.

Packaging

As most of the tanning extracts are hygroscopic and light sensitive, they are packed in bituminised polythene lined gunny bags in 25 kilo packs. The bags will bear markings such as batch number and lot number, date of manufacture, and warnings like 'use no hooks' and keep in cool and dry place etc. It is very essential to note that iron hooks will produce darker colour extracts.

Solid and liquid wastes from Extract Manufacturing units

As such the process of extract manufacture does not involve the use of any toxic/hazardous/risky chemicals. Also no inflammable solvents are used. The bleaching agents are used in small quantities (< 1 %).

During the process of manufacture of vegetable tannin extract the fall lowing solid/liquid solid/liquid/gaseous wastes are expected.

The only solid waste is spent tanning material (residual plant material after leaching/extraction of tannins). Since this is a natural plant material from which tannins were extracted with water and the plant material has not been subjected to any chemical treatments, the spent material can be used after suitable drying as boiler feed.

The extract manufacturing process uses storage tanks and the liquid is transferred through pipes, as such there is no possibility of any liquid waste except for normal plant spillages and leakages which are not likely to pose any environmental problem in disposal. Since the extract contains valuable tannins, maximum care is taken to avoid any such leakages/ spillages.

The gas that is likely to evolve is sulfurdioxide that too in very small quantities during bleaching operation and this can easily be controlled by using scrubbers and this does not pose any environmental problem.

Chapter - 6

Vegetable Dyes

Before the mid – 19th century, until the discovery of synthetic mauveine by H.Perkin in 1856, the only colorants available were dyes of natural (animal/ vegetable/geologica) origin. The use of these natural dyes over the centuries especially the middle ages on, laid the foundations of the art and later the science of the modern dye industry.

Dyeing, as the term is generally understood, occurs only when the dye is in solution, usually in aqueous medium. Some dyes, whose solubility is less are called disperse dyes, because they are dispersed rather than dissolved in water. Some colorants called pigments are completely insoluble. The term "Colorants" is used to describe both dyes and pigments.

By definition a dye is "a colorant that has substantivity for a substrate either inherent and induced by reactants" and a pigment is a substance in a particular form that is substantially insoluble in a medium but which can be mechanically dispersed in these medium to modify its colour and/or light scattering properties.

This definition has to be understood clearly as solvent (or fat) soluble colouring matter which do not appear to conform to the definition as it stands, should be called 'dyes' and may be termed as "stains". This is more so in the case of natural dyes which in addition to dyes, contain colouring matter and stains which do not have any dyeing properties on fabrics. Many natural dyes are mixtures of two or more colouring matter.

By definition, the natural dyes and pigments comprise all those that are obtained from vegetable/animal kingdom with no or very little chemical processing.

Although most of the natural dyes have very little commercial significance, their use has not totally disappeared from the market. The handicrafts worker believes that nature knows the best. This natural industry is a major employer of natural dyes in India.

Though the use of natural colorants for textiles and fibres has declined, their use for colouring foods and ingested products has recently increased. This has been prompted, in part, by the Government regulations, environmental consciousness, concern regarding the carcinogenecity and mutangenecity etc.

Sources of Natural Dyes

As already mentioned most of the natural dyes in use are of plant origin (hence the term "Vegetable dye" is used in this booklet). The sources of natural dyes include:

(i) Plant kingdom – e.g. indigo, logwood, fustic etc.

(ii) Animals and insects – e.g lac, cochineal, carminic etc.

iii) Marine (shell fish) – e.g. Tyrian (royal) purple etc.

iv) Earth crust (mineral) – e.g. chromates, iron oxide, coal etc.

Occurrence

The vegetable dyes occur in almost all parts of the plants. Perhaps in any plant material the dyes are concentrated in a particular part only. That part is used commercially of course, after considering other factors like the chemical nature of the dyes and their reactivity with the substrate concerned, the shade, intensity and light fastness, wash fastness, penetrating properties wherever required etc.

Flowers	e.g. safflower, toon, bengal kino,
Fruits/pods	e.g. kamela,
Berries	e.g. black berries,
Seeds	e.g. annato,
Nuts	e.g. myrobalan
Bark	e.g. quercus spp,
Leaves	e.g. henna, ipdigo plant,
Roots	e.g. maddar,
Heart wood	e.g. red sanders,
Wood	e.g. logwood, sappan wood,
Fruit rind	e.g. pomegranate,

Classification of dyes

There may be several methods of classifications possible like e.g. the classification based on the part of the plant, based on the colour etc., but the scientific method is based on the chemical nature of the dyes.

Structurally the dyes are classified into:

(i) **Polyene Dyes** – based on isoprene unit e.g. carotenoids,

(ii) **Quinonoid dyes** – based on 1, 4 – naphthaquinone and 9, 10 – anthraquinone,

(iii) **Flavonoid dyes** – based on chalcones, flavones, flavans, aurones, anthocynanins, isoflavones etc. Structurally this group of dyes are related to and commonly occur in condensed type vegetable tannins. The famous phenomenon – "Tannin Reds", the red colour associated with condensed tannins – either as such or with the leather tanned with condensed tannins is mainly due to this class of dyes which are mainly authocyanidins.

(iv) **Dihydropyran dyes** – e.g. logwood, sappan wood, brazil wood. This group of dyes are one of the most important and were used in leather industry. As already mentioned still logwood retains its commercial importance.

(v) **Diarylmethane dyes** – e.g. turmeric

(vi) **Indigo dyes** – based on 3 - hydroxy indole (Indoxyl).

e.g. Indigo, Tyrian (Royal) purple and berberine (the only basic dye of natural occurrence).

(vii) **Porphyrin dyes** – based on pyrrole e.g. chlorophyll, haem etc.

In addition to these, there are several other colouring matter present in plant materials. These include purines, iso-alloxazines, phenoxazines, melanins, betalains etc. However their dyeing properties on a particular substrate have to be studied in detail.

Advantages of vegetable dyes

(i) Harmonising colours,

(ii) Possibility of rare colour ideas,

(iii) More challenges due to element of chance (quite often the natural dyes are mixtures of more than one dye constituent),

(iv) Minimum pollution problems – most ecofriendly, environmentally safe, green, healthy etc.

Constraints

As against these advantages, there are some constraints considered important. These include:

(i) non-sustained availability of dye - yielding plant rnaterims, and the likelihood of ecological damages due to unplanned telling of the flora,

(ii) technology for the extraction of dyes yet to be prefected,

(iii) availability of limited shades and colours,

(iv) unfavourable cost factor as compared to synthetic dyes,

(v) unsatisfactory fastness properties to light, washing etc.,

(vi) require mordants for dyeing,

(vii) quality and quantity (yield) depend on method and timing of harvesting/collection.

Dye yielding plants of India

There are several dye yielding plants available in the country. Most of the plants are useful for cotton/wool/silk.

(i)	Khair/Cutch *Acacia catechu heart wood*	flavonoids - condensed tannins CI Natural Brown 3 CI 75250
(ii)	Annatto *Bixa orellana seeds*	Polyene - Bixin CI Natural Orange 4 CI 75120
(iii)	Sappan *Caesalpinia sappan wood*	Dihydropyran-Brazilin and Brazilein CI Natural Red 24 CI 75280
(iv)	Safflower (kusum) *Carthamus tinctorius* florets	Flavonoids – chalcones CI Natural Red 26 CI 75140
(v)	Indigo *Indigofera tinctoria* leaves	N-Heterocyclics - Indigo CI Natural Blue 1 CI 75780

(vi)	Henna *Lawsonia inermis* *(L.alba)*, leaves	Naphthaquinone - Lawsone CI Natural orange 6 CI 75480
(vii)	Indian Mulberry *Morinda citrifolia* root bark	Anthraquinone - Morindine CI Natural Red 18 CI 75380, C1 75390
(viii)	Kamela *Mallotus phillippensis*	Flovonoids – Chalcones CI Natural Orange 2 CI 75310
(ix)	*Myrica nagi (M. esculanta)* bark	Flavonoids – flavonol bark
(x)	Indian Maddar (Manjith) *Rubia cardifolia* roots	Anthraquinone - Purpurin, Manjistin, CI Natural Red 16,
(xi)	Indian Mahagani (Toon) *Cedrella toona* flowers	Polyene - Nycanthin & Quercetin CI Natural Red 1 CI 75670 CI 785100
(xii)	Red sanders *Pterocarpus santalinus* wood	Naphthaquinone – Santalin CI, Natural Red 22 CI 76540
(xiii)	Pitti *Ventilago madraspatana* root bark	Anthraquinone CI Natural Orange 1

General Methods of Preparation

The general methods for the preparation of these plant dyes can be divided into:

(i) Physical methods like - beating/shaking the raw material e.g. Kamela.

(ii) Extraction with water –

(a) As such e.g. henna, kamela, Indian mahagony,

(b) As such followed by concentration – cutch, logwood,

(c) As such followed by fermentation e.g sappan wood,

(d) As such followed by fermentation and oxidation – indigo.

(iii) Extraction with acidulated water –

(a) as such – Indian Mulberry

(b) the residual plant material re-extracted with aqueous sodium car – bonate followed by acidification – e.g. safflower.

(iv) Extraction with aqueous sodium carbonate solution followed by acidification and coagulation with NaCl e.g. annato.

Leather dyes from vegetable sources

Leather manufacturing involves the use of several chemicals/ auxiliaries/formulations during the process of converting the raw materials – hides and skins into finished leather. These chemicals are generally classified into: i) general purpose chemicals, ii) basic tanning agents and iii) tailor made speciality performance chemicals which are meant for specific end use. These performance chemicals are further sub-divided in to : (a) wet processing (finishing) chemicals like dyes, fatliquors etc. and : (b) finishing agents like pigments, top coats etc.

With the growing awareness to protect environment, there is now a tendency in all processing industries to : (i) use environmentally safe and ecofriendly chemicals/auxiliaries/formulations and (ii) avoid/eliminate environmentally sensitive chemicals which are toxic/hazardous during such processing industries. This can be achieved by several ways and one such method is to use natural materials as far as possible. In leather manufacturing process quite a good number of natural products are used. These include, natural tannins, vegetable dyes, oils/fats, protein binders, natural preservatives etc.

Leather is a high value fashion oriented commodity in the International trade and commerce and is dyed with a mixture of dyes to get the desired shades and intensities to cater for aesthetic aspects and competitive market.

Leather differs from other fibrous materials. Generally the textile fibres can be grouped into : (i) cotton/jute/coir/sisal etc., (ii) silk, (iii) wool, (iv) synthetics like polyamide, polyesters, acrylics, polyens etc. Leather differs from these textile materials due to its reactive 3-dimensional structure. Chemically leather is very close to silk and wool as a result the natural dyes useful for silk and wool may be screened for use in leather, of course keeping in view the 3-dimensional structure of leather where penetration plays a greater role. Also the surface charge characteristics of leather play a greater role.

The chemical reactivity of collagen, the main fibrous protein of hides and skins is modified by various physical and chemical treatments during pretanning and tanning operations of leather manufacturing process. During these processes the raw materials are subjected different pH conditions, both on the acidic and alkaline sides. These chemical treatments and the resulting pH conditions result in the modification of the reactivity and surface charge of collagen (Figure 3).

Leather dyeing has to be implemented on a system consisting of collagen – tanning agents – water molecules present in the fibre pores. Leather dyeing with natural dyes has an advantages in that the incorporated tannins (mineral) act as mordants for the natural dyes.

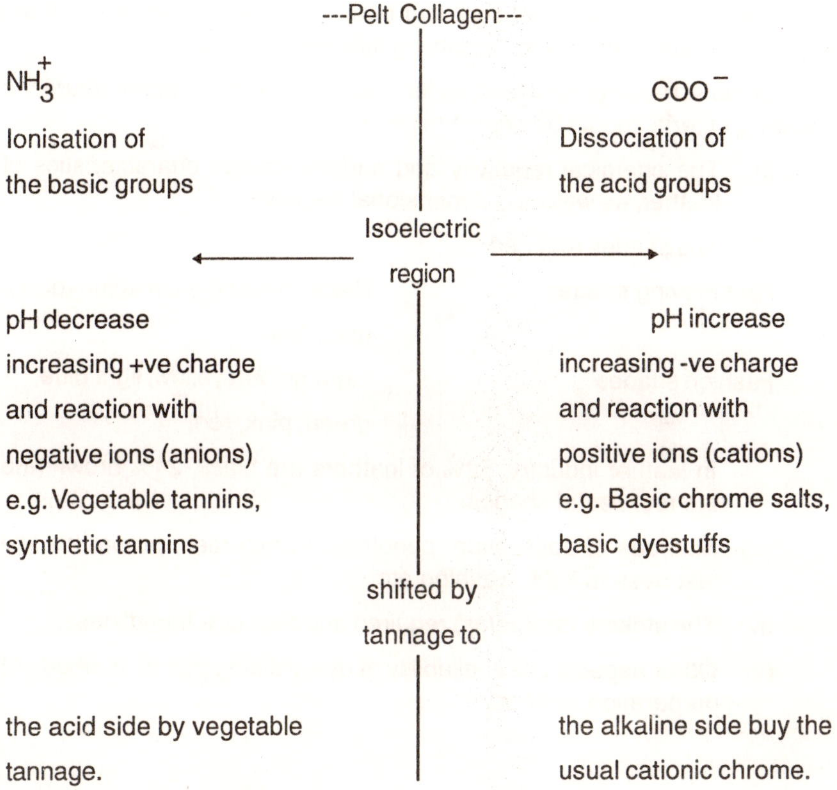

FIGURE 3: SURFACE CHARGE CHARACTERISTICS OF LEATHER

The special/additional advantages vegetable dyes in leather processing are:

(i) both flesh and grain sides can be dyed with same shade,

(ii) a more level shade is produced,

(iii) grain defects are not emphasized,

(iv) full handle is imparted to mineral tanned leathers,

(v) grease dispensing effect is exerted,

(vi) buffing properties of suede and nubuck leathers are improved,

(vii) ecofriendly/environmentally safe and

(viii) biodegradability.

The most important leather dyes include: (i) logwood (Haematoxylon *campachianum*), (ii) fustic (*Chlorophoro tinctoria*), (iii) osage orange (*Maclura ponifera*), (iv) oak (*Quercus tinctoria*) bark, (v) hypernic etc. All of them require different mordants for achieving different colours.

While screening, natural dyes for their use in leather manufacture the following criteria should be kept in mind. V

(i) The chemical reactivity and surface charge characteristics of leather, as well as 3-dimensional net work,

(ii) The shades required

Fast moving shades	:	Black, brown (light/medium/dark), grey, fawn.
Fashion shades	:	Light/golden yellow, light blue, green, pink, red.

In leather industry, 52% of leathers are black, 24% brown and the rest pastal shades.

(iii) Methods of application, penetration properties, properties like fast ness to light, washing etc.

(iv) The strikers (mordents) required and their eco-friendliness,

(v) Other aspects like availability of dye-yielding plants, methods of preparation, cost etc.

Chapter - 7

Preparation Of Chrome Liquor

I. Chrome Liquor of 331/3rd Basicity

Sodium Dichromate crystals	– 10 kg.
Water *85 - 90°)	– 20 Kg.
Sulphuric Acid (66°)	– 9.5 kg.
Glucose	– 2.5 kg.
Water	– 5.0 kg.
Sodium Bisulfite	– 0.25 kg.

Take 20 litres of hot water at 85° – 90° in a lead lined wooden and dissolve the dichromate in water. Add 9.5 kg. Sulphuric acid to bichromate solution. Stir well while adding.

Prepare glucose solution by dissolving glucose in 0.5 litres water. Add this in slow feeds during a period of 40, all the time stirring well. Add 0.25 kg. Sodium bisulfite as powder in slow feeds during a period of 10 – 15 with stirring.

Test for reduction. Leave overnight.

Dilute to a known volume 28 to 30 litres. Determine the Cr_2O_3 content. on volume basis and also the basicity. If necessary make it to a convenient volume by correcting the basicity to 33 1 /3rd. If the basicity is less than 33 1 /3rd add necessary amount of soda ash which is calculated as follows: -

Amount of Na_2CO_2 at T./. purity = $0.0209 \times 11 \times P \times \frac{100}{T}$

N = the no. of degrees to arrive at 33 1 /3rd
P = the weight of Cr_2O_3 in the stock liquor.

T = the % of purity of Na_2CO_3

Add the calculated amount of soda ash dissolved in water (1:15) slowly to the stock chronic liquor with constant stirring. Finally make up such that 1 litre contains about 150 gm Cr_20_3.

If the basicity is more than 33 1/3rd add necessary amount of Sulphuric acid (1.84 ap Gr) to bring it to 33 1 /3rd%

Amount of Sulphuric acid = 0.019 x N x P

N = the no. of degrees to arrive at 33 1 /3rd %

.P = the wt. of Cr_20_3 in the stock chrome liquor.

Make it to a known volume.

II. Chrome Liquor (50% Basicity).

Sod. dichromate	– 10 kg.
Water (85 - 90°)	– 20 kg.
Sulphuric Acid	– 8.4 kg.
Glucose	– 2.5 kg.
Water	– 5 Kg.
Sod. bisulfite	– 0.25 to 0.5 kg.

Prepare as in 1. Check for reduction. Leave overnight. Make up to a known volume. Determine the basicity and Cr_20_3 content.

Adjust the basicity to 50% by adding the calculated quantity of soda ash.

Make up to a known volume.

Chrome liquor I can also be made 50% basic by adding calculated amount of soda ash.

In I and II, glucose can be replaced by 3.25 to 3.5 kg. of molasses.

CHROME LIQUOR

Tests for Complete Reduction

(i) Place a drop of chrome liquor in a filter paper. Absence of yellow or yellowish green colour indicates that the chrome liquor is reduced well and does not contain unreduced dichromate.

(ii) Take a few drops of chrome liquor in a test tube. Dilute with distilled water. Add excess ammonia. Boil and filter. If filtrate is yellow, then unreduced dichromate is present provided the reducing e\agent. used does not cause yellow colouration.

(iii) To ensure this, a few drops of chrome liquor are heated with dilute H C I. Starch iodide paper is dipped in the this. A blue colour developed indicates the presence of unreduced biohromate.

(iv) Two grams of Diphenyl Carbazide are dissolved in 10 cc. glacial acetic acid and alcohol is added to make up the volume to 200 cc.

A few drops of this reagent are added to small amount of diluted chrome liquor. Formation of violet colouration indicates presence of unreduced dichromate.

III. $\dfrac{\text{Preparation of Chrome Liquor from}}{\text{Chrome Alum } K_2SO_4\,Cr_2(SO_4)_3\,24\,H_2O}$

Parts by weight of soda ash for 100 part of chrome alum	% of Basicity
0	0
2.65	8.33
5.30	16.66
7.95	25.00
10.60	·33.33
13.25	41.60
15.90	50.00

IV. Preparation of Basic Aluminium Sulphate Liquor (45% Basicity approx.)

(Iron free) Aluminium Sulphate – 10 kg.)

(Boilding) Water – 50 kg.) Dissolve.

Add with string 0.9 kg. Sodium citrate till dissolved.

Add 2.5 kg. Soda, ash dissolved in 10 litres water slowly during a period of 40 rats with constant stirring.

Make up the solution such that Al_2O_3 content is 2% on volume basis.

This will give a basic aluminium sulphate liquor of approximately 45% basicity.

Ph. Indicators

Thymol blue	1.2 to 2.8	Red to yellow
Bromophenol blue	3 to 4.6	Yellow to blue
Methyl orange	3 to 4.4	Red to yellow
Bromocresol green	3.8 to 5.4	Yellow to blue
Methyl red	4.2 to 6.2	Red to yellow
Litmus	4.5 to 8.3	Red to blue
Bromocresol purple	5.2 to 6.8	Yellow to purple
Bromothymol blue	8 to 9.6	Yellow to blue
Phenolpthalein	8.2 to 10.0	Colourless to red.

Indicator for checking whether combined lime is present : -

Alizarine Red B 1 is used. The pelt should show yellow colouration for absence of combined lime when tested with Alizarine Red B 1 while a brown or even violet colouration indicates that capilaoeously or chemically fixed lime is present.

V Preparation of Common Indicators used in Tannery

Phenolpthalein: Weigh 0.1 gm. and make up to 100 cc with alcohol.

Bromocesol green: 0.1 gm. in 14.3 cc of 0.01 N NaOH and make up to 250 cc. with distilled water.

Bromocresol purple: 0.1 gm. in 18.5 cc of 0.01 N NaOH and make up to 250 cc. with distilled water.

Relation between density (B°) of Sodium Sulphide Solution (Approximate Value)

B°	B^k	Na_2S (60-62%) Concentration m/litre.
1	6.0	12
2	13.8	23
3	20.9	35
4	28.0	46
5	35.3	58

Contd...

B°	B^k	Na_2S (60-62%) Concentration m/litre.
6	42.6	69
7	50.1	81
8	57.6	92
9	65.3	104
10	73.1	115
11	81.0	127
12	89.0	138
13	97.1	150
14	105.4	161
15	113.8	173

Leather Thickness

1 oz = 1/64" = 0.4mm.

1 iron = 1/48" = 0.5 mm.

Useful Conversion Factors

Centimeters x 0.3937 = inches.

Cubic centimeters x 0.0610 = cubic inches.

Cubic centimeters x 0.00176 = pints.

Cubic feet x 0.0283 = cubic meters.

Cubic feet x 6.229 = gallons.

Cubic feet x 28.33 = litres.

Cubic inches x 0.0036047 = gallons.

Cubic inches x 16.4 = cubic centimeters.

Cubic meters x 35.315 = cubic feet.

Cubic meters x 1.308 = cubic yards.

English gallons x 1.2 = U.S.A. gallon.

Feet x 0.3048 = meters.

Gallons x 0.160 = cubic feet.

Gallons x 4.546 = litres.

Gallons x 10 = pounds of water.

Grams x 0.002205 = pounds.

Grams per litre x .016 = oz. per gallon.

Grams per litre x 0.001 = US per gallon.

Inches x 2.54 = centimeters.

Kilograms x 2.2046 = pounds.

Kilograms per centimeter x 14.22 = pounds per sq. inch.

Horsepower x 0.746 = kilowatts.

Kilowattes x 1.341 = Horsepower.

Litres x 0.220 = gallons.

Litres x 0.0353 = cubic feet.

Meters x 3.281 = feet.

Kgm x 2.2046 = pounds.

1 kgm = 2 lbs. 3 ozs.

1 1b = 0.454 kgm.

Meters x 30.37 = inches.

Meter x 1.094 = yards.

Ounce per gallon x 62.5 = grams per litre.

Pints x 567.936 = cubic centimeters.

Pounds x 0.016053 = cubic feet of water.

Pounds x 0.4536 Kilograms.

Pounds per gallon x 100 = grams per litre.

Pounds per square inch x 0.0703 = kilograms per sq. cm.

Square inches x 6.452 = square centimeters.

Tons x 35.962 = cubic feet of water.

Tons x 1015.6 = kilograms.

Tons per square inch x 152.4 = atmospheres.

USA gallons x 0.833 = Imperial gallons.

Atmospheres x 14.7 = pounds per sq. inch.

1 sq. ft.. = 9.29 sq. decimeters.

sq. ft. x 9.29 = sq. decimeters.

Chapter - 8

Physical Testing Of Leathers

Leather has a variety of uses. The quality of Leather is assessed by its properties or specific characteristics. The properties are dependent on the physical structure and chemical composition and the mechanical finishing operations during the manufacture of leather. Physical structure decides the properties of the finished products to a large exent. Thus, goat or sheep skin are not suitable for the manufacture of sole leather but heavy steer hides and buffalo hide can be used. The properties are also influenced by chemical composition and mechanical handling.

After the leathers are produced, it will be necessary to test them to assess whether they will serve the ultimate purpose and if required to improve the properties of these leathers and to counter increasing competition from the substitute materials. As the properties of leather are affected by atmospheric temperature and varying humidity and as in the same place in different seasons of the year and with the hour of the day, it is essential to condition the leather, prior to testing, in a room under controlled conditions. The conditions specified by the Indian Standard Specifications are 80°F ± 4 and 65% r.h. ± 2 (r.h. = relative humidity)

The conditioned samples are tested for various properties. It should be borne in mind that no two leathers are exactly alike, and even in the same leather, values of the properties show variations with the different locations. However, a minimum and a maximum value can be given for a particular lot of leathers if sufficient samples are taken. The samples for testing are cut out from a specified region of the hide or skin. The principles involved in testing various properties and the methods are given below..

(1) Tensile Strength

It is the load per unit area of cross-section required to pull apart or break a strip of leather.

Good tensile strength is obviously a good attribute in general for all types of leather. It is a valuable guide for judging the quality of leather.

A dumb-bell shaped sample is punched out using a steel die of standard and dimension : this particular shape aids in concentrating the stresses in the narrow portion forcing sample to break there or otherwise the sample may break near the jaws of the machine and this will give a wrong value.

The conditioned samples are tested in a motor-driven testing machine, which is generally of constant loading rate or constant traverse rate type of pendulum testing machines. Usually, provision is made in these machines to record the stress-strain diagram while the testing is being carried out.

The thickness of the specimen is measured at three equidistant points on the straight portion of the specimen using a thickness gauge and the average calculated. The width is measured using a graduated scale or Vernier Caliperd correct to 0.02 inch, at the corresponding positions, and these values are used in calculating tensile strength of the sample, were

$$\text{Tensile strength} = \frac{\text{Breaking load in lb. or kg.}}{\text{Thickness (in inch or cm.)} \times \text{width (in inch or cm.)}}$$

(2) Elongation

The percentage elongation of a leather is also a useful index of the stretching quality in many cases. Usually if a leather has a more-than normal elongation, then it is probably weak or if it has a subnormal elongation, it has perhaps been hardened and has become brittle. A minimum requirement of tensile strength and elongation is specified for each type of leather.

The elongation is measured simultaneously with the measurement of tensile strength. Two reference marks are made in the narrow portion of the specimen before testing and the distance between these points is measured. The machine is run for some time and stopped, and the corresponding load are noted. The extension can be expressed as the percentage elongation at that load.

(3) Breaking Strength

This test is very similar to that for tensile strength, and is particularly suited for light-weight leathers. Here, the sample is cut simply in the form of a rectangle instead of dumb-bell and clamped between the laws so that the tension is applied parallel to the longer dimension of the sample. The load at which the sample breaks is noted.

(4) Tearing Strength

This is the load required to continue a tear in leather, once started.

Various types of tearing tests, depending on the way in which the sample is torn in the tensile strength tester, are known, which are out lined below.

(5) Tongue tear

A sample of leather is split along its centre line to form two tongues, each of which is clamped to one jaw of the tensile strength tester, and the test performed.

(6) Split tear

If the sample is split by cutting as nearly as possible along the middle of its thickness so as to form two tongues (one on the flesh and the other on the grain side) then the test gives the value of trans split tear.

(7) Buckle tear

Two pieces of leather are joined together by a buckle and pulled apart. The maximum load indicated is the buckle tear strength.

(7) Stitch tear

In stitch tear strength test, steel wires are used to stitch since ordinary threads extend during the test. Two holes of specified dimension are made at one end of a rectangular piece of leather and a steel wire of specified diameter in the form of a 'U' is inserted such that the bend is on the grain side. The wire is fixed to one clamp and the leather to the other clamp in the tensile strength testing machine and the load required to start the tear is noted. This load divided by the thickness is recorded as the double hole stitch tear strength.

For thicker leathers like sole leather, only one hole is made and instead of the wire one steel wire is passed through the hole and the test performed in the same way.

(8) Cracking

This is a test performed to assess the quality of the grain of a leather.

The specimen, cut in the forrn of a rectangle, is bent slowly by hand over a mandrel of specified diameter through an angle of 180° with grain side out and the grain is scrutinised for any crackiness.

More accurately, the test can also be done as follows: The specimen, again in the form of a rectangle, is bent into a loop with the grain side out. A mandrel of required diameter is placed in the loop, and a metal bar (with the thickness approximately the same as the diameter of the mandrel) is placed in a vise with the loop downward. The specimen is bent around the mandrel against the bar by slowly closing the jaws of the vise till the bar can no more be moved by hand. The grain side is then examined for any crack around the bend.

(9) Piping

Pipiness is defined as the formation of wrinkles transverse to the direction in which the specimen is bent, the wrinkled tissue extends subsequently through the grain layer of the leather, while the corium remains undisturbed.

The specimen, cut in the form of a rectangle is bent slowly by band over a mandrel of required diameter, through 180°, with grain side in, much the same way, as is done for cracking. The mandrel is removed and the specimen held in the bent position is viewed along the edges and on the grain side for any pipiness and assessed according to the extent of piping as good, very fair and so on.

(10) Resistance to Perspiration

The test is useful in measuring the effect of perspiration on leather. The sample, here also, is cut in the form of a rectangle and immersed in a standard artificial perspiration solution at room temperature until its weight increases by about 20%. The wet specimen is immediately transferred to a constant temperature air oven maintained at the specified temperature for the specified time. The sample is removed and cooled to room temperature. The specimen is bent slowly, grain side out, through 180° over a mandrel 2 inches in diameter and the bent specimen is examined for cracks, if any.

(11) Grain Crack and Bursting Strength

The bursting strength tester has, in principle, a plain surface with an aperture which registers with an exactly similar aperture, one of which is movable along a common axis. A rubber diaphragm is provided to the lower aperture which closes it and also functions as a means of applying hydraulic pressure. The hydraulic pressure is applied manually by a hand bar. The liquid used is glycerine, a non-compressible liquid. The pressure is continuously registered as the piston is moved. The sample is cut and conditioned in the usual way. It is then clamped, in the bursting strength tester with the grain side up holding securely without slippage. Pressure is applied gradually. The end point is reached when ultimately the leather fails. The point at which the grain befo cracks below the point of ultimate failure is a measure of its resistance to grain cracking.

(12) Abrasion Resistance

The abrasion resistance, which is a measure of wear resistance, is the shrinks reciprocal of the loss in thickness of leather after a definite amount of abrasive action on it. It is a valuable property in sole leather.

The sample is cut into a rectangular shape, and conditioned. The sample is then clamped rigidly between two jaws on a lever arm, after in the measuring its thickness. The recorder is adjusted so that it reads zero. The lever is placed over the abrasive wheel and the machine is started. After a certain number of revolutions (generally 100) the lever is taken out, the wheel and the sample are cleaned with a vacuum cleaner and the thicnkess is measured. The differences in thickness is a measure of its wearing property.

(13) Flexibility

The ability of the leather to bend is a determining factor in many of its uses. In practice, flexibility is expressed as the force required to bend the leather through a given angle or as the angle through which the leather is bent by a given force.

One end of a rectangular leather piece is fixed and the load applied to the other end (at a specified rate) to bend the leather through a specified angle is recorded. From the dimensions of the leather, the load and the angle, a flexibility index is arrived at.

On release of the load, the leather will recover its original shape to a greater or lesser extent. This ability to recover combined with the ease of bending is given the name "temper".

(14) Compressibility and Resiliency

Compressibility is the change in thickness under a given load resiliency is the percentage rebound after a standard force is applied to the surface of leather under standard conditions. Both the above properties can be measured in a compression and resiliency tester in a simple manner.

It is, in principle, thickness gauge the lower end of the leg being planer for being placed on the leather piece. There is also provision to load and unload the leather without impact. A known load is applied to the sample and after a specified time thickness is measured After some time, the load is removed and the thickness read as before.

Per cent compression is given by $\frac{a-b}{a}$ x 100, where **'a'** is the original thickness before applications of load, and **'b'** its thickness with load.

per cent recovery is given by $\frac{c-b}{c-b}$ x 100, where **'c'** is the thickness after the removal of load, the other symbols having the same meaning as before.

(15) Shrinkage Temperature

Leather has the unique property of shrinking abruptly at a particular critical temperature, if heated in a liquid. The temperature at which it shrinks is defined as the shrinkage temperature in that liquid (T). It is measured by means of a shrinkage test meter.

Each sample is cut into 2" x 0.5" size and fixed between the clamps. The liquid used is water (for most leathers) or a glycerine-water mixture in the ratio of 3 : 1 for temperatures above 100°C and below about 120°C. In some cases, liquid paraffin may also be used. After filling up the vessel to completely immerse the samples in bath heated at the rate of 2-3°C a minute. A stirrer distributes the heat uniformly while a thermometer denotes the temperature of the bath. At one moment, when the leather suddenly shrinks, the pointer in the dial moves in the opposite direction rapidly over the scale. The temperature is read from the thermometer at this point and noted as the T_S.

(16) Water Absorption

Water resistance is a desirable property in many leathers whereas water absorption is required in certain others. Both of these can be easily measured by immersing a piece of leather in water for a known amount of time and noting difference in weight before and after the experiment.

The experiment is carried out using Kubelka's sample with the sample cut in a circular form. The conditioned sample is weighed, 25 ml. water is added in the cup of the apparatus, so that its level stands at the zero mark of the graduations marked in the tubular portion. The sample is put in the cup and the apparatus tilted so that the water flows from the graduated portion to the cup and comes into contact with the coming into contact with the bottom of the dish, thereby exposing a large surface of water. The level of water is noted after intervals of ½ hour, 2 hrs. and 24 hrs. by tilting the apparatus carefully. Finally, the sample is removed, pressed gently between two filter papers and weighed immediately.

$$\frac{\text{100 x volume of water be absorbed (after a specified time)}}{\text{Initial conditioned wt. of the sample}}$$

No correction is made for the removal of water solubles.

(17) Water Penetration

For some purposes, it is necessary to know the time taken for water to pass through leather from one surface to the other. This is easily measured in the following way. A piece of leather sample is fixed between two glass cylinders and the joint is sealed with molten paraffin wax along the edges. 50 ml. water is added on the top cylinder such that water stands over the grain surface of the leather. The time taken for the first drop of water to penetrate through the leather from the grain to the flesh surface, is noted and this gives a measure of the resistance to water penetration.

(18) Water Vapour Permeability

Water vapour can go through even pores which are too small to allow the passage of water through them. It is a very important property to be measured in garment leathers, as it is this property which allows the escape of perspiration from the body.

It is measured by a very simple method. The sample is cut in the form of a disc, and a bottle is nearly filled with fused calcium chloride and is covered with the leather sample and tightly closed by means of a special cap. The whole assembly is weighed, as such, initially. After known intervals of time, the apparatus is weighed. The increase in weight of the bottle gives a measure of the water vapour that has permeated and the leather sample during the specified time and it is expressed in terms of mg. water vapour/ unit cross-section/unit time.

(19) Air Permeability

This is a measure of comfort in garment leathers. Sometimes, a low permeability is also required in some cases as in washer and seal leathers. There are a number of instruments to test the air permeability. The principle is to measure the quantity of air passing through in a given time under a given difference of pressure or measure the time taken for a given volume of air to pass through the leather by starting with a given excess pressure and timing till this pressure falls to that of the atmosphere.

(20) Real And Apparent Densities

Apparent Density: The density of a substance is its mass per unit volume. The mass of leather is easily measured while the determination of its volume offers some problems. As leather is porous, the volume measured may be (i) its over-all volume (including the volume occupied by air in the interfibre spaces between fibers) or (ii) merely the volume of tanned fibres. The density in the former case is the apparent density while that in the latter case is denoted as the real density of the material.

The apparent density of a leather can be computed roughly by weighing a piece of leather of known dimension and of some regular shape like a square, rectangle, or circle. The area, thickness and hence the volume areall calculated. Then, by dividing the weight by the calculated volume, apparent density is obtained.

More accurateiy, the apparent density can be determined using a mercury trough. The sample is weighed in air and then sufficient weight is added in "Edwards Densimeter" to immerse the sample completely in the mercury. The apparent density is equal to

$$\frac{\text{wt. in air x density of mercury}}{\text{(wt. in air + wt. added immerse the sample)}}$$

(21) Real Density : The measurement of real density is difficult because of the fibrous structure. A simple method is to find the weight of the sample in air and its apparent weight in an inert liquid like kerosene whose density is known. Assuming that no matter has been removed from the real density is given by

$$\frac{\text{wt. in air}}{\text{(wt. in liquid x density of liquid (sp. gravity)}}$$

It can also be measured by a gas displacement method. The leather sample whose real volume is v is kept in a bulb of volume v_1 under a pressure of p_1. If the pressure is now increased to p_2, the volume occupied by the air and leather will be reduced to v_2. If both leather and air are dry, then according to Boyle's !aw,

$$v = \frac{(P_2V_2 - P_1V_1)}{(P_2 - P_1)}$$

(22) Special Tests For The Finishing Or Surface Properties Crocking

The rubbing off colouring of finishing materials from leather on to other materials is termed crocking. This may be dry rubbing wet rubbing.

The specimen is tested in the crockmeter. This consists of a base covered with an abrasive material over which the leather sample, cut in the form of a rectangle, is kept. Rubbing action is provided using a mechanical hand-operated device which rubs over the surface of leather such that the rubbing is done parallel to the length of the sample. A white cloth is mounted on the finger type device and the sample is rubbed for a specified number of times, at the end of which time, the cloth is taken out and compared with a control white cloth for any crocking. This gives the dry rub resistance.

To determine the resistance to wet rubbing, the above experiment is repeated with the cloth wetted so as to contain 75 to 100 per cent moisture by weight. If the cloth is not stained when dry or wet, the colour fastness is designated as "good"; if stained only in the wet condition but not in the dry, it is 'fair'. If stained even in the dry condition, it is "poor".

(23) Staining

This test is used to test whether leathers at elevated temperatures stain other materials. A white cloth is cut in the form of a square and kept between two rectangular pieces of the test leather. The leather piece are covered with glass plates and the whole assembly is kept in an oven maintained at the required temperature for the specified time. At the end of the test, the pad is removed and tested for any staining.

(24) Bleeding

Diffusion of uncombined materials from the interior of the leather to the outer surfaces, where they may contaminate other materials or spoil the appearance of the leather is called bleeding.

The leather is kept in contact with water for a specified time and the water is then tested for its transparency. This test is very important in all kinds of finished leathers, whether dyed, pigmented or coated.

(25) Tackiness

Tackiness is the tendency of leathers to stick to foreign substances with which they come into contact. This is likely to happen specially in warm conditions.

The following method is used to test this property. The leather is brought to a uniform temperature of 120° + 2°F and a piece of bleached cheese cloth is spread on the finished surface at this temperature and held under standard conditions of pressure for a specified time. The cloth is then stripped off and any tackiness noted.

(26) Lightfastness

Some leathers have a tendency to darken or fade after exposure to sun light atmosphere for some time. This is underneath in leathers used for fancy articles, car upholstery and for similar purposes. This property can be assessed in the following way.

Strips of leathers dyed or finished are exposed, along with standards to light from a standard source, keeping them at a fixed distance away. After exposure for some time, both the control and test pieces are taken out and compared for their fastness to light.

Apart from these properties, there are also some other characteristics of leather like feel, break, fall, run, firmness, anti-fog, etc., which are judged by hand. Also, it is not necessary to carry out all the tests for each sample of leather. Below are given some indications for carrying out the physical tests in some of the more important commercial leathers.

Sole

Abrasion resistance, water absorption, thermal conductivity, air permeability and apparent density.

Upper

Grain crack, stitch tear and flexibility.

Belting

Tensile strength, elongation and permanent stretch (i.e., the portion that the leather cannot recover on release of load after stretching).

Chamois

Water absorption, wettability and ability to retain water in water-petroleum mixture and breaking strength.

Clothing

Water absorption, air-permeability, water-vapour permeability, thermal conductivity, draping qualities, resistance to perspiration and stitchtear.

Glove

Flexibility, temper and elongation.

Picking band

Tensile strength, elongation and heat resistance.

Seal and Washer leathers

Air permeability, water penetration and bursting strength.

All finished leathers must also be tested for crackiness, staining, bleeding, and other tests described above. Grain crack strength must be determined for all leathers.

(Adopted from publication by Central Leather Research Institute Chennai).

Gas Meter Leather: In addition to the above lists for seal leather, it is necessary to conduct tests for the presence of pin holes and ensure that there are no pin holes, to free passage of air or gas. This is best done by examining the samples in a dark room against light.

VARIOUS OTHER CHEMICALS L.R. QUALITY

Ammonium chloride, Ammonium Nitrate, Ammonium Thiocyanate, Ammonium Oxalate, Barium Chloride, Barium Sulphate, Bromine, Calcium Carbonate, Calcium Hydroxide Chrome Alum, Ferrous Ammonium sulphate, Copper Sulphate, Hydrogen peroxide, Iodine, Formaldehyde, Gelatine, Iron Alum, Potassium Chromate, Potassium Dichromate, Potassium Oxalate, Potassium Sulphate, Potassium Iodide, Kaolin, Lead Acetate, Orthophosphoric Acid, Potassium Permanganate, Rochelle Salt, Sodium chloride, Sodium Bisulphite, Sodium Sulphate (Anhydrous), Sodium Thiosulphate, Sodium Ammonium Hydrogen Phosphate (Microcosmic Salt), Ethylene Diamine Tetra-Acetic acid EDTA (sodium salt), Starch, Oxalate, Silver Nitrate, Zinc Sulphate.

Commercial Chemicals, etc.

Glycerine, Calcium Chloride, Liquid Paraffin, Paraffin Wax, Sodium Dichromate. Sulphuric Acid, Sodium Stearate, Sand (iron free), Hide Powder (CLRI).

Physical Testing Laboratory

Tensile Strength Testing Machine with standard dies.

Shrinkage Tester

Kubelka Water Absorption Apparatus (CLRI)

Abrasion Tester

Flexometer

Lastometer

Thickness Measuring Gauge

Grey's Scale

Hand Clicking Press

Humidity Control Chamber.

[For Preconditioning of Leathers for physical testing strict control of temperature of humidity are essential and this will require at air-coreditioned room with good humidity and temperature controlling facility.]

CHEMICAL TESTING

1.	Absorbent cotton	2 x 500 g.
2.	Air-oven (up to 200°C)	1 No.
3.	Adjustable screw for rubber tubing	12 Nos.
4.	Balance (analytical) (* naivivity 0.1 mg.)	1 No.
5.	Balance (analytical) (* naivivity 10.0 mg.)	1 No.
6.	Barkometer (0-120° BK)	2 Nos.
7.	Beaker (2L)	2 Nos.
8.	Beaker (1 L)	2 Nos.
9.	Beaker (600 ml)	6 Nos.
10.	Beaker (500 ml)	6 Nos.
11.	Beaker (400 ml)	24 Nos.
12.	Beaker (200 ml)	1 No.
13.	Beaker (100 ml)	12 Nos.
14.	Beaker (50 ml)	12 Nos.
15.	Bucket (Plastic/Enamelled) (10 L)	3 Nos.
16.	Bucket (Stainless steel) (10 L)	2 Nos.
17.	Burette (50 ml)	3 Nos.
18.	Burette stand	3 Nos.
19.	Clay pipe triangle	12 Nos.
20.	Colorimeter (electrically operated)	1 Nos.
21.	Conical flask (500 ml)	12 Nos.
22.	Conical flask (250 ml)	12 Nos.
23.	Cork borer set	1 Nos.
24.	Crucible with lid (30 ml)	24 Nos.

25.	Denn & Stark apparatus for the determination of water-content (e.g. in sulphated oils)	2 Nos.
26.	Desiccator (5 L)	3 Nos.
27.	Desiccator (3 L)	3 Nos.
28.	Disintegrator (for grinding barks & other veg. tanstuffs: Cap. 1 kg/hr)	3 Nos. 3 Nos.
29.	Distilled water flask (1 L)-flat-bottomed-polythene/glass	3 Nos.
30.	Distilled water still (e.g. Manesty)	1 No.
31.	Electric hot-plate	1 No.
32.	Enamelled basin (31)	2 Nos.
33.	Evaporating basin (50 ml) flat-bottomed both sides glazed	36 Nos.
34.	Filter paper (18.5 cm) - Whatman No.1-Box	2 Nos.
35.	Filter paper (18.5 cm) - Whatman No.11-Box	2 Nos.
36.	Filter paper (18.5 cm) - Whatman No.42-Box	1 No.
37.	Filter paper sheet - Whatman No.1	20 Nos.
38.	Filter stand - six-in-one	2 Nos.
39.	Filter stand - two-in-one	3 Nos.
40.	Flask holder	2 Nos.
41.	Frigidaire	1 No.
42.	Funnel - 4" dia	12 Nos.
43.	Funnel - 1" dia	12 Nos.
44.	Gas burner	12 Nos.
45.	Gas plant (or Domestic gas cylinders)	1 No.
46.	Glass bottle (wide-mouthed) - 1 L	6 Nos.
47.	Glass bottle (wide-mouthed) - 500 ml	12 Nos.
48.	Glass bottle (wide-mouthed) - 250 ml	12 Nos.
49.	Glass for making thimbles (soxhlet)	2 Nos.
50.	Glass marking pencil (Blue)	3 Nos.
51.	Glass marking pencil (Red)	3 Nos.
52.	Glass rods (different dia)	3 Kg.
53.	Glass sintered crucible (30 ml)	6 Nos.

54.	Glass-tube	3 Nos.
55.	Glazed porcelain tile	3 Nos.
56.	Gooch crucible (30 ml)	6 Nos.
57.	Indicator bottle (glass/polythene)	12 Nos.
58.	Iodine flask B 24 with stoppers (250 ml)	6 Nos.
59.	Kjeldahl digestion flask (500 ml)	24 Nos.
60.	Kjeldahl digestion unit (-do-)	1 No.
61.	Kjeldahl distillation unit (-do-)	1 No.
62.	Litmus paper (Blue) box	1 No.
63.	Litmus paper (Red) box	1 No.
64.	Measuring cylinder (1 L)	1 No.
65.	Measuring cylinder (500 ml)	2 Nos.
66.	Measuring cylinder (250 ml)	2 Nos.
67.	Measuring cylinder (100 ml)	3 Nos.
68.	Measuring cylinder (50 mi)	3 Nos.
69.	Measuring cylinder (25 ml)	3 Nos.
70.	Measuring cylinder (10 ml)	2 Nos.
71.	Mechanical shaker (50-60 r.p.m.)	1 No.
72.	Muffle furnace (1100°C)	1 No.
73.	Mull cloth	5 met.
74.	Muslin cloth	3 met.
75.	Nessler's tube (100 ml)	4 Nos.
76.	Nickel crucible (30 ml)	6 Nos.
77.	Nickel spactula - 15 cm	6 Nos.
78.	Pair of Tongs (Long-for use with muffle furnace)	2 Nos.
79.	Pair of Tongs (Long-for use with muffle short)	3 Nos.
80.	Pestle & Mortar	1 No.
81.	pH Meter	1 No.
82.	Pipette (100 ml)	2 Nos.
83.	Pipette (50 ml)	3 Nos.
84.	Pipette (25 ml)	6 Nos.

85.	Pipette (10 ml)	3 Nos.
86.	Pipette -Graduated (20 ml)	3 Nos.
87.	Pipette -Graduated (10 ml)	6 Nos.
88.	Polythene bags (different sizes)	1 kg.
89.	Polythene Carbuoys (20 L)	2 Nos.
90.	Polythene Carbuoys (5 L)	3 Nos.
91.	Porcelain basin (glazed inside) - 1 L	3 Nos.
92.	Porous earthenware pieces	1 kg.
93.	Quickft flask (Conical/flat-bottomed, with B 24 joint) - 500 ml	6 Nos.
94.	Quickfit flask (Conical/flat-bottomed, with B 24 joint) 250 ml	12 Nos.
95.	Reagent bottle (Polythene) - 500 ml	12 Nos.
96.	Reflux condenser with B24 joint	12 Nos.
97.	Ring stand for separating funnel	6 Nos.
98.	Rubber adaptor for gooch crucible	6 Nos.
99.	Rubber bungs of various sizes (For Sl. Nos.46-48 & other sizes)	48 Nos.
100.	Rubber tubing including pressure tubing	10 met.
101.	Separating funnel (500 ml)	3 Nos.
102.	Separating funnel (250 ml)	3 Nos.
103.	Specific gravity bottle (25 ml)	2 Nos.
104.	Soxhlet Extraction glass apparatus, including flasks (250 ml) with B24 joints/middle units and condensers	12 Nos.
105.	Soxhlet Extraction Heating mantle (six-in-one) unit	2 Nos.
106.	Standard flask (2L)	3 Nos.
107.	Standard flask (1 L)	6 Nos.
108.	Standard flask (500 ml)	6 Nos.
109.	Standard flask (250 ml)	6 Nos.
110.	Standard flask (200 ml)	6 Nos.
111.	Standard flask (100 ml)	12 Nos.
112.	Standard flask (50 ml)	6 Nos.

113. Suction flask (1 L) 2 Nos.
114. Test Tube 12 Nos.
115. Test Tube brush (big) 2 Nos.
116. Test Tube brush (small) 2 Nos.
117. Test tube holder 2 Nos.
118. Thermometer (0-110°C) 3 Nos.
119. Thermometer (0-360°C) 1 No.
120. Tintometer (Lovibond) 1 No.
121. Tripod stand 6 Nos.
122. Twine ball 2 Nos.
123. Vacuum Pump 1 No.
124. Watch glass 10 em.dia 24 Nos.
125. Water bath-stainless steel-12 holes (with concentric rings) 1 No.
126. Weighing bottle with lids 6 Nos.
127. Wiley mill (for grinding leather) 1 No.
128. Wire gauze 12 Nos.
129. Wire gauze with asbestos centre 4 Nos.
130. Working Table (150 x 75 x 90 cm): & Fume cupboard: 1 No.

CHEMICALS (A.R. GRADE)

1. Acetic acid 2 x 500 g.
2. Ammonium carbonate 500 g.
3. Ammonium Chloride 500 g.
4. Ammonium Hydroxide 500 g.
5. Ammonium nitrate 500 g.
6. Ammonium oxalate 500 g.
7. Ammonium thiocyanate 500 g.
8. Asbestos (for gooch crucibles) 500 g.
9. Barium chloride 500 g.
10. Benzene 2 x 500 g.

11.	Boric acid	3 x 500 g.
12.	Bromine	250 g.
13.	Buffer tablets for pH 9 (BDH) Pockets	2 each
14.	Calcium carbonate	500 g.
15.	Calcium hydroxide	500 g.
16.	Carbon tetrachloride	3 x 500 g.
17.	Chloroform	2 x 500 g.
18.	Chrome alum	500 g.
19.	Copper sulphate	500 g.
20.	Dichloromethane	5 x 500 g.
21.	Diethyl ether	3 x 500 g.
22.	Dimethyl aniline	50o g.
23.	Disodium hydrogen phosphate	500 g.
24.	Ethyl alcohol (absolute)	3 x 500 ml.
25.	Ethylene Diamine Tetra Acetic acid (sodium salt)	500 g.
26.	Ferrous ammonium sulphate	500 g.
27.	Formaldehyde	500 ml.
28.	Gelatine	500 g.
29.	Gum Arabic	100 g.
30.	Hide powder (CLRI/International)	6 x 500 g.
31.	Hydrochloric acid (Conc.)	5 kg.
32.	Hydrogen peroxide (20 volumes)	500 g.
	Indicators : (SI: Nos.33-43) Smallest packing in each.	
33.	Bromocresol green	
34.	Bromocresol purple	
35.	Bromophenol blue	
36.	Calcon	
37.	Cresol red	
38.	Eriochrome Black T	
39.	Methyl orange	
40.	Methyl Red	

41.	Murexide	
42.	Phenolphthalein	
43.	Thymol bluc	
44.	Iodine	500 g.
45.	Iron alum	500 g.
46.	Isopropyl alcohol	3 x 500 g.
47.	Kaolin	500 g.
48.	Lead-acetate	500 g.
49.	Liquor ammonia	3 x 500 ml.
50.	1-histidine monohydrochloride monohydrate	500 g.
51.	Magnesium sulphate	500 g.
52.	Nitric acid (conc)	5 kg.
53.	Oxalic acid	500 g.
54.	Petroleum ether (40-60°C)	10 x 500 g.
55.	Perchloric acid	4 x 500 g.
56.	Phosphoric acid (ortho)	500 g.
57.	Potassium carbonate	500 g.
58.	Potassium chromate	500 g.
59.	Potassium dichromate	500 g.
60.	Potassium fluoride	500 g.
61.	Potassium hydrogen phthalate	500 g.
62.	Potassium hydroxide	500 g.
63.	Potassium iodide	2 x 500 g.
64.	Potassium oxalate	2 x 500 g.
65.	Potassium Permanganate	500 g.
66.	Potassium sulphate	2 x 500 g.
67.	Rochelle Salt	500 g.
68.	Sand	2 kg.
69.	Silver nitrate	100 g.
70.	Starch	500 g.

71.	Sodium ammonium hydrogen phosphate (Microcosmic salt)	500 g.
72.	Sodium bicarbonate	500 g.
73.	Sodium bisuiphite	500 g.
74.	Sodium carbonate	500 g.
75.	Sodium chloride	500 g.
76.	Sodium hydroxide	6 x 500 g.
77.	Sodium sulphate (anhydrous)	500 g.
78.	Sodium tetraborate (dibasic)	500 g.
79.	Sodium thiosulphatd	500 g.
80.	Sulphuric acid (conc)	5 kg.
81.	Zinc sulphate	500 g.

CHEMICALS (Commercial)

1.	Acetone	5 kg.
2.	Calcium chloride	3 x 500 g.
3.	Caustic soda	3 kg.
4.	Glycerine	6 x 500 ml.
5.	Liquid paraffin	3 x 500 ml.
6.	Potassium dichromate	2 kg.
7.	Sulphuric acid	5 kg.
8.	Washing soda	10 kg.
9.	Xylene	2 ltr.

PHYSICAL TESTING

Equipment / Apparatus

1.	Abrasion Tester (Catalogue No. 9D 400)	Taber Instruments Corn., North Tonawada, New York, U.S.A.
2.	Apparatus for testing bursting strength and grain crackiness strength - Lastometer	Baird & Tatlock (London) Ltd. 14/17 St. Cross St., London, England.

3. Apparatus for testing bursting strength and grain crackiness strength - Lastometer	B.F. Purlins & Sons Inc., Holyoke, Massachusetts U.S.A.
4. Apparatus for testing fastness to rubbing	Shoe and Allied Trades' Research Association Satra House, Rockingham road, Kettering, Northampton, U.K.
5. Bally Flexometer	Bally CTU Bally Schuhfabriken AG CH-5012 Schonenverd, Switzerland
6. Bally Penetrometer	Bally CTU Bally Schuhfabriken AG CH-5012
7. Bally Permeometer	Bally CTU Bally Schuhfabriken AG CH-5012
8. Bally Tensometer	Bally CTU Bally Schuhfabriken AG CH-5012
9. Compressibility & Resilience Tester	Custom Scientific Instruments Inc., 541, Devon St., Kearny, New Jersy, U.S.A.
10. Kubelka apparatus	CLRI, Madras.
11. Shrinkage tester	CLRI, Madras.
12. Stiffness Tester	Tinius Olsen Testing m/c Co. Easton Road, Willow Grove U.S.A.
13. Tensile strength tester with automatic load extension recorder (1000 kg)	M/s. Kamal Metal Industries Arun Park, Bhaipura, Khokhara, Mahemdabad, AHMEDABAD - 8.
14. Thermostat apparatus	SET ? 101-103, Rue is Seze 69, Lyen 6e, France
15. Water vapour Permeability apparatus St. James Road, Croydon,	H.W. WALLACE & Co., Ltd.

U.K.

MISCELLANEOUS

1. Adjustable Table Lamp
2. Balance (Sensitivity 10 mg)
3. Calculator - Electronic
4. Clicking Press
5. Dies for cutting test specimens
6. First aid Box
7. Foot scale
8. Graph paper
9. Grey scale for assessing change in colour
10. Grey scale for assessing change in staining
11. Hand lens 10 cm. dia
12. Knives
13. Planimeter
14. Scissors
15. Stop Watch
16. Thickness gauge 0.1 mm
17. Tool box
18. Tracing paper
19. Vernier calipers
20. Wail clock
21. Weather controlled (A/C) unit for maintaining temp and relative humidity as per test conditions

PHYSICAL TESTING OF LEATHER

Sl. No.	Test 2	Equipment 3	Reagent 4	Note 5
1.	Measurement of thickness of test pieces	Dial micrometer gauge: – load applied 393 ± .10 gm [1500 gm/cm]^2 – flat circular pressures foot of diameter 10 mm – anvil shall be flat horizontal surface of a cylindrical of 10.00 mm, which shall be projected 3 mm from the surface of a flat circular platform of diameter 50 cm error should not exceed 0.005 mm – graduated dial guage to read 0.01 mm directly		BIS or BSS
2.	Measurement of thickness of leather	Spring type gauge: – graduate in 0.1 mm, having a flat pressure foot 10.2±0.6 mm in diameter and a flat anvil 10.2±0.6 mm in diameter OR – spring shall exert a force of 450 gm on the foot when the guage reads 0.8 mm and 900 gm when the gauge reads 4.8 mm OR Standard wedge type gauge – having one leg gradually in 0.1 mm preferably constructed of stainless steel, in which legs enclose an angle of about 4		BIS or BSS

3.	Measurement of width	Steel scale-graduated in 0.5 mm Steel tape-graduated in 1 mm Vernier caliper		BIS or BSS
4.	Measurement of area	Graduated sheet-sheet of transparent flexible material, ruled in square centimeter. The sheet should be large enough to cover the test piece completely		BIS or BSS
5.	Apparent density	Steel press knife-inner wall of which shall be a right circular cylinder of diameter 70 mm Dial micrometer gauge		BIS or BSS
6.	Tensile strength, Modulus elongation at specified load and elongation at break	Tensile tester- A tensile strength testing machine having a uniform speed for separation of the jaws of 100 ± 20 max/min. The faces of the jaws shall measure at least 40 mm in the direction of the applied load.		BIS or BSS
7.	Tear strength	– Press knife – Tensile testing machine, same as used in tensile strength – Test piece holders – A pair of test piece holders each consisting of a strip of steel 10 mm wide and 2 mm thick, bent through a right angle at one end, and welded to a bar which makes the strip		BIS or BSS

8.	Double hole stitch tear strength	Metal wire – A piece of soft steel wire 1.00 ± 0.025 mm in diameter and not less than 100 mm in length Punch or other instrument for making holes 2 mm diameter Testing machine-same as used in tensile strength test except that the jaws of the grips of the machine shall be covered with a material suitable for protecting the gripping surface from possible damage by the metal wire		BIS or BSS
9.	Tongue tear test	A low inertia recording tensil strength machine, with a load range of 0 to 50 kg and one or more lower load range, and a speed of transverse of 75 mm	.	BIS or BSS
10.	Shrinkage temperature	Apparatus for wetting test piece – desiccator – vacuum pump capable of reducing the pressure in the vessel to less than 30 mm of Hg within two minutes – test tube Apparatus for shrinkage temperature measurement; – glass beaker-500 ml – brass rod of diameter 4mm		BIS or BSS or ISO

		– other rods – circular scale having diameter 45 mm, with division of 1 mm of the rim – light pointer having diameter 10 mm - hook made of copper wire – thermometer – a 80 to 100 watt electric heater		
11.	Absorption of water – gravimetric method	Glass vessel Press knife-a press knife, the inner wall of which is a right circular cylinder of diameter 70 mm		BIS or BSS or ISO
12.	Absorption of water-Kubelka method	Kubelka apparatus		BIS or BSS or ISO
13.	Resistance to cracking of grain and crack index	Apparatus consists of – clamp device to hold – a mandrel of the desired diameter – roller of diameter 25 mm Mondrel No. Diameter 1 61.57 ± 0.03 2 5.00 ± 0.03 3 23.57 ± 0.03 4 17.22 ± 0.03 5 13.22 ± 0.03 6 10.38 ± 0.03 7 8.33 ± 0.03 8 6.76 ± 0.03		BIS or BSS or ISO
14.	Measurement of two-dimensional extension	– A metal head to clamp test piece with an oil resistance rubber diaphragm beneath it		BIS or BSS or ISO

		– A constant rotary oil pump pressure up to kgf/cm^2 in 30 seconds – A manometer having range 0 to 25 kgf/cm^2 and having no errors greater than 0.1 kgf/cm^2 at any part of its range or – Means for recording automatically in graphical form the pressure applied to the leather		
15.	Resistance to compression	Standard measurement guage – micrometer guage as used in measurement of thickness of test pieces		BIS or BSS or ISO
16.	Compressibility of leather	Press-either hand or power driven, having a capacity of at least 5450 kg. permitting a pressure of 250 ± 5 kgf/cm^2 rate of increase shall not exceed 14 kgf/cm^2 – two flat plates and an indicator for reading the applied force. A suitable testing may also be used stop watch		BIS or BSS or ISO
17.	Indentation index	Thickness guage as used in measurement of thickness of test pieces modified by removing the flat pressure foot and replacing it with a steel ball of diameter 3 mm Total load on the ball 15±5gm		BIS or BSS or ISO

18.	Dynamic water proofness of boot and shoe sole leather	The apparatus consists of a) a brass roller of diameter 120 mm width 50 mm which rests on a rectangular leather test piece 100 x 40 mm b) a clamp c) Pieces of absorbent cellulose board-100 x 60 mm, 1.5 to 1.7 mm thick weight of 1200 gm/cm^2 d) Apparatus for measuring time either atomic or semiatomic balance		BIS or BSS or ISO
19.	Flexing endurance	Bally flexometer The apparatus consists of – upper clamp-movable – lower clamp-fixed		BIS or BSS or ISO
20.	Dynamic water proofness test of upper leather	Penetrometer. The apparatus consists of a) two cylinders, 30 mm in diameter b) an electric motor-crank motion 50 cycles/minute and with amplitude 1.0, 1.5,2.0, or 3.0 mm c) ting-shaped clamps d) tan kcontaining distilled water e) an electrically operated device which provides a signal f) absorption cloth for absorbing water g) apparatus for measuring time		BIS or BSS or ISO

21.	Water vapour permeability	The apparatus consists of a) bottles b) bottle holder in the shape of wheel which is rotated at 78 ± 5 re/min by electric motor c) a fan	Silica jel-dried at least for 16 hours in a ventilated oven at 125° ±5°c and cooled at least 6 hours in closed bottle	BIS or BSS of ISO
22.	Water proofness of gloving leather	Apparatus for measurement of waterproofness of gloving leathers consists of – a brass anvil – a hammer – a shaft – a counter – a suitable electric circuit and auxiliary apparatus which provide an audible or visual signal when penetration of water through test piece occurs. – an automatic or semi-automatic balance for weighing test piece to the nearest milligrams.		BIS or BSS of ISO
23.	Bond strength laminated leather	The testing machine consists of a) tension testing machine b) grips c) recorder		BIS or BSS or ISO
24.	Thermal conductivity constant of leather	– Cenco Fitch conductivity apparatus – Galvanometer – Immersion heater		BIS or BSS or ISO

		– Micrometer – Stop watch – Weight-5 kg.		
25.	Area stability of leather on Immersion in water and oil	Thermometer Immersion thermometer having a range from –20° to 150°c	Distilled water immersion	BIS or BSS or ISO
26.	Spray test for estimating water repellency of clothing leathers	(a) A spray device (b) Stand (c) Test-piece holder		BIS or BSS or ISO
27.	Colour fastness test of leather to *Daylight *Artificial light *Heat *Organic solvents *Perspiration *Water phobing *Wet rubbing *Masking *Washing	Felt pads Geometric grey (grey scale) Geometric staining scale Colour fastness tester Crook meter-wet & dry rubbing Glass rotating drum with rotating device		BIS or BSS or ISO
28.	Shrinkage temperature	Ts apparatus		BIS or BSS or ISO

	temperature			ISO

CHEMICAL TESTING OF LEATHER

S.No	Test	Equipment	Capacity	Reagents
1	2	3	4	5
1.	Volatile matter	– Desiccator – Oven – Weighing bottles & dishes flat, shallow with ground in stopper, or flat open dishes	102°C ± 2°C	
2.	Moisture	– Flask – Glass reflux condenser jacket – Receiver	500 ml 400 ml long	– Potassium – Sulphuric acid – Toluene
3.	Total ash	– Crucible-Platinum or silica – Desicator – Muffle furnace with pyrometer and thermometer control		
4.	Solvent extractable substance	– Desiccator – – Filter paper thimbles or glass filter bells – Oven – Soxhlet Extraction Apparatus with extraction flask	102°C ± 2°C	Dichlorom hand – Petroleu Hydro carbon Solvent [40/60]
5.	Nitrogen and hide substances	– Distillation apparatus – Kjeldol flask	200 to 300 ml 300 to 400 ml	– Fuming sulphur acid – Catalyst mixture anhydrous copper sulphate + potassium

		– Receiver		sulphate – Phenol halein indicate – Sodium hydrox solution – Solution of boric and – Sulphuric or hydro-chloric acid
6.	Water soluble matters	– Desiccator – Evaporating basin with flat bottom quarge, porcelain or platinum – Flask – Oven – Shaker	500 ml 102°± 2°C 50 ± 10 rev/min.	
7.	Sulphate ash of water solubles	– Apparatus as in water		– Sulphuric Acid
8.	Water insoluble ash	– Crucible – Desiccator – Muffle furnace – Other apparatus as in – water soluble matter		– Ammonium Nitrate Solution
9.	Water soluble organic substance	– Apparatus as in water soluble matter		
10.	Chromic oxide	– Kjeldehl or Erlenmeyer flask with round stopper – Conical flask – Crucible [iron or nickel]	300 ml	– Conc. sulphuric acid – Perchloric acid – Phosphoric acid

				– Starch solution – Sodium thio sulphate solution – Potassium iodide solution
11.	Aluminium Method A	– Conical flask – Hot plate – Muffle furnace provided with pyrometer and thermometer control	100 ml	– Potassium Hydroxide Solution – Conc. Hydro Chloride Acid – Thymol Blue and Cresol Red Indicator – Potassium Tartrate Solution – Potassium Fluoride Solution – Standard Hydro Chloric Acid
12.	Aluminium Method B	– Analytical balance, Burette – Conical flask, Filter apparatus – Glass beaker, Magnetic stirrer – pH mesuring apparatus – Pippets – Platinum crucible	100 ml	– Hexa methylene tetram – Fusion mixture – Hydro chloric acid – Oxidizing mixture – Sodium hydroxide solution – Ammonia

		– Muffle furnace – Tall-form beaker – Volumetric beaker		– CDTA – Zinc chlorid – Xylenol Orange [indicator]
13.	Zirconium	– Analytical balance, sensitivity—0.001 – Conical flasks – Desiccator – Filter apparatus, acid resistance filter paper – Muffle furnace – Measuring cylinders – Pippets – Platinum basin or crucible – Tuff form beaker	250ml–500ml	– Potassium bisulphate – Sulphuric acid – Hydrogen peroxid – Barium chloride – Hydro-chloride acid – Ammonium Phosphate – Ammonium nitrate
14.	Formaldehyde presence			– Dilute hydro chloric acid – Sodium sulphite solution – Gross Bohle reagent – Dilute sulphuric acid – Chro motropic acid

15.	Free-formaldehyde	– Kjeldahal flask – Burettes – Beakers – Conical flask	500 ml	– Dilute sulphuric acid – Sodium bisulphite solution – Standard iodine solution – Starch solution – Sodium carbonate solution
16.	Combined oil condenser	– Flask with reflux – Oven	120°C ± 2°C	– Alcoholic potassium hydroxide solution – Conc. hydro-chloric acid – Ether
17.	Epsom salt	– Conical flask – Pipette – Burette – Measuring cylinder	250 ml 25 ml 100 ml 100 ml	– Hydro chloric acid – Ammo-nium chloride solution – Feric chloride solution – Nitric acid – Ammonium hydroxide solution – Zinc granules – Ammo-nium oxalate solution – Ether

				– Ethyl alcohol – Sodium hydroxide solution – Sodium chloride solution
18.	Glucose			– Lead acetate solution – Potassium oxalate – Conc. hydro-chloric acid – Anhydrous sodium carbonate – Fehlings Solution No. 1 & No. 2 – Rectified spirit – Ether
19.	pH and difference figure of water soluble matter	– Flask – pH meter, range 0 to 14 accuracy 0.05 – Electrode system – Glass electrodes with spherical or chlindrical membranes	200 ml	– Buffer solution – Distilled water
20.	Total chlorides	– Glass apparatus		– Conc. Nitric Acid – Standard Silver Nitrate Solution – Calcium Carbonate

				– Potassium Chromate Solution
21.	Total sulphate			– Cone. Hydro chloric acid – Barium Chloride Solution
22.	Bound organic substances and degree of tannage			
23.	Corrosion produced by leather in contact with metal	– Desiccator – Analytical balance – Forceps – Metal plates – Non-abrasive cloth – Piece of glass – Weight	10 ± 1 g	– Non-corrosive oil – Petroleum hydro carbon solvent
24.	Silicon [Method A]	– Analytical balance – Beaker – Graduated flask – Parr bomb – pH meter – pipettes – Spectrometer or photoelectric absorption meter	250 ml	
25.	Silicon [Method B]	– Analytical balance – Extraction flask – Measuring cylinder – Oven	100° ± 2°C 50 ml 100 ml 30 x 100 mm	– tetra hydrofuran – hydro chloric acid – n-propanol – hydro carbon solvent

		– Platinum basin – Soxhlet extractor – Soxhlet thimble		
26.	Iron	Nessler cylinder	50 ml	– fuming nitric acid – bromine water – conc. hydro chloric acid – ammonium hydroxide – dil. hydro chloric acid – dil. sulphuric acid – potassium-permanga-nate solution – potassium or ammonium thiocyanate solution
27.	Copper	Nessler cylinder	50 ml	– tetra sodium pyro phosphate solution – gum arabic solution – sodium diethyl dithio carbonate solution – stock solution of copper – standard

				solution of copper
28.	Phosphorus	– Analytical balance with sensitivity – Burettes – Kjeldahl or conical type fitted with splash bulbs – Measuring cylinders – Pipettes – Spectrophoto meter or absorption meter with suitable filler – Volumetric flasks		– sodium sulphite – conc. nitric acid – oxidizing mix.
29.	For all chemical tests	Cutter mill with a knife velocity of 700 to 1000 revolution per minute and a 4 mm diameter mesh sieve - Willey Mill		

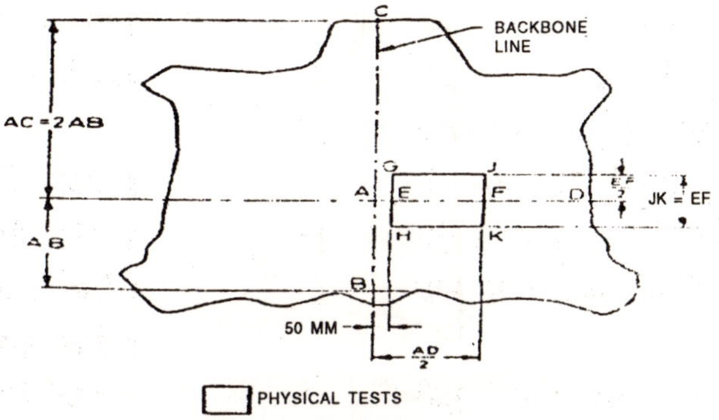

LOCATION FOR CUTTING OUT TESTS PIECES IN A WHOLE SKIN, HIDE AND SIDE FOR PHYSICAL TESTS

Methods for random sampling.

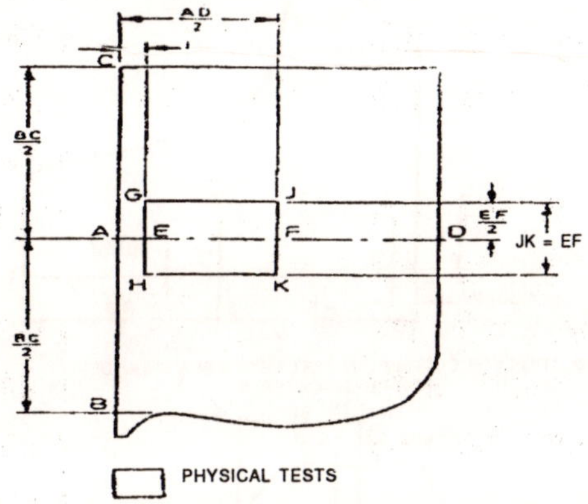

LOCATION FOR CUTTING OUT TESTS PIECES IN A BEN FOR PHYSICAL TESTS

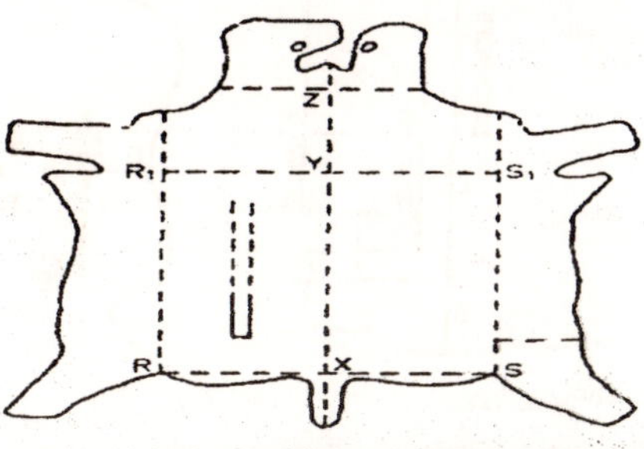

LOCATION FOR CUTTING OUT TESTS PIECES FOR PICKING-BAND BELTING LEATHER FOR PHYSICAL TESTS

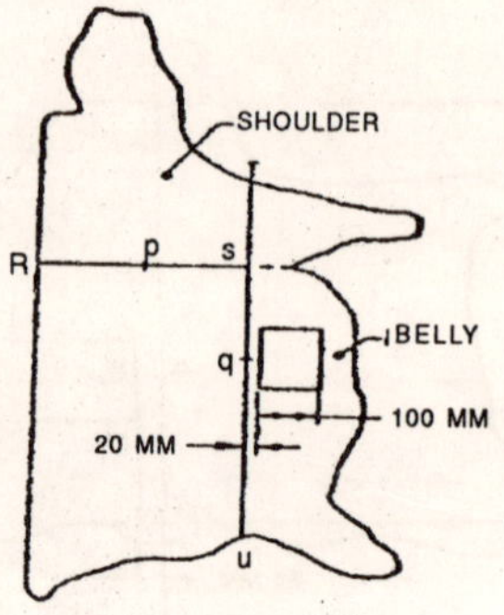

LOCATION FOR CUTTING OUT TEST PIECES IN A BELLY FOR PHYSICAL TESTS

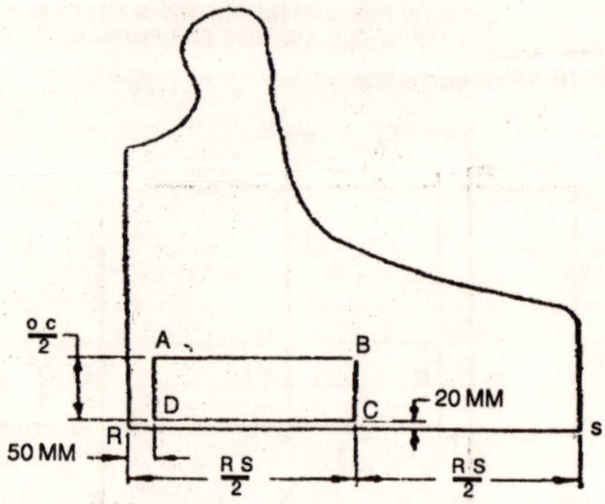

LOCATION FOR CUTTING OUT TEST PIECES IN A SHOULDER FOR PHYSICAL TESTS

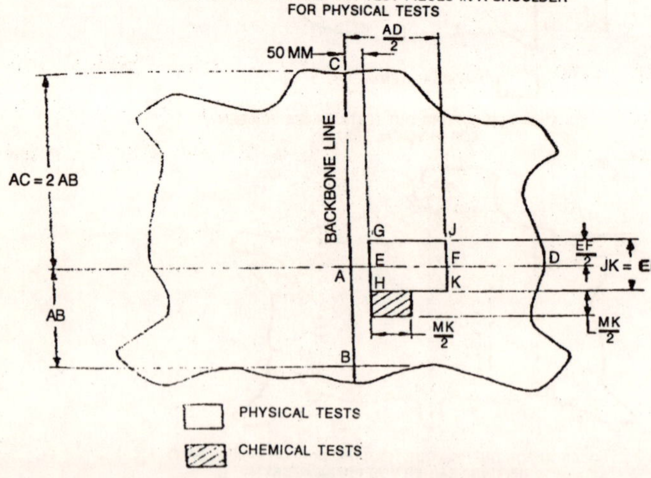

LOCATION FOR CUTTING OUT TEST PIECES IN A WHOLE SKIN, HIDE AND SIDE FOR CHEMICAL TESTS

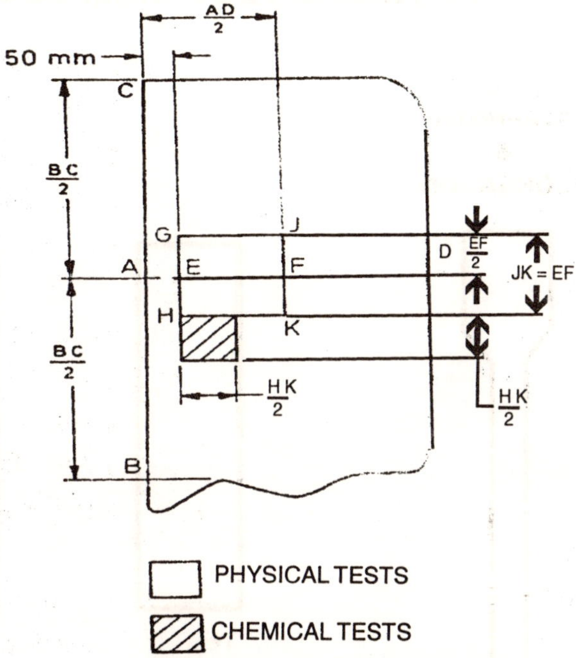

LOCATION FOR CUTTING OUT TEST PIECES IN A BEND (BUTT) FOR CHEMICAL TESTS

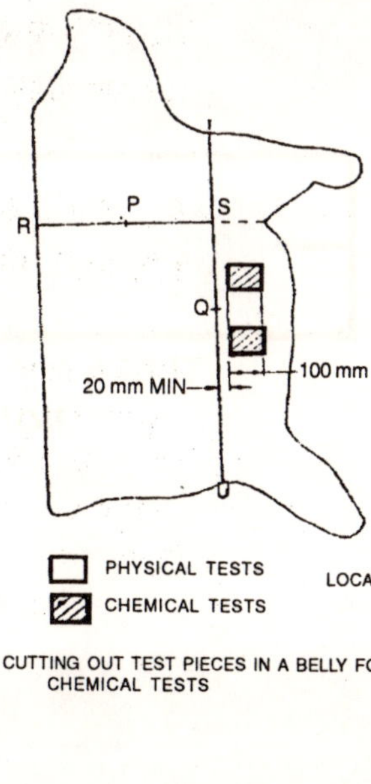

LOCATION FOR CUTTING OUT TEST PIECES IN A BELLY FOR CHEMICAL TESTS

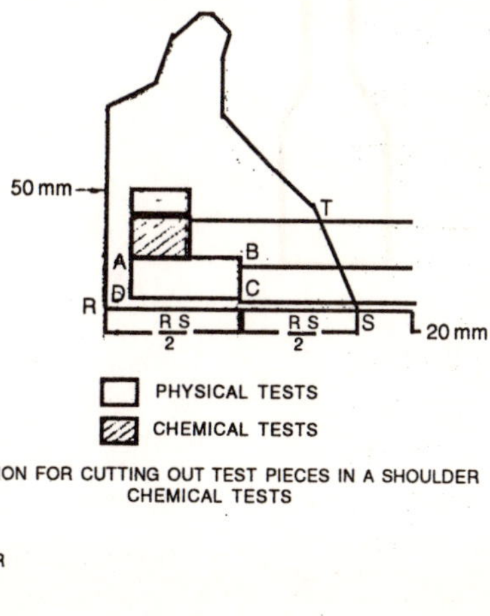

LOCATION FOR CUTTING OUT TEST PIECES IN A SHOULDER CHEMICAL TESTS

PHYSICAL TEST SAMPLES

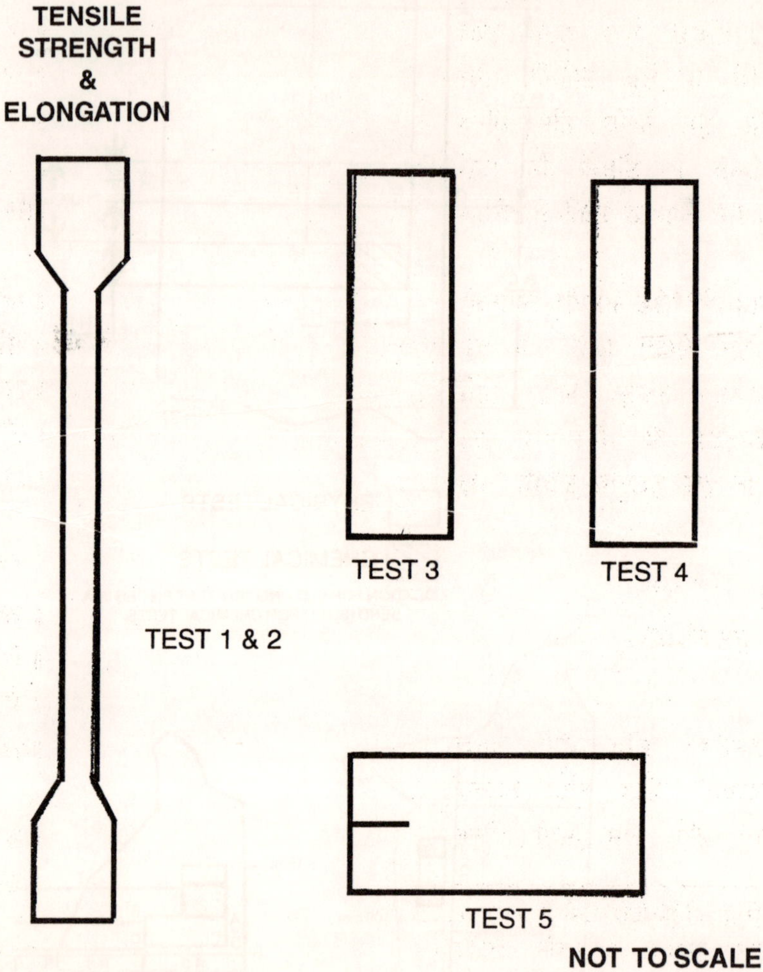

PHYSICAL TEST SAMPLES

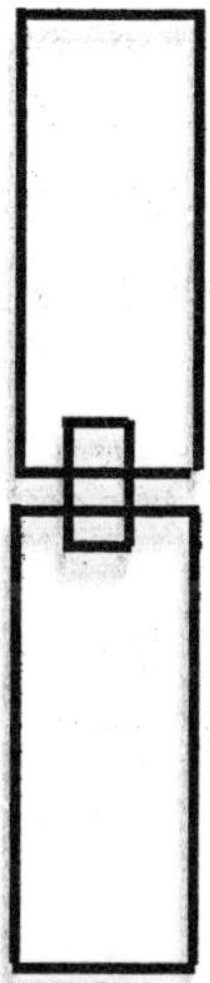

TEST 6

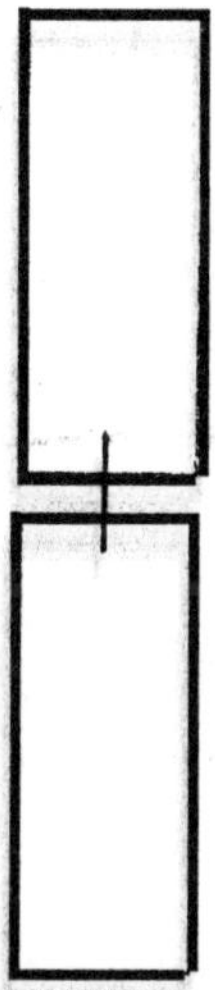

TEST 7

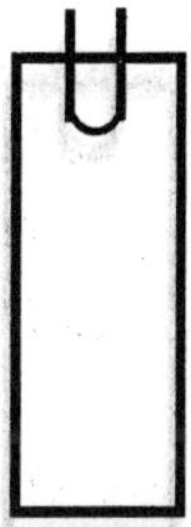

TEST 8

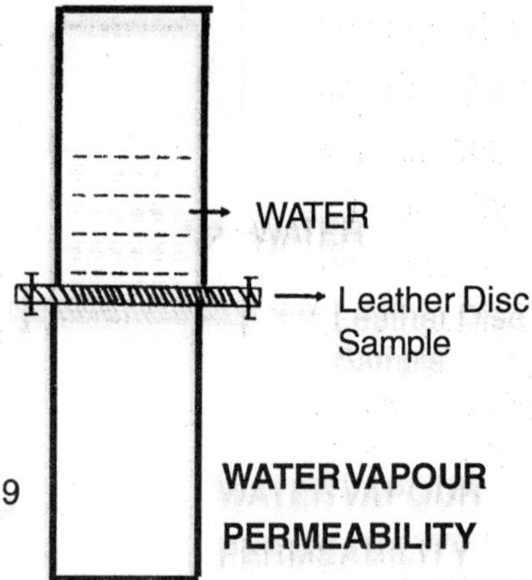

TEST 9

WATER VAPOUR PERMEABILITY

NOT TO SCALE

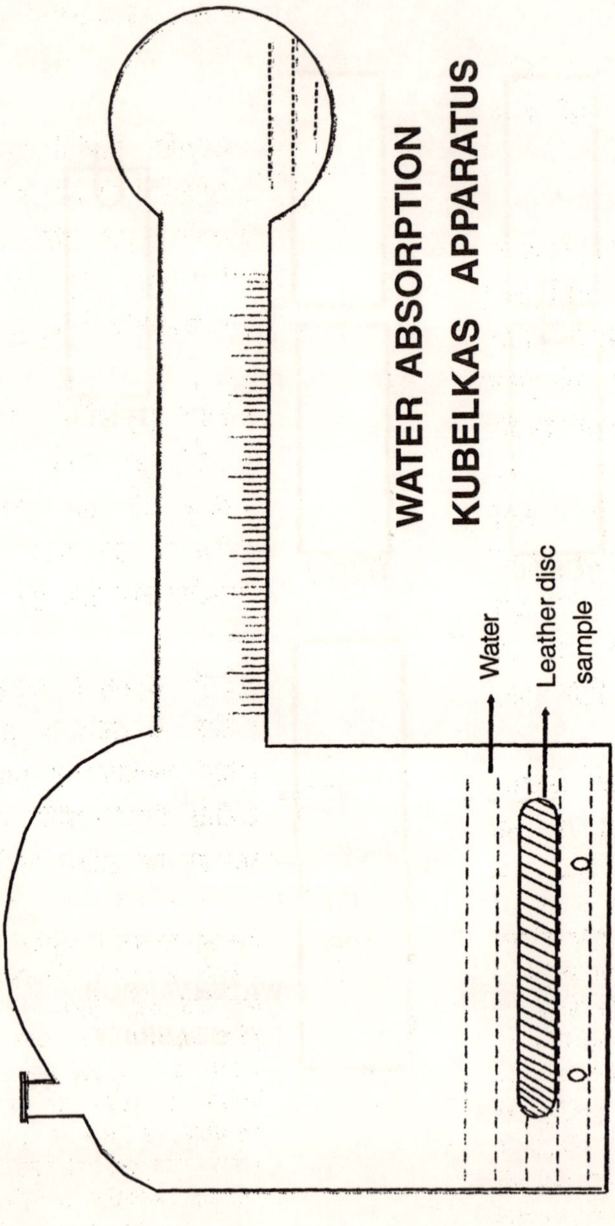

WATER ABSORPTION KUBELKAS APPARATUS

SUPPLIERS OF INDIGENOUS TESTING MACHINES

	MACHINES FOR
(1) **PROLIFIC ENGINEERS** **Office: (a)** 4787/23, Dariya Ganj New Delhi 110 002 **Works: (b)** D-91, Sector 2 Noida 201301 District Ghaziabad (U.P)	Tensile Strength Elongation Bursting Strength, Flexometer, Penetrometer Lastometer Water Proofness, Sole Adhesion, Shoe Flexing Static, Toe Cup-ImpactTester
(2) **P S I SALES (PVT.) LTD.** **Office:** 809, Hemkunt House 6 Rajendra Place New Delhi 110 008	Tensile Strength & Elongation Specimen Cutting Die (Dumbel Shape Sample) Thickness Gauge, Compressibility, Ross Flexometer, Shore Hardness, Lastometer, Colour Fastness, Water Penetrometer
(3) **SRI K RANGA RAMANUJAM** Project Promoters Old No.32/1, Melpadi Muthu - Naicken Street, Nungambakkam, Chennai 600 034	Shrinkage Temperature

PHYSICAL TESTING

EQUIPMENT/APPARATUS (IMPORTED)

(1) **Mr K R Ramakrishnan** **SPINCO** Special Instruments Consortium PO. Box No.2927, Block G-8 81, Luz Church Road, Mylapore, Chennai 600 004. *Telephone:* 044-499 3714 Fax : 044-4990479	Tensile Strength Elongation Monitoring Continuous Record

(2)	**INSTRON** Toshniwal Brothers Old No. 268, Kilpauk Garden Road Chennai 600 010.	(Instron) Tensile Strength Elongation Monitoring (Fully Computerised)

EQUIPMENT/APPARATUS (IMPORTED)

(3)	**MEGATECH** A 2/10, Dangre Park Post Box No. 17652 Chembur, Mumbai 400 074 Telephone: 555 7798 Fax: 91-22-556 4317	As above
(4)	**SATRA** Shoe and Allied Trades Association U.K.	Whole Range of Testing Machines And Guidelines For Accredition.
(5)	**ABRASION TESTER** (Catalogue No.9D 400)	Taber Instruments Corpn. North Tonawala, New York, U.S.A.
(6)	Apparatus for testing bursting strength and grain crackiness strength - Lastometer	Baird & Tatlock (London) 14/17 St. Cross St., London, England.
(7)	-do- Mullen	B.F. Perkins & Sons Inc. Holyoke, Massachusetts, U.S.A.
(8)	Apparatus for testing fastness to rubbing	Shoe and Allied Trades' Research Association, Satra House, Rocking Road, Kettering, Northampton, U.K.
(9)	Bally Flexometer	Bally CTU Bally Schuhfabriken AG, CH 5012, Schonewered, Swizerland
(10)	Bally Penetrometer	-do-
(11)	Bally Permeometer	-do-

	Equipment	Supplier
(12)	Bally Tensometer	-do-
(13)	Compressibility & Resilience Tester	Custom Scientific Inst Inc. 541, Devon St., Kearny New Jersey, U.S.A.
(14)	Kubelka apparatus	CLRI, Madras.
(15)	Shrinkage tester	-do-

EQUIPMENT/APPARATUS (IMPORTED)

	Equipment	Supplier
(16)	Stiffness Tester	Tinius Olsen Testing Co. Easton Road, Willow G1, U.S.
(17)	Tensile strength tester with automatic loadextension recorder (1000 kg)	M/s Kamal Metal Industry Arun Park, Bhaipura, Khokhara, Mahemdabad, Ahmedab - 8.
(18)	Thermotest apparatus	Set Aram 101-103, Rue de Seze 69, Lyon 6e, France
(19)	Water Vapour Permeability apparatus	H.W. Wallace & Co, LTD., St. James Road, Croydon, U.K.

MISCELLANEOUS

1. Adjustable Table Lamp
2. Balance (Sensitivity 10 mg)
3. Calculator - Electronic
4. Clicking Press
5. Dies for cutting test specimens
6. First Aid Box
7. Foot scale
8. Graph paper
9. Grey scale for assessing change in colour
10. -do- staining
11. Hand lens 10 cm. dia
12. Knives

13. Planimeter
14. Scissors
15. Stop Watch
16. Thickness gauge 0.1 mm
17. Tool box
18. Tracing paper
19. Vernier calipers
20. Wall clock
21. Weathering (A/C) unit for maintaining temp. and relative humidity as per test conditions.
22. Wool blue standard patterns
23. Working Table (180 x 75 x 75 cm) 4 Nos.

Chapter - 9

Manufacture of Exotic Leather From Ray Fish

Introduction

Fish skin has a characteristic appearance peculiar to each of the species. Some twenty species have so far been transformed into a viable leather material and then marketed as raw material for shoes and clothing. The skins of ray fish are easily available and cheaper to traditional skins. Moreover, these skins, which are normally wasted, could be used as desirable leather after processing. Method of processing is similar to that of processing conventional raw material, but one should take special care while processing, in order to maintain its uniqueness.

Ray Fish

Ray Fish also known as Sting Cray fish, commonly known as Thirukkai fish in Tamil by the local inhabitants, is available at Rayapuram area in Chennai. The denticles of the ray skins, known as bucklers are generally quite large and and deeply rooted with their basal plates in the connective tissues of the corium. The corium of all fish consists of collagen fiber whose water content is higher than those of the skins of reptiles and mammals as also in their amino acid composition. Owing to this different chemical composition, the unpreserved and untanned skin is very sensitive to temperature, acids and alkali with swelling effect, enzymes and severe Mechanical stress.

Process:

	Wet Salted
Raw material	: Ray fish skins
Quantity	: 8 pieces
Weight	: 5 kg
Thickness	: 1.8.4.0 mm

Process	*Chemicals used*	*Percentage*	*Duration*	*Remarks*
Soaking	Water	300%	2-3 Days	Weight based on wet
	Soap Oil	0.5%		salted weight.
	Preservative	0.25%		After soaking do green fleshing
Liming	Water	200%		Handle the skins
	Lime	8.0%		thrice a day for 3 days
	Sodium bi			if necessary add
	sulphite	2.0%		0.25% sodium
	Soda ash	0.2%		sulphide in order to
				improve the liming.
			2-3 Days	Check for plumping and then do fleshing and note the pelt weight
Deliming	Water Ammonium	70%		Check deliming with the help of phenolpthalein
	Sulphate	0.8%	20 min	indicator throughout
Bating	Alkaline enzyme	0.5%	30 min	cut section and then do bating. Check bating and wash well and do picking.
Pickling	Water	75%		Run the skin in the
	Salt	8%	10 min	liquor for min and then feed the acid Check the pH to 2.8.3.0
	Formic acid	0.5%	15 min	throughout the cross
	Sulphuric acid	1.0%		section and drain 50% Of the liquor
Chrome Tanning	Chrome powder	4.0%	30 min stable	Check the penetration of the chrome before
	Chrome stable fatliquor	0.5%	30 min	starting the basification

Process	Chemicals used	Percentage	Duration	Remarks
	Chrome powder	4.0%	30 min	
	Sodium Formate	1.0%	20 min	
	Water	100%	20 min	
	Basification	Masking and		Check pH to 3.8-4.0
	basifying agent	1.0%	30 min	Drain wash. Drain pile
	Sodium bi			for 48 hours and then
	carbonate	0.8%	30 min	do mechanical
			min	operation
	Preservative	0.2%	15 min	

*Final year B.Tech students, BIST, Chennai

**Sudhakar & Co., Chromepet, Chennai.

After basification the skins are piled for 48 hours and then they are sammed, set and then shaved to required thickness. Shaved weight is noted. Percentage is based on shaved weight.

Process	Chemicals	Percentage	Duration	Remarks
Acid wash	Water	300%	30 min.	Check wetback and
	Acetic acid	0.5%	15 min.	then drain wash drain
	Surfactant*	0.5%		
Rechroming	Water	100%		Check pH to 3.8-4.0
	Chrome powder	3.0%	15 min.	Drain wash drain pile overnight.
	Chrome	3.0%	30 min.	Next day do
				neutralization
	Chrome stable			
	fatliquor	1.0%	20 min.	
	Sodium			
	formate	1.0%	10 min.	
	Sodium Bi			
	Carbonate	0.5%	30 min.	
	Neutralization	Water	150%	Check the pH to 5.0 if
	Neutralization			necessary adjust

Process	*Chemicals*	*Percentage*	*Duration*	*Remarks*
	syntans	1.0%	20 min.	bicarbonate, Drain
	Sodium			wash drain
	formate	0.5%	10 min.	
	synthetic			
	fatliquor	2.0%	30 min.	
Retanning,	Water	100%		
dyeing and	Synthetic	1.0%		
fatliquoring	fatliquor			
	based on			
	natural			
	and			
	mineral oil			
	Synthetic			
	fatliquor	1.0%		
	Replacement		30 min	
	syntan	1.0%		
	Melamine			
	based			
	resin syntan	4.0%		
	Suitable dye			
	Synthetic fatliquor			
	Formic acid	4.0%	40 min.	
		4.0%	40 min.	Check penetration
		4.0%	40 min.	I
		3.0%	30 min.	Check exhaustion
				drain wash drain pile
				overnight

Next day sam set hook to dry condition stake trim toggle and then finish.

Finishing process	*Chemicals*	*Quantity*	*Spray coat*	*Remarks*
Base coat	Protein binder	100 parts	Spray 3-4	After drying
	(MS)		cross coats	do plain plating
	Protein binder Soft	100 parts	dry well	
	Polyurethane	100 parts		

process	*Chemicals*	*Quantity*	*Spray coat*	*Remarks*
Season coat	Protein binder (MS)	100 parts	Spray 2-3 cross cost dry well	First add dye sol. along with the protein
	Protein binder Soft	100 parts		binder and add water to this finally add polyurethane and wax emulsion.
	Polyurethane	100 parts		
	Dye solution	70 parts		
	Wax emulsion	20 parts		
	Water to make	1 litre		
Top Coat	Protein binder (MS)	100 parts		
	Protein binder Soft	100 parts		
	Water	100 parts		
	Wax emulsion	20 parts		
	Polyurethane	100 parts	Spray two cross coat dry well	Do plain plating

Physical testing results:

Testing	*Perpendicular* ·	*Parallel*	*Average*
Tensile strength (kg/sq.cm)	190	207	198.5
Percentage elongation	60	53	56.5
Stitch tear strength (kg/sq.cm)	85	90	87.5
Tongue tear strength (kg/sq.cm)	40	42	41
Grain crack (kg/sq.cm)	250	257	253.5

Chapter - 10

Formaldehyde Free Finishing Recipe For Glazed Kid Leather

Introduction

The production of eco-friendly leathers and eco-labelling has gained paramount importance today and the Indian tanners are being forced to look at new eco-friendly options for leather manufacture to meet to the current trend of eco-labelling which is prevailing globally. Limits on the concentration of free formaldehyde in leathers and formaldehyde vapours permissible in the work place have been established in many countries. Under this circumstance, the production of glaze kid, which is a novelty product and a unique product with traditional speciality of India, right from the yester years have to be modified in a way so as to come under eco-labelling, without the traditional heritage and the quality being impaired.

In the traditional receipt, the syntans and other products used were prone to contain formaldehyde, which is a suspected carcinoge. The permissible limit of formaldehyde, present has been defined by various institutions depending upon the limits set by the respective governments and health organisations of various countries.

Formaldehyde is all ubiquitous chemical and a thorough understanding of any health important hazards associated with its use is extremely important to the society. So the importance of formaldehyde free leather is of prime concern from the environmental point of view. Hence, a new recipe has got to be formulated, which will produce formaldehyde free glaze kid leather without impairing its original unique properties.

Detection of HCHO

The presence of formaldehyde may be detected in many ways. But the most accredited way which is followed is the method in which it is complexed with 2,4 Dinitrophenyl hydrazine after which it is passed through the **High Performance Liquid Chromatography (HPLC)** in which it is detected in the anode.

There are other complexing methods available, they are:

Acetyl Acetone Complexation

Chromatropic Acid Complexation

Dimedone Complexation

In the above complexations the analysis is being done in an alkaline pH which makes the quantification complexed and the accuracy may be a problem.

The 2,4 Dinitro Phenyl hydrazine complexation is best as this is being done in an acidic pH condition and the final leather is also in the same condition. Moreover, the accuracy of the experiment will be perfect in an acidic condition. This method of detection is being followed by the European Union and the Din. The results obtained by the HPLC method is more accurate.

Importance of Formaldehyde in Leather Manufacture

As in many cases the formaldehyde treated collagen behaves like leather, formaldehye by virtue of its property to react and harder protein is being used in the leather industry as tanning agent.

Formaldehyde is a strong polymerizing agent, and is used to polymerize phenolic compounds in the production of syntan, and in leather finishing, formaldehyde is used as a preservative and to coagulate the various binders used in finishing in order to increase the fastness property of the leathers. In finishing, formaldehyde topcoat is given, which will fix the protein and enhance the film formation.

Importance of Formaldehyde in Glaze Kid

In the traditional receipes of glaze kid, formaldehyde based syntans played a major role in the retaining system. Some of the syntans in which formaldehyde is used are discussed here.

Aromatic Syntans

These syntans are condensation products of phenolic compounds with formaldehyde. The properties imparted by these type of syntans on leather are softness, fine/firm grain pattern, heat resistance, fine break and level shade dyeing. Free formaldehyde has been detected and the amount depends upon the manufacturing process employed. Free formaldehyde present in these syntans is notably in a free form.

Few commercially available products were analyzed for free formaldehyde content following IUC (doc. no.): 9550207e-Photometric procedure for the determination of formaldehyde in leather, which involves the derivatization of formaldehyde with acetylacetone at 40°C and measuring the intensity of the diacetyl 1,4- lutidine developed at 412 mm. The results obtained were compared with HPLC method, which involved derivatization of formaldehyde with 2,4-di-nitro phenyl hydrazine followed by effected separation through C 18 column and monitoring at 350 mm. The results were consistent.

Free formaldehyde content of commercial aromatic resin syntans.

S.No.	Product	Free fromaldehyde ppm
1.	Phenol formaldehyde condensates	6000-8000
2.	Naphthalene formaldehyde condensates	12000-15000
3	Naphthalene, Phenol formaldehyde condensates	1500-3000

Formaldehyde free syntans

S. No.	Name of the product	Nature of the Product	Character imparted
1.	Polymeric tanning agents	The polymeric tanning agents consist of polymers of acrylic acid.	Good light fastness, softness, fullness and tight grain leathers.
2.	Protein based products	These are based on modified proteins.	Fullness, softness without causing looseness or reduction in tensile strength. Increase the elasticity of the grain.
3.	Resin tanning agents		Improves the fullness of the leather and tightens the bellies, enhances good buffing.

Free formaldehyde content of commercial resin tanning agents

S.No.	Product	Free formaldehy ppm
1.	Urea formaldehyde based product	16,000-18,000
2.	Aldehyde based syntans	10,000-15,000
3.	Melamine formaldehyde syntan	30,000-40,000
4.	Dicyandiamide formaldehyde syntan	85,000-1,35,000
5.	Carbamide formaldehyde precondensate product	80,000-85,000
6.	Heterocyclic-N-metholol compound	60,000-70,000
7.	Styrene maleic anhydride copolymer based product	0

Permissible Limits of Formaldehyde

Eco-Labelling Schemes and Formaldehyde Limits

Eco-labelling Scheme	Formaldehyde Limit (ppm)
Oeko-Tex Standard 100	20 (baby) - 75 (adult, skin contact)
SG (Schadstoff Gepruft)	50 (children wear) - 150 (adults wear)
Addidas A-01	13
R Griggs & Co. Ltd.	300
EU eco-label for footwear (1999/ 179/EC)	150 (adultwear) - 75 (childwear)
Audi	10
Mercedes	10
Din	100 (adultwear) - 50 (kidwear)

Introduction

The glace-kid, also called glazed-kid, is a highly glazed Fancy leather manufactured from special quality goat skin and is used for the manufacture of fancy ladies' and gents' shoes and also fancy leather goods. The gloss of glace- kid has some speciality and differs from the gloss of other types of upper leathers like box and willow sides, calf leather, corrected grain chrome retanned upper leathers, katais, etc. These latter leathers, when glazed after finishing, reflect light in the same way as is done by a big piece of mirror.

Properties of Glaze Kid Leathers

One of the major consumers of finished leather is the footwear industry where leather uppers still continue to enjoy a pride place. The glazed kid is a highly glazed kid fancy leather manufactured from special quality goat skin and is used for the manufacture of fancy ladies' and gents' shoes and also fancy leather goods. The gloss of glace- kid has some speciality and differs from the gloss of other types of upper leathers like box and willow sides, etc. These latter leathers, when glazed after finishing reflect light in the same way as is done by a big piece mirror.

Properties of Glaze kid Leathers

One of the major consumers of finished leather is the footwear industry where leather uppers still continue to enjoy a pride place. The glazed kid is a highly glazed kid fancy leather manufactured from special quality goat skin and is used for the manufacture of fancy ladies and gents shoes and also fancy leather goods. The gloss of glazed kid after glazing should reflect light in the same way as is done by a big piece of mirror. But on the other hand if we look to the surface of a glaze-kid through a microscope against reflected light, it will appear like the night sky of winter - a cloudless with millions of shining stars in it. This indicates that the glaze-kid surface. Other imporant properties of glazed kids are:

Glaze-kid should be made practically non-stretchy and only that much stretchiness is allowed which is absolutely necessary for wearing comfort. It should have some degree of roundness when folded with grainside out.

3. Tensile strength - sufficient to withstand stitch, flexing and wear.
4. Water resistance generally, the higher the resistance the better. However, higher water resistance should not materially affect air and water vapour permeability.
5. Abrasion resistance - sufficient to resist scuff in wear.
6. Good air and water vapour permeability.
7. Among the other desired attributes are included lightness in weight, foot comfort, resistance to cracking, peeling, shining or ceiling.

Physical requirements of Glazed Kid Leather Indian Standards (Minimum)

1.	Tensile strength kg/cm^2	–	250
2.	Elongation at Break	–	40-65%
3.	Tongue tear resistance kg/cm	–	30

4.	Stitch tear resistance kg/cm	–	100
5.	Flexular endurance	–	75000 flexes without crankiness of grain
6.	Dry rub fastness	–	32 revolutions
7.	Wet rub fastness	–	4 revolutions

Chemical Requirements of Glazed Kid Leather – Indian Standards

1.	% Solvent extractable substance	–	2.5-7.5
2.	Chromium content (as Cr_2O_3)%	–	3.0
3.	Water soluble matter	–	5.0
4.	Hide substance	–	65
5.	pH of water soluble	–	3.5
6.	Differential number	–	Shall not exceed 0.7
7.	Bound organic matter	–	9.0

Finishing Recipe for Formaldehyde Free Glaze Kid Leather Clear Coat

Clear Coat

IPA	–	100 gms
Water	–	900 gms Spray one coat

Stain Coat

Cationic casein binder	–	100 gms
Cationic polishable PU binder	–	50 gms
Cationic dye solution	–	75 gms spray one coat
Water to make one ltr.	–	Stone polish

Season Coat

Medium soft protein binder	–	100 gms
Hard protein binder	–	75 gms
Polishable PU binder	–	50 gms
Anionic dye solution	–	100 gms
Pigment	–	20 gms
Filler		10 gms
Wax	–	15 gms

IPA	–	40 gms Spray 3 to 4 coats slightly snuff with 900 grit paper.

spray 3 to 4 coats

Tinted Top

Medium Hard Protein binder	–	100 gms
Medium Soft protein binder	–	50 gms
Polishable PU binder	–	75 gms
Dye solution	–	100 gms Spray 2 coats

Fixing

Formaldehyde free fixing agent	–	1 part
Acetic acid	–	50 gms
Water	–	1 part Spray 2 coats

Final glaze, iron, mollisa stake and contilux at $100^{\circ}C$ and 120 kg/cm^2 pressure.

Conclusion

The various properties of formaldehyde its toxicity, properties, contribution of formaldehyde in leather industry, the permissible limits, have been discussed. The properties of glaze kid leathers, its requirement have also been discussed. The relevance of formaldehyde free glaze kid leathers has also been discussed.

Hence, by developing a new recipe, which is formaldehyde-free, the eliminated. Hence a 100% formaldehyde free glaze kid could be manufactured without the quality being impaired to a great level.

The phenol-formaldehyde condensate products were replaced by protein syntan, styrene maleic copolymer based syntan and veg. tanning agents.

With respect to protein fixing new agents developed were used which were free of the hazards of formaldehyde but also has the same effect of formaldehyde with respect to coagulating property.

By following the formaldehyde free recipe the tanners can have a Cutting edge over the other competitors and at the same time, the eco-criteria is also fulfilled.

Chapter - 11
Canvas Shoes

Introduction

Canvas shoes are extensively used by Armed Forces, Police, Home Guard and NCC etc. and are also used by civilians for casual wear and sports. These shoes are gaining popularity among students and children. As the name indicates the shoes are made with upper of canvas and with rubber sole by vulcanization process. The increasing popularity of canvas shoes for general use is due to its cheap cost and comfort in use. Student also use them for physical training and other sports and games.

Process of Manufacture

The process is divided in four departments viz :

1. Rubber Mixing Section.
2. Canvas upper Checking and sewing Section.
3. Assembly Section.
4. Finishing and packing section.

1. In rubber mixing section, rubber mixture for sole is mixed, taking 100 parts rubber, 50 parts filler, 4 to 5 parts sulpher, ½ part of organic accelerators and 3 to 4 parts pine oil. The fixing gum contains 15% more raw rubber and 3 to 5% resin. This cement is also prepared by mixing this mixture in mixing well thoroughly and then pacing it in a chamber which has a tank fitted with electrically operated paddle. Naptha is added to the mixture where the mixture is churned out for calendaring the cloth for making rubberized cloth for tongue thick inlose and for applying this binder for lasting. Thick cement is used for tongue and then for sole. Neptha is added accordingly for outer sole, rubber is spread and soles are checked.

2. The various components of canvas uppers are cut stitched, eyelets are fixed on upper by machine. The innersole is placed lasts and the upper pressed with hand roller and the bottom is pasted.

3. Cement is applied on bottom of shoes and sole is placed on it and pressed with roller. Noak is pasted on toe. For cement fixing a string of proper length is taken in extender and is pasted all around the edge of shoes. Pressure is applied through metal roller. The pasted shoes are placed on metal lears of metal framed trollies for vulcanizing. The vulcaniser is a horizontal circular shaped shell boiler with steam coils. Air pressure is used for compacting the rubber and to shorted the vulcanizing time. The trollies with the lasted shoes are pushed into the vulcaniser. The vulcaniser is closed and air pressure is applied. There must be sufficient steam in the coils to let up to 275 F. Afer the vulcanization is complete the goods are taken out. The time is 5 to 15 minutes depending upon the accelerator used.

4. After cooling the shoes are stripped from lasts inspected for defects, laced and packed.

PROCESS FLOW CHART

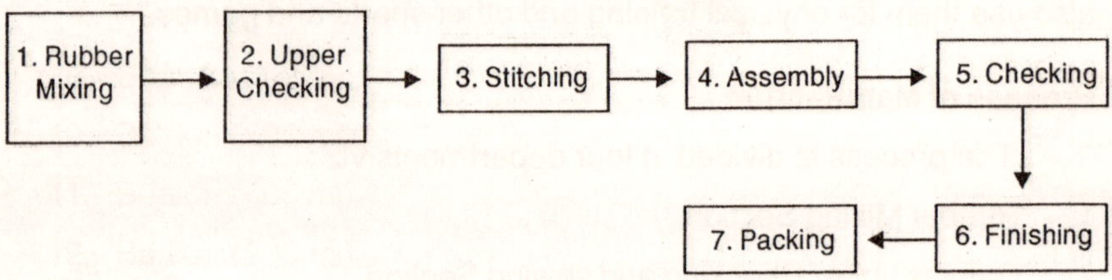

COST ESTIMATIONS

Machinery And Equipments

Production Unit

Name of machine with specification

1. Mixing mill 14" x 36" with chilled cast rolls with reducing gear 50 HP motor
2. Rubber spreading m/c 12"x 30" with HP motor
3. Vulcaniser 9' x 5'
4. Boiler 10 NHP (Baby)
5. Embossing machine
6. Chunner with 1 HP motor

7. Eyeleting m/c.
8. Clicking press 5 tonne power operated with 5 HP motor
9. Sewing machine industrial power operated with ¼ HP motor
10. Aluminium and Iron Shoe lasts
11. Extruder for fixing
12. Moulds and dies for upper and bottom clicking
13. Trollies
14. Office equipments
15. Printing and making m/c. power operated with 2 HP motor
16. Storing tank for naptha etc.
17. Calendering m/c. for cloth 8" x 24" with 20 HP motor
18. Miscellaneous equipments
19. Installation and electrification @10%

Raw Material (per month)

1. Canvas
2. Lining
3. Rubber sole/insole
4. Rubber Patti
5. Rubber sheet for toe
6. Tape Cotton
7. Insole calender cloth
8. Counter for rubberized cloth
9. Laces
10. Packing
11. Other grinderies

CAPITAL INVESTMENT

1. FIXED CAPITAL	Rs.	17,22,900.00
2. WORKING CAPITAL FOR 3 MONTHS	Rs.	16,04,925.00
TOTAL	**Rs.**	**33,27,825.00**

TURNOVER (PER ANNUM)

BY SALE OF 1,20,000 PAIRS OF CANVAS SHOES RS. 84 LACS.

NET PROFIT RATIO = 15.26%

RATE OF RETURN = OPRATING PROFIT/NET PROFIT X 100 = 38%

BREAK EVEN POINT (B.E.P) = 59.21%

Chapter-12

Shoe Upper Leather

Introduction

Eco- Friendly shoe upper Leather is generally manufactured from raw-hides and skins by using eco- friendly chamicals and by reducing polluting materials during its manufacturing process. Footwear made out of eco-friendly upper leather are exported to different countries to fulfil the demand of local market as well as the demand of local market. Apart from footwear this leather is also used for the manufacturing of sports goods items such as sports shoes, travelling kits etc. which are also exported to different countries. Products made out of eco- friendly leather are evergreen and there is good demand for these items by every category of the people.

Process of Manufacture

Raw-materials: wet salted cow hides lower quality ave.

Wt. = 15 kg. each.

De-Salting : Remove the salt by mechanical method to Reduce the pollution.

Soaking : The hides are soaked in pits containing 1 to 2% lime 100% water.

Soaked well washed and soaked wt. is noted.

Liming : Paddle liming

Water : 200%

Clarizyme : 0.5%

Sodium sulphide : 2%

On soaked wt.

Time 18 to 20 hours.

Unhairing, fleshing and fleshed wt. is to be noted.

Deliming : Drum Process) - 1st wash with water

Water : 100% Run 30 to 45 minutes.

Ammonium sulphate: 1% to 1.5%

and check pH.

Drain and wash well

Pickling: Water 50 to 100%

Salt 5% Run for 20 minutes

Add : Sulphuric acid = 1% (Dilute with10% water)

Formic Acid =25% (on Acide wt.)

Run for 1 hr. and get the cross section pH equal to solution of drum. Left over night. Run for 30 minutes and check pH = 2.8 to 3.0

Drain 50% of pickle bath and add.

Chrome powder = 4%

Run for 1 hr. and add.

Chrome powder = 4%

Run for 1 hr. check penetration, add water 100% and basified with sodium formate

Or

Ammonium bicarb = 0.5%

sodium bi-carbonate = 1%

Feed in 4 to 6 feed after de-solving in water.

Run for 1 hr. check pH = 3.8 to 4

Drain the chrome bath and collect it for chrome recovery.

Preserve the pelt in separate bath with sutaible eco- friendly preservative, pile the stock for 1 to 2 days. Then samming and conditioning splitting shaving operation is done and shaved wet is noted.

Wet back with working the hides with 200% water and pile for over night.

Rechroming:

Water = 50%

Basic chrome powder = 4%

Run for 1 hr. add water = 50%

Run for 30 minutes

Add : Sodi-bi-carb. 1%

Sodi- formate = .5%

Run for 1 hr., check

pH 3-8 to 4 pile O/N

Neutralisation :

Water = 100%

Sodi-formate = 1% Run for 30 minutes to

Vernaten EKM 2% 45 minutes check

pH- 4.8 to 5.8

Drain, Wash well

Dyeing and Fat Liquoring and Retanning :

Hot water =10%

Suitable dye = ½% to 1%

Run for 30 minutes and

Add :

Suitable fat liquor = 4 to 6%

Run for 1 hr. and add

Retanning syntan = 3% and run for 30 minutes

Fixed with formic acid = 0.25%

Run for 15 minutes check and drain.

Wash the pelt in hot water and pile for over night.

Next day sammed, setting and drying operation is done. Then the goods are ready for finishing. The goods are finished as per requirement by using pigments and binder and finally top coat with lacquer is applied to prevent the bleeding of colour. The leather is then assorted, measured and packed for despatch.

Machinery and Equipments

1. Wooden paddle with motor starter etc. ((compete in all respect) size 8′ × 7′ with 10 HP motor 1000 RPM.
2. Tanning drum 8′ × 6′ with 10 HP motor and starter (Complete in all respect)
3. Fleshing machine 1800mm working width with 20 HP motor and starter.
4. Experiment drum 3′ × 3′ with 5 HP motor and starter.
5. Shaving machine single width 7.5 HP motor and starter.
6. Dyeing and fat liquiring drum size : 8′ × 6′ with 10 HP motor and starter.
7. Reverseable type setting machine 1800mm working with 15 HP motor and starter.
8. Through feed buffing machine 1800mm working width with 15 HP motor and starter.
9. Toggle chamber with 10 Plate toggle drier unit (Complete unit).
10. Slow comb staking M/c. with 75 HP motor.
11. Spray chamber with one compressor and two spray systems with exhaust system (complete in all respect)
12. Electronic area measuring machine 1800mm working width with motor (Complete).
13. Weighing scale working table and other hand tools, Lab Equipment and Misc. Items etc.
14. Cost of pollution control system.
15. Cost of tube well, OHD, Water Supply system, Oil fired baby Boiler etc.
16. Diesel generator set 50KVA with standard accessories etc.
17. Cost of transformer and other electrical accessories and other legal expenses etc.
18. Electrification and installation charges. @ 10% on Rs. 32,50,000
19. Cost of furniture and office equipment.

Raw Materials

1. Wet salted cow hides (Lower quality) Ave. of wt. 15 kg. each.
2. Chemicals from soaking to finishing including service charges for spliting and processing and other charges outside etc.

Cost Estimations

FIXED CAPITAL

1. LAND & BUILDING		
(AREA 2000 SQ.MT.)	Rs.	20,00,000.00
2. PLANT & MACHINERY	Rs.	40,00,000.00
TOTAL	**Rs.**	**60,00,000.00**

TOTAL WORKING CAPITAL(PER MONTH)

1. RAW MATERIAL	Rs.	32,50,000.00
2. SALARY & WAGES	Rs.	1,46,400,00
3. UTILITIES & OVERHEADS	Rs.	70,000,00
TOTAL	**Rs.**	**34,66,400,00**

TOTAL CAPITAL INVESTMENT

FIXED CAPITAL	Rs.	60,00,000.00
WORKING CAPITAL FOR 3 MONTHS	Rs.	1,03,99,200.00
TOTAL	**Rs.**	**1,63,99,200.00**

TURN OVER/ANNUM

BY SALE OF FINISHED LEATHER AS PER GRADE I, II, III & IV AND NATURAL SPLIT LEATHER 60%

NET PROFIT RATIO = 11.72%

RATE OF RETURN = OPERATING PROFIT / T.C.I X 100 = 36%

BREAK EVEN POINT (B.E.P) = 40%

Chapter - 13
PVC Footwear

Introduction

Full PVC footwear such as chappal, Sandals and Shoes are popular in Indian Market due to their cheap prices, durability and easy maintenance and affordability by a common man. Used PVC footwear containing basic raw-material i.e PVC can again be used for making cheaper types of footwear. The plant and machinery and raw materials are available indigenously. The PVC Footwears are generally light weight and very comfortable to wear in rainy seasons.

Process of Manufacture

As per the design of the sample, PVC Footwear to be manufactured, the moulds are obtained and fitted in the machine. Then the PVC compound is fed according to requirement into a heated cylinder from sopper either in strip, granular of powder form. Ceramular form is more common. The injection Cycle starts with closing and locking of the moulds under pressure either applied by hand or mechanical levers of automatically by hydraulic or pneumatic power. When PVC in the cylinder is sufficiently softened by heat, the same forced forward by ram or screw action through an intermediate channel known as 'SPRUE' into the mould untill it has cooled down to a state of sufficient rigidity and the pressure in the mould relaxed. The time cycle, therefore, can be adjusted into several stages, namely, mould filling time, dwell time under pressure, cooling time usully is the longest of all and has to be cut especially in small machine and the same has been recommended in the project.

PVC compounds are available as natural/transparent granules. Prior to use, colour concentrate granules known as master batches are mixed with the proportitonto give the desired colour. Initial mixing can be done in any convenient container units, a scoop or small showel. The final mixing is automatically achieved in the cylider of the moulding machine.

The PVC compound, suitably mixed with the master batch is fed into the sopper of the machine. Normally 10 to 12 kg. PVC compound are fed at a time. Shore hardness of 70 to 78 for PVC granules temperature of 160°C and pressure of 80 lbs/ square inch gives satisfactory results.

The main operations are :

1. Feeding of PVC granules into the sopper
2. Trimming of surplus materials
3. Cleaning and spraying (if required)
4. Fixing of fittings
5. Checking and packing.

Quality Control And Standards

Following specifications are followed to customer's requirements :

(1) PVC Sandals IS 2167 : 1972

(2) Polyvinyl Chloride Resins Method of text IS 4669 : 1968.

Production Capacity

Quantity : 75,000 pair

Value : Rs. 41,25,000.

COST ESTIMATIONS

FIXED CAPITAL

1. LAND & BUILDING		Rs.	6,000.00
2. PLANT & MACHINERY		Rs.	11,40,000.00
	TOTAL	**Rs.**	**11,46,000.00**

Machinery and Equipments

1. Six Station PVC Injection Moulding Machine fully automatic Rotary.
2. Moulds 4 Sets each consists of four sizes sandal and shoes.
3. Tools and Equipments/Jigs and Fixtures.
4. Office Equipments, Working Table, Racks, Trollies, Stools etc.

Raw Materials

1. PVC Granules
2. Master Batch (Colour)
3. Fittings, Buckles, Button and Lacer etc.
4. Packing Materials

WORKING CAPITAL (PER MONTH)

1. PERSONNEL	Rs.	42,500.00
2. RAW MATERIAL	Rs.	1,74,500.00
3. UTILITIES	Rs.	4,000.00
4. OTHER EXP	Rs.	20,000,00
TOTAL	**Rs.**	**2,41,000,00**

TOTAL CAPITAL INVESTMENT

1. FIXED COST	Rs.	12,00,000.00
2. WORKING CAPITAL FOR 3 MONTHS	Rs.	7,23,000.00
TOTAL	**Rs.**	**19,23,000.00**

TURNOVER (PER ANNUM)

BY SALE OF PVC SHOES AND SANDALS 75000 PAIRS = RS. 41,25,000,00

NET PROFIT RATIO = PROFIT / SALES X 100 = 17%

RATE OF RETURN = OPERATING PROFIT / NET PROFIT X 100 = 38%

BREAK EVEN POINT (B.E.P) = 53 %

Chapter - 14
Industrial Hand Gloves

Introduction

Industrial hand gloves serve as an item of protective apparel for workers in factories. Hand gloves are of various types and sizes. Fast moving sizes are 14", 16", 18", etc. The materials that go in the production of hand gloves vary from cotton fabrics and asbestos to variety of leathers. Leather, however since supreme in the production of industrial hand gloves. Amongst leather chrome tanned split leather is predominantly in use possibly because of its cheap price and peculiar qualities needed for hand gloves as compared to other kind of leather. Chrome tanned split leather impacts special qualities to withstand roughness of the handling material and gives enough flexibility and softness for the hand to move in the gloves easily and swiftly while working in the workshop. Such industrial gloves are widely used in industry, Railway and Defence. Due to rapid industrialization and expansion of railway the use of industrial hand gloves is expected to grow considerably.

Process of Manufacture

The leather is checked for uniform thickness, holes and flying cuts, if any. It is then marked with the pattern and then cut with the help of scissors or clicking knife into different components. After stitching all the components. suitably, the gloves are turned inside out. The gloves are then ready for packing and despatch.

Production Capacity

(a)	Industrial hand gloves	:	75,000 pairs (per annum)

COST ESTIMATIONS

FIXED CAPITAL

1. LAND & BUILDING	Rs.	3,000.00
2. PLANT & MACHINERY	Rs.	90,500.00
3. OTHER FIXED ASSETS	Rs.	90,500.00
TOTAL	**Rs.**	**1,84,000.00**

Machinery and Equipments

1. Flat bed single needle industrial sewing machine power operated 1/2 HP motor
2. Cylinder bed single needle industrial sewing machine power operated 1/2 HP motor
3. Tools and fixtures
4. Office furniture and workshop furniture
5. Electrification and Installation of machinery

Raw Materials Including Packing Requirements

1. Chrome tanned split leather (3.5 Pairs Per Kg.)
2. Thread
3. Cartons for packing (Carton pack for 100 pairs)

TOTAL WORKING CAPITAL (PER MONTH)

1. RAW MATERIALS	Rs.	67,525.00
2. STAFF AND LABOUR	Rs.	38,500.00
3. UTILITIES	Rs.	1,500.00
4. OTHER CONTINGENT EXPENSES	RS.	6,400.00
TOTAL	**Rs.**	**1,13,925.00**

TOTAL CAPITAL INVESTMENT

1. FIXED CAPITAL	Rs.	90,500.00
2. WORKING CAPITAL FOR 3 MONTHS	Rs.	3,41,800.00
TOTAL	**Rs.**	**4,32,300.00**

TURNOVER (PER ANNUM)

BY SALE OF 75,000 PAIRS OF INDUSTRIAL HAND GLOVES = RS. 15,75,000.00

NET PROFIT RATIO = PROFIT / SALES X 100 = 8.3%

RATEOF RETURN = OPERATING PROFIT / NET PROFIT X 100 = 30.3%

BREAK EVEN POINT (B.E.P) = 77 %

Chapter - 15
Leather Chappals

Introduction

Since time immemorial man has been using footwear of different kinds to protect feet from the extremities of weather and external injuries. In addition to functional utility chappal has also become an item of fashion and also forms a part of dress. Today chappals are used by simple villagers, farmers, farmers, common people of urban areas and also by the rich people. To cope with the requirement of different users chappals are made of different type of materials.

Process of Manufacture

As per the graded patterns of various sizes of both upper and bottom, the components are cut. The edges of cut components are skived and stitching operation, decorative treatment on the upper such as punching, fixing of buttons, metal fittings etc. is done either by hand or machine. The straps of the upper are inserted in the slots of the insoles. The inserted portion of the flesh side of the insloe are roughened and cemented. Finally the flesh sides of both the insole and bottom sole are roughened and the adhesive is applied. The cemented soles and insole are stuck and pressed in Cementing press to make the bond permanent.

The next operation is finishing in which the edges of sole and heel are trimmed, inked and set on the machine or by hand. The upper is cleaned and dressed before packing into boxes.

Machinery and Equipments

1. Strap Cutting Machine 300 mm hand operated
2. Upper Sewing machine Power operated
3. Sole Cementing press, 4 Power operated
4. Double ended buffing machine with exhaust motor
5. Trade mark embossing machine with heating device
6. Electrification and installation of machine

7. Wooden Cast
8. Tools and Equipments
9. Office equipments and furniture

Raw Materials

1. Upper leather @ 1.5 Sq.ft./pair
2. Lining Leather @ Sq.ft./pair
3. Insole
4. Sole and heels (Rubber)
5. Grinderies
6. Packing materials

COST ESTIMATION

FIXED CAPITAL

Land and Building

2000 Sq. Ft. Area Rented

@ Rs. 4,000.00 Per Month

TOTAL RECURRING EXPENDITURE (PER MONTH)

1. RAW MATERIALS	Rs.	2,70,000.00
2. STAFF AND LABOUR	Rs.	87,600.00
3. UTILITIES	Rs.	4,000.00
4. OOTHER CONTINGENT EXPENSES	RS.	25.000
TOTAL	**RS.**	**3,86,600.00**

TOTAL CAPITAL INVESTMENT

1. FIXED CAPITAL	Rs.	1,90,000.00
2. WORKING CAPITAL	Rs.	11,59,800.00
TOTAL	**Rs.**	**13,49,800.00**

TURNOVER (PER ANNUM)

BY SALE OF 30,000 PAIRS LEATHER CHAPPALS = RS. 52,50,000,00

NET PROFIT RATIO = PROFIT / SALES X 100 = 7.28%

RATEOF RETURN = OPERATING PROFIT / NET PROFIT X 100 = 28.31%

BREAK EVEN POINT (B.E.P) = 68.12 %

Chapter - 16
Leather Garments

Introduction

Leather Garments are one of the sophisticated products of finished leather. Leather Garments consist of articles of leather apparel and other cloth accessories as per ITC Classification which would include more specifically Gents leather Jackets, Long Coats, Waist/Shorts, Leather Pants/ Shorts (Gents), Waist Coats/Shirts, Pant/Shorts and Children Garments. These are used only in cold places and usually garments made for autumn – winter are made of some what heavy leather from hides with thick lining of either wool or artificial fur. Demand for Goat suede and light sheep nappa is generally high for European markets in spring summer while that for cow hides and somewhat heavy sheet skin is high for the autumn-winter in Europe and the U.S.A.

Process of Manufacture

The manufacturing process in the industry does not involve much complicated techniques. Leather garment industry is normally based on strict specification of buyer and country to which items are exported. Due care has to be taken in the manufacturing garments as follows:

(i) The component of the article is to cut from the materials as per specification or keeping in view the quality. This comprises a complete list of properly evaluated materials both leather and auxiliaries, components in addition to correct pattern for cutting leather, lining etc.

(ii) The design evaluation may be conducted in a small batch or trial production to find out the production difficulties so that these can be sorted out and timely corrected.

(iii) The items should be manufactured as per strict design and specification of the buyer or standards.

(iv) Component Specification: This consists of details of materials plus dimensional stability or tolerance so that the component will fit up or stand satisfactorily.

(v) Process and Production Control: This is an area where control could be actually implemented. As for materials, leather lining and auxiliaries should be tested for tear, stich tear and tensile strength. Fastness of colours of leather has to be tested repeatedly.

Threads: One of the most important requirement in thread is a level of properly balanced twist, particularly in Garment Industry, stiching plays a vital role and synthetic thread is much stronger than cotton and does not absorb moisture so readily.

Glue and Cements: Adhesive plays a dominant role in the fabrication of leather joints and testing of emblem. Invariably, the closing of joints is first secured by adhesives and later by means of stiching.

Grindery and Hardware: These are known as metal grindery or hardware and some of the embellishments and fittings are also grouped in this category.

Zip Fastener: In Garment Industry Zip Fastener plays a key role and oftenly tear and wear related complaint come from buyers. So the imported fastener may be used duly tested by repeated closing and opening method. Finally in the assembling section, which is mainly concerned with the workmanship is carried out at each stage. The final inspection takes place before the goods are packed and sent for stores.

Embellishment: Due care should be taken while doing this job, a small negligence will damage the whole product.

Quality Control and Standards

No particular specification of this product is available. The specifications in the export market mainly relate to the quality of leather i.e. colour fastness, softness and resistance to moisture and cold. Other specification like pattern, design would be as per the requirements of the buyer. However, the following specification for accessories has been given below which are as per BIS.

Standards Related to Leather Garments Industry and Related Items

Elastic Tapes	IS 9686
Metal Buckles	IS 96986:1980
Threads	IS 1376/1803
Leather Garment Sizing System	IS 10397

Care of Leather	NIL
Garments Metalic Slide Fastner	IS 3148:1983
Guide Leather For Garments	IS 12718
Fur Leather	IS 3840/2961
Fusible Lining	IS 12806
Zip Fasteners	IS 8894/3184/4829

Production Capacity

It is proposed to manufacture 60,000 pieces of Leather Garments for Men, Women and Children valued at Rs. 15,00,00,000.

Quantity : 60,000 pieces

Machinery and Equipments

1. Flat bed, lock stitch sewing Machine.
2. Flat bed two thread, double needle lock stitch sewing machine.
3. Zig-Zag stitch sewing machine.
4. Cylinder bed lock stitch sewing machine.
5. High speed single thread lock stitch sewing machine.
6. Strape cutting machine.
7. Post bed lock stitch sewing machine.
8. High speed single thread chain stitch sewing machine.
9. Button stitching sewing single thread.
10. Hem turning machine clicking press.
11. Skiving machine.
12. Cliking press.
13. Tools and equipments.
14. Office and workshop furniture.
15. Electrification and installation of machinery.

Raw Material

1. Nappa Leather, Suede Leather, Cow Softy Leather, Cow/Sheep/ Goat 1st grade Leather.

2. Lining, Non Woven/Woven fusible, Interlining, Ribcloth, Satin, Jacqards, polyester, staple yarns.
3. Zip, Buttons, Threads, Adhesive, Embellishments and Other Accessories.
4. Packing Materials.

COST ESTIMATION

FIXED CAPITAL

1. LAND & BUILDING	Rs.	16,00,000.00
2. PLANT & MACHINERY	Rs.	14,63,000.00
TOTAL	**Rs.**	**30,63,000.00**

WORKING CAPITAL (PER MONTH)

1. RAW MATERIAL	Rs.	85,75,000.00
2. SALARY & WAGES	Rs.	97,750.00
3. UTILITIES & OVERHEADS	Rs.	22,000.00
4. OTHER	RS.	18,000.00
TOTAL	**Rs.**	**87,12,750.00**

TOTAL CAPITAL INVESTMENT

FIXED CAPITAL	Rs.	30,63,000.00
WORKING CAPITAL FOR 3 MONTHS	Rs.	2,61,38,250.00
TOTAL	**Rs.**	**2,92,01,250.00**

TURN OVER/ANNUM

BY SALE OF LEATHER COATS MEN/WOMEN, JACKETS, SHIRTS, BLOUSES AND TROUSERS, LEATHER SHORTS, SKIRTS AND CHILDREN GARMENTS 60000 NOS/YEAR = RS. 11.95 CR.

PROFIT SALES RATIO = PROFIT / SALES X 100 = 8.6%

RATE OF RETURN = OPERATING PROFIT / T.C.I X 100 = 35.3%

BREAK EVEN POINT (B.E.P) = 33.8%

Chapter - 17

Leather Sandal With P.U. Sole

Introduction

Leather Sandals and Chappals in different designs and forms are made of leather which is a natural protective material for the foot. The purpose of using sandals is mainly to protect the feet from injury, thorn, insects, heat and cold. With the rapid increase of population and civilization more and more people are using footwear. It may be either chappal or sandal or shoe.

The term footwear covers mainly:

(i) Chappal

(ii) Sandal

(iii) Shoe and

(iv) Boot

The project profile deals with sandals with top made of upper leather and the bottom made of PU sole, which are available in the market readily. PU sole, being more durable, will eliminate a number of operations.

Process of Manufacture

The upper components i.e. leather straps, split lining leather for outside straps and inside straps are cut. The straps are skived wherever necessary and pasted with latex or rubber solution. The front straps, which are having self-lining, are folded and stitched. The outside and inside straps are pasted and nicked at the deep carved portion to facilitate folding. The split linings are pasted and attached with the outside and inside straps. The buckle holder pieces are also cut and buckles are fixed. The buckle holder piece, which is carrying the buckle, is fixed on the outside by rivets. The ends of the straps and lining, and inside strap and lining. The upper is secured by stitching.

The bottom surface of synthetic insoles (PVC) is buffed lightly. These are temporarily fixed under the bottom of the sandal last. The uppers are fitted on the last and lasted under the insole by pasting. Adhesive is applied under the buffed surface of the PVC insole and lasted upper. Mock welts (4 to 5 mm width) are attached on the PU soles all round the edges.

The top surface of PU soles treated by primer and then halogenated by chemical. Slight heat treatment is given on PU. The top surface of PVC insoles are buffed lightly and adhesive (SR-NL) is applied and slight heat treatment is given. After proper drying, both the surfaces are stuck together by cementing press. The upper complete with sole is removed from the last. The sandals are cleaned, polished and packed.

Quality Control and Standards

Quality and specifications are as per buyer's specification and for export, certain quality and specifications are maintained, but for local market, no strict quality standards are followed.

IS 578:1971 and IS 3890:1966 can be seen for chrome tanned upper leather and lining leather respectively.

The upper leather should be uniform in thickness and colour and should have water fastness property. Very good quality adhesive and chemicals are to be applied for fixing sole and insole. Proper care should be taken while doing final inspection before packing.

Production Capacity (per annum)

Quantity	:	36,000 pairs
Value	:	Rs. 1,08,00,000

Motive Control Power 3 HP.

Pollution Control

There is hardly any pollution except a little noise pollution on account of running of the machine.

Energy Conservation

Normally it is not required.

Machinery and Equipments

1. Flat bed single-needle stitching machine, power operated with 0.33 H.P. Motor.
2. Strap cutting machine, power operated with 0.5 H.P. Motor

3. Upper leather skiving machine complete with table, stand with 0.5 H.P. motor.
4. Hand operated strap folding machine.
5. Buffing and roughening machine with 0.5 H.P. motor.
6. Polishing Machine with 0.25 H.P. motor.
7. Sole cementing press-4 bed operated with Air compressor 1 H.P. motor.
8. Trademark embossing machine hand operated.
9. Wooden sandal last.
10. Tools, equipment etc.
11. Office equipment, furniture etc.
12. Electrification and Installation Charges.

Raw Materials

1. Chrome upper leather lower quality.
2. Split lining leather (approx. 1/2 sq. ft. to be used for buckle strap and side strap only)
3. PVC readymade insole.
4. P.U. Sole.
5. Grinderies like Mock welt, Adhesive Thread, Buckle etc.
6. Packing.

COST ESTIMATION

FIXED CAPITAL

1. LAND & BUILDING (RENTED)		
2. PLANT & MACHINERY	Rs.	2,61,000.00
3. OTHER FIXED ASSETS	Rs.	29,000.00
TOTAL	**Rs.**	**2,90,000.00**

WORKING CAPITAL (PER MONTH)

1. RAW MATERIAL	Rs.	6,60,000.00
2. SALARY & WAGES	Rs.	1,03,200.00
3. UTILITIES & OVERHEADS	Rs.	35,000.00
TOTAL	**Rs.**	**7,98,200.00**

CAPITAL INVESTMENT

FIXED CAPITAL	Rs.	2,90,000.00
WORKING CAPITAL FOR 3 MONTHS	Rs.	23,94,600.00
TOTAL	**Rs.**	**26,84,600.00**

TURN OVER/ANNUM

BY SALE OF 36,000 PAIRS OF GENTS SANDALS WITH P.U. SOLE = RS. 1,08,00,000,00

PROFIT SALES RATIO = PROFIT / SALES X 100 = 7.25%

RATE OF RETURN = OPERATING PROFIT / T.C.I X 100 = 29.2%

BREAK EVEN POINT (B.E.P) = 59.44%

Chapter - 18

Leather Travelling Bag

Introduction

Travelling bag is one of the convenient goods used for carrying the belongings such as clothes, daily-use articles and other essentials during travelling from one place to other. Some other types of products are also used for carrying important documents and office use equipments by the executives and high profile personnel. Although this product is manufactured from various types of materials such as textile, jute, coated fabrics, yet leather travelling bag is having wider acceptance due to its superior strength, aesthetic look and up-man-ship among middle and high-income group people. A wide range of travelling bags are in use for various purposes. The cost of the leather bags depends upon the type of leather, space and/or style of it. This project aims at manufacturing two types of bags i.e.:

(i) Bags of single large pocket with one or two zips usually made from heavy cow or buffalo leather; and

(ii) Bags of multi pockets with interling and re-enforcement, flap type, fitted with magnetic press buttons, commonly made from cow nappa leather. C

Process of Manufacture

The leather travelling bags proposed to be manufactured in this project are mainly of two types. One is of single large pocket with a space of 3 to 6 ft. fitted with one or two fasteners and a long strap handle and other one is of multi-pockets (3 to 5) fitted with different types of fasteners like zips, velcro or press buttons. While heavy cow or buffalo bag leather with the thickness of 2.0 to 2.5 mm without lining is preferred for making the former, the softy type of leather like cow nappa leather with inter-lining and reinforcement is ususlly used for the later.

First of all the components are cut from suitable materials. The basic raw material is the finished leather, which is not uniform irregular in shape and size, variation with grain structure and presence of defects on the surface. On the other hand, the components are generally regular or rectangular shape and the adjacent components should have similar shade and structure. Therefore, necessary care should be taken in cutting the components. The cut components are then skived to the edges for ease of folding and/or stiching. The edges are then beaded attached as per the specification. The outer surface (leather), the inner surface (lining) and the re-enforcement materials if required so, are attached first with the adhesive and then by stiching. The linings and thread-ends are trimmed and sealed. The surface is cleaned and polished and made ready for packing.

Quality Control and Standards

The quality of this product has to be maintained as per buyer's specification. However, the main criterial for quallity control are selection of suitable materials, (especially the leather with required thickness, shade, strength and softness) cutting components from suitable portions of leather, uniform folding, fastener attachment, regular stitching with suitable thread with specified stitch length and finishing.

Production Capacity (per annum)

(i) Leather travelling bag 9000 Pcs. of single pocket with one Rs. 54,00,000 handles (20″ × 5″ × 18″)

(ii) Leather travelling 600 0 Pcs. of bag-multi pocket flap Rs. 488,00,000 type with one long and two small handles (18″ × 5″ × 15″)

MOTIVE POWER

Pollution Control

The proposed unit does not produce any effluent. However, the scraps of leather and other materials are to be collected and disposed-off at appropriate place or are burnt at an isolated place.

Energy Conservation

All machines are power driven and are run individually, whenever required.

Machinery and Equipments

1. Strap cutting machine Straight (12 knives)
2. Pneumatic stamping machine-stamping wheel (0-9 nos.) (A-Z)

3. Upper Skiving machine.
4. Flat bed single needle sewing machine.
5. Heavy duty flat bed single needle sewing machine.
6. Cylinder bed sewing Single.
7. Combined finishing machine.
8. Rivetting machine Ind.
9. Electriflication and erection of machine.

Tools and Equipments and other Fixed Assets

1. Leather goods makers tool kit.
2. Machine maintenance and electricians tool kit.
3. Testing equipments thickness gauge measuring scales etc.
4. Workshop working tables, racks etc.
5. Office furniture and equipments.
6. Misc. equipments.

Raw Material Including Packaging Materials

1. Heavy cow or buffalo Chrome tanned Bag Leather (2.0 mm)
2. Cow nappa/softee leather (1.4 mm)
3. Linings and reinforcements
4. Magnetic press buttons.
5. Zips, Threads, adhesive, Finishing and other misc, materials.
6. Packaging materials.

Cost Estimation

FIXED CAPITAL

1. LAND & BUILDING			(RENTED)
2. PLANT & MACHINERY		Rs.	5,18,100.00
3. OTHER FIXED ASSETS		Rs.	1,42,000.00
	TOTAL	**Rs.**	**6,60.100.00**

WORKING CAPITAL (PER MONTH)

1. RAW MATERIAL	Rs.	6,53,000.00
2. SALARY & WAGES	Rs.	37,500.00
3. UTILITIES & OVERHEADS	Rs.	3,000.00
TOTAL	**Rs.**	**6,93,500.00**

CAPITAL INVESTMENT

FIXED CAPITAL	Rs.	6,60,000.00
WORKING CAPITAL FOR 3 MONTHS	Rs.	20,80,500.00
TOTAL	**Rs.**	**27,40,500.00**

TURN OVER/ANNUM

BY SALE OF 15000 PIECES LEATHER TRAVELLING BAG SINGLE POCKET AND MULTI POCKETS = RS. 1,02,00,000 = 00

PROFIT SALES RATIO = PROFIT / SALES X 100 = 12.51%

RATE OF RETURN = OPERATING PROFIT / T.C.I X 100 = 48.71%

BREAK EVEN POINT (B.E.P) = 37.06%

Chapter - 19

Leather Waist Belt

Introduction

Leather waist belt is an item of dress used by young and old. It has a functional value beside being a fashion item. The actual use of this belt is to keep the pant tight at the waist. They are made in different widths and lengths to suit customers of all age groups and build. The leather used is plain or chrome tanned cowhides of even substance in different colours and shades of mainly black and brown. The buckles used are in different attractive designs and plated. They are detachable and fitted as per customers choice. Leather belts are more comfortable in use and long lasting than belts made of other materials. The manufacturing process of these belts are very simple. This item can easily be fabricated by small scale/cottage scale units.

Process of Manufacture

After selection of suitable leather, the belts of different sizes are cut by strap cutting machine and skived from the edges. Similarly the lining of the same sizes of required leather is also cut. The skived edges are folded. Then the lining attached by paste. After pasting the belts are stiched with help of stiching machine. The excess of lining are to be trimmed. The other operations like buckle attaching edge setting punching are then carried out according to the design. The belts are then finally inspected and packed.

Quality Control and Standards

The belts are generally manufactured as per buyer's requirements and specifications. However the quality of this item will be maintained by the good quality of raw materials, selection of appropriate designs and strict supervision during manufacturing process.

Production Capacity

Leather waist belts - 18,000 pieces - value : Rs. 12,2400

Motive Power 3 HP.

Pollution Control

This industry does not create any kind of pollution and as such there is no need to take any preventive measures for pollution control.

Machinery and Equipments

1. Strap cutting machine.
2. Upper Leather skiving machine.
3. Single Needle flat bed Industrial sewing machine 31 ND 15 Merrit.
4. Side creasing machine.
5. Hand tools and other equipments.
6. Office equipment and working table etc.
7. Electrification and installation charges @ 10% of machinery.

Raw Materials (per month)

1. Chrome Tanned upper Leather.
2. Splid Upper.
3. Buckle, thread, solution etc.
4. Packing material.

COST ESTIMATION

FIXED CAPITAL

1.	LAND & BUILDING (75 sq. mt.)		(RENTAL)
2.	PLANT & MACHINERY	Rs.	1,06,000.00
3.	OTHER FIXED ASSETS	Rs.	10,000.00
	TOTAL	**Rs.**	**1,16,000.00**

WORKING CAPITAL (PER MONTH)

1. RAW MATERIAL	Rs.	58,500.00
2. SALARY & WAGES	Rs.	21,600.00
3. UTILITIES & OVERHEADS	Rs.	8,700.00
TOTAL	**Rs.**	**88,800.00**

CAPITAL INVESTMENT

TOTAL FIXED CAPITAL	Rs.	1,16,400.00
TOTAL WORKING CAPITAL FOR 3 MONTHS	Rs.	2,66,400.00
TOTAL	Rs.	3,82,800.00

TURN OVER/ANNUM

BY SALE OF 18,000 PES. OF LEATHER WAIST-BELTS = RS. 12,60,000.00

PROFIT SALES RATIO = PROFIT / SALES X 100 = 9.82%

RATE OF RETURN = OPERATING PROFIT / T.C.I X 100 = 32.34%

BREAK EVEN POINT (B.E.P) = 35.26%

Chapter - 20

Manufacturing of Batting Gloves

Introduction

The Cricket Batting Gloves are used as safety by the players while playing the Cricket to save hand from any injury being caused by the cricket ball and these gloves also observes the shock caused by hitting the ball, thus also help to keep the hand in comfortable condition during the play for longer period by absorbing the perspiration, etc. Initially, Batting Gloves were manufactured of leather but due to fast changing technology, the new synthetic material has been developed which is suitable, more durable and cheaper than the leather material. The process of manufacturing the Batting Gloves is the same as for other industrial gloves. The only difference is that for the safety of fingers, pads are used made out of woolen rug or foam attached on the upper side of the gloves.

Process of Manufacture

As per graded pattern, the components are clicked manually or by clicking process:

- Pre or post printing of monogram log etc. is carried out. This depends upon the price of the product agreed upon.
- Components are stitched together and padding is attached separately over the post bed machine.
- Fixing of buckle and button etc.
- Finishing i.e. excess thread/material or oily matter etc. is removed.
- Inspection and signing of Tag with full description, etc.
- Packing as per buyer's instruction.

Production Capacity

Cricket Batting Gloves	:	60,000 Pairs (Per annum)
Value	:	Rs. 85,20,000.00
Motive Power		3 HP (approx.)

Pollution Control

This industry does not create any pollution, therefore, State Pollution Control Board's permission is not binding to start the industry.

Energy Conservation

There is no scope of energy conservation in this unit.

Machinery and Equipments

1. Cylinder bed compound, Feed Machine (JUKI) No. MS-335).
2. Post bed Lock Stitching Machine (Juki No. Ms-810).
3. Electrification and Installation Charges @ 10%.
4. Tools and Equipments.
5. Cost of Furniture and Fixture.

Raw Materials (per pair)

1. Single Thick Cloth.
2. PVC (fingers).
3. Sweat Band.
4. PVC for quirk.
5. Thread No. 50.
6. Gusset-Nylon tape.
7. Velcro 2* H/L.
8. Thimbla.
9. Logo/Monogram Printing.
10. Packing and forwarding

COST ESTIMATION

FIXED CAPITAL

1. LAND & BUILDING		(RENTED)
2. PLANT & MACHINERY	Rs.	3,09,000.00
3. OTHER FIXED ASSETS	Rs.	10,000.00
TOTAL	**Rs.**	**3,19,000.00**

WORKING CAPITAL (PER MONTH)

1. RAW MATERIAL	Rs.	5,20,000.00
2. SALARY & WAGES	Rs.	46,000.00
3. UTILITIES & OVERHEADS	Rs.	29,000.00
TOTAL	**Rs.**	**5,95,000.00**

CAPITAL INVESTMENT

TOTAL FIXED CAPITAL	Rs.	3,19,000.00
TOTAL WORKING CAPITAL FOR 3 MONTHS	Rs.	17,85,000.00
TOTAL	**Rs.**	**21,04,000.00**

TURN OVER/ANNUM

BY SALE OF 60,000 PAIRS CRICKET BATTING GLOVES = RS. 85,20,000.00

PROFIT SALES RATIO = PROFIT / SALES X 100 = 12.05%

RATE OF RETURN = OPERATING PROFIT / T.C.I X 100 = 48.79%

BREAK EVEN POINT (B.E.P) = 43.33%

Chapter - 21

Shower Proof Garment Leather

Introduction

The Shower Proof Garment Leather is a special type of leather with some unique characteristics. The shower proof garment industry for making shower proof leather garments like coat, jacket, trousers etc. It is a type of leather which protects the garments from rain and snow shower. This can be made by processing cow hides or goat or sheep skins as per the demand. The present project envisages to produce the shower proof garment leathers by processing the cow hides. The garment leather should be very soft, defectless and shower proof should have a good run to withstand the stretch of the garment while in wear. The leather should have a good colour fastness property both dry and wet rub fastness. Such type of leather are in great demand in the export market.

Process of Manufacture

Soaking : Suitable quality of raw-cow hides is selected for manufacturing of the shower proof garment leathers for garments. The selected raw-cow hides are taken in the paddle. The hides are washed in the running water for about 2 hours to remove all the dirts. The soaking process is carried out as follows:

Water	–	250%
Detergent	–	0.2%
preservative	–	0.5%

The paddle is run for about 3 to 4 hours till proper soak back of the raw-hides.

Liming : the soaked hides are then limed as follows in the paddle:

Water	–	25%

Sodium Sulphide	–	5-6%
Lime	–	6-7%

The paddle is run for 2 hours continuously. Then the paddle is run intermittently for 10 to 15 minutes per hour. In this way the liming is carried out for about 24 hours. Then the pelts are checked as regards the completion of liming and are taken out of the paddle for fleshing. After fleshing of the pelts are over, the pelt weight is taken.

Deliming : The limed pelts after fleshing are taken into the drum and thoroughly washed in running water for about 2 hours. Then, deliming is done as follows:

Water	–	25%
Ammonium Chloride	–	1.5% to 2%

The deliming is carried out for about one and a half hours. Then the Deliming is checked with the phenolphthalein.

Pickling : The deliming bath is drained out and the pickling is done as follows:

Water – 75% to 80% : The drum is run for about 10 minutes.

Add : 1.5% sulphuric acid previously diluted in water (1:10) is added to the drum in three equal installments at an interval of 30 minutes. The pickling is carried out for 2 hours and is checked at a *p*H of 3.0.

Chrome tanning : The chrome tanning is carried out in the same bath as follows:

Add : Basic chrome sulphate : 7%

The drum is run for 10 hours. Then, the penetration of the chrome liquor into the pelt is checked. Then, basification is done with the sodium basification is done with the sodium bicarbonate and boil test is carried out to check the completion of tanning.

The tanned hides in this stage are called wet blue. The wet blues are then sammed under the sun or in the samming machine. The shaving of the wet blue is done to proper thickness of around 0.8 to 0.9 mm in the shaving machine. The shaved wet blues are then taken into the drum to carry out the following processes.

Neutralisation : The neutralisation of the blues are carried out as follows:

Water	:	200%
Sodi-bi-carb	:	2% (On shaved weight)
Sodium formate	:	0.5%

The drum is run for 6 minutes. The neutralisation is checked at *p*H around 6.0 and the wet blues are washing in running water for 15 minutes.

Retanning : It is done as follows:

Water	:	250%
Basyntan OS	:	2%
Basyntan DI	:	3%

The drum is run for 60 minutes and the exhaustion of the bath is checked and washed in running water for 10 minutes.

Flat liquoring and dyeing : The fat liqouring and dyeing of the leathers is done as follows:

Water	:	200% (50C–60C°)
Sulphited vegetable oil	:	8%
Densodium, EN	:	1%
Synthetic oil	:	7%
Raw oil	:	1%
Water proofing agent	:	0.5%
Preservative	:	0.5%
Liquor Ammonia	:	0.3%

The oil emulsion is added to the drum which is run for about one hour. Then the exhaustion of the fat is checked. Then 0.5% formic acid is added for fixing of the fat and the drum is run for 30 minutes.

Then add : Direct Dye – 1.0 to 1.5% (As per the required shade).

The drum is run for 30 minutes and the dye is fixed with 0.5% formic acid and the drum is run for 30 minutes.

Add : preservative : 0.5%

Drum is then run for another 20 minutes.

The materials are washed in running water for 10 minutes and then drained out and piled up in the horse overnight.

Next day, the crusts are sammed, set and dried. Then the crusts are conditioned with the saw dust, toggled and trimmed off. Then buffing and dusting off the crusts is done and sent for finishing.

Finishing : This is one of the most important operations in making the shower proof garment leather. The crusts are first of all snuffed on the grain surface with 420 emery paper on the buffing wheel. This is done to remove the defects on the grain surface and bring uniformity on the surface. The snuffed crusts are then dusted off to remove the loose from the crusts. The crusts dusts are remoulded from the crusts. The crusts are then sprayed with a soft impregnating resin binder in the spray booth and dried. The impregnated crusts are then embossed in the hydraulic press with a fine hair-cell plate. The fine hair-celled crusts are then padding table twice and dried properly. The padding season is made with the following elements:

Lipton Pigment	:	100 parts
Polyurethene binder and other binder	:	300 parts
Impregnator	:	10 parts
Plasticiser and Wax	:	10 parts
Lipton filler	:	20 parts
Preservative	:	5 parts
Water	:	1000 parts

The padded shower proof garment leathers are then sprayed with the above season twice to ensure complete coverage. The sprayed leather are then dried properly.

Top coat : The sprayed leathers are then sprayed with water proofing agent and lacquered with a lacquer solution to impart colour fastness and shower fastness after which it is dried.

The garment leathers are then plane plated in the hydraulic press under light pressure and low temperature. The garment leathers thus finished is measured in the measuring machine and then packed for despatch.

Quality Control and Standards

BIS specification to be followed or as per the customer's specification.

Production Capacity

a) Quantity : 30000 pcs. of shower proof leather for leather garments.

Equivalent to 7,50,000 sq.ft. (per annum)

b) Value : Rs. 4,12,50,000

Motive Power 110 KW.

Pollution Control

As the project is envisaged to be set up in Industrial Estate for tanneries with Common Effluent Treatment Plant, separate pollution control plant is not considered in the project. However, a cost of about Rs. 10,000 will be incurred per month for maintenance of CETP.

Energy Conservation

There exists a lot of scope of energy conservation in the tannery, since a lot of energ is spent in the tannery in the form of electricity and fuel. As a measure of energy conservation, the workers should be properly trained to operate the machinery as and when required and maintain them in good condition and check wastage of energy.

Plant and Machineries

1. Wooden paddle of vat size 8″ x 7″ one 10 HP 1000 RPM AC motor Starter and Vee Belt.
2. Wooden Drum 8″ x 8″ with starter and motor 15 HP and starter.
3. Shaving machines single width 7.5 HP motor and starter.
4. Slocomb staking machine with motor 7.5 HP and starter.
5. Toggling machine with 20 boards of size 9″ x 5″ suitable for hides.
6. Hydraulic Press with 25 HP motor and starter.
7. Reversible setting M/c. 2400 mm Working width with 25 HP and Starter.
8. One spray booth of 9″ x 5″ with top booth cover, 2 nos. of 18" exhaust fan and starter.
9. Fleshing machine (2400 mm) working width with 20 HP motor/starter.
10. Tools and equipments L.S.
11. Electrification and Installation @ 10% of the cost of machinery.
12. Office furniture, workshop furnitures etc.

Raw Materials

1. Raw-cow hides.
2. Processing and finishing chemicals.

COST ESTIMATION

FIXED CAPITAL

1. LAND & BUILDING (AREA 1200 SQ. MT.)	Rs.	35,16,000.00
2. PLANT & MACHINERY	Rs.	29,33,500.00
3. OTHER FIXED ASSETS	Rs.	15,000.00
TOTAL	**Rs.**	**64,64,500.00**

WORKING CAPITAL (PER MONTH)

1. RAW MATERIAL	Rs.	25,62,500.00
2. SALARY & WAGES	Rs.	1,45,800.00
3. UTILITIES & OVERHEADS	Rs.	1,06,300.00
TOTAL	**Rs.**	**28,14,600.00**

CAPITAL INVESTMENT

FIXED CAPITAL	Rs.	67,70,000.00
WORKING CAPITAL FOR 3 MONTHS	Rs.	84,43,800.00
TOTAL	**Rs.**	**1,52,13,800.00**

TURN OVER/ANNUM

BY SALE OF 7,50,000 SQ. FT OF SHOWER PROOF GARMENT LEATHER - RS. 4,12,50,000.00

PROFIT SALES RATIO = PROFIT / SALES X 100 = 11.48 %

RATE OF RETURN = OPERATING PROFIT / T.C.I X 100 = 31.13%

BREAK EVEN POINT (B.E.P) = 45.45%

Chapter - 22
Suede Leather

Introduction

Suede Leather can be manufactured from cow hide, goat skin, buffalo hide and even from sheep skins. This leather is finished on the flesh side and has a velvety nap. The velvety nap on the flesh side is the beauty of this leather. Shoe Upper, garment and other fancy products are manufactured from this leather but mostly it is manufactured from cow hide or goat skins.

Process of Manufacture

Raw Material : Wet salted hair-slip quality cow hides.

Soaking : The hides are washed thoroughly and soaked in a paddle containing Na_2S (Sodium Sulphide) 0.2% and water 400-500%. The hides are kept in the paddle overnight and next morning checked for proper soaking and then washed in running water. The water is drained out and soaked weight is taken.

Liming (in drum) : The following chemicals are taken on soaking weight-water 300%. Sodium sulphide 5%, Staked lime 4 to 6%, salt 3%. Total liming is done for 18-20 hours and the drum is run 2-3 minutes after every two hours. The stock is rinsed in soft water for 10 minutes. The hides are fleshed and the weight determined.

Deliming : The fleshed pelt is washed in running water in drum for 20 minutes. The water is drained out and the following chemicals are taken on pelt weight. Ammonium sulphate 1.2-1.7%, Sodium bi-sulphate 0.4-0.6% water 250%.

The drum is run for 30-40 minutes and checked by phenolphthalein and test should show 20-25% red. Drain out the water and wash thoroughly with 2 changes of water for 20 minutes.

Pickling : The pelt are picked with the following chemicals : Water 30-60%, salt 8%, Drum run for 10 minutes and then add H_2SO_4 (1.84 Conc.) 1.5%.

The acid is diluted with water and added in 3 instalments after the interval of 10 minutes and after last instalment drum run for 45 minutes and then Formaldehyde 0.5% is added.

Drum run for 5 minutes and checked *p*H of pelt with bromophenol blue indicator, which should be 2.3 to 3.0 and the PH of the float be about 8.

Chrome Tanning : Half of the pickle liquor is drained out and the hides are run for 15 minutes and B.C.S. powder 3%, sodium Acetate 0.5% is added. The following chemicals are fed in two instalments after the interval of 15 minutes and drum run for further 2-2.5 hours. Next day Samming, setting, splitting and shaving 1.3-1.4 mm is done. The shaved leather is washed for 10 minutes in warm water of 30-35°C.

Retannage : Basic Chrome crystal (33%) 5% (without float-dissolved 1:1, sodium formate 1%, Let the drum run for 10 minutes and then add sodium formate 0.5%, and Sodium bi-carbonate 0.7% (dissolved 1.10) the drum is run for 45 minutes and *p*H should be 4.5-4.6 and then add wattle extract powder 4% and Tanigan PR (Bayer) 1%. The drum is run for 45 minutes and rinsed for 5 minutes.

Dyeing and Fat Liquoring : Acid dye in powder 3%, the drum is run for 25 minutes and 100% water is added. Drum run for 20 minutes and Sandozol KS 6% is added. Drum run for 20 minutes and traffnilon 210A-1% is added. Drum run for 20 minutes and then horse up. The leather are sammed, set up saw dusted, staked, toggled, buffed on grain side with 400 grit emery paper, dust off and dry miled.

Quality Control and Standards

1. Indian Standard Specification IS 8170 : 1983 will be used in maintaining standards for cow suede leather.
2. As per the buyer's specification.

COST ESTIMATION

Production Capacity

Quantity	:	60,000 cow hides.
Value	:	Rs. 5,04,00,000
Motive Power		130 HP.

Pollution Control

The tanning process require a huge quantity of water for processing and generates a large quantity of waste water. Non-degradable organic matter and organic salt. Most of the chemicals used in the tanning process are bio-non-degradable and pose a serious threat to the environment. Thus the tannery waste water contains a variety of different substances like salt, Sulphide, chrome sulphate, solvents, dyes and other materials.

In view of the above, the leather tanning industry is identified as the most highly polluting industry and marked as "RED CATEGORY" in the list of polluting industry.

Therefore, the unit requires an "Effluent Treatment Plant: of its own in the unit premises.

For the treatment of tanning waste water the following steps may be adopted:

1. Change in process, segregation and recovery, reuse of water.
2. Primary treatment of waste water.
3. Secondary treatment of the effluents.
4. Disposal of solid wastes.

Since the complete tanning waste treatment is very expensive and it is also not possible for any small-scale unit, therefore, the tanning waste treatment system has been classified in to two sections:

1. Primary Treatment
2. Secondary Treatment

The primary treatment should be done by respective tanning unit, and secondary treatment should be done by Municipalities corporations, Waste Treatment Organisation.

The basic objectives of the primary treatment plant are screening, sedimentation, reducing effluents volume, settling, filtration and evaporation.

Energy Conservation

(i) Common drive system to run the paddles may be adopted.

(ii) Thorough checking of the motors, driving system etc. should be done from time to time.

FIXED CAPITAL

1. LAND & BUILDING (AREA 1500 SQ. MT.)	Rs.	40,00,000.00
2. PLANT & MACHINERY	Rs.	26,50,000.00
3. OTHER FIXED ASSETS	Rs.	2,50,000.00
TOTAL	**Rs.**	**69,00,000.00**

WORKING CAPITAL (PER MONTH)

1. RAW MATERIAL	Rs.	32,50,000.00
2. SALARY & WAGES	Rs.	1,38,000.00
3. UTILITIES & OVERHEADS	Rs.	75,000.00
TOTAL	**Rs.**	**34,63,000.00**

CAPITAL INVESTMENT

TOTAL FIXED CAPITAL	Rs.	69,00,000.00
TOTAL WORKING CAPITAL FOR 3 MONTHS	Rs.	1,03,89,000.00
TOTAL	**Rs.**	**1,72,89,000.00**

TURN OVER/ANNUM

BY SALE OF 13,80,000 SQ. FT. OF GRADE I, II, III & IV SHEDE LEATHER = RS. 5,04,00,000.00

PROFIT SALES RATIO = PROFIT / SALES X 100 = 33.8%

RATE OF RETURN = OPERATING PROFIT / T.C.I X 100 = 11.60%

BREAK EVEN POINT (B.E.P) = 40.96%

Chapter - 23
Upholstery Leather

Introduction

Upholstery leather manufacture, like many other branches of the industry, is in a rapid state of flux at this time. Although the manufacture of upholstery leather has been characterised for years by rocker tannage, with vegetable extracts, the majority of the industry has shifted or is in the process of shifting to lime-split drum-tanned upholstery leather.

At times mineral salts such as chrome or zirconium may be used alone or in combination with the vegetable tannis. The primary purpose of such usage is to achieve certain leather effects such as softness but also to "tie-down" the excess vegetable tannins and thus prevent migration which might lead to a colour change of light coloured finishes.

The finishing of upholstery leather is also undergoing major changes which have been largely brought about the specifications applied by the automotive industry in efforts to improve the surface characteristics of the leathers used. Other changes in finish materials have been brought about the extensive use of white and pastel leather, both for furniture and automobiles.

The major grades of upholstery are :

(i) Full top grains (top grain, full grain and full top grain)

(ii) Top grains snuffed (corrected top grains or hand buffs)

(iii) Deep buffs

(iv) Splits

Process of Manufacture

Raw materials : Wet sated cow hides.

Soak : Soaked in a drum for 1 hour and then drum at 3 rpm in running cold water for 20 minutes using a lattice door.

Lime : Suspend 2 days or rocking frames in old lime liquor mended with 0.25% lime and 0.2% sodium sulphide (fused) on volume of liquor.

Liquor : Pelt 5:1 ratio. Follow by 4-6 days in new lime containing 1% lime suspension and 0.1% soda ash. This liquor after use.

Unhair : By machine.

Flesh : By machine. Examine hides to check selection.

Plump for 1-2 days in 1% lime suspension

Split : to required substance.

Surface delime : in a paddle, using 0.5% ammonium chloride or sulphate (% on grain split weight at 33°C.

Bate : 0.5% weak pancreatic bate at 35°C for 1 hour (% on split weight).

Scud : By hand.

Vegetable tannage : In a set of 12 suspender pits the first liquor is 10oBK and *p*H 5.0 and is raised in steps of 2-30 BK per pit finishing at 40° BK and *p*H 4.0.

The bottom 3 pits have rocker movement. The desired blend of extract is diluted with water to slightly over 40 degree barko meter and run into the top pit. If myrobalans alone is used, alkali must be added to the diluted liquor to reduce the natural acidity and so raise the *p*H from 3.2–4.0. The hides spend one day in each pit and as they are moved the liquors are run in the opposite direction.

Scour : The grain in drum, using warm sumac leaf in fusion at 33°C for 30 minutes. Wash off and Horse up.

Fatliquor : In drum using 0.25 kg sulphated codlever oil per hide at 35 degree centgrade for 45 minutes.

Horse up to drain.

Dry : slowly over poles.

Finishing : Fashions in this type of leather range from the flexible to the very soft in the case of cushion, upholstery. In all cases it is essential that the finish should be rub-fast in colour, gloss or non-gloss and should be cleanable with a damp cloth. Originally, it was finished by application of a bottom sealing coat of polyacrylate dispension, dried and then spray finished with pigmented on tinted nitro-cellulose lacquers, usually plated or embossed. Unless carried out carefully, there is always the possibility of the film becoming brittle due to plasticiser migration or yellowing on exposure to sunlight. Polyurethane finishes have distinct advantages.

Coat (1) is sprayed to give good wetting and anchorage to the leather. Coat (2) is sprayed to cover, dried and plated at 73°C and 150 kg per sq. cm. A second levelling spray coat (2) may be necessary. At this stage the leather may be boarded or preferably dry-drummed until the plated effect is lost and an attractive broken or natural grain is achieved. Finally, the urethane coat is applied as before.

Quality Control and Standards

The upholstery leather industry has done far more than any other segment of the leather industry in developing test method and specifications for the product. A major reason for these developments is the result of the relatively large percentage of the product sold to the automotive industry which buys on specification. The work of the upholstery industry has been done through the technical committee of the upholstery leather group working, very effectively, with the technical staff of the various auto motive companies and suppliers. Although all the leather sold to the automotive industry is sole on definite specifications, the upholstery leather industry has extended this principle into the furniture leather field. In a number of instances very extensive work has been carried out by the technical committee in attempting to set specifications and develop method that can be related realistically to service performance. Particular tests and specifications that have been done are resistance to fading, resistance to flex and resistance to cold. The following test methods are used as basis of specifications on upholstery leather :

1. Breaking (strench)
2. Elongation (stretch)
3. Stitch tear resistance-static
4. Stitch tear resistance-dynamic
5. Colour fastness–fademeter
6. Colour fastness–south florida exposure
7. Abrasion resistance
8. Cold temperature resistance
9. Flex resistance
10. Resistance to cracking
11. Resistance to bleeding
13. Resistance to sulfides
14. Resistance to perspiration

The common chemical requirements covered include moisture, fat, *p*H. The more subjective requirement of satisfactory upholstery leather such as colour, grain, embossing, depth, temper hand etc. are covered descriptively. Of course, all specifications include a statement of the requirements of thickness, area, type of finish etc.

COST ECONOMICS

Production Capacity

Quantity : 30,000 pcs. of upholstery leather i.e. equivalent to 7,50,000 sq.ft. (per annum).

Value : Rs. 3,60,00,000

Motive Power 75 kW.

Pollution Control

The pollution control measures are to be given utmost attention as the Affluents coming out of the process are very toxic and they are likely to affect the flora and fauna of water, if disposed off into the river. Moreover, effluents are also, likely to degrade the fertility of the soil. So proper effluent treatment plants are to be installed in the tannery to treat the effluent and make the treated water go out into river.

Energy Conservation

Energy is spent in the tannery in the form of electricity and fuel. Hence, there exists a lot of scope for conservation of electricity and fuel as a measure of energy conservation. The workers should be properly trained to operate the machines as and when required. They should be trained to yield maximum units during the machine operation and should not allow the machines to run by motive power unnecessarily. The electrical lines should be properly made and checked at regular intervals. In respect of fuel, proper attention is to be taken care of. The boiler should be properly maintained. Misuse of fuel in the form of wood, petrol, kerosene should be avoided.

Machinery and Equipments

1. Wooden paddle of vat size 8′ × 7′ on 10 HP-1000 rpm A.C. Motor, starter and V belt.
2. Wooden drum 8′ × 6′ with starter and motor 10 HP and starter.
3. Fleshing machine 1800 mm with 15 HP motor and starter.
4. Splitting machine 1800 mm with 15 HP motor and starter.
5. Unhairing machine 1800 mm with 15 HP motor and starter.
6. Hydraulic press with 25 HP motor and starter.
7. Spray booth with compressor.

8. Measuring machine 1800 mm width with 5 HP motor.
9. Generator set 50 KVA.
10. Working table, toggles etc.
11. Testing equipments.
12. Pollution Control Equipments (Effluent tratement plant).
13. Cost of power connection including transformer.
14. Electrication and installation.
15. Cost of office equipment including furniture.

Raw Materials

1. Raw cow hides.
2. Processing and finishing chemicals.

FIXED CAPITAL

1. LAND & BUILDING (AREA 1000 SQ. MT.)		Rented
2. PLANT & MACHINERY	Rs.	33,00,000.00
TOTAL	**Rs.**	**33,00,000.00**

WORKING CAPITAL/MONTH

1. RAW MATERIAL	Rs.	23,75,000.00
2. SALARY & WAGES	Rs.	95,000.00
3. UTILITIES & OVERHEADS	Rs.	75,000.00
TOTAL	**Rs.**	**25,45,000.00**

TOTAL CAPITAL INVESTMENT

TOTAL FIXED CAPITAL	Rs.	33,00,000.00
TOTAL WORKING CAPITAL FOR 3 MONTHS	Rs.	76,35,200.00
TOTAL	**Rs.**	**1,09,35,200.00**

TURN OVER/ANNUM

BY SALE OF @ 750000 SQ. FT. = 3,60,00,000.00

PROFIT SALES RATIO = PROFIT / SALES X 100 = 9.75%

RATE OF RETURN = OPERATING PROFIT / T.C.I X 100 = 32%

BREAK EVEN POINT (B.E.P) = 45.16%

Chapter - 24
Cricket Ball (Leather)

Introduction

Cricket ball leather is used for the manufacture of cricket balls. Cricket is now considered as the most popular sport in our country. This game is also played in Common Wealth countries and is now gaining popularity in many other countries. Cricket ball leather is manufactured from Vegetable retanned cow leather or from chrome- Zirchonium tanned leather.

Manufacturing Process

Wet-salted cow hides free from flay cuts are selected for the manufacture of cricket ball leather. The hides are washed in running water and then soaked overnight if necessary. Next day, liming is done in paddles with sodium sulphide and lime. The following day, the stock is shifted to drums and delimed with 2% ammonium sulphate & 1% bate deliming is checked and then the stock is washed and pickled with 1.5-2% sulphuric acid & 8-10%, common salt. After attaining a PH of 2.5-3, the stock is left in the pickled bath overnight. Then chrome tanning is done with 8% basic chromium sulphate, penetration is checked, banifide with sodium bicarbonate & hypo till PH-4 is attained.

The stock is aged for few days after which selection is done. The selected wet blue is sammed and split to uniform thickness. Shaving is done and the shaved leather is then given a mild acid treatment and retanned with 6-10% vernatan ZR, rinsed for 5 minutes and neutralized with 3% Neutranol F & 0.5% sodiumbicarbonate, PH adjusted 4-8-5, washed for 10 minutes & fatiquored with 3% vernol liquor W.G & fixed with fornic acid. The leather is then washed and piled overnight.

The leather is then sammed, set to dry, conditioned, shacked, toggled, buffed and plated if necessary measured and packed for delivery.

Cricket balls can also be manufactured from vegetable retanned leather.

For manufacture of vegetable retanned leather for cricket ball the vegetable tanning is done as usual either by pit system for which construction of leach pits is required or a combination of pit leaching & drum tannage system. The vegetable tanned leather is then shaved, retanned and fat-liquored. It is then hand set, dried and packed.

Quality Specification

ISI specification for leather for cricket and hockey ball is IS: 416-1963.

Production Capacity (p.a.)

(a) Quantity

(i)	GR-I Cricket balls leather	5,00,000 sq. ft.
(ii)	GR-II Cricket ball leather	7,00,000 sq. ft.
(iii)	Split leather (by- product)	2,00,000 sq. ft.

(b) Value

	Rs.
(i) 5,00,000 sq. ft. of Gr. I Cricket balls leather @ Rs. 24 per sq. ft.	1,20,00,000.00
(ii) 7,00,000 sq. ft. of GR-II cricket balls leather @ Rs. 17.50 per sq. ft.	1,22,50,000.00
(iii) 2,00,000 sq. ft.of split leather crust @ Rs. 5/- per sq. ft.	10,00,000.00
Total	2,52,50,000.00

4. Power Requirement (p.m.)

Total power requirement per month for the unit

(200 HPX 0.74) X 8 X 25

= 29,600 KWH

Say = 30,000 KWH

5. Pollution Control

The effluents from proposed unit will be treated in a primary effluent treatment plant costing Rs. 50,000.

6. Energy Conservation

No particular machinery is required for energy conservation.

1. Fixed Capital

(a) Land and Building	**Rs.**
Land one acre @ Rs. 50,000 per acre	
150 Sq. m. office/store etc. @ Rs. 500 per Sq. m	65,000
600 Sq. m. working shed @ Rs. 300 per Sq. m.	1,80,000
Overhead tank, water connection boundary wall etc.	45,000
Total cost of land & bulding	3,50,000

Machinery and Equipments

1. Paddle size 8'x7' with 10 HP motor & starter.
2. Drum size 8'x8' with 15 HP motor.
3. Drum size 8'x6' 10 HP with motor.
4. Fleshing machine working width 2100mm with 25 HP motor.
5. Reversible setting machine working width 2100 mm with 25 HP motor.
6. Baby boiler with accessories.
7. Shaving machine 1200mm working width with 7.5 HP motor & starter.
8. Slocomb staking machine with 15 HP motor & starter.
9. Sammying maching 7½' with 7.5 HP motor & starter.
10. Band knife splittng machine 2100mm working width with motor & starter.
11. Double width buffing machine with motor & starter.
12. Toggle drying equipments with 20 frames, blower & thermostat equipment.
13. Computerised electronics leather area measuring machine with 2100 mm working width with motor.
14. Hydraulic press 6.5 tonnes capacity 15 HP motor & starter.
15. Pollution control equipments.

Raw Materials (p.m)

1. Raw cow hides
2. Different chemicals for processing

COST ESTIMATION

FIXED CAPITAL

1. LAND & BUILDING (AREA 4000 SQ. MT)	Rs.	3,50,000.00
2. PLANT & MACHINERY	Rs.	5,90,000.00
TOTAL	**Rs.**	**9,40,000.00**

WORKING CAPITAL/MONTH

1. RAW MATERIAL	Rs.	16,50,000.00
2. SALARY & WAGES	Rs.	57,400.00
3. UTILITIES & OVERHEADS	Rs.	34,600.00
TOTAL	**Rs.**	**17,42,000.00**

CAPITAL INVESTMENT

FIXED CAPITAL	Rs.	40,10,700.00
WORKING CAPITAL FOR 3 MONTHS	Rs.	52,26,000.00
TOTAL	**Rs.**	**92,36,700.00**

TURN OVER/ANNUM

BY SALE OF CRICKET BALL (LEATHER) OF GRADE I & II 12,00,000 NOS YEAR AND 2,00,000 SPLIT LEATHER (BY PRODUCT) = RS. 25250,000.00

PROFIT SALES RATIO = PROFIT / SALES X 100 = 9.1%

RATE OF RETURN = OPERATING PROFIT / T.C.I X 100 = 25%

BREAK EVEN POINT (B.E.P) = 50%

Chapter - 25
Football (Leather)

Introduction

Fooball leather is used in the sports goods industries for making football. Football leather should be tight, non-stretchy and of high tensile strength and stitch-tear resistant. For this reason football leather is semi-chorme tanned leather from cattle hides. The demand for football and football leather is increasing day in India and abroad.

Process Outline

Football leather should be tight, non-stretchy of high tensile strength and stitch tear resistant. For this reason, vegetable and synthetic retanned chrome leather or semi- chrome leather is preferred for football making. This profile considers semi-chorme leather process only, which is more popular for football making. The process is given from raw hide stage but E.I kips can also be used as raw material and in that case vegetable tanning portion given in this project may be avoided.

(a) 500 pieces of wet salted cow hides of average weight 10 kgs are socked in plain water for 4 to 6 hours. After proper socking they are lined with:

Water	400%
Detergent	0.2%
Sodium sulphate flackes	4%
Lime	8%

Paddle is run initially for 2 hours and thereafter 5 minutes per hour. Total duration of liming is about 40-48 hours. Hair loosening plumping should be checked to understand the completion of liming. After liming the hides are dehaired, flashed and the fleshed pelt weight is noted. The pelts are then delimed with 1% ammonium chloride and 1% sodium bisulphite.

After deliming the pelts are pickled with 8% salt and 1% sulphuric acid. The drumming is continued for 30 to 45 minutes. Tanigan PR, a pre- tanning syntan is added in the pickle leath and the drum run for an hour. One per cent starasol K.B. 70 is added and run for 30 minutes. 50% powdered myrebalan nuts equivalent to leached liquor is added and run for 2 hours; 10-12% of wattle extract is added and drumming continued for 2 hours. Add 100% water and bleaching syntan (TaniganBLIM) and drumming is done for 20 minutes and the leathers are piled.

The tanned leathers are struck out and dipped one by one in 5% solution of epsom salt to fix the tanning and piled overnight. The following morning the leathers are sammed.

The leaching of myrobalan is done by adding 4 times hot water to it containing 7% sodium sulphite, 4% sodium bisulphite, 2% neutralised napthalene sulphuric acid syntan (Tanigan P.R.) (Percentages are calculated on myrobalan powder weight). Myrobalan is leached overnight and the following morning the liquor is filtered and used for tanning. The barkometer of the liquor should preferably be 5.0 to 5.5

(b) Leathers are rounded discarding the loose portion and then shaved to 2.3 to 2.5 m for football. Shaved weight is noted and the leathers put into drum with sufficient water and stripped with soda ash and washed. Then they are chorme powder and ½% of salt. The goods are piled overnight and washed thoroughly next day followed by neutralisation with ½% soda bicarb and then fat liquoring with 6% to 7% TRO and 1% ground nut oil. The leathers are sammed and stretched with slickers. The leather is worked, so as to remove the stretch as far as possible. For more stretchless leather they are stretched on angle frame with toggles. Then the leathers are dried completely and snuffed lightly. The pigmentseason is prepared and 4 to 6 coats are applied for complete coverage. After drying a tallow mixture of 2 parts tallow and 1 part mustard oils applied on the flesh side and the leathers are kept overnight. Next day they are hand staked and packed.

Quality Specifications

IS 4207 – 1967.

COST ESTIMATION

Production Capacity

Tanning of 1,50,000 cattle hides per annum. Producing 34,50,000 sq.ft. of football leather worth Rs. 3,62,25.000.

Motive Power Requirement

20,000 KWH @ Re. 1 - 20,000 per month.

Pollution Control

Low cost waste treatment method is suggested for such project, the process for which may be outlined as under.

The effluents may be screened first for removal of coarser impurities and hair and settling for at least 4 hours in continuous settling tanks. The settled wastes can then be treated by an aerobic lagoon wherein the wastes are impounded for a period of 10 days. Later the wastes are further treated by aerated lagoon, the detention period here being about 6 days. By this treatment effluent can be treated quite satisfactorily.

The technical know-how of the treatment and disposal of tannery waste is available with Central Leather Research Institute and National Environmental Engineering Research Institute, Nagpur.

IS specification for tolerance limits for tannery effluents are according to IS : 2490 (Part 3) - 1985.

Machinery and Equipment

1. Paddle size 8' x 4' with 7.5 H.P. motor
2. Drum size 8' x 8' with 10 H.P. motor
3. Drum size 8' x 6' with 7.5 H.P. motor
4. Dehairing machine working width 2,100 mm with 15 H.P. motor
5. Fleshing machine working width 2,100 mm with 20 H.P. motor
6. Reversible setting out machine working width 2,100 mm with 25 H.P. motor
7. Stacking machine with starter and 5 H.P. motor
8. Buffing machine 12" working width with 3 H.P. motor
9. Baby boiler
10. Working table, tools, and equipment
11. Testing equipment, furniture etc.
12. Installation and electrification @ 10%
13. Pollution control machinery

Machinery Utilisation

It is expected that about 70% of the capacity utilisation of the machinery will achieve the desired target of the project. According to 2nd All India SSI Census, Leather and Leather Product Industries utilised 79% of the capacity. However, it is should be noted that the following problems may hamper the rate of production, viz. (1) drying of the crust and finishing coats in rainy season; (2) unforeseen break-down of machinery and motor.

Raw Materials

Raw hides 12500 per. @ Rs. 125.

Chemicals for 12,500 pcs @ Rs. 56 per pc.

FIXED CAPITAL

1. LAND & BUILDING (AREA 4000 SQ. MT.)	Rs.	13,20,000.00
2. PLANT & MACHINERY	Rs.	21,14,500.00
3. OTHER FIXED ASSETS	Rs.	5,500.00
TOTAL	**Rs.**	**34,40,000.00**

WORKING CAPITAL/MONTH

1. RAW MATERIAL	Rs.	23,75,000.00
2. SALARY & WAGES	Rs.	36,400.00
3. UTILITIES & OVERHEADS	Rs.	33,600.00
TOTAL	**Rs.**	**24,45,000.00**

CAPITAL INVESTMENT

FIXED CAPITAL	Rs.	34,40,000.00
WORKING CAPITAL FOR 3 MONTHS	Rs.	73,35,000.00
TOTAL	**Rs.**	**1,07,75,000.00**

TURN OVER/ANNUM

BY SALE OF 34,50,000 SQ. FT. FOOTBALL LEATHER RS. 3,62,25,000.00

PROFIT SALES RATIO = PROFIT / SALES X 100 = 12.86%

RATE OF RETURN = OPERATING PROFIT / T.C.I X 100 = 43.24%

BREAK EVEN POINT (B.E.P) = 34.60%

Chapter - 26

School Bags

Introduction

School bags made out of non-leather materials like canvas, foam etc. School bags are used by the school and college going students as they have to carry many items like books, note-books, pen, pencils, tiffin boxes etc. These items cannot be carried in hand by the students while going to the school/college. Since they have to go to their academic institutions by walking or travelling in crowded vehicles or in other transport, there is every possibility of missing or damaging any item. It is safer to carry all necessary items in school bags. It is very easy also for the students to carry school bag either in hand or on the shoulder making themselves free for easy movement.

Process Outline

After selection of required design and size of bag various components of canvas/foam are cut. The lining components are also cut in a similar way. The lining components are then stitched with canvas components as per the design. The zip is then attached by way of stitching wherever required. The D-ring buckles and rivets etc. are then fitted properly. The shoulder strap and handle straps are then fixed and the bags are then finally finished and packed.

These bags are manufactured as per the buyers' requirements and specifications. However, the quality of such bags can be maintained by using good quality of raw materials.

COST ESTIMATION

Production Capacity (p.a.)

(a) Quantity	–	30,000 pcs. school bags
(b) Value	–	Rs. 39,00,000

This industry does not create any kind of pollution and there is no need to take preventive measures for pollution control.

There is no scope of energy conservation in this unit.

FINANCIAL ASPECTS

1. Fixed Capital

Land & Building

Constructed Area - 2000 sq. ft.

Rented - Rs. 4,000 p.m.

Machinery Utilisation

Initially 60% utilisation of machinery will be made and thereafter it will increase @10% per year and 100% utilisation will be achieved during the course of next 4-5 years.

The costs of machinery, equipments and raw materials as indicated are approximate and refer to a particular make. Hence the prices of raw materials and machinery may vary depending upon place, type and various suppliers or manufacturers of these items.

Machinery and Equipments

1. Single needle flat bed Ind. sewing m/c Singer make 31-T with motor.
2. Equipment for screen printing.
3. Tool & Equipment Ind.
4. Electrification & installation charges.
5. Office furniture & fixtures.

Raw Materials

1. Waxed canvas/rubberised foam.
2. Canvas Plain.
3. Nylon straps, D-Rings, Zip, Fastners, rivets, cotton tape, buckles, locks, etc.
4. Packing charges.

FIXED CAPITAL

1. LAND & BUILDING (AREA 2000 SQ. FT.)		(RENTED)
2. PLANT & MACHINERY	Rs.	1,82,000.00
TOTAL	**Rs.**	**1,97,000.00**

WORKING CAPITAL/MONTH

1. RAW MATERIAL	Rs.	1,93,750.00
2. SALARY & WAGES	Rs.	60,200.00
3. UTILITIES & OVERHEADS	Rs.	22,600.00
TOTAL	**Rs.**	**2,76,550.00**

CAPITAL INVESTMENT

FIXED CAPITAL	Rs.	1,97,000.00
WORKING CAPITAL FOR 3 MONTHS	Rs.	8,29,650.00
TOTAL	**Rs.**	**10,26,650.00**

TURN OVER/ANNUM

BY SALE OF 30,000 PCS. SCHOOL BAGS = 39,00,000.00

PROFIT SALES RATIO = PROFIT / SALES X 100 = 9.5%

RATE OF RETURN = OPERATING PROFIT / T.C.I X 100 = 36%

BREAK EVEN POINT (B.E.P) = 63%

Chapter - 27

Indian and Overseas Trade Directory of Leather & Leather Products, Chemicals and Machineries

A Kumar & Company Pvt. Ltd.
10, Shriram Market, Hing-KI-Mandi,
Agra-282003 (U.P.)
Tel : + 91-0562-2267772
Fax : + 91-0562-2640160
E-mail : akumar_co@yahoo.com
Products Manufactured/Marketed:
Shoe Components

Aastropure Electro Systems Pvt. Ltd.
Plot No. 404, Phase-IV,
Gidc Estate, Naroda
Ahmedabad, Gujarat
Products Manufactured/Marketed:
R.O. Plant

Abhilash Chemicals Pvt. Ltd.
26-D, Ganesapuram, K. Pudur,
Madurai-625007 (Tamil Nadu)
Tel : + 91-0452-2569286, 2569566
Fax : + 91-0452-2567663
E-mail: abhichem@sancharnet.in
Products Manufactured/Marketed:
Finished Leather

Abrameq
Rua Lucas De Oliveira,
49, Sala 204, 93510-110,
Novohamburgo, RS Brazil
Tel. : 55 51 594 2232
Fax : 55 51 594 2232
E-mail : abrameqe@abrameq.com
Products Manufactured/Marketed:
Machinery and Equipment

A.G.G. Leather SRL
Via Giuriolo, 5-36071 Arzignano (VI)
Italy
Tel. : 0039-0445-491507
Fax : 0039-0445-497729
E-mail : agg.leather@keycomm.it

Products Manufactured/Marketed:
Wet Blue hides, Crust leather

Ajanta Labels Company Pvt. Ltd.
6202/2, Block No. 1, Dev Nagar,
(Near Tank Road) Karol Bagh,
New Delhi-110005
Tel. : 91-011-25850025, 25760010
Fax : 91-011-25752595, 25862660
E-mail : ajanta@bol.net.in
Products Manufactured/Marketed:
Fashion Accessories

Al Ganoub Tanning Factory
P.O. Box No. 1133, Khamis Mushayt,
Saudi Arabia
Tel. : 966-7-2271497, 2271005
Fax : 966-7-2271537
E-mail :
alganoub_tannery@yahoo.com
Products Manufactured/Marketed:
Wet Blue skins

Aleem Leathers
13, M.V. Badran Street, Periamet,
Chennai-600003
Tel. : 91-44-25321436
Fax : 91-44-52175331
E-mail : aleemleathers@hotmail.com
Products Manufactured/Marketed:
Shoe Components, Travelware,
Fashion Accessories

Alert India
C-1, SMA Industrial Estate,
G.T. Karnal Road,
Delhi-110033
Tel. : 91-011-27220499, 27463356, 57
Fax : 91-011-27227482
Products Manufactured/Marketed:
Shoe Components

Alig International
126, Iqbal Street, Jajmau,
Kanpur-208010 (U.P.)
Tel. : 91-0512-2461591, 2461244
E-mail : info@aligtannery.com
Products Manufactured/Marketed:
Finished Leather, Leather Goods,
Leather Garments, Upholstery

Allied Chemicals International Co. Ltd.
255/2, Bangpoo Industrial Estate
SOI 3, Prakasa, Muang,
Samuthprakarn-10280 (Thailand)
Tel. : 00662-3239930-1
Fax : 00662-3231627, 7094672
E-mail : acicth@allied-chemical.co.th, acicth@yahoo1.com
Products Manufactured/Marketed:
Chemicals for Leather Industry

Alpha Leather Products
80, Anna Salai, Nagalkeni,
Chrompet, Chennai - 600044
(Tamil Nadu)
Tel. : 91-044-22385541
Fax : 91-044-22414758
E-mail :
alphaleatherproducts@vsnl.com
Products Manufactured/Marketed:
Finished Leather, Footwear

Alpha Systems Pvt. Ltd.
55, Thomas Nagar, Little Mount,
Saidapet,
Chennai-600015 (Tamil Nadu)
Tel. : 91-044-22201796, 22352733
E-mail : rajesh@alphasysindia.com
Products Manufactured/Marketed:
ERP Software for Leather Industry
(tannery, shoes, leather garments
and goods)

Anand Cutting Profiles Pvt. Ltd.
340, Phase-IV, Udyog Vihar,
Gurgaon-122016 (Haryana)
Tel. : 91-0124-5013075
Fax : 91-0124-5013076
E-mail : anandbro@del3.vsnl.net.in
Products Manufactured/Marketed:
Shoe Components: injection moulds for unit soles in PVC, PU, TPR, EVA, rubber, etc., embosing and perforating plates; round punches and prickers; fancy tubes; automobile dies for nonmetallic components; matrix dies with punches; forged dies for soles, insoles

Anywhere Corporation
SF-2, No.68, Dong-Nan Street,
401, Taichuang, Taiwan R.O.C.
Tel. : 886-4-22126483, 5
Fax : 886-4-22126486
E-mail : anywhereshoes@seed.net.tw
Products Manufactured/Marketed:
Leather Goods, Footwear Shoe, Components

Apex Footwear Ltd.
Celebration Point, 1st Floor,
Road No. 113A, Plot No. 3 & 5
Gulshan-2, Dhaka-1212, Bangladesh
Tel. : +880-2-8828258
Fax : +880-2-8813038
E-mail : afl@ranksitt.net
Products Manufactured/Marketed:
Footwear

APL Polyfab (P) Ltd.,
5, Dr. Ranendra Prasad Salai,
Kolkatta-700001
Tel. : 91-33-22200373, 9574
Fax : 91-33-22205125
E-mail : polyfab@vsnl.com
Products Manufactured/Marketed:
Shoe Components

Apsom Infotex Ltd.
A-53, Okhla Industrial Area, Phase-II,
New Delhi-110020
Tel. : 91-011-26387729, 26384443
Fax : 91-011-26385097
E-mail : apsom@vsnl.com
Products Manufactured/Marketed:
Footwear upper designing CAD/CAM Software solutions

Ares (Yanchen) Machinery Co. Ltd.
Dagang Industrial Park Zone,
Yangcheng, (China)
Tel. : 0086-515-8804088
Fax : 0086-515-8803267
E-mail : James@aresmachine.com
Products Manufactured/Marketed:
Machinery & Equipment

Argolanda B.V.
Weena 693, 3013 AM Rotterdam
The Netherlands
Tel. : +31-10-2800000
Fax : +31-10-4045794
E-mail : info@argolanda.nl
Products Manufactured/Marketed:
Raw, Pickled, Wetblue, Crust, Goat/ Sheepskins, Hides

Asia Pacific Leather Fair Ltd. (APLF)
17/F, China Resources Building,
26, Harbour Road,
Wanchai, (Hong Kong)
Tel. : 852-25856135, 28276211
Fax : 852-28277831
E-mail : gracelee@cmpasia. com
Products Manufactured/Marketed:
APLF show brochures and folders

Asialink Agencies Pvt. Ltd.
7, 2nd. Floor, Paschim Enclave,
Main Rohtak Road,
New Delhi-110087
Tel. : 91-011-25268285, 86
Fax : 91-011-25262539
E-mail : asianlink@rediffrmail.com
Products Manufactured/Marketed:
Machinery & Equipment

Asiatic Colour Chem Ind. Ltd.
1503, GIDC, Phase-I, Naroda,
Gujarat
Tel. : 91-079-22821066
Fax : 91-079-22820766
E-mail : ceo@asiaticcolor.com
Products Manufactured/Marketed:
Fashion Accessories, Leathers Chemicals and Dyes

Assomac (National Association of Italian Manufacturers of Footwear Leather goods & Tannery Machines and Accessories
Via Matteotti, 4/A
P.O. Box 73-27029 Vigevano (PV)
Italy
Tel. : 0039 0381 78883
Fax : 0039 0381 88602
E-mail : info@assomac.it
Products Manufactured/Marketed:
Trade Association

Astral Impex
126, Rama Street
Nungambakkam, Chennai-600034
Tel. : 91-44-28277546, 52045294
Fax : 91-44-28225680
E-mail : astralimpex@hotmail.com
Products Manufactured/Marketed:
Fashion Accessories

ATC Chemicals India Pvt. Ltd.
89, Annasalai Nagalkeni, Chrompet,
Chennai-600044
Tamil Nadu
Tel. : 91-044-22362708, 22381638
Fax : 91-044-22380152
Products Manufactured/Marketed:
Chemicals

Atlas Copco Compressor Sales
16, Race Course Road, Guindy,
Chennai-600032 (Tamil Nadu)
Tel. : 91-044-22455033
E-mail :
sreekumar.nambiar@in.atlascopco.com
Products Manufactured/Marketed:
Machinery & Equipment

Auro Electronics
A-2, Industrial Estate, Thattan Chavadi,
Pondicherry-605009
Tel. : 91-0413-2248286, 5
Fax : 91-0413-2248285
E-mail : svswamy@vsnl.net
Products Manufactured/Marketed:
Machinery & Equipment

A.V. Thomas Leathers & Allied Products Pvt. Ltd.
118 Velachery Main Road,
Guindy, Chennai-600032
Tel. : 91-44-22201954, 22201965
Fax : 91-44-22201954
Products Manufactured/Marketed:
Men's & Ladies Wallets, Men's & Ladies Bags, Organizers Note book covers, Money Clips & Card cases, Keyfobs/Keyrings, Desktop items, Travel Belts, Shoe uppers, Full shoes etc.

Baco Metallic Industries
D-31, Sector - 59,
Noida-201301 (U.P.)
Tel. : 91-0120-2580231
Fax : 91-0120-2580484
E-mail : baco@vsnl.com
Products Manufactured/Marketed:
Shoe Components

Basmalah Marketing (P) Ltd.
No. 289, 1st Floor, Dr. Natesan Road,
ICE House,
Chennai-600005 (Tamil Nadu)
Tel.: 91-044-28475666, 9444120394
E-mail :
basmalahbasmalah@yahoo.com
Products Manufactured/Marketed:
Fashion Accessories

Bathija International
3, K.K. Mansion, 289/91 Nagdevi Street,
Mumbai-400003 (Maharasthra)
Tel. : 91-022-23421004
Fax : 91-022-23415034
E-mail :
bathijainternational@rediffmail.com
Products Manufactured/Marketed:
Machinery & Equipment

Bay Footwear Ltd.
21, Hazaribagh,
Dhaka-1209 (Bangladesh)
Tel. : +880-2-8611468
Fax : +880-2-8618716
E-mail : baytann@citechco.net
Products Manufactured/Marketed:
Footwear

Bertin Ltda
Rodovia BR 153, KM 179,
Lins-SP-Brazil : CEP 16400-000
Tel. : 55-14-35332141
Fax : 55-14-35332142
E-mail :
bracol.directoria@bertin.com.br
Products Manufactured/Marketed:
Finished Leather

Bharath & Co.
99/3, Poonakutty Tannery, Nagalkeni,
Kannayiram Street, Chrompet,
Chennai-600044 (Tamil Nadu)
Tel. : 91-044-22368429
Fax : 91-044-22211090
E-mail : bharathco@vsnl.net
Products Manufactured/Marketed:
Finished Leather, Leather Good, Footwear, Shoe Components

British United Shoe Machinery Shoemat
USM House, Warren Park Way,
Enderby, Leicester-LE19 4ZW
United Kingdom
Tel. : 0044-116-2862840
Fax : 0044-116-2847600
E-mail : bmoore@busm.co.uk
Products Manufactured/Marketed:
Shoemaking CAD/CAM Software/ hardware

Central Leather Research Institute
Adyar;
Chennai-600020
Tel. : 044-24915238, 24911386
Fax : 044-24911589, 2150
E-mail : bbdclri@yahoo.com
Products Manufactured/Marketed:
Finished Leather, Footwear, Shoe Components, Leather Garments, Leather Goods, Fashion Accessories.

Central Footwear Training Institute
Ministry of SSI, Govt. of India
65/1, G.S.T. Road, Guindy,
Chennai-600032
Tel. : 91-44-22341529
Fax : 91-44-22336876
E-mail : cfti@vsnl.net
Products Manufactured/Marketed:
Footwear

Chemcrown Exports Ltd.
18 (Old No. 30), Balfour Road, Kellys,
Chennai-600010 (Tamil Nadu)
Tel. : 91-044-26454992, 93
Fax : 91-044-26452257
E-mail : cemcrown@eth.net
Products Manufactured/Marketed:
Shoe Components

Chander Shoe Components
Toplatex Products
126, P.S. Sivaswamy Salai, Mylapore,
Chennai-600004 (Tamil Nadu)
Tel. : 91-044-24992432
Fax : 91-044-24992286
E-mail : chandershoe@eth.net
Products Manufactured/Marketed:
Shoe Components

Cinturones Alvi (India) Pvt. Ltd.
B-1/45, Safdarjung Enclave,
New Delhi
Tel. : 91-011-51411062
Fax : 91-011-51411063
E-mail : alviindia@touchtelindia.net
Products Manufactured/Marketed:
Shoe Components, Leather Goods

CICB - Center of Brazilian Tanning Industries
Sas Quadra 01, Bloco 'N', ED.
Terra Brazilis, Brasilia, DF - Brazil
Tel. : 55-61-2241867
Fax : 55-61-3237943
E-mail : lucchese.cicb@sinos.net
Products Manufactured/Marketed:
Finished Leather

Classic Home Furnishing (P) Ltd.
Plot No. 16, CSEZ Kakkanad,
Kochi-680237 (Kerala)
Tel. : 91-0484-2413046, 2413047
E-mail : classichome@satyam.net.in
Products Manufactured/Marketed:
Leather/seude protection/anti-stain chemical

Clri - Ascent
Central Leather Research
Institute, Adyar,
Chennai-600020 (Tamil Nadu)
Tel. : 91-044-24917216
Fax : 91-044-24917216
E-mail : vbmclri@hotmail.com
Products Manufactured/Marketed:
Footwear

Classic Enterprises
R-22, Khaneja Complex, Shakarpur,
Delhi-110092
Tel. : 91-011-22523304
Fax : 91-011-22432927
E-mail : aggarwal@vsnl.com
Products Manufactured/Marketed:
EVA sheets plain/laminated, Moulded cup insole

Components & Equipments Ltd.
18 (Old No. 30), Balfour Road, Kellys,
Chennai-600010 (Tamil Nadu)
Tel. : 91-044-26454992, 93
Fax : 91.044-264252275
E-mail : cemcrown@eth.net
Products Manufactured/Marketed:
Chemicals

Conceria Marca Toro Spa
Via Dei Conciatori, 56024,
Ponte A Egola,
Pisa, Italy
Tel. : 0039-0571-498367
Fax : 0039-571-498771
E-mail : marcatoro@marcatoro.it
Products Manufactured/Marketed:
Finished Leather

Conceria Virginia
50, Raja Muthia Road, Peramet,
Chennai-600003 (Tamil Nadu)
Tel. : 91-044-25361634
Fax : 91-044-25366187
E-mail : forward@vsnl.com
Products Manufactured/Marketed:
Shoe Components

Conserve H.R.P.
A-116, Madhuban, Vikas Marg,
New Delhi-110092
Tel. : 91-011-22439274
Fax : 91-011-22413112
E-mail : conserve@vsnl.net
Products Manufactured/Marketed:
Bags and Fashion Accessories

Cordinal Industries
4/8, Ganpathy Nagar, 1st Street,
Ekkaduthnagal,
Chennai-600097 (Tamil Nadu)
Tel. : 91-044-22316505, 22326473
Fax : 91-044-22316505
E-mail : cordinal_industries@vsnl.net
Products Manufactured/Marketed:
Machinery & Equipment

Cortume Krumenauer S.A.
Rua Julio De Castilhos, No. 7979,
Portao-cep: 93180-000
RS - Brazil
Tel. : 55-51-5621200
Fax : 55-51-5621862
E-mail : joel@krumenauer.com.br
Products Manufactured/Marketed:
Finished Leather

Couros Nobre Beneficiamento Ltda.
Estrada Da Integracao Leopoldo
Petry500 93425-320-Novo
Hamburgo-RS
Brazil
Tel. : (55) 51 595 8822
Fax : (55) 51 595 8506
E-mail :
paulo.xavier@courosnobre.com.br
Products Manufactured/Marketed:
Finished Leather

Coim India Pvt. Ltd.
202-203, Deepshikha Building,
Rajendra Place,
New Delhi-110008
Tel. : 91-011-51538902, 3, 4
Fax : 91-011-51538901
E-mail : vipul@coimindia.com
Products Manufactured/Marketed:
Shoe Components

Creative Home Fashions Pvt. Ltd.
B-44/45, Sector-58,
Noida-201301 (U.P.)
Tel. : 91-0120-2584662/3, 2584296/7/8
Fax : 91-0120-2584662, 2584299
E-mail :
leather@creativehomefashions.net
Products Manufactured/Marketed:
Fashion Accessories, Leather Goods

Crispin Systems Ltd.,
C-51, Kendriya Vihar Apartments,
Sector-51, Noida (U.P.)

Tel. : 91-0120-2480961
E-mail : ragarwal@crispinsystems.com
Products Manufactured/Marketed:
CAD/CAM for footwear design

Crab Industry Co. Ltd.
No. 8-3, 2 Sec., Tan-Fu Rd.,
Tan-Tzu Hsiang, Taichung,
Taiwan R.O.C.
Tel. : 886-4-25324177
Fax : 886-4-25324166
E-mail : crab.tds@msa.hinet.net
Products Manufactured/Marketed:
Machinery & Equipment

Curtume Aimore S.A.
Rua Presidente Vargas, No. 505, Bairro: Aimore, Arroio Do Meio-Cep: 95940-000
RS - Brazil
Tel. : 55-51-37161313
Fax : 55-51-37161353
E-mail : importexport@aimore.ind.br
Products Manufactured/Marketed:
Finished Leather

Curtume Kern Mattes S.A.
Rua Julio De Castilhos, No. 2554,
Bairro: Portao Velho,
Portao-Cep: 93180-000,
RS - Brazil
Tel. : 55-51-5621300
Fax : 55-51-5621157
E-mail : kernmattes@vol.com.br
Products Manufactured/Marketed:
Finished Leather

Curtipelli Industria E Comercio De Couros Ltda
Avenida Irinev Becker, No. 501, Bairro: Florestal, Dois Irmaos-
Cep: 93950-000
RS-Brazil
Tel. : 55-51-5641088
Fax : 55-51-5641088
E-mail : curtiplli@curtipelli.com.br
Products Manufactured/Marketed:
Finished Leather

D2 International
P-78, Kasba Industrial Estate,
Phase-II,
Kolkata-700107 (West Bengal)
Tel. : 91-033-24427539
Products Manufactured/Marketed:
Leather Goods

Dagger Die Cutting
31/A5, North Phase,
Sidco Industrial Estate, Ambattur,
Chennai-98
Tel. : 91-044-26258261
Fax : 91-044-26254140
E-mail : dagger@vsnl.com
Products Manufactured/Marketed:
Cutting Knives, Cutting dies.

DCP Synthetics (P) Ltd.
6535, Hardhian Singh Road,
Dev Nagar, Karol Bagh,
New Delhi-110005
Tel. : 91-011-51333333 (6 lines)
Fax : 011-25824244
E-mail : dcp@puleather.net
Products Manufactured/Marketed:
Leather Goods, Shoe Components

Deeco
2/188, Dayasadan Road
Nerkundram,
Chennai-600107
Tel. : 98840 77060
Fax : 044-52143576
E-mail : decco@sify.com
Products Manufactured/Marketed:
Wooden Wallet and belt boxes

Dermatech International Limited
1404/1410 High Road,
Whetstone, London N20 9BH
United Kingdom
Tel. : 44-20-83437372
Fax : 44-20-83437288
E-mail : sales@dermatechint.com
Products Manufactured/Marketed:
"THE BEST OUT OF AFRICA AND ASIA"
A) Wetsalted - Drum salted - Pickled and wetblued
• Hides, Wool sheep skins, Skivers, Hair Sheep Skins, Goat Skins, Calf Skins, Reptile Skins.
B) Drum dyed and undyed crust and finished leathers for shoe uppers, Garments, Leather Goods, Linings, Glove, Hair-on and Chamois,
• Chrome free, Full vegetable and vegetable combinations, Full Chrome, Chrome Retan, Oil tanned, Semi Chrome

DESPA + PIDIGI
Via Della Meccanica, 27,
37139 Verona,
Italy
Tel. : 0039-045-8393811
Fax : 0039-045-8393812
E-mail: despa@degara.com
Products Manufactured/Marketed:
Machinery and Equipment, Shoe Components, Spare Parts, Consumable Accessories etc.

Dharmsee Parpia
11, Kothari Road, Nungambakkam,
Chennai-600034 (Tamil Nadu)
Tel. : 91-044-28251566, 28251577
Fax : 91-044-28251650
E-mail : dharmsee@dishnetdsl.net
Products Manufactured/Marketed:
Finished Leather, Footwear Machinery & Equipment Leather, Garments, Chemicals Etc.

Dornbusch Gravuren GMBH
AM Selder 31, 47906 Kempen,
Kempen, Germany
Tel. : 02152-9165-0
Fax : 02152-518394
E-mail : info@dornbusch-gravuren.de
Products Manufactured/Marketed:
Machinery & Equipment

Dow Chemical Intl. P. Ltd.
A-6, Sector 58,
Noida-201304 (U.P.)
Tel. : 91-0120-2589447/48
Fax : 91-0120-2589446
E-mail : tbediedow.com
Products Manufactured/Marketed:
Shoe soles made of PU chemicals

Dyna Creations Pvt. Ltd.
M-576, Guru Harkishan Nagar,
Paschim Vihar, 1st Floor,
New Delhi-110087
Tel. : 91-011-55496285
Fax : 91-011-25274297
E-mail : yf8dnag8@nda.vsnl.net.in
Products Manufactured/Marketed:
Machinery & Equipment

Dynamic Techno Medicals Pvt. Ltd.
Post Box No. 45, Ashokapuram,
Aluva-683101 (Kerala)
Tel. : 0484-2637788/970
Fax : 0484-2637688
E-mail : dynamicortho@sity.com
Products Manufactured/Marketed:
Footwear

E.H. Turel & Company
7, Haddows Road,
Chennai-600006.
Tel. : 91-44-28278591/28275308
Fax : 91-44-28274662
E-mail : turel@md3.vsnl.net.in
Products Manufactured/Marketed:
Machinery & Equipment

ECO Sales
C-32, Sector 10,
Noida-201301 (U.P.)
Tel. : 91-0120-2532101
Fax : 91-0120-2519537
E-mail : dipens@satyam.net.in
Products Manufactured/Marketed:
Machinery & Equipment

Elastic India
62, Jermiah Road, Vepery,
Chennai-600007 (Tamil Nadu)
Tel. : 91-044-26650107, 52176866
Fax : 91-044-26481022
E-mail : elasticindia@msn.com
Products Manufactured/Marketed:
Footwear

Elgi Equipment Ltd.
S-2, IInd Floor, 'Amar Sindur'
No. 43, Pantheon Road, Egmore,
Chennai-600008 (Tamil Nadu)
Tel. : 91-044-28586699, 28513599
Fax : 91-044-28586499
E-mail : padmakumarls@elgi.co.in
Products Manufactured/Marketed:
Machinery & Equipment

Elite India Rubber Products Pvt. Ltd.
61, Topsia Road (South),
Kolkata-700046 (West Bengal)
Tel. : 91-033-23447319, 23440149
Fax : 91-033-23439067, 8385
E-mail : eliterbr@vsnl.com
Products Manufactured/Marketed:
Shoe Components

Enkay (India) Rubber Co. Ltd.
B-3, SMA, Industrial Estate,
G.T. Karnal Road, Delhi-110033
Tel. : 91-011-27450510, 27130036
Fax : 91-011-27211952
E-mail : contact@enkayrub.com
Products Manufactured/Marketed:
Shoes, Heels, Resin Rubber Sheets, Top lifts, Shoe Concepts

Ess Aar Universal Pvt. Ltd.
A-40/1 Site-4, Sahibabad
Industrial Area,
Ghaziabad-201010 (U.P.)
Tel. : 91-0120-2896012, 74
Fax : 91-0120-2895951
E-mail : essaar@vsnl.com
Products Manufactured/Marketed:
PU soles, Insoles, Footbeds

Essegi Moulds India Pvt. Ltd.,
New No. 6, Velmurugan Colony Street,
Vadapalani, Chennai-600026
Tel. : 91-44-56138658
E-mail : essegiindia@yahoo.co.in
Products Manufactured/Marketed:
Mould for shoes

Euro Leathers Pvt. Ltd.
Plot No. 1345, Road No. 68,
Jubilee Hills,
Hyderabad-500033 (Andhra Pradesh)
Tel. : 91-040-23543847
Fax : 91-040-23608475
E-mail : hyd_nadella@sancharnet.in
Products Manufactured/Marketed:
Finished Leather

Euro Shoe Components & Co.
New No. 48, North Phase,
Sidco Industrial, Estate, Ambattur,
Chennai-600098 (Tamil Nadu)
Tel. : 91-044-26251545, 26253441
Fax : 91-044-26251545
E-mail : euroshoe@eth.net,
euroshoeco@yahoo.com
Products Manufactured/Marketed:
Toe caps, Heels & Wedges, Plastic Trims, Buckles, Shoe Horms, Soles, Shank, Lables, Plastic Eyelets, etc.

Exportadora Bom Retiro Ltda
Rua Carlos Arn, No. 715A,
Bairro: Canabarro,
Teutonia-Cep: 95890-000
RS - Brazil
Tel. : 55-51-37625800
Fax : 55-51-37629166
E-mail :
teutonia@courosbomretiro.com.br
Products Manufactured/Marketed:
Finished Leather, Upholstery Leather

Finicap Chemicals
Tatia House, 18, Ritherdon Road,
Vepery, Chennai-600007 (Tamil Nadu)
Tel. : 91-044-25325050, 266050210
Fax : 91-044-253225142
E-mail : tatia@md3.vsnl.net.in
Products Manufactured/Marketed:
Chemicals

First Computers
2nd Floor, Ceebros Centre,
45, Montieth Road,
Egmore, Chennai-8
Tel. : 28554559 / 28554568
Fax : 28553703
E-mail : firstc@vsnl.com
Products Manufactured/Marketed:
Application Software for Leather Manufacturing Companies

Freudenberg Non-Wovens India Pvt. Ltd.
A-324, TTC Industrial Area,
4 Ahape, Navi Mumbai (Maharashtra)
Tel. : 91-022-27781456, 27781371
Fax : 91-022-27781857
E-mail : bramji@fnindia.net
Products Manufactured/Marketed:
Shoe Components

Galvano Technica SNC
Via Bertagalla 14, 17014,
CA RO Montenotte (SU),
Italy
Tel. : 0039-019-504753-4
Fax : 0039-019-500025
E-mail : info@galtec.it
Products Manufactured/Marketed:
Plates & rollers for tanning machines

G.B. Leathers SPA / Concerie Riunite G.B. SPA
Via Dei Conciatori, 8/10, 56024
Ponte A Egola - San Miniato,
Pisa, Italy
Tel. : 0039-0571-415299
Fax : 0039-571-485271
E-mail : gbleathers@gbcuoio.it
Products Manufactured/Marketed:
Finished Leather

GE. MA. TA. SPA
Via Rampa Dell 'Agno, 6, Trissino
(Vicenza), Italy
Tel. : 0039-0445-492711
Fax : 0039-0445-490111
E-mail : info@gemata.com
Products Manufactured/Marketed:
Machinery & Equipment

Gopi Engineering Works
2/73, M.C. Road,
Madanur-635804 (Tamil Nadu)
Tel. : 91-04174-256237
Fax : 91-04174-256273
E-mail : gopigroups@eth.net
Products Manufactured/Marketed:
Machinery & Equipment

Gopi International
141, M.B.T. Road, Ranipet
(Vellore District).
Ranipet-632401 (Tamil Nadu)
Tel. : 04172-270054
Fax : 04172-270055
E-mail : vir_gopisons@sancharnet.in
Products Manufactured/Marketed:
Machinery & Equipment

Gopl Engineering & Sons
141, M.B.T. Road, Ranipet,
Vellore Distt.,
Ranipet-632401 (Tamil Nadu)
Tel. : 91-04172-270054
Fax : 91-04172-270055
E-mail : vir_gopisons@sancharnet.in
Products Manufactured/Marketed:
Machinery & Equipment

Gusbi Officina Meccanica SPA
27029, Vigevano (PV),
Italy Via Alessandria, 35,
Italy
Tel. : 0039-2054516
E-mail : gusbitv@gusbi.com
Products Manufactured/Marketed:
Machinery & Equipment

Gupta Enterprises
3159/34 IInd Floor,
Beedon Pura, Karol Bagh,
New Delhi-110005
Tel. : 98100 70027
Fax : 011-51548782
Products Manufactured/Marketed:
Leather Garments, Machinery &
Equipment

Harman Ambur Clicking Dies
No. 1/359, Pernambut Road,
Kadambur, Kailasagiri Village,
Oomerbad Post-635808 (Tamil Nadu)
Tel. : 91-04174-249907
Fax : 04174-249907
E-mail : harmanambur@rediffmail.com
Products Manufactured/Marketed:
Cutting dies

Harman Chennai Clicking Dies
New No. 115 (Old No. 51), IInd Floor,
Maddox Street, Choolai,
Chennai-600112 (Tamil Nadu)
Tel. : 91-044-52041704, 5
Fax : 91-044-26651902
E-mail : harmanchennai@eth.net
Products Manufactured/Marketed:
Cutting dies

Harman Sales Pvt. Ltd.
201-A, Byculla Service Indl. Estate,
Dadoji Konddeo Marg, Byculla,
Mumbai-400027 (Maharashtra)
Tel. : 91-022-23712893, 99
Fax : 91-022-23738814
E-mail : hrmngrpbyc@vsnl.net
Products Manufactured/Marketed:
Machinery & Equipment

Hari Chand Anand & Co.
A-94/1, Okhla Indl. Area, Phase-II,
New Delhi - 110020
Tel. : 91-011-26383820, 11, 04
Fax : 91-011-51612614, 26383802

E-mail : hca@vsnl.net,
hca@touchtelindia.net
Products Manufactured/Marketed:
Machinery & Equipment

Hawk Leathers Pvt. Ltd.
Plot No. 23, Leather Complex,
Kapurthala Road,
Jalandhar, (Punjab)
Tel. : 91-0181-2650568, 2651617
Fax : 91-0181-2650568
E-mail : hawkleathers@vsnl.com
Products Manufactured/Marketed:
Finished Leather, Wet Blue

Huni Deri Makinalari V.E.
Tycarct AS, Buluani, No. 210,
34841 Aucilar, Turkey
Tel. : 0090-212-6902244
Fax : 0090-212-6905525
E-mail : hueni@hueni.com
Products Manufactured/Marketed:
Machinery & Equipment: Wooden, steel and polypropylene drums & accessories; process control equipment; automatic water mixing and dosing systems; automatic weighing, mixing and dosing system for liquid chemicals; process control system for tanneries; Batching/dispensing for powder products; waste water treatment, tannery filteration; batching systems for finishing chemicals; turnkey tannery projects; engineering and special software; service and spare parts.

Hyde Park India Pvt. Ltd.
C-50, Sector-63,
Noida-201301 (U.P.)
Tel. : 91-0120-2402908, 2403950
Fax : 91-0120-2403949
E-mail : hydepark@vsnl.net,
hydepark@eth.net
Products Manufactured/Marketed:
Fashion Accessories, Shoe Components

Indchem Distributors Private Limited
'Vaibhav', 62 EVK Sampath Road,
Vepery, Chennai-600007 (Tamil Nadu)
Tel. : 91-44-26618035, 26618095
Fax : 91-44-26618480
E-mail : indchem@vsnl.com
Products Manufactured/Marketed:
Machinery & Equipment

Indchem Marketing Corporation
No. 62, EVK Sampath Road,
Vepery, Chennai-600007 (Tamil Nadu)
Tel. : 91-44-26618900, 26618095
Fax : 91-44-26618480
E-mail : indchem@vsnl.com
Products Manufactured/Marketed:
Shoe Components, Buffing Paper

Indian Shoe's Accessories
186, Purasawalkam High Road,
F-10, City Centre,
Chennai-600010 (Tamil Nadu)
Tel. : 91-044-25325272, 26430753
Fax : 91-044-26428652
E-mail : isac@satyam.net.in
Products Manufactured/Marketed:
Footwear, Shoe Components, Etc.

Indian Shoe Federation (ISF) & Indian Finished Leather Manufacturers Exporters Association (Iflmea)
3rd Floor, CMDA Tower II,
Gandhi Irwin Road, Egmore,
Chennai-600008 (Tamil Nadu)
Tel. : 91-044-2858794
Fax : 91-044-28413704

E-mail : indshoeted@eth.net
Products Manufactured/Marketed:
Association

Indofil Chemicals Company
Nirlon House, 3 RD Floor,
DR. Annie Besant Road,
Mumbai-400030 (Maharashtra)
Tel. : 91-022-56637373
Fax : 91-022-24938109
E-mail : sjha-icc@modi.com
Products Manufactured/Marketed:
Finished Leather

Intek Tapes Private Limited
No. 13,9th Main, 3rd Block, Jayanagar,
Bangalore-560011 (Karnataka)
Tel. : 91-080-26655691
Fax : 91-080-26656693
E-mail : intek@vsnl.com
Products Manufactured/Marketed:
Shoe Components

International Leather Materials
No. 4B, Vepery High Road, Periamet,
Chennai-600003
Tel. : 91-44-55663722, 9381015043 / 9840039692
Fax : 91-44-52142437
E-mail : saltas@vsnl.com
Products Manufactured/Marketed:
Footwear, Shoe Components, Leather Garments, Fashion Accessories

I.S.T. S.R.L.
Via Selve 28,
62010 Montecosaro (MC)
Italy
Tel. : 390733567
Fax : 390733567301
E-mail : info@istmachinery.it
Products Manufactured/Marketed:
Machinery & Equipment

Italia Heels (Div. of: Jupiter Power Transmissions Pvt. Ltd.)
B-177, Sanjay Building No. 5,
Mittal Indl. Estate, M. Vasanji Road,
Andheri (East),
Mumbai-400059 (Maharashtra)
Tel. : 91-022-28508857, 58
Fax : 91-022-28500866
E-mail : italiaheels@horseshoeindia.com
Products Manufactured/Marketed:
Footwear, Shoe Components

Jarvis International
6 Valmeek Street,
Kolkata-700026 (West Bengal)
Tel. : 91-033-24765551
Fax : 91-033-24762990
E-mail : jarvis@cal2.vsnl.net.in
Products Manufactured/Marketed:
Machinery & Equipment

Jasch Industries Ltd.
5105/1, Jasch House,
Behind Khalsa College, Dev Nagar,
New Delhi - 110005
Tel. : 91-11-25733745-750
Fax : 91-11-25733748, 2823732
E-mail : Kaushal@jaschindia.com
Products Manufactured/Marketed:
Shoe Components

Jennys Shoes Ltd.
Jennys House, H-6, Road 68/A,
Gulshan-2, Dhaka-1212,
Bangladesh
Tel. : +880-2-8824885
Fax : 880-2-8823372
E-mail : jennys@optimaxbd.net
Products Manufactured/Marketed:
Footwear

Jesons Industries Ltd.
904 Penninsula Tower-1,
Ganpat Rao Kadam Marg, Lower parel,
Mumbai-400013 (Maharashtra)
Tel. : 91-022-56615253
Fax : 91-022-56515252
E-mail : kirti@jeson.net
Products Manufactured/Marketed:
Synthetic adhesives

Jet Graphics
Flat No. 6, 995-A, Koleta Court,
11th Main Road, 2nd AVN., Annanagar,
Chennai-600040 (Tamil Nadu)
Tel. : 91-044-52170656
Fax : 91-044-26161532
E-mail : jetgraphics@eth.net,
jetgraphics@touchtelindia.net
Products Manufactured/Marketed:
Fashion Accessories

J.M.J. Textile Pvt. Ltd.
J-147. Ashok Vihar, Phase-I,
Delhi-110052
Tel. : 91-011-27314292, 227318129
Fax : 91-011-27865180, 27312892
E-mail : jmj@del3.vsnl.net.in
Products Manufactured/Marketed:
Sewing & Stiching Thread, Lamination EVA Fabric

K.H. Shoes Private Ltd.
2, Thirunarayana Guru Road, Choolai,
Chennai-600112 (Tamil Nadu)
Tel. : 91-044-25322731, 25323335
Fax : 91-044-25321185, 26434117
E-mail : khgroups@vsnl.com
Products Manufactured/Marketed:
Finished Leather, Leather Goods, Footwear, Shoe Components, Leather Garments, Leather Goods, Upholstery, Leather Belts Etc.

K.S.R. Agencies
17/13, First Floor,
Kattur Sadayappan Street, Periamet,
Chennai-600003 (Tamil Nadu)
Tel. : 91-044-25387892
Fax : 91-044-25365998
E-mail : ksrleathers@vsnl.net
Products Manufactured/Marketed:
Machinery & Equipment

K.S.R. Leathers
17/13, First Floor,
Kattur Sadayappan Street, Periamet
Chennai-600003 (Tamil Nadu)
Tel. : 91-044-25387892
Fax : 91-044-25365998
E-mail : ksrleathers@vsnl.net
Products Manufactured/Marketed:
Finished Leather

Kaeser Compressors (I) Pvt. Ltd.
AG 55/2, IIIrd Street,
River View Colony, Anna Nagar,
Chennai-600040 (Tamil Nadu)
Tel. : 91-044-26200425, 26200439
Products Manufactured/Marketed:
Air compressors & cooling towers

Kailash Trade Links Private Limited
174/2, Vanagaram Road, Athipet,
Chennai-600058 (Tamil Nadu)
Tel. : 91-044-26545035
Fax : 91-044-26545036
E-mail : ktrade@eth.net
Products Manufactured/Marketed:
Shoe Components

Kaiser Exports Private Limited
140-B, Zamrudpur Community Centre,
New Delhi-110048
Tel. : 91-011-26442755, 26442640
Fax : 91-011-51634911

E-mail : schandhok@hotmail.com
Products Manufactured/Marketed:
Finished Leather, Shoe Components, Leather Garments

Kanan Plastic Product Pvt. Ltd.
386, M.I.E. Bahadurgarh,
Haryana
Tel. : 91-0-9810002826, 9899128211
Fax : 28117051
E-mail : kananplastic@vsnl.net
Products Manufactured/Marketed:
PU Soles

Kanna Chemie (P) Ltd.
No. 11, Thiruneermalai Main Road,
Nagalkeni, Chrompet,
Channai-600044 (Tamil Nadu)
Tel. : 91-044-22383379
Fax : 91-044-22383816
E-mail : kannachemie@eth.net
Products Manufactured/Marketed:
Chemicals

Kemia Tau
Sagar Tech Plaza, B-Wing, 309-310,
Andheri-Kurla Rd., Sakinaka, Andheri (East), Mumbai-400072 (Maharashtra)
Tel. : 91-022-56430474
Fax : 91-022-28524955
E-mail : indiakta@vsnl.com

Kenda Farben S.P.A.
Via Tramia No. 72,
27026 Garlasco (PV),
Italy
Tel. : 0039-0382-820201
Fax : 0039-0382-820205
E-mail : info@kendafarben.com
Products Manufactured/Marketed:
Chemicals for the footwear and leather goods industries

Khaiser International
5, Nabi Khan Subedar Street,
Periamet,
Chennai-600003 (Tamil Nadu)
Tel. : 91-044-25380703
Fax : 91-044-25362225
E-mail : khaiser-intl@dishnetdsl.net
Products Manufactured/Marketed:
Finished Leather, Leather Goods, Footwear, Shoe Components, Leather Garments, Shoe Finishes

Khas (Pvt.) Ltd.
Plot # 80/1, Sector 7-A,
Korangi Industrial Area,
Karachi, Pakistan
Tel. : 009221-5054411, 3
Fax : 009221-5056558, 9
E-mail : khas@khas.com.pk
Products Manufactured/Marketed:
Finished Buff - calf & cow calf leather for shoes leather, goods and all kinds of leather products.

KLJ Group's of Industries
No. 63, Rama Marg, Najaf Garh Road,
New Delhi-110015
Tel. : 91-011-25459706 to 709
Fax : 91-011-25436254
E-mail : kljint@vsnl.com
Products Manufactured/Marketed:
TPR/PVC compound, sole applications

Kurt O John Shoe Components (India) Pvt. Ltd.
C-12 & 13, Phase-II Extn.,
Hosiery Complex,
Noida (U.P.)
Tel. : 91-0120-2568992, 993, 994
Fax : 91-0120-2568991
E-mail : india@kurtojohn.com

Products Manufactured/Marketed:
Shoe Components

Lanxess India Private Limited
No. 749. Anna Salai,
Chennai-600002 (Tamil Nadu)
Tel. : 91-044-28420165
Fax : 91-044-28419974
E-mail :
azhar.mohammed@lanxess.com
Products Manufactured/Marketed:
Chemicals

Leather Connections (Pvt.) Ltd.
Alam Porvair City,
Bhoptian Chowk, 9th KM
Raiwing Road, Rohi Nala,
Lahore-53700 Pakistan
Tel. : 0092-42-5321401, 6
Fax : 0092-42-5321407
E-mail :
buckleup@leatherconnections.com
Products Manufactured/Marketed:
Permair leather for shoe upper and belts; leather belts & accessories

Leather Industries Development Corporation of Andhra Pradesh
5/77/27 Darga Hussainshaw Ali
Golkoda, Hyderabad-500008
Tel. : 91-40-23568690, 23568691
Fax : 91-40-23568977
Products Manufactured/Marketed:
Finished Leather, Footwear, Leather Goods, Infrastructure facilities in Leather parks especially in International Leather Complex, Nellore, AP.

Leather Links
FF 302 E, Sushant Lok,
Shopping Arcade,
Sushant Lok Phase-I,
Gurgaon, Haryana
Tel. : 91-0124-5046880
Fax : 91-0124-5046990
E-mail : vijay@leather-links.com
Products Manufactured/Marketed:
Fashion Accessories, Footwear, Shoe Components, Saddlery & Harness, Leather Garments, Upholstery, Synthetic Leather, Ultra Suede, Fabrics

Lederchem Private Limited
Salma House, New No. 334
(Old No. 142),
Purasawalkam High Road, Kellys,
Chennai-600010 (Tamil Nadu)
Tel. : 91-044-26421907, 26426063
Fax : 91-044-26422239
E-mail : info@salmagroup.com
Products Manufactured/Marketed:
Chemicals, Leather

M & B Footwear P. Ltd.
D-32, Sector-59
Noida-201301 (U.P.)
Tel. : 91-0120-2580173, 2581839
Fax : 91-0120-2580913
E-mail : amit@mbfootwear.com
Products Manufactured/Marketed:
Finished Leather, Upholstery, Brazil Wet Blue, Crust, Sole, Leathers

M. Muhammad Shafi & Co.
Plot # 50, Sector 7-A,
Korangi Industrial Area,
Karachi, Pakistan
Tel. : 009221-5061151/5
Fax : 009221-5061156
E-mail : mmsc@cyber.net.pk
Products Manufactured/Marketed:
Finished Leather for Garments and Gloves

Mac-India International
820 (Old No. 401), 1st Floor,
Anna Salai, Nandanam,
Chennai-600035 (Tamil Nadu)
Tel. : 91-044-24355454, 52178079
E-mail : macindia_int@hotmail.com
Products Manufactured/Marketed:
Machinery & Equipment

Madura Coats Pvt. Ltd.
H-85, Old Madras Road, PB-1600
Doorvaninagar,
Bangalore-560016 (Karnataka)
Tel. : 91-080-28510911
Fax : 91-080-28518046
E-mail : sk.raja@coats.com
Products Manufactured/Marketed:
Sewing Threads for Footwear, Leather Garments and Leather Goods

Main Group S.P.A.
V.L.E. Dell Industria 65,
35129 Padova (PD),
Italy
Tel. : 0039 049 8290111
Fax : 0039 049 8290122
E-mail : mktg@maingroup.com
Products Manufactured/Marketed:
Machinery

Mario Caime S.R.L.
Via Villoresi 64/G
20029 Turbigo,
Milano (MI) Italy
Tel. : 0039 0331 899323
Fax : 0039 0331 871502
E-mail : caimi@caimi.net
Products Manufactured/Marketed:
Accessory & tool for tannery - Transfer foils.

Mascot Automation Pvt. Ltd.
Plot No. 16, Mira Co-operative
Indl. Area, Off Western Express
Highway No. 8, Mira,
District Thane-401101 (Maharashtra)
Tel. : 91-022-28454358, 6359, 7360
Fax : 91-022-28455362
E-mail : mapl@mtnl.net.in
Products Manufactured/Marketed:
P.U. Soles

Max Speciality Products
SCO-86 / 87, Sector 8-C,
Chandigarh-160018 (Punjab)
Tel. : 91-0172-2544320, 2544232
Fax : 91-0172-2544559
E-mail : maxstar@maxmsp.com
Products Manufactured/Marketed:
Leather finishing transfer foils for upgradation and high fashion garments. Also foils for designs, Metallic and special effects. Special range of laminated foils for Shoe, Goods and Belts. An ISO 9001:2000 Certified Company

Mayur Uniquoters Ltd.
28, IV Floor, Lakshmi Complex,
M.I. Road,
Jaipur-302001 (Rajasthan)
Tel. : 91-0141-2361132, 2361133
Fax : 91-0141-2365423, 2368005
E-mail : info@mayur.biz
Products Manufactured/Marketed:
PU/PVC synthetic leather

M.D. Industries
'Sundaram' 46F,
Rafi Ahmed Kidwai Road,
2nd Floor, Room No. 2B,
Kolkata-700016

Tel.: 91-33-22294284/3334
Fax : 91-33-22804776
E-mail : medi@colz.vsnl.net.
Products Manufactured/Marketed:
Leather Embossing Plates and Hydraulic fully automatic machines

Medi-Tek International
C-43, DSIDC Packaging Complex,
Kirti Nagar, New Delhi-110015
Tel.: 91-11-51420775, 51420776
Fax : 91-11-25927635
E-mail : meditek@bol.net.in
Products Manufactured/Marketed:
Machinery & Equipment

Meridian Specialities Private Limited
No. 33, E.V.K. Sampath Road, Vepery,
Chennai-600007 (Tamil Nadu)
Tel. : 91-44-25612627
Fax : 91-44-25612627
E-mail : meridianchennai@vsnl.net
Products Manufactured/Marketed:
Leather chemicals

Meridian Synthetics (P) Ltd. (MSPL)
No. 434-A, Vazhudavur Main Road,
Muthiraiyarpalayam,
Pondicherry-605009
Tel. : 9345400497
Fax : 91-0413-2273075
E-mail : suresh_dtc@yahoo.co.in
Products Manufactured/Marketed:
Leather chemicals

Metavogue (India)
75C, Park Street, Suite No. 2/1,
IInd Floor,
Kolkata-700016 (West Bengal)
Tel. : 91-033-22166861, 62
Fax : 91-033-22166863
E-mail : kcclzips@cal.vsnl.net.in
Products Manufactured/Marketed:
KCCL branded zips & sliders. Importers of latest fashion accessories for leather goods, garments and shoes, Locks Magnetic Button, Hidden Magnets, Dog Hook, Rings etc.

Milan Foils Pvt. Ltd.
Plot No. 29-30, Industrial Area,
Bhambla (District Mandi),
Bhambla (Himachal Pradesh)
Tel. : 91-01905-256750
Fax : 91-01905-256750
E-mail : milanfoils@yahoo.co.in
Products Manufactured/Marketed:
Leather finishing foils, hot stamping foils, etc.

Millennium Leather Foils Pvt. Ltd.
SCO 39, Ist Floor, Sector 41-D,
Ghandigarh· (Punjab)
Tel. : 91-0172-2636094
Fax : 91-0172-2636093
E-mail : millimatts2000@yahoo.com
Products Manufactured/Marketed:
Others: Leather finishing transfer foils

Mostardini & Figli S.R.L.
Via Piovola 138 - 50053,
Empoli (FI), Italy
Tel. : 0039 0571 591341
Fax : 0039 0571 592995
E-mail : mostardini@mostardini.it
Products Manufactured/Marketed:
Machinery & Equipment: Hydraulic ironing and embossing presses, rotary multiroller ironing and embossing machines, electronic surface measuring machines, polishing machine, buffing and airdusting machines

N.V.S. Manian
No. 14 (Old No. 33), V.V. Koil Street, Periamet
Chennai-600003 (Tamil Nadu)
Tel. : 91-044-25389586
Fax : 91-044-25368215
E-mail : nvsmanian@vsnl.com
Products Manufactured/Marketed:
Finished Leather, Shoe Components, Machinery & Equipment

Nadeem Leatherware Exports
TF4 & TF6, III Floor Golden Enclave,
No. 184/99 Poonamallee High Road,
Kilpauk, Chennai-600 010
Tel. : +91-44-26650016 & 17
Fax : +91-44-52178743
E-mail : nadeemle@vsnl.com
Products Manufactured/Marketed:
Finished Leather, Fashion Gloves, Leather Goods

National Institute of Fashion Technology
Nift Campus,
Old Mahabalipuram Road,
Taramani, Chennai-600 013
Tel. : 91-44-22542766
Fax : 91-44-22542769
E-mail : niftchi@vsnl.com
Products Manufactured/Marketed:
Footwear, Leather goods, Fashion Accessories, Publications

Navkar
4866/24, Sheeltara House,
Darya Ganj, New Delhi-110002
Tel. : 91-11-55351665
Fax : 91-11-51562665
E-mail : navkar_india@hotmail.com
Products Manufactured/Marketed:
Finished Leather, Shoe Components

Noble Exports
No. 3, Salai Street, First Floor, Choolai,
Chennai-600112 (Tamil Nadu)
Fax : 91-044-25324874
E-mail : ashmain@md3.vsnl.net.in
Products Manufactured/Marketed:
Raw material (Leather)

Orient Express
Race View Towers 2B,
71 Mount Road,
Guindy, Chennai-600 032
Tel. : 91-44-22349112, 22330036
Fax : 91-44-22347375
E-mail : orient@vsnl.in
Products Manufactured/Marketed:
Finished Leather, Leather Garments

Orlando S.R.L.e Italfrese S.A.S.
Via Noventana, 200-35027
Noventa Padovana (PD) Italy
Via Asolana, 27L, 31017
Crespano Del Grappa (TV) Italy
Tel. : 0039 049 8959104 / 0423 930195
Fax : 0039 049 8959104 / 0423 930196
E-mail : oriando.macchine@libero.it / info@italfrese.com
Products Manufactured/Marketed:
Shoe Machinery, Leather goods machinery, Cutting tools in steel - carbide and diamond for shoes.

Oswal Sewing Threads
D-52, East of Kailash,
New Delhi
Tel. : 91-011-26448851, 52, 53
Fax : 91-011-26448872
Products Manufactured/Marketed:
Sewing threads

Ozdersan Tannery Machines Co. Ltd.
10006 Sok No. 68, A.O.S.B. Cigl
Izmir, Turkey

Tel. : 0090 232 3280645 (5 Lines)
Fax : 0090 232 3767345
E-mail : Ozdersan1@superonline.com
Products Manufactured/Marketed:
Machinery & Equipment, Pictures and Posters

P.R. Engineering
14/53, V.V. Koil Street,
Chinmaya Nagar, Stage-I,
Chennai-600111 (Tamil Nadu)
Tel. : 91-044-24792864, 24793053
Fax : 91-044-24792864
E-mail : prbaskar@vsnl.net
Products Manufactured/Marketed:
Machinery & Equipment

P.R. Overseas
14/53, V.V. Koil Street,
Chinmaya Nagar, Stage-I,
Chennai-600111 (Tamil Nadu)
Tel. : 91-044-24792931
Fax : 91-044-24792864
E-mail : prbaskar@vsnl.net
Products Manufactured/Marketed:
Machinery & Equipment

Pak Leather Crafts Ltd.
Plot # 16, Sector 7-A,
Korangi Industrial Area,
Karachi, Pakistan
Tel. : 009221-5064100-4
Fax : 009221-5060809
E-mail : leather@pakleather.com
Products Manufactured/Marketed:
Finished Leather, Leather Garments

Perfect Trading Company L.L.C.
H.O.: P.O. Box: 26475
Sharjah, UAE
Tel. : +971-6-5732535
Fax : +971-6-5728465

Peekay Lamcoats (P) Ltd.
3, Balakrishna Street,
Nehru Nagar, Erukancherry,
Chennai-600118 (Tamil Nadu)
Tel. : 91-044-25585166, 25612827
Fax : 91-044-25610221
E-mail : peekay@md3.vsnl.net.in
Products Manufactured/Marketed:
Inter Lining Fabrics

Perma Colours & Chemicals Pvt. Ltd.
5-A, Chandarlok Apartments, No. 59,
Baker (RTM) Street, Choolai,
Chennai-600112 (Tamil Nadu)
Tel. : 91-044-25381540
Fax : 91-044-25367503
E-mail : perma@md3.vsnl.net.in
Products Manufactured/Marketed:
Finished Leather, Leather/Goods

Picard Bangladesh Ltd.
Sky Lark Point (9th Floor)
Suit No. 9J1, 24/A Bijoy Nagar,
Dhaka-1000, Bangladesh
Tel. : +880-2-9354993-4
Fax : +880-2-9332569
E-mail : picard@bdmail.net
Products Manufactured/Marketed:
Leather Goods

Pidilite Industries Ltd.
Ramakrishna Mandir Road,
P.O. Box 17411, Andheri (East)
Mumbai-400059 (Maharashrta)
Tel. : 91-022-28357584
Fax : 91-022-28367459
E-mail : krishnaraj@pidilite.com
Products Manufactured/Marketed:
Shoe Components

Pielcolor - Agk Synthetics
30/23. Second Main Road,
New Colony, Chrompet,

Chennai-600044 (Tamil Nadu)
Fax : 91-044-22368928
E-mail : agk_synthetics@vsnl.net
Products Manufactured/Marketed:
Finished Leather

Polar Couros Ltda
Rua Passo Do Leao, S/N,
Bairro: Lomba Grande,
Nova Hamburgo-Cep: 93490-000,
RS – Brazil
Tel. : 55-51-5962680
Fax : 55-51-5962680
E-mail : vania@polarcouros.com.br
Products Manufactured/Marketed:
Finished Leather

Poletto Technology
Via Risorgimento 90-36070,
S, Pietro Mussolino (VI)
Italy
Tel. : 0039-0444-472472
Fax : 0039-0444-472450
E-mail : info@polettotechnology.it
Products Manufactured/Marketed:
Fleshing Machines, Splitting Machines, Shaving Machines, Sammying and Setting-out Machines, Drum for Tanning & Dyeing, Rotary Toggling Drier with Frames, Finishing Lines, Fumes Cleaners, Drying Tunnel, Chiller Cells, Milling Drums.

Poplon Chemie
C/O Palar (India),
Adam Tannery Compound,
70, Anna Salai,
Chennai-600044 (Tamil Nadu)
Tel. : 91-044-22486151
Products Manufactured/Marketed:
Leather chemicals & auxillaries, Fatliquors, Etc.

Presidency Kid Leather Limited
476, Kilpauk Garden Road, Kilpauk,
Chennai-600 010 (Tamil Nadu)
Tel. : 91-044-26461837, 26441853
Fax : 91-044-26445837
E-mail : panther@pklindia.com
Products Manufactured/Marketed:
Finished Leathers

Prime International India Pvt. Ltd.
9, Vgp Murphy Square-I,
Cross Street, St. Thomas Mount,
Chennai-600016 (Tamil Nadu)
Tel. : 91-044-22313332
Fax : 91-044-22313331
E-mail :
prime@prime-international.com
Products Manufactured/Marketed:
Finished Leather

Priya Impex Consulants
B-1, P.A. Towers, 869,
P.H. Road, Kilpauk,
Chennai-600010 (Tamil Nadu)
Tel. : 91-044-52133590
Fax : 91-044-26650308
E-mail :
priyaimpex@mantraonline.com
Products Manufactured/Marketed:
Machinery & Equipment

Psm Udyog
RR 127, Ananda Pur,
East Kolkata Township,
Kolkata-700107 (West Bengal)
Tel. : 91-033-24431389
Fax : 91-033-24431389
E-mail : psmudyog@sify.com,
bagchisoumen@hotmail.com
Products Manufactured/Marketed:
Machinery & Equipment

Q & Q Holding Co. Ltd.
55/188-189 Moo 6, Sukhumvit 103 Rd.,
Nongbon Pravase,
Bangkok-10250 (Thailand)
Tel. : 662-7471313
Fax : 662-3990106, 3615984
E-mail : sales@qandq.co.th
Products Manufactured/Marketed:
Shoe Components

R. Cube Enterprises
15/1, Avadhana Pappiah Road,
Choolai,
Chennai-600112 (Tamil Nadu)
Tel. : 91-044-26692898, +9282106830
Fax : 91-044-26692416
E-mail : aargee@md4.vsnl.net.in
Products Manufactured/Marketed:
Fusible & Self-adhesive Linings and Interlinings, Pressure Sensitive Reinforcement Tapes

R.Y. Gaitonde & Company
58, Harrington Road, Chetput,
Chennai-600 031
Tel. : 91-044-52137480
Fax : 91-044-28363101
E-mail : gaitondeagency@vsnl.net
Products Manufactured/Marketed:
Finished Leather, Machinery, Raw Material

Ridhi Sidhi Laminations Pvt. Ltd.
C-68, Sector 4,
Noida (U.P.)
Tel. : 9810031791, 9313779672
Fax : 91-0120-27135326
E-mail : rathis4n@rediffmail.com
Products Manufactured/Marketed:
Linings & Interlinings (foam & EVA laminated fabric & coated fabric)

Rishi Overseas
184, Sukhdev Vihar, Mathura Road,
New Delhi-110025
Tel. : 91-011-26916587, 26311023
Fax : 91-011-26846525
E-mail : rimpex@vsnl.com
Products Manufactured/Marketed:
Shoe Components

River Walk Design Studio
256-257, 3rd Floor, Shri Fort Havelli,
New Delhi
Tel. : 91-011-51798737
E-mail :
riverwalkdesign@rediffmail.com
Products Manufactured/Marketed:
Fashion Accessories, Leather Goods

Rock Chemie Co.
43, Iranshahr Avenue,
Tehran, Iran
Tel. : 98-21-8843227
Fax : 98-21-8826168
E-mail : sales@rockchemie.com
Products Manufactured/Marketed:
Chemicals for leather

Romega Foam (P) Ltd.
No. 81, Mc Nichols Road, Chetpet,
Chennai-600031 (Tamil Nadu)
Tel. : 91-044-28362009, 28365002
Fax : 91-044-28361124
E-mail : romega@vsnl.com
Products Manufactured/Marketed:
Shoe Components, Upholstery

Rossetti Leather Italia
Via Industria 48, 36071, Arzignano
Vicenza, Italy
Tel. : 39-0444 67 36 08
Fax : 39-0444 67 56 66

E-mail : rosetti@rosette_leather.com
Products Manufactured/Marketed:
PU coated split, Upholstery leather, Wet blue split, Upsplitted wet blue

Rotopia International
88/100, Mouda Ibrahim Street, Nagalkeni, Chrompet,
Chennai-600044 (Tamil Nadu)
Tel. : 91-044-22485442, 22485808
Fax : 91-044-22485441
E-mail : roto@vsnl.net
Products Manufactured/Marketed:
Machinery & Equipment

Rssr Overseas (Pvt.) Ltd.
B-12, Manohar Apartments,
1, Easwaran Koil Street,
West Mambalam
Chennai-600033 (Tamil Nadu)
Tel. : 91-044-24898259
Fax : 91-044-24894967
E-mail : vasanbio@yahoo.com
Products Manufactured/Marketed:
Shoe Components

Rudra Blades & Edges P. Ltd.
36, Veerabhadran Street,
1st Floor, Nungambakkam,
Chennai-600034 (Tamil Nadu)
Tel. : 91-044-28265222, 28229022
Fax : 91-044-28262750
E-mail : rudhraa@eth.net
Products Manufactured/Marketed:
Industrial blades

S.E. Marketing (P) Ltd.
S-5, Site-IV, Panki Industrial Estate,
Kanpur-208020 (U.P.)
Tel. : 91-0512-2691865, 6
Fax : 91-0512-2691197
E-mail : sales@sempl.com
Products Manufactured/Marketed:
Metal fitting and accessories for leather goods and footwear

S.M.S. Footwears Pvt. Ltd.
56257/77, Regar Pura, Karol Bagh,
New Delhi-110005
Tel. : 91-11-51547528, 25810329
Fax : 91-11-25741528
E-mail : smsfootwearltd@yahoo.co.in
Products Manufactured/Marketed:
Shoe Components

Saba Group - Sabri Systems & Surya Pelle
1703, Phase-II, Sathuvachary,
Vellore-632009 (Tamil Nadu)
Tel. : 91-0416-2252952, 2252954
Fax : 91-0416-2253035
E-mail : sabri@sabagroup.org
Products Manufactured/Marketed:
Finished Leather

Saba Soles (P) Ltd.
AJ-122, 9th Main Road,
Anna Nagar,
Chennai-600040 (Tamil Nadu)
Tel. : 91-044-26280275, 26284633
Fax : 91-044-26280821
E-mail : sabach@md4.vsnl.net.in
Products Manufactured/Marketed:
Shoe Components

Sachina Engineering Pvt. Ltd.
9/1A, Hayes Cross Road,
Richmond Town,
Bangalore-560025 (Karnataka)
Tel. : 0091-080-25228615
Fax : 0091-080-25228889
E-mail : sachina@sachina.com
Products Manufactured/Marketed:
Machinery & Equipment

Sagittarians International Ltd.
46/4, Rafi Ahmed Kidwai Road,
Kolkata-700016 (West Bengal)
Tel. : 91-033-22292517, 3494
Fax : 91-033-22290420
E-mail : sil@cal.vsnl.net.in
Products Manufactured/Marketed:
Machinery for Leather Industries

Salma International
Salma House, New No. 334
(Old No. 142),
Purasawalkam High Road, Kellys,
Chennai-600010 (Tamil Nadu)
Tel. : 91-044-26421907, 26426063
Fax : 91-044-26422239
E-mail : info@salmagroup.com
Products Manufactured/Marketed:
Leather, Aquamix, Chemicals etc.

Sant Rubbers Ltd.
373-374 Leather Complex,
Kapurthala Road,
Jalandhar City (Punjab)
Tel. : 91-44-0181-2651623/33
Fax : 91-44-0181-2650743
E-mail : gbains@jla.vsnl.net.in
Products Manufactured/Marketed:
Shoe components

Sanghavi Shoe Accessories (P) Ltd.
11, Hari Krupa, 10th Road, Chembur,
Mumbai-400071 (Maharashtra)
Tel. : 91-022-25281126, 25288272
Fax : 91-022-25280785
E-mail : mumbai@sanghavishoe.com
Products Manufactured/Marketed:
Shoe Components

Schum-Mac International
48-A Sydenhams Road, Periamet,
Chennai-600003 (Tamil Nadu)
Tel. : 91-044-25387562, 25393387
Fax : 91-044-25367641
E-mail : schuhmac@vsnl.com
Products Manufactured/Marketed:
Machinery & Equipment

Sellam Chemicals
Thekkupattu Post, Ambalur 635 801,
(Vaniyambadi. TK., Vellore District),
Ambalur-635801 (Tamil Nadu)
Tel. : 91-04174-225927, 226583
Fax : 91-04174-232957
E-mail : Sellam@sancharnet.in
Products Manufactured/Marketed:
Chemicals for leather, Casein Products, anionic & Cationic Compact products for upgradation of selection

Serafini S.R.L.
Via Ccattolica, 62 Zona Ind L.E.B.
62012 Civitanova
Marche (MC) Italy
Tel. : 39-0733-892200
Fax : 39-0733-892202
E-mail : info@serafini.it
Products Manufactured/Marketed:
Shoe Components

Seta S.A. Extrativa Tanino De Acacia
AV. 10 Demaio 1109, 93600-000
Estancia Velha
RS-Brazil
Tel. : 55-51-5612233
Fax : 55-51-5612424, 56122366
E-mail : sales@seta-sa.com.br
Products Manufactured/Marketed:
Chemicals Wattle Extract, G.S. Powder, Setafiller

Sethsons International
113, Pratap Chamber,
Gurudwara Road, Karol Bagh,
New Delhi-110005

Tel. : 91-011-25718104, 25757125
Fax : 91-011-25754104
E-mail : seth@ndf.vsnl.net.in
Products Manufactured/Marketed:
Lining, Interlining and Moulding Insock

Sgs India Private Limited
21, New Street,
Kottur, Chennai
Tel. : 91-44-24470184, 24473929
Fax : 91-44-24470317
E-mail : anitha@sgs.com
Products Manufactured/Marketed:
Consumer Testing Services

Sim Exports
AJ-83, 10th Main Road,
Anna Nagar,
Chennai-600040 (Tamil Nadu)
Tel. : 91-044-26287582
Fax : 91-044-26263987
E-mail : iqbal_modi@rediffmail.com
Products Manufactured/Marketed:
Shoe Components

Sivagami Micro Processors
No. 10, Kundrathur High Road,
Gerugambakkam,
Chennai-602101 (Tamil Nadu)
Tel. : 91-044-23820811, 23820911
Fax : 91-044-23820811, 23820911
E-mail : sivagami@vsnl.net
Products Manufactured/Marketed:
Machinery & Equipment

Sky Industries Ltd.
C-58, Ttc Industrial Area,
Thane-Belapur Road, Pawani,
Navi Mumbai-400705 (Maharashtra)
Tel. : 91-22-26400660, 661
Fax : 91-22-27632224
E-mail : janak@chennai.skgroup.com
Products Manufactured/Marketed:
Shoe Components

Solar Soles Pvt. Ltd.
829/1 Periar Evr High Road, Kilpauk,
Chennai-600010 (Tamil Nadu)
Tel. : 91-044-26412433
Fax : 91-044-26427528
E-mail : headoffice@ahindia.com
Products Manufactured/Marketed:
Shoe Components

Sperry Plast Ltd.
H-88A, Kirti Nagar,
New Delhi-110015
Fax : 91-011-51424375, 76
E-mail : sperry@del2.vsnl.net.in
Products Manufactured/Marketed:
Shoe Components

Srinala Leathers India Pvt. Ltd.
28/2A, Ammoor Road, Manthangal,
Ranipet-632402 (Tamil Nadu)
Tel. : 91-04172-226298
Fax : 91-04172-227409
E-mail : vor–slirpt@sancharnet.in
Products Manufactured/Marketed:
Cow Wet Blue, Hides & Splits

Srinivasa Special Equipment Engineers
1, Pammal Main Road,
Chennai-600005 (Tamil Nadu)
Tel. : 91-044-22484477, +9383077044
E-mail : ssee@vsnl.com
Products Manufactured/Marketed:
Machinery & Equipment

Srivathsa Industries
1-A, Rajaji Salai, Madhavaram,
Chennai-600060 (Tamil Nadu)

Tel. : 91-044-25530511
Fax : 91-044-25530928
E-mail : svi@vsnl.net
Products Manufactured/Marketed:
Finished Leather, Woven Leather Etc.

Staill India Private Limited
1-A, Sargunar Salai, Nagalkeni,
Chromepet,
Chennai-600044 (Tamil Nadu)
Tel. : 91-044-22485102
Fax : 91-044-22484389
E-mail : stahlind@stahl.com
Products Manufactured/Marketed:
Finished Leather

Standard Embossing Plate
129 Pulaski Street, Newwark,
NJ. U.S.A.
Tel. : 91-973-344-6670
Fax : 91-973-344-6730
E-mail :
standardembossing@yahoo.com
Products Manufactured/Marketed:
Embossing Plates, Embossing Supplies

Star International Pvt. Ltd.
109/366-2, R.K. Nagar, G.T. Road,
Kanpur-208005 (U.P.)
Tel. : 91-0512-2544133, 2544134, 2544195, 2544196
Fax : 91-0512-2557925, 2216285
E-mail : sales@stargroupindia.com
Products Manufactured/Marketed:
Machinery & Equipment: Clicking press; shoe machinery; industrial machines including sewing machines for shoes, garments, leather goods; stitching machines for soles, moccassins; machines for eyelet & D-ring fixing and skiving

Sts S.R.L.
Via L. Galvani 8
48100 Ravenna (RA)
Italy
Tel. : 0033-0544-456731
Fax : 0039-0544 456733
E-mail : info@stsitaly.it
Products Manufactured/Marketed:
Shoe Machinery, Chemical Products and systems for washing of soles in plastic material and for the cleaning of the moulds.

Sukhia Agencies (P) Ltd.
Atkinson Palace, 2nd Floor, No. 2,
Jothi Venkatachalam Salai, Vepeery,
Chennai-600007 (Tamil Nadu)
Tel. : 91-044-25610194
Fax : 91-044-25610094
E-mail : rakesh_retch@satyam.net.in
Products Manufactured/Marketed:
Machinery & Equipment

Sun Footwear Industries (P) Ltd.
F-1/A, Panki Industrial Area,
Site-1, Kanpur (U.P.)
Tel. : 91-044-2691940, 2692415
Fax : 91-0512-2691941
E-mail : sunfootwear@hotmail.com
Products Manufactured/Marketed:
Shoe Components

Suolificio Chennai
50 Raja Muthiah Road, Periamet,
Chennai-600 003 (Tamil Nadu)
Tel. : 91-044-25385658, 25361634
E-mail : suolificiochennai@vsnl.com
Products Manufactured/Marketed:
Shoe Components

Super Edge Australia Pty. Ltd.
Unit 5 & 6/17 Norfolk Court,
Coburg 3058,

Melbourne, Australia
Tel. : 61-3-93505588
Fax : 61-3-93505880
E-mail :
superedgeaustralia@optusnet.com.au
Products Manufactured/Marketed:
Machinery & Equipment

Sushma International
New No. 21, Sydoji Street, Triplicane,
Chennai-600005 (Tamil Nadu)
Tel. : 91-044-28525757
Fax : 91-044-28525757
E-mail : sushmainter@vsnl.net,
Sushma_inter@hotmail.com
Products Manufactured/Marketed:
Machinery & Equipment

T. Abdul Wahid & Co.,
26, Vepery High Road, Periamet,
Chennai-600 003
Tel. : 91-044-25610500
Fax : 91-044-25611277
E-mail : wahid@tawahid.com
Products Manufactured/Marketed:
Finished Leather

Tai Yang Rollers Mould Manufactory
Yang Wu Park, Dalinsan Town,
Guang Dong Province,
Dong Guang City,
China
Tel. : 486-769-5617926 & 8
Fax : 486-769-5612929
E-mail : tybeauty@changan.net
Products Manufactured/Marketed:
Embossing rollers and plate moulds for leather

Tanext Chemicals
21, Gandhipuram Main Road,
Kamarpalayam, Namakkal Dist.
Kamarpalayam-638183 (Tamil Nadu)
Tel. : 0-9840169669
Fax : 91-04288-265705
Products Manufactured/Marketed:
Vegetable leather tanning chemicals

Tata International Limited
47-A (NP), Thiru-Vi-Ka Industrial Estate
Ekkaduthangal, Guindy,
Chennai-600032 (Tamil Nadu)
Tel. : 91-044-22329686, 22345547
Fax : 91-044-22346641
E-mail :
tichennai@tatainternational.com,
pvr@tatainternational.com
Products Manufactured/Marketed:
Finished Leather, Leather Goods, Leather Garments, Footwear

Taurus International
Vasant Complex 502, Shubham,
Mahavir Nagar, Kadiv Ali (W),
Mumbai-400067 (Maharashtra)
Tel. : 91-022-56264453
Fax : 91-022-28010600
E-mail : taurusi@vsnl.com
Products Manufactured/Marketed:
Machinery & Equipment

Techno Concepts
No. 37, Chennai-Bangalore Road,
Varadharajapuram, Poonamallee,
Chennai-602103 (Tamil Nadu)
Tel. : 91-044-26494025
Fax : 91-044-24314952
E-mail : technojp@md3.vsnl.net.in
Products Manufactured/Marketed:
Machinery & Equipment

Techno Impex
905, Periyar Evr High Road Lane,
First Floor,
Chennai-600084 (Tamil Nadu)

Tel. : 91-044-52029219, 52029319
Fax : 91-044-52029419
E-mail : etsmontels@touchtelindia.net
Products Manufactured/Marketed:
Machinery & Equipment

Technogi India Pvt. Ltd.
Eagle Plaza, 12 Roshanara Road,
Delhi-110007
Tel. : 91-011-23821726, 23825449
Fax : 91-011-23824318
E-mail : techogi_tn@touchtelindia.net
Products Manufactured/Marketed:
Shoe Components

Teja Industries
306, Vasan Udyog Bhavan,
Senapati Bapat Marg, Lower Parel,
Mumbai-400013 (Maharashtra)
Tel. : 91-022-56607977
Fax : 91-022-56607978
E-mail : tejaindustries@vsnl.com
Products Manufactured/Marketed:
Leather Goods

Texon (India) Pvt. Ltd.
11-A, (29 III), Sarathy Nagar, Velachery
Chennai-600042 (Tamil Nadu)
Tel. : 91-044-22430148, 22430695
Fax : 91-044-22434696
E-mail : texonmadras@texon.com
Products Manufactured/Marketed:
Shoe Components

Textile Tapes Corporation
14/53, V.V. Koil Street,
Chinmaya Nagar, Stage-I,
Chennai-600111 (Tamil Nadu)
Tel. : 91-044-24792931
Fax : 91-044-24792864
E-mail : prbaskar@vsnl.net
Products Manufactured/Marketed:
Shoe Components

Tfl Quinn India Pvt. Ltd.
54, Thiruneermalai High Road,
Nagalkeni, Chrompet,
Chennai-600 044
Tel. : 91-044-22212040-44
Fax : 91-44-22212045
E-mail : Vimala@tflindia.com
Products Manufactured/Marketed:
Finished Leather, Chemicals, Dyes & Dye Auxillaries

Thejo Engineering Services (P) Ltd.
No. 41, 'Whites Road' Aysha Building
2nd Floor, Royapettah,
Chennai-600014 (Tamil Nadu)
Tel. : 91-044-28588936
Fax : 91-044-28522547
E-mail : teschennai@vsnl.net
Products Manufactured/Marketed:
Primers and tackifiers

Tien Kang Plastic Machinery Co. Ltd.
No. 427, Hsi Hu Rd.,
412, Tali Taichung,
Taiwan R.O.C.
Tel. : 00886-4-24938669
Fax : 00886-4-24938801
E-mail : tienkang@tcts.seed.net.tw
Products Manufactured/Marketed:
Machinery & Equipment

Toetech Footwear Machines Pvt. Ltd.
S-6 Dhruv Appt. Sector-13
Rohini, New Delhi-110 085
Tel. : 91-011-27867752, 27862460
Fax : 91-011-27862460
E-mail : info@toetechindia.com
Products Manufactured/Marketed:
Machinery & Equipment

Top Light Labels
S-6, Alankar Anugraha Apartments,
501, M.K.N. Road, Alandur,

Chennai-600016 (Tamil Nadu)
Tel. : 91-044-22344912
Fax : 91-044-22344912
E-mail : toplight@eth.net,
toplightchennai@yahoo.com
Products Manufactured/Marketed:
Fashion Accessories

Torielli India Pvt. Ltd.
10, Siri Fort Road, II Floor,
Ormes Road, Kilpauk,
Chennai-110049 (Tamil Nadu)
Tel. : 91-44-26602810, (011) 26258572
Fax : 91-44-26602810, (011) 26258571
E-mail : tordel@sify.com,
torielli@vsnl.com
Products Manufactured/Marketed:
Machinery & Equipment, Shoe Components & "Shoemaster"

Toscana Lasts Ltd.
E-6, 7, 8, Sector-59
Noida-201301 (U.P.)
Tel. : 91-0120-2580792
Fax : 91-0120-2580791
E-mail : toscana@bilt.com
Products Manufactured/Marketed:
Shoe Components

Tropical Shoe Industries Ltd.
A.R. Tower (3rd Floor),
24 Kemal Ataturk Avenue, Banani, Dhaka-1213 (Bangladesh)
Tel. : +880-2-8815142
Fax : +880-2-8860448
E-mail : bdexport@bangla.net
Products Manufactured/Marketed:
Footwear

Turel Sales Corporation
7, Haddows Road,
Chennai-600006
Tel. : 91-44-28278591/28275308
Fax : 91-44-28274622
E-mail : turel@md3.vsnl.net.in
Products Manufactured/Marketed:
Machinery & Equipment

V. Sreenivas
20 (Old No. 30) V.V. Koil Street,
Periamet
Chennai-600003 (Tamil Nadu)
Tel. : 91-044-25385919, 25381847
Fax : 91-044-25389185
E-mail : vsree@vsnl.com
Products Manufactured/Marketed:
Finished Leather, Chemicals

V.S.K. Enterprises
1/53, Q-2, Paul Wells Road,
Sripuram Colony, St. Thomas Mount,
Chennai-600016
Tel. : 91-44-55855565, 94440 70134
E-mail : vske33@hotmail.com
Products Manufactured/Marketed:
Machinery & Equipment

Van Hoorn's Handelmij B.V.
P.O. Box 76, 5140 AB, Waalwijk,
The Netherlands
Tel. : 0031-416-333831
Fax : 0031-416-332445
E-mail : info@van-hoorn.com
Products Manufactured/Marketed:
Finished Leather

Vansun Intermediates P. Ltd.
No. 3, Wellingdon Estate,
2nd Floor, 24, Ethiraj Salai,
Chennai-600 105 (Tamil Nadu)

Tel. : 91-044-28272462, 28276002
Fax : 91-044-28257335
E-mail : vansun@md4.vsnl.net.in
Products Manufactured/Marketed:
Chemicals

Vardhman Threads Ltd.
212, Deen Dayal Upadhyay Marg,
Urdu Ghar, New Delhi-110002
Tel. : 91-011-23232630, 31, 32
Fax : 91-011-23232608
E-mail :
speciality@cmo.vardhman.co.in
Products Manufactured/Marketed:
Shoe Components

Vibhuti Industries
158-B, Kheora, Nawabganj,
Kanpur-208002 (U.P.)
Tel. : 91-0512-2583709
Fax : 91-0512-2584054
E-mail : vibhuti_Trivedi@hotmail.com
Products Manufactured/Marketed:
Non-Woven Fabrics, Needle-Punched, Anti-Static, Strobel Insoles

Vicar S.R.L.
Viole Colomba 36-38, Fucecchio,
Italy
Tel. : 0039-0571-242481
Fax : 0039-0571-260988
E-mail : info@vicarsrl.it
Products Manufactured/Marketed:
Machinery & Equipment

Viswaat Chemicals Ltd.
Viswaat 7, Satsang Complex,
Upper Govind Nagar,
L.S. Raheja Marg, Malad (East)
Mumbai-400097 (Maharasthra)
Tel. : 91-022-28740365, 28742341
Fax : 91-022-28745321
E-mail : viswaat@vsnl.com
Products Manufactured/Marketed:
Leather Chemicals

Vrs Leathers P. Ltd.
64, (Old No. 78-B) Annasalai,
Nagaalkeni, Chromepet,
Chennai-600 044
Tel. : 91-44-22484428/6669
Fax : 91-44-22485010
E-mail : vrs@vsnl.com
Products Manufactured/Marketed:
Finished Leather

Vsl Sa
88 Avenue De La Poterie
33170 Gardignan
France
Tel. : 0033 5 56 8923 00
Fax : 0033 5 56 75 52 64
E-mail : pilippe@vsl.fr
Products Manufactured/Marketed:
Multi colour patterns, special design effect for sude skins, metallic transfer film, worn look and cracking effect foil and real glitters transfer foil.

Wel Tech India Pvt. Ltd.,
A-22, 70, Najafgarh Road, Indl. Area,
New Delhi
Tel. : 91-11-27438282, 27465206
Fax : 91-11-27465206
E-mail : viginternational@hotmail.com
Products Manufactured/Marketed:
Shoe Components

Wilhelm Textiles India P. Ltd.
Plot No. 15, 2/401, Karpagambal Nagar,
Kottivakkam,
Chennai-600041 (Tamil Nadu)
Tel. : 91-44-24512341, 24512944
Fax : 91-44-24510615
Products Manufactured/Marketed:
Shoes Components

Winners
95-A. Mittal Tower,
Nariman Point
Mumbai-400021
Tel. : 91-022-22021767, 22021779, 22820618
Fax : 91-022-22026397, 24229494, 24304250
E-mail : sales@winners-india.com
Products Manufactured/Marketed:
Accessories for Leather Goods (ring binder machanisms)

Worldwide Associates
#3 Anna Indira Gandhi Street, Kilpaukk Garden Road,
Chennai-600010 Tamil Nadu
Tel. : 91-044-26454182
Fax : 91-044-26454182
E-mail : worldwideassociates@vsnl.net
Products Manufactured/Marketed:
Adhesives

Youngman Woollen Mills Pvt. Ltd.
Village-Seera, Rahon Road,
Ludhiana-141007 (Punjab)
Fax : 91-0161-2690133
E-mail :
marketing@youngmanwm.com
Products Manufactured/Marketed:
Artificial Fabrics / Lining

Zahonero Virgili S.L.
Pol. Ind. Campo Auto-AVPA. Benelux 91,
P.O. Box 26, 03600 ELDA,
Alicante, SPAIN
Chennai-600041 (Tamil Nadu)
Tel. : 0086-20-82977633
Fax : 0086-20-82978377
E-mail : slveas@zahonero.com.in
Products Manufactured/Marketed:
Shoe Components

Zahur Sancho (Pvt) Ltd.
Plot # 46, Sector 7-A,
Korangi Industrial Area, Karachi
Tel. : 009221-5061786 to 90 (5 Lines)
Fax : 009221-5060343
E-mail : sales@zahursancho.com
Products Manufactured/Marketed:
Finished Leather : from goat and sheep for shoes, garment and gloves.

117. MANUFACTURE OF TIN CONTAINERS
118. MANUFACTURE OF STORAGE TANKS, PRESSURE VESSELS, HEAT EXCHANGERS
119. MARK II HAND PUMPS
120. MARUTI WORKSHOP CUM - SERVICE STATION
121. MECHANICAL JACKS
122. METAL CUTTING DIE DESIGN
123. METAL CUTTING OF AND GRINDING WHEELS (ABBRASIVE CUTTING WHEELS)
124. METAL HOOKS & CLIPS
125. METAL SEPARATION (COPPER, TIN, LEAD) FROM SPENT WASH ACID
126. METALLIC RING JOINTS
127. METALLIC GASKET (SPIRAL WOUND)
128. MICROVEE & ABSOLUTE FILTER
129. MICROWAVE OVEN
130. MILD STEEL INGOTS
131. MINI STEEL PLANT
132. MODERN VEHICLE WORKSHOP
133. MOPED
134. M.S.HINGES
135. M.S.INGOT AND HR. STEEL STRUCTURALS
136. M.S.INGOT BY INDUCTION FURNACES
137. M.S.PIPES
138. M.S. WELDING ELECTRODE
139. MUFFLERS & SILENCERS FOR THREE WHEELERS
140. NAIL CUTTER WITH FILER & MANICURE
141. NICHROME WIRE
142. NICKEL LINED SCREENS
143. NON-FERROUS ALLOY ROLLING
144. NON-FERROUS FORGING
145. NON-FERROUS FOUNDRY
146. NON PRESSURE
147. INCANDESCENT LAMP
148. NUMBER COMBINATION LOCKS FOR LUGGAGES
149. NUTS & BOLTS
150. PAPER COATED ALUMINIUM AND COPPER WIRE
151. PETROMAX CONTAINER
152. PHOTO ETCHING OF STAINLESS STEEL PLATES
153. PIPE GALVANIZING PLANT
154. PISTON RING-AUTOMOBILE
155. PLANT PROTECTION EQUIPMENTS
156. PLATINUM LABORATORY APPARATUS
157. PRESSURE COOKER & ALUMINIUM UTENSILS
158. PRESSURE COOKER (ALUMINIUM)
159. PRESSURE DIE CASTING
160. PRINTED ALUMINIUM COLLAPSIBLE TUBES
161. PRINTED TIN CONTAINERS
162. PRINTING PRESS (CYLINDER MACHINE)
163. PUMPS FOR CHEMICAL INDUSTRY (SPECIAL)
164. RAILWAY SLEEPERS (M.S.)
165. RAZOR TWIN BLADE
166. R.C.C SPUN PIPES
167. RECONDITIONING OF M.S. DRUMS/BARRELS
168. RE-ROLLING COPPER AND BRASS SHEET AND RODS
169. RE-ROLLING MILLS
170. RESIN COATED SAND
171. RESIN CORED SOFT SOLDER WIRES
172. ROLLING MILL (BY INDUCTION FURNACE) & MANUFACTURE OF BARS, ANGLES, SQUARES, TUBES AND OTHERS
173. ROLLER BEARING & FORGING
174. ROLLING OF STAINLESS STEEL PATTA
175. RUBBER INSULATED PLIERS (HAND TOOLS)
176. RUBBING COMPOUND FOR AUTOMOBILES
177. SCIENTIFIC LABORATORY EQUIPMENTS
178. SCOOTER ASSEMBLING
179. SECONDARY LEAD EXTRAC -TION BY SCRAP BATTERY PLATES,PIPES & SHEET
180. SEAMLESS M.S. TUBES & PIPES
181. SELF TAPPING STEEL SCREW
182. SEWING NEEDLES
183. S.G. IRON & ALLOY STEEL
184. SHEET METAL PRODUCTS, (FERROUS/NON-FERROUS)
185. SHIP/MARINE CONTAINER
186. SHOCK ABSORBERS
187. SHOE EYELETS
188. SHOT AND GRITS BY AUTOMIZATION PROCESS
189. SHOVELS
190. SILICO MANGANESE ALLOYS
191. SILENCERS (MUFFLERS) EXHAUST & TAIL PIPE FOR ALL TYPES OF VEHICLES
192. SINTERED BEARING
193. SINTERED BUSHES
194. SINTERED METAL PRODUCTS
195. SOFT AND HARD FERRITES
196. SPANNERS
197. SPARK PLUGS
198. STEEL PLANT (ELECTRIC ARC FURNACE BASED- EAF)
199. SPHERIODAL GRAPHITE CAST IRON
200. SPRAY DRYER
201. STAINLESS STEEL HINGES
202. STAINLESS STEEL SHEET ROLLING TO PRODUCE STAINLESS STEEL UTENSILS
203. STAINLESS STEEL UTENSILS
204. STAPLE PINS,PAPER PIN, GEM CLIPS ETC.
205. STEEL CASTINGS
206. STEEL CHAIN
207. STEEL FOUNDRY
208. STEEL FURNITURES AND ELECTRICAL APPLIANCES
209. STEEL PLANT (MINI)
210. STEEL RODS AND COILS FROM SCRAPS
211. STEEL ROLLING MILL
212. STEEL STRIPS (COLD ROLLED) SILICON WITH GRAIN RIENTED FOR ELECTRIC USE
213. STEEL TRANSMISSION LINE TOWERS & ROLLING MILL TO PRODUCE STEEL SECTION
214. STEEL FURNITURES AND ELECTRICAL APPLIANCES
215. STEEL WIRE DRAWING AND GALVANIZING
216. STEEL WOOL
217. SUBMERGED ARC WELDED PIPES
218. SUBMERSIBLE PUMP MANUFACTURING
219. SUPER ENAMELLED COPPER WIRE
220. THREE WHEELERS
221. TIE-ROD ENDS
222. TIN CONTAINERS
223. TOOLROOM AND SHEET METAL PRODUCTS
224. TRACTOR TRAILERS
225. TRANSMISSION POWER FITTING
226. TUBULAR POLES
227. SUPER ENAMELLED COPPER WIRES
228. TUBULAR POLES FOR ELECTRICAL TRANSMISSION (BY FABRICATION PROCESS)
229. TUBULAR POLES OF M.S. & HIGH TENSILE STEEL
230. VACUUM CLEANERS
231. VACUUM FLASK (STAINLESS STEEL)
232. VALVES FOR REFRIGERA TION AND AIR-CONDITION
233. VEHICLE WELDING & PAINTING
234. VENETION BLIND
235. WASHING MACHINES (AUTOMATIC & COMPUTERISED)
236. WATER CONTROLLER (AUTOMATIC)
237. WATCH STRAPS/CHAINS/ BRACELETS/BELT BRASS & STAINLESS STEEL
238. WATER COOLERS
239. WELDED WIRE MESH
240. WELDING ELECTRODES
241. WICK STOVES
242. WIND MILL WINDOW FRAME (FERROUS & NON-FERROUS)
243. WRIST WATCH

359. DI ETHYL OXALATE
360. DI METHYL ORTHOPHTHALATE
361. DI-METHYL PHTHALATE
362. DICLOFENAC GEL
363. DIOCTYL PHTHALATE (DOP)
364. DI PHENYL GLYCERINE
365. DI PHENYL OXIDE
366. DINITRO-CHLORO BENZENE
367. DISTILLED WATER
368. DODECYL BENZENE SULPHONATE
369. DUSTLESS CHALK
370. EDTA & ITS SALTS
371. ELECTROLESS NICKEL PLATING ON PLASTICS
372. ENDOSULFAN
373. EPOXY RESIN BASED COMPOUND
374. ETHYL ACETATE
375. EHTYL ETHER
376. ETHYL ALCOHOL (POTABLE LIQUOR)
377. ETHYL HEXANOL
378. EXTRACTION OF ESSENTIAL OILS BY SUGAR CRITICAL FLUID (CARBON DIOXIDE) METHOD FROM FLOWERS, HERBAL & SPICES
379. FERRIC ALUM
380. FERRO CHROME LIGNO SULPHONATE
381. FERRO MANGANESE
382. FERRO SILICONE
383. FERRO VANADIUM FROM VANADIUM SLUDGE
384. FERROUS SILICATE
385. FERROUS SULPHATE
386. FERTILIZER FROM ANIMAL BLOOD & LEATHER WASTE
387. FLUORESCENT TUBE LIGHT POWDER
388. FOAMED PVC COMPOUNDING & ITS PRODUCTS
389. FORMALDEHYDE
390. FRACTIONAL DISTILLATION OF D.M.O (DEMENTHOLIZED OIL)
391. FRACTIONAL DISTILLATION OF ESSENTIAL OIL & MEDICINAL PLANT EXTRACT
392. FRICTION DUST (LIQUID & POWDER) FROM CNSL
393. FRUIT FLAVOURS
394. FURFURAL FROM RICE HUSK
395. GARLIC ACID
396. GASKET SHELLAC COMPOUND
397. GEAR OIL
398. GIBBERELLIC ACID
399. GLASS PUTTY
400. GLYCERINE
401. GOSSYPOL (POLY PHENOL) FROM COTTON SEED OIL
402. GUAR GUM POWDER
403. HAIR FIXER (HAIR GEL TYPE)
404. H - ACID
405. HENNA PASTE MAKING
406. HEPTAL DEHYDE
407. HIGH CARBON FERRO CHROME
408. HYDRATED CALCIUM SILICATE BRICK
409. HYDRATED LIME FROM SEA SHELL
410. HYDROCHLORIC ACID
411. HYDRO FLUORIC ACID
412. HYDROGEN PEROXIDE (BY AUTO-OXIDATION PROCESS)
413. ICE PACKS (SOLUTIONS TYPE, WHITE GEL TYPE, VIOLET SEMI SOLID POLYMER TYPE)
414. IMPROVING DROP POINT PARAFFIN WAX FROM 45-50°C TO 75-80°C
415. INDUSTRIAL ALCOHOL
416. INTEGERATED COMPLEX OF EASTER & ALLIED PRODUCTS (D.O.P, D.B.P, ETHYL ACETATE WIRE ENAMEL & CABLE JELLY)
417. IMFL (WHISKY) & COUNTRY LIQUOR
418. IRON OXIDE FOR MAKING FERITTE
419. IRON SULPHIDE
420. JUTE BATCHING OIL
421. KESH KALA TEL (HAIR DYE LOTION) (VASMOL 33, BLACK NITE TYPE)
422. L-LYSINE MONOHYDROCHLORIDE
423. LACTIC ACID FROM WHITE SUGAR BY FERMENTATION PROCESS
424. LDPE GRANULES FROM VIRGIN (LDPE RESIN)
425. LEAD EXTRACTION FROM BATTERY SCRAP
426. LEAD OXIDE (A) LEAD MONOXIDE (B) LEAD TETRA OXIDE (C) GREYLEAD OXIDE
427. LIQUID GLUCOSE & ITS BY PRODUCTS
428. LIQUID OXYGEN BOTTLING PLANT
429. LIQUID SHOE POLISH
430. LIQUID FLOOR POLISH
431. LUBE OIL VISCOSITY IMPROVED FOR P.P.G/P.E.G.
432. LUBRICANTS ASHLESS 100% COMBUSTION
433. MAGNESIUM CARBONATE AND MAGNESIUM BICARMONATE
434. MAGNESIUM HYDROXIDE POWDER
435. MAGNESIUM SILICATE
436. MAGNESIUM SULPHATE
437. MALACHITE GREEN
438. MALEIC ANHYDRIDE
439. MANGANESE SULPHATE
440. MANUFACTURING OF CARBON MONO-OXIDE WATER GAS
441. MENTHOL BOLD CRYSTALS FROM FLAKES
442. MENTHOL CRYSTAL & MENTHA OIL
443. MERCURIC OXIDE
444. METAL PRE-TREATMENT CHEMICALS
445. METHANE GAS BY SODIUM ACETATE & SODA LIME
446. METHYL ACETYL RICINOLATE
447. METOL
448. METOL FROM HYDROQUINONE & METHYLAMINE
449. MICANITE
450. MICRO NUTRIENT MIXTURE
451. MINERAL WATER
452. MINERAL WATER AND PET BOTTILNG PLANT
453. MINERAL WATER IN BOTTLES, GLASS AND POUCHES
454. MINI CEMENT PLANT (BY ROTARY KILN PROCESS)
455. MIXED FERTILIZER
456. MOSQUITO & FLIES REPELLENT AGARBATTI (INCENSE STICKS)
457. MONO CHLORO ACETIC ACID
458. MONOCROTOPHOS (TECHNICAL)
459. MOSQUITO COIL
460. MOSQUITO COIL & MAT
461. MOSQUITO MAT
462. MOTHER TINCTURE & BIO CHEMIC MEDICINES
463. NAPHTHALENE & PHENYL (INTEGRATED UNIT)
464. NATURAL MINERAL WATER BY REVERSE OSMOSIS PROCESS
465. NICKEL PLATING BRIGHTNER (PRIMARY OR CARRIER BRIGHTNER & SECONDARY BRIGHTNER)
466. NICKEL SULPHATE
467. NICOTINE FROM TOBACCO WASTE
468. NICOTINE SULPHATE FROM TOBACCO WASTE
469. NITRO BENZENE
470. NITRO CELLULOSE SANDING SEALER/LACQUER
471. NITRO MUSK
472. NITROGEN & OXYGEN GAS PLANT
473. NON-IONIC SURFACTANT (WETTING AGENT)
474. NO-CARB PASTE
475. OCTANOL
476. ORTHO NITRO PHENOL
477. OXALIC ACID FROM MOLASSES
478. OXALIC ACID FROMRICE HUSK
479. OXALIC ACID FROM TREE BARK
470. OXALIC ACID FROM WASTE VEGETABLES
471. OXYGEN GAS PLANT
472. OXYGEN GAS PLANT (AIR SEPERATION METHOD)
473. PARA-AMINO BENZOIC ACID
474. PARA-AMINO PHENOL
475. PARA TOLUENE SULPHONIC ACID
476. PECTIN FROM RAW PAPAYA
477. PERFUME (LEMON & OTHERS)

Pay Rs. 8,000/- Only

for Tailor made Report
We (EIRI) are fully capable
to prepare any report
as per your requirements

478. PESTICIDE PREPARATION USING NEEM FRUIT & SEEDS (MARGOSA)
479. PET BOTTLES FROM PRE-FORM
480. PET PREFORM FROM RESIN FOR PET BOTTLES
481. PETROLEUM JELLY
482. PHENOL
483. PHENYL
484. PHENYL (BLACK) IN LIQUID FORM
485. PHTHALIC ANHYDRIDE
486. PHOSPHORIC ACID FROM ROCK PHOSPHATE
487. PHOSPHORUS BY CHEMICAL PROCESS
488. PHOTO EMULSION FOR ROTARY SCREEN PRINTING
489. PHTHALOCYANINE BLUE
480. PIGMENT EMULSION FOR TEXTILE
481. PIGMENT GUM
482. PLANT GROWTH REAGEN BASED CHLOROTHYL TRIMETHYL AMMONIUM CHLORIDE
483. PLANT HARMONES BASED ON 2,4-DICHLORPHENOXY ACENTIC ACID & NAPHTHALENE
484. PLASTICINE (MODELLING CLAY)
485. PLASTIC WASTE REPROCESSING
486. PLASTER OF PARIS BANDAGES
487. POLYESTER RESIN (G.P. GRADE LAMINATE GRADE, ELECTRICAL GRADE)
488. POLY VINYL ACETATE
489. POLYVINYL ACETATE EMULSION
490. POLYURETHENE FOAM
491. POTASSIUM DICHROMATE/ BICHROMATE
492. POTASSIUM IODATE
493. POTASSIUM NITRATE
494. POTASSIUM PERMAGNATE
495. POTASSIUM PER SULPHATE
496. POTASSIUM SULPHATE (FERTILIZER GRADE)
497. POTASSIUM PER OXY DI-SULPHIDE
498. POTASSIUM SILICATE
499. POTASSIUM STEARATE
500. POWER ALCOHOL
501. PVC RESIN FROM ETHYL ALCOHOL
502. PYRIDINE & ITS DERIVATIVES
503. RAPID FAST DYES (ONLY PROCESS)
504. REACTOR (CHEMICAL)
505. RECLAMATION OF USED ENGINE OIL (BY CLAY & VACUUM DISTILLATION PROCESS)
506. RECLAMATION OF SPENT BLEACHING EARTH
507. RECLAMATION OF NICKEL SPENT CATALYST FROM VANASPATI INDUSTRY
508. RECTIFIED SPIRIT FROM MOLASSES & MAHUA FLOWERS
509. RECTIFIED SPIRIT FROM RICE STRAW
510. RED OXIDE PAINT/PRIMER (ANTI CORROSIVE) BASED ORGANIC RED PIGMENTS
511. REMOVAL OF ANTIMONY FROM LEAD SCRAP
512. RESORCINOL
513. ROSIN SIZING AGENT
514. RESORCINOL
515. SALINE AND INJECTION WATER
516. SALICYLIC ACID
517. SANTONIN
518. SENNOSIDES FROM SENNO LEAF
519. SHOE POLISH
520. SILICA GEL (BLUE SELF INDICATING PROCESS)
521. SILICONE EMULSION
522. SILICONE FROM RICE HUSK
523. SILICON FROM SILICA (SEMI CONDUCTOR GRADE)
524. SILICONE RESINS
525. SILICONE SPRAYSILVER BRAZING FOIL
526. SILVER EXTRACTION FROM WASTE HYPO SOLUTION
527. SILVER NITRATE
528. SILVER PARTS FOR CERAMIC CAPACITOR SINGLE SUPER PHOSPHATE & MIXED FERTILIZER (NPK)
529. SINGLE SUPER PHOSPHATE (S.S.P) & SULPHURIC ACID
530. SODA ASH
531. SODA ASH FROM NATRON
532. SODA WATER BOTTLING PLANT (CARBONATED BEVERAGE)
533. SODIUM ALUMINATE
534. SODIUM BI-CARBONATE (BAKING SODA) FROM SODA ASH
535. SODIUM CHLORITE
536. SODIUM CHROMATE SODIUM CYCLAMATE
537. SODIUM DI-CHROMATE
538. SODIUM DI-CHROMATE & SODIUM SULPHATE AS BYE PRODUCTS
539. SODIUM HEXA META PHOSPHATE
540. SODIUM HYDROSULFITE
541. SODIUM HYPO CHLORIDE (BLEACH LIQUOR)
542. SODIUM ISO-PROPYL XANTHATE
543. SODIUM LAURYL SULPHATE
544. SODIUM LAURYL SULPHATE & SODIUM LAURYL ETHER SULPHATE
545. SODIUM NITRATE
546. SODIUM PETROLEUM SULPHONATE (EMULSIFIER)
547. SODIUM SILICATE FROM SILICA & SODA ASH
548. SODIUM SILICATE FROM (1) PADDY SILK HUSK 2) & SILICA
549. SODIUM CARBONATE & SILICA
550. SODIUM SULPHATE
551. SODIUM SULPHIDE BY BARIUM SULPHATE PROCESS
552. SODIUM SULPHIDE FROM AMMONIA & SODIUM CHLORIDE
553. SODIUM SULPHITE
554. SODIUM TRI-POLY PHOSPHATE
555. SOFTENER (CATIONIC ANIONIC & NON-IONIC)
556. SPIRIT FROM PINE APPLE
557. STANNOUS CHLORIDE
558. STEARIC ACID
559. STEARATES MANUFACTURE (CALCIUM, ZINC, ALUMINIUM, MAGNESIUM STEARATES)
560. SULPHUR FROM PYRITES & SLAG
561. SULPHUR CRYSTALS/LUMPS
562. SULPHURIC ACID
563. SULPHURIC ACID FROM DCDA PROCESS
564. SUPER PHOSPHATE (S.S.P)
565. SYNTHETIC IRON OXIDE (YELLOW)
566. SYNTHETIC RED & WELLOW IRON OXIDE FROM IRON FILLING & PICKLE LIQUOR
567. TARTARIC ACID
568. TOILET CLEANER
569. TOLUENE AND SBP FROM

Above all the Detailed Project Report are available at *"ENGINEERS INDIA RESEARCH INSTITUTE"*. 4449, Nai Sarak (D), Main Road Delhi - 110 006
● Ph : 91-11-23918117, 2391 6431, 2392 0361, 31082370 ● Fax : 91-11-2391 6431
● E-Mail : eirisidi@bol.net.in

CRUDE NAPHTHA
570. TRIMETHYL AMMONIUM CHLORIDE
571. TRIPHENYL PHOSPHITE (T.P.P)
572. ULTRAMARINE BLUE (LIQUID)
573. UREA FORMALDEHYDE & MELAMINE FORMALDEHYDE POWDER
574. UNDECYLINIC ACID
575. VINYL ACETATE MONOMER
576. VITAMIN C
577. VITAMIN E
578. WASTE WATER TREATMENT PLANT FOR INDUSTRIAL SECTOR IN INDIA (ONLY MARKER SURVEY)
579. WIRE DRAWING LUBRICANT
580. WIRE ENAMEL
581. XANTHATES
582. YELLOW DEXTRIN
583. ZINC CHLORIDE
584. ZINC OXIDE
585. ZINC PHOSPHATING BY COLD PROCESS
586. ZINC SILICATE
587. ZINC STEARATE
588. ZINC SULPHATE
589. ZINC SULPHATE MONOHYDRATE
590. ACID BLACK
591. AURAMINE'O'
592. AZO DYES STUFF
593. DYE & DYE INTERMEDIATE
594. DYE INTERMEDIATES
595. MALACHITE GREEN
596. METHYLENE BLUE
597. PHTHALOCYANINE BLUE
598. PHTHALOCYANINE BLUE & GREEN
599. REACTIVE DYES
600. SULPHUR BLACK DYE
601. VAT DYES
602. WATER CHILLING PLANT
603. WADDING OIL (100%) FOR WADDING OF COTTON HOSIERY CLOTH IN THE DYEING PROCESS
604. WHITE OIL
605. WAX FLOOR POLISH

ELECTRICAL, ELECTONICS, COMPUTERS AND INFOTECH/IT PROJECTS

606. AIR CONDITIONING
607. ALUMINIUM ALLOY CONDUCTOR
608. ALUMINIUM CABLE
609. ALUMINIUM ELECTROYTIC CAPACITORS
610. AUDIO CASSETTE ASSEMBLING & RECORDING
611. AUDIO CASSETTES DUPLICATING RECORDING
612. AUDIO CASSETTES & AUDIO STUDIO
613. AUDIO CASSETTES PLANE & RECORDED
614. AUDIO MAGNETIC HEADS
615. AUDIO MAGNETIC TAPE
616. AUDIO/VIDEO CASSETTES
617. AUTO BULB/LAMPS
618. AUTOMATIC VOLTAGE STABILIZER
619. BATTERY PLATES
620. BACK OFFICE (Rs. 5000/-)
621. B/W TV & COMPUTER MONITOR PICTURE TUBE
622. BREAD BOARDS
623. CALL CENTRE
624. CAMERA (35 MM)
625. CAPACITORS
626. CARBON ELECTRODE USED FOR BATTERY CELL
627. CARBON POTETIOMETERS
628. CEILING FAN
629. CERAMIC INSULATOR
630. CHILDREN INFOTECH TRAINING INSTITUTE (Rs. 5000/-)
631. CHOKE AND PATTI
632. CHOKE AND STARTER
633. CHOKE USED FOR FLUORESCENT LAMPS
634. COLOUR TELEVISION
635. COLOUR AND BLACK & WHITE TELEVISION
636. COMPACT DISC
637. COMPACT DISC PLAYER (AUDIO/VIDEO)
638. COMPUTER EDUCATION INSTITUTE
639. COMPUTER ASSEMBLY
640. COMPUTER HARDWARE
641. COMPUTER KEYBOARD
642. COMPUTER PERIPHERALS
643. COMPUTER PRINTERS
644. COMPUTER RIBBON
645. COMPUTER RIBBON REINKING OR REFILLING
646. COMPUTER STATIONERY
647. COMPUTER STATIONERY &

IMPORTED HARDWARE PARTS
648. COMPUTER TERMINALS
649. COMPUTERISED WASHING MACHINE (AUTOMATIC)
650. COMPUTER SOFTWARE
651. CONDENSER FOR MOTOR USING MPP FILM
652. CONTENT DEVELOPMENT CENTRE (EOU) (Rs. 5000/-)
653. CONTROL PANEL BOARD
654. COOLING COIL FOR AIR CONDITIONERS
655. COPPER STRIP COIL FROM SCRAP
656. CORDLESS TELEPHONES
657. CYBER CAFE
658. CYBERKIOSK (Rs. 5000/-)
659. DATA PROCESSING CENTRE (Rs. 5000/-)
660. D.C. MICRO MOTORS
661. D.G.SETS
662. DISH ANTENNA AND CABLE T.V. NETWORK EQUIPMENT
663. DISTRIBUTION TRANSFORMERS & REPAIRS
664. DOMESTIC ELECTRICAL APPLIANCES- ROOM COOLER, WASHING MACHINE, WATER HEATER, ELECTRIC ROOM HEATER
665. E-SCHOOL
666. E-COMMERCE/BUSINESS
667. ELECTRIC ENERGY METER
668. ELECTRIC FANS
669. ELECTRIC HORN FOR AUTOMOBILE
670. ELECTRIC LAMP/GLS (INCANDESCENT LAMP)
671. ELECTRIC MIXER
672. ELECTRIC MOTORS UP TO 10 HP. REWINDING OF ALL TYPES OF MOTORS WATER PUMPS
673. ELECTRIC MOTOR WINDING (FOR FAN, MIXIES, ETC.)
674. ELECTRIC STEAM IRON
675. ELECTRICAL APPLIANCES
676. ELECTRICAL FIXTURES
677. ELECTRICAL STAMPING
678. ELECTROLYTIC CAPACITORS
679. ELECTROMAGNETIC RELAY
680. ELECTRONIC BALAST/CHOK
681. ELECTRICAL CHOKE
682. ELECTRONIC DIGITAL WATCHES
683. ELECTRONIC DIGITAL WEIGHING MACHINE
684. ELECTRONIC FIRE ALARM
685. ELECTRONIC GAS STOVE LIGHTERS
686. ELECTRONIC PRESSURE INDICATORS, ELECTRICALS, ELECTRONIC LIQUID LEVEL INDICATORS, ELECTRONIC TEMPERATURE INDICATOR, DIGITAL TACHOMETER
687. ELECTRONIC TELEPHONE INSTRUMENTS
688. ELECTRONIC TOYS
689. ELECTRONIC WATCHES & CLOCKS
690. FAX MACHINES
691. F.H.P MOTORS
692. FLOPPY DISKETTES
693. FLUORESCENT LAMP STARTER
694. FLUORESCENT TUBULAR

Above all the Detailed Project Report are available at *"ENGINEERS INDIA RESEARCH INSTITUTE"*. 4449, Nai Sarak (D), Main Road Delhi - 110 006

● Ph : 91-11-23918117, 2391 6431, 2392 0361, 31082370 ● Fax : 91-11- 2391 6431

● E-Mail : eirisidi@bol.net.in

LAMPS WITH INTRODUCTION TO MERCURY VAPOUR LAMP
695. FRANCHISEE COMPUTER EDUCATION CENTRE (Rs. 5000)
696. GAS DETECTOR (L.P.G)
697. GENERATOR SET & PUMP SETS
698. GENERATOR (BATTERY OPERATED)
699. GIS SERVICE CENTRE (GEOGRAPHICAL INFORMATION SYSTEMS)
700. HARDWARE FITTING FOR TRANSMISSION LINE OVERHEAD LINE MATERIAL
701. HEADERS FOR TRANSISTOR ICS SEMI CONDUCTOR
702. H.T & L.T INSULATORS
703. H.T & M.V INDUSTRIAL CUBICAL SWITCH BOARD
704. INFORMATION MOVING DISPLAY (L.E.D TYPE)
705. INSURANCE CLAIM PROCESSING CENTRE (EOU) (Rs. 5000/-)
706. INTEGRATED CIRCUITS
707. INTERNET BASED STOCK TRADING (Rs. 5000/-)
708. INTERNET SERVICE PROVIDER (I.S.P.)
709. JELLY FILLED TELEPHONE CABLES
710. LAP TOP COMPUTERS
711. LEAD ACID BATTERIES
712. LEAD ACID BATTERY PLATES AND ASSEMBLING OF BATTERY
713. LEGAL TRANSCRIPTION & SECRETARIAL SERVICES CENTER (EOU)(Rs. 5000/-)
714. LIGHT EMITTING DIODES (L.E.D)
715. LINEAR ICS TRAINER KIT
716. LOUD SPEAKER
717. L.T TRANSFORMER REPAIRING
718. MEDICAL TRANSCRIPTION CENTRE
719. METAL FILM RESISTORS
720. METALLISED POLYPROPYLENE, POLYESTER FILM CAPACITOR
721. MICA BASE ELECTRONIC COMPONENTS
722. MICA PAPER WASTE PAPER FROM MICA WASTE
723. MICRO PROCESSORS TRAINER KITS BASED ON MICRO PROCESSORS
724. MINI COMPUTER (PERSONAL COMPUTER)
725. MINIATURE CIRCUIT BREAKER (M.C.B)
726. MINIATURE WATCH BATTERIES (BUTTON CELL)
727. MIXER/GRINDER (MIXI)
728. MONO CHROME COMPUTER MONITOR
729. MOTOR START ELECTROLYTIC CAPACITOR
730. MULTI LAYER P.C.B
731. MULTIPLE RELAY FOR LOW VOLTAGE
732. NEON INDICATOR
733. NEON SIGN MANUFACTURE
734. OPTICAL FIBRE CABLES
735. ON LINE SHOPPING MALL (Rs. 5000/-)
736. OPTO MECHANICAL & ELECTRICAL EQUIPMENTS
737. PHOTO COLOUR LAB
738. PICTURE TUBE (B/W)
739. PLAIN PAPER COPIER
740. PLASTIC FILM CAPACITORS
741. POLYESTER CAPACITORS
742. PORTABLE GENERATOR SET
743. PORTAL
744. PORTABLE TELEVISION(TV)
745. POWER CAPACITORS
746. POWER INVERTERS
747. POWER PLANT
748. POWER TRANSFORMERS UP TO 600 KVA
749. PRINTED CIRCUIT BOARD
750. PVC WIRES & CABLES
751. RE-CONDITIONING OF PICTURE TUBE
752. RESIN CAST CT & PT (1 KV)
753. SEMI CONDUCTOR DEVICE
754. SEMI CONDUCTORS FOR TRANSISTORS & DIODES
755. SETTING UP OF A VIDEO STUDIO
756. SMOKE DETECTORS
757. SOLAR CELLS
758. SOLAR MODULES
759. SOLAR PHOTO VOLTAIC SYSTEM
760. SOLDER FLUXES
761. SOLAR WATER HEATING PANELS
762. STEEL FURNITURE & ELECTRICAL APPLIANCES
763. STEREO AMPLIFIERS
764. STEREO CASSETTE RECORDERS/PLAYERS
765. STREET LIGHT FITTINGS SURGE SUPPRESSOR
766. TANTALUM CAPACITORS
767. TEFLON COATED ELECTRIC CABLE
768. TELEMEDICINE (DISTANCE HEALTH CARE) (Rs. 5000/-)
769. TELEPHONE CORD/CABLE
770. TELEPHONE (PUSH BUTTON TYPE)
771. TELEPHONE (PUSH BUTTON & CORDLESS)
772. TELEVISION (CTV & B/W)
773. TELEVISION (3-D)
774. TELEVISION DEFLECTION COMPONENTS
775. TELEVISION SIGNAL BOOSTERS
776. TELEVISION TUNERS
777. TRACTION BATTERIES
778. TRAINING INSTITUTE OF MEDICAL TRANSCRIPTION
779. TRANSFORMER FOR B/W TV
780. TRANSFORMER FOR VOLTAGE STABILIZER & E.H.T
781. TRANSMISSION POWER LINE FITTING
782. TRANSMISSION TOWER FITTING
783. TV AUDIO EQUIPMENT CABINETS & THEIR ASSEMBLING UNIT
784. UN-INTERRUPTED POWER SUPPLY (U.P.S)
785. VARIABLE FREQUENCY
786. VARIABLE VOLTAGE A.C. DRIVE
787. VIDEO CASSETTES (COMPLETE MANUFACTURING & ASSEMBLING)
788. VIDEO CASSETTES RECORDER (V.C.R)
789. VIDEO FILM STUDIO
790. VOLTAGE REGULATOR FOR AUTOMOBILES
791. VOLTAGE STABILIZERS
792. VOLTAGE STABLIZER & T.V. GAIN BOOSTER
793. WAX AND CHEMICAL COATED, BRAIDED TINSEL WIRE
794. WEBSITE DESIGN & E-MAIL REGISTERING
795. WELDING ELECTRODES
796. WIND ENERGY POWER PROJECT (10 MW)
796A WIRES (METAL)

FOOD, AGRO FOOD, PROCESSED FOOD, AGRO PLANTATION, CULTIVATION, FARMING, DAIRY/MILK, TOBACCO/PAN MASALA, BREWERY & DISTILLERY, EDIBLE OILS, EOU FOOD PRODUCTS AND ALLIED PRODUCTS

797. ALCOHOLIC BEVERAGES & VENEGAR FROM COCONUT WATER
798. ALCOHOL DRINKS FROM ETHYL ALCOHOL BY MIXING OF VARIOUS FLAVOURS
799. ANTI SCALE COMPOUND FOR ADDING INTO SUGAR JUICE BOILING
800. APPLE JUICE CONCENTRATED & DEHYDRATED FRUIT & VEGETABLES
801. ARTIFICIAL FISH MEAL FOR POULTRY FEED
802. AUTOMATIC BISCUIT PLANT
803. BABY CEREAL FOOD AND MILK POWDER
804. BACTERIA FOR CANE JUICE
805. BAKER'S YEAST
806. BAKERY INDUSTRY
807. BANANA PUREE
808. BEER & WINE
809. BEER PLANT (BREWERY)
810. BIDI
811. BIDI & CIGARETTE
812. BISCUIT PLANT

813. BREAD (AUTOMATIC PLANT)
814. BLACK PEPPER (SPICES)
815. BREAD AND BISCUITS
816. BREEDING FARM
817. BROILER CHICKEN
819. BUTTON MUSHROOM CULTIVATION & PROCESSING
820. CANNING OF RASAGULLAS IN METAL CANS
821. CAFFEIN FROM TEA WASTE
822. CANNING OF FRUITS & VEGETABLES
823. CASEIN AND BY-PRODUCTS
824. CASHEW FRUIT JUICE FROM CASHEW FRUIT APPLE
825. CASHEWNUT KERNEL EXTRACTION FROM CASHEWNUT FRUIT
826. CASHEWNUT SHELL LIQUID & KERNEL PROCESSING
827. CASHEW FENI
828. CATECHEU (BY CHEMICAL PROCESS)
829. CATTLE FEED FROM TAPIOCA
830. CHEWING & BUBBLE GUM
831. CHICKEN/SHEEP MEAT PROCESSING
832. CHOCOLATE (MILK)
833. CIGARETTE AND BEEDIES
834. COCOA BUTTER FROM COCOA MASS
835. COCONUT PRODUCTS & BY PRODUCTS PROCESS COMPLEX
836. COLD/SOFT DRINKS
837. COLLECTION OF MILK AND MILK MAKING POWDER
838. COLLECTION OF MILK AND PACKING IN POLYTHENE POUCH (1/2 KG.1 KG. & 2 KG.)
839. CONDENSED MILK (SWEETNED)
840. CONFECTIONERY INDUSTRY (TOFFEE & CANDY, SEMI-AUTOMATIC PLANT)
841. COUNTRY LIQUOR FROM MOLASSES
842. CIGARETTE
843. DAIRY FARM AND DAIRY (MILK) PRODUCTS (PASTEURISED MILK, BUTTER, GHEE, PANEER)
844. DAIRY FARM TO PRODUCE MILK & PACKING IN POUCHES (50%) & CAN(50%)
845. DAIRY FOR MILK PROCESSING
846. DAIRY FARM (BUFALO)
847. DAL (PULSE) MILL UNIT
848. DEHYDRATION OF CARROT & GARLIC
849. DEHYDRATION & CANNING OF FRUITS & VEGETABLES
850. DEHYDRATION OF FIGS
851. DEHYDRATION OF FRUITS AND VEGETABLES
852. DEHYDRATED ONIONS AND ONION POWDER
853. DRY ICE BY BREAKING OF AIR
854. DRYING OF RED CHILLIES, HALDI, DHANIA, AND GREEN PEAS
855. EGG POWDER (40,000 EGGS PROCESSING PER DAY)
856. EXPORT OF PROCESSED FOODS AND MARINE PRODUCTS
857. FISH CANNING & POUCHING
859. FISH FARMING (PRAWN & OTHER MARINE PRODUCTS)
860. FISH MEAL
861. FLOUR MILL AND MUSTARD OIL
862. FOOD COLOUR & ORASTED GROUNDNUT GRAM PEAS, ETC IN POUCHES
863. FROG LEGS PROCESSING
864. FROZEN MEATS PROCESSING
865. FOOD FLAVOURS (WHISKY) VODKA, GRAPE, BUTTER SCOTCH)
866. FOOD PRODUCTS COMPLEX (DEHYDRATED ONIONS, GARLIC POWDER & FLAKES, CATTLE FEED, TOMATO POWDER, TOMATO PRODUCTS, CANNED FRUITS & VEGETABLES, TOMATO PURE, GROUN NUT OIL, REFIND OIL, DEHYDRATED GRAPES, BANANA POWDER & WAFFERS)
867. FRUIT JUICE, JAM, JELLIES & ALLIED PRODUCTS
868. FRUIT JUICE, PICKLES PROCESSING AND CANNING
869. FRUIT JUICE MAKING & PACKING IN PLASTIC CONTAINER/POUCHES
870. FRUIT PROCESSING (JAM & JELLIES)
871. FRUIT PULP & JUICE CONCENTRATES
872. FRUIT & VEGETABLE DRYING (FREEZE DRYING METHOD)
873. GOAT & SHEEP FARMING
874. GRAM DALL/PULSE MILL
875. GRAPE DEHYDRATION
876. HARD BOILED CANDY (TOFFEE & CANDY)
877. HERBAL CIGARETTES
878. HONEY PROCESSING & PACKAGING
879. ICE CREAM OF DIFFERENT FLAVOURS
880. ICE CREAM STABILIZER
881. ICE MAKING PLANT
882. INDIAN MADE FOREIGN LIQUOR (I.M.F.L)
883. INSTANT FOOD (IDLI MIX, DOSA MIX, GULAB JAMUN MIX)
884. INSTANT FOOD (INSTANT FOOD & FAST FOOD PARLOUR)
885. INSTANT NOODLES
886. INSTANT TEA
887. INSTANT TEA FROM BLACK TEA
888. INTEGERATED STARCH BAKING POWDER/YEAST INDUSTRY
889. IODIZED SALT
890. IODIZED SALT (ORDINARY MOISTURE-LESS/FREE FLOWING IN PLASTIC BAGS AND CONTAINERS)
891. JAM, JELLIES, FRUIT JUICE & ALLIED PRODUCTS
892. KATHA AND CUTCH
893. KHANDSARI SUGAR
894. KHANDSARI SUGAR & IMFL
895. LACTIC ACID FROM WHITE SUGAR BY FERMENTATION PROCESS
896. LACTOSE & BY PRODUCTS PROCESSING FROM MILK
897. LIQUID GLUCOSE AND ITS BYE PRODUCTS
898. MACRONI AND VERMICILLI
899. MALT EXTRACTION FROM BARLEY
900. MANGO PROCESSING (MANGO PULP, JUICE & SLICES)
901. MAYUR BRAND TYPE CHEWING TOBACCO
902. MINERAL WATER
903. MILK PRESERVATION & MARKETING TO WHOLE SELLERS (INPOUCH PACKING BY UHT TECHNOLOGY)
904. MILK PROCESSING AND PACKAGING OF MILK PRODUCTS
905. MILK PRODUCTS (CASEIN, LACTOSE, GHEE & WHEY POWDER)
906. MILK TOFFEE
907. MINI FLOUR MILL
908. MINI SUGAR PLANT
909. MISRI (PEARL SUGAR CANDIES)
910. MODERN RICE MILL
911. MURABBA
912. MUSTARD OIL EXTRACTION & REFINING
913. MUTTON TALLOW
914. NAMKEEN INDUSTRY (BHUJIA, CHANA CHUR ETC.)
915. NAMKEEN & SWEETS
916. NON-BASMATI RICE FROM PADDY
917. OLEORESIN, ESSENTIAL OIL, DYES & POWDER OF SPICES
918. OLEORESIN EXTRACTION FROM DIPTERO-CARPUT TURMINATUS AND PINUS KHASYANA
919. OLEORESIN EXTRACTION FROM CHILLI
920. PAN MASALA AND POUCH

1059. BUFFALO HORN TIP, HOOF
1060. BANQUET HALL
1061. BUTTON
1062. CALCINED PETROLEUM (C.P) COKE
1063. CANVAS SHOES
1064. CANVAS SHOES, JUNGLE BOOTS
1065. CARBON BRUSH, BRUSH HOLDER & SLIP RING
1066. CEMENT SHEETS WITH COIR FIBRE & OTHER SEGMENTS
1067. CERAMIC TILES (GLAZED) BY DOUBLE FIRING/HEATING
1068. CHILDREN RECREATION CENTRE
1069. COAL BRIQUETTES
1070. COLD STORAGE & ICE
1071. COLD STORAGE FOR FRUITS AND VEGETABLES
1072. COMPRESSOR (HERMETIC) FOR AIR CONDITIONER
1073. COSTUME JEWELLERY/ IMITATION JEWELLERY
1074. DECORATIVE LAMINATED SHEET (SUNMICA)
1075. DIAMOND CUTTING & EXPORTS
1076. DRINKING STRAW FROM PROPYLENE
1077. ENGINEERING COLLEGE
1078. ENTERTAINMENT CLUB
1079. FASHION TECHNOLOGY INSTITUTE
1080. FAST FOOD PARLOUR
1081. FAST FOOD (INSTANT FOOD & FAST FOOD PARLOUR)
1082. FIRE EXTINGUISHERS (SODA ACID TYPE)
1083. FISH NET
1084. FLORICULTURE (CUT FLOWER ROSE) WITH GREEN HOUSE
1085. FLOOR COVERING SHEET
1086. FILM STUDIO (VIDEO)
1087. FLUSH DOOR, CHIP BOARD, WOOD WOOL & OTHER INSULATING BOARDS
1088. GAS DETECTORS OF L.P.G
1089. GEMS MANUFACTURING
1090. GLASS BOTTLE BY SCRAP
1092. GOAT & SHEEP FARMING
1093. GOLD ELECTROPLATING
1094. GOLD JEWELLERY (E.O.U)
1095. GOLD PLATED SILVER JEWELLERY & CUTLERY
1096. GRANITE SLAB AND TILES
1097. GREEN HOUSE
1098. HARD CHROMIUM PLATING
1099. HEALTH CLUB AND BEAUTY PARLOUR CUM HAIR SALOON WITH SONA BATH
1100. HEALTH CLUB CUM BEAUTY PARLOUR TRAININGINSTITUTE
1101. HORN TIP,HOOVE BUTTON
1102. HOSPITAL
1103. HOSPITAL (100 BEDS)
1104. HOSPITAL (200 BEDS)
1105. ICE MAKING PLANT
1106. IMITATION AND COSTUME
1107. JEWELLERY (NECKLACE, EARRINGS EAR TOP ETC.)
1108. INITMATE SCENT CHEMICALS FROM ALL TYPES OF FLAVOUR
1109. INVESTMENT CASTING
1110. JUTE, COIR, GLASS ROPE/ SUTLI
1111. JUTE TWINE
1112. L.P.G BOTTLING PLANT
1113. L.P.G REGULATOR (DOMESTIC PURPOSE)
1114. LAMINATED PARTICLE BOARD & HARD BOARD
1115. LAMINATED SAFETY AND TOUGHENED GLASS
1116. LEASING & HIRE PURCHASE
1117. LICHEN (CHARILA)
1118. MANILA ROPES
1119. MEDICAL COLLEGE
1120. MATCH UNIT FROM WAXED PAPER
1121. MEDIUM DENSITY FIBRE BOARD
1122. MELAMINE CROCKERY
1123. MINERAL WATER
1124. MINI CEMENT PLANT
1125. MIRROR SILVER, GOLDEN, PINK, BLACK & SMOKES
1126. MODERN ADVERTISING AGENCY WITH DTP & FILM STUDIO
1127. MOTEL/SMALL HOTEL
1128. MULTI COLOUR PRINTING
1129. MULTI STOREY COMMERCIAL COMPLEX ALONGWITH RESIDENTIALAND DELUX FLATS FOR FOREIGN TOURISTS & REVOLVING RESTAURENT AT THE TOP
1130. MULTIPLE LAMINATION INDUSTRY
1131. MUSHROOM GROWING AND PROCESSING (BY DEEP FREEZING METHOD)
1132. NEWS PAPER PRINTING
1133. NICKEL LINED INDUSTRIAL SCREEN
1134. OFFSET COLOUR PRINTING PRESS (SIX COLOUR)
1135. OFFSET PRINTING PRESS
1136. P.C.C ELECTRIC POLES
1137. PHOTOGRAPHIC DEVELOPER & FIXER
1138. PVC EXTRUSION PROFILE (DOOR & WINDOWS)
1139. POP-CORN
1140. PHOTO ETCHING OF S.S.
1141. PRE STRESSED CEMENT CONCRETE PIPES
1142. PILFER PROOF CAPS
1143. PILFER PROOF CAPS AND CROWN CAP
1144. POUCH MAKING & GRAVURE PRINTING (ROTO PRINTING)
1145. POULTRY & FISH FARMING (INTEGERATED UNIT)
1146. PRINTING OF TIN SHEETS
1147. READYMADE GARMENTS
1148. RESTAURANT
1149. ROSE PLANTATION AND ROSE OIL EXTRACTION
1150. ROTOGRAVURE PRINTING
1151. SAFETY BELTS
1152. SAFETY MATCHES
1153. SHOE LACES
1154. SILK COCOON CULTIVATION (GROWING OF SILK COCOON WARM)
1155. SILK SCREEN PRINTING FORMULATIONS FOR PLASTIC, PAPER & CLOTH
1156. SPIKENARD (JATAMANSI)
1157. STENCIL COATING SOLUTION
1158. SUGAR CANDY (MISRI)
1159. SUGAR CANE PLANTATION
1160. SUGAR CANE JUICE PRESERVATION
1161. SURAT ZARI
1162. SYNTHETIC SHOES & SOLES
1163. TEA PACKAGING INDUSTRY
1164. TENNIS BALLS
1165. THREE STAR HOTEL
1166. TRAVELLING AGENCY
1167. TRAYS, TROLLEYS FOR HOSPITAL WITH SCRATCHLESS COATING
1168. WAX EXTRACTS (TANNING POWDER)
1169. WIRE ROPE SLINGS
1170. WOOD WOOL SLAB
1171. WOODEN CANE FURNITURE WITH EXPORT POTENTIAL
1172. WOODEN FURNITURE
1173. WOODEN PANEL INCLUDING KILN SEASONING
1174. WOODEN FURNITURE
1175. WATCH CASE BUFFING
1176. WATCH DIAL
1177. WRIST WATCHES
1178. WATCHES (ELECTRONIC)
1179. ZEDOARY (KACHUR)

EDIBLE OILS, ESSENTIAL OILS LURICATIING OILS, GREASES, VEGETABLE OILS, WAXES, CAMPHOR, PERFUMES & PERFUMERY COMPOUNDS AND REFINED OILS ETC.

1180. AROMATIC PERFUMERY COMPOUND
1181. AEROSOL
1182. AGARBATTI PERFUMERY COMPOUND
1183. BEES WAX MANUFACTURE
1184. CAMPHOR
1185. CARDANOL FROM CASHEW NUT SHELL LIQUID
1186. CASTOR OIL
1187. CASTOR OIL DERIVATIVE OLEORESINS
1188. CHILLI OIL
1189. CITRONELLA OILS
1190. CLOVE OIL
1191. CONCENTRATE OF ROSE JASMINE & LILY ETC.
1192. COLOURED FLAME CANDLE

1193. CANDLES (SEMI-AUTOMATIC)
1194. CORN OIL (MAIZE OIL)
1195. DEHYDRATED CASTOR OIL
1196. EUGENOL FROM CINNAMON LEAF OIL
1197. EXTRACTION OF ESSENTIAL OIL (CARDAMON, JEERA, AJOWAN, GINGER OILS ETC. & PACKAGING OF GROUND SPICES)
1198. EXTRACTION OF JASMINE ESSENCE
1199. EXTRACTION OF ESSENTIAL OILS BY SUPER CRITICAL FLUID METHOD FROM FLOWERS, HERBS & SPICES
1200. EUCALYPTUS OIL
1201. EXTRACTION OF OIL FROM OIL SEED EXPANDEREXTRUSION TECHNOLOGY)
1202. FAT LIQUOR SULPHATED OIL
1203. FLAVOURS FOR FOOD
1204. GARLIC OIL & POWDER
1205. GINGER OIL, SANDALWOOD OIL AND NAGARMOTHA OIL
1206. GINGER OIL
1207. GINGER OIL & GINGER DUST
1208. INTEGERATED WAX COMPLEX
1209. IONONE FROM LEMON GRASS OIL
1210. JASMINE & LILLY FLOWER OIL
1211. LEMON GRASS OIL
1212. LIQUID PARAFFIN
1213. LUBE OIL & GREASE
1214. LUBRICATING OIL
1215. MENTHOL CRYSTALS
1216. MENTHOL OIL & CRYSTAL
1217. MICRO CRYSTALLINE WAX
1218. MUSTARD OIL (EDIBLE OIL)
1219. OIL FROM ARTEMISIA HERBS
1220. PALM OIL CRUSHING UNIT
1221. PAN MASALA
1222. PARAFFIN WAX
1223. PARAFFIN WAX FROM SLACK WAX
1224. REFINED OIL-SUN FLOWER OIL, GROUNDNUT OIL, STAFF FLOWER OIL & COTTON SEED OIL
1225. REFINED VEGETABLE OIL
1226. RECLAMATION OF USED ENGINE OIL
1227. RICE BRAN OIL (R.B.O)
1228. ROSE OIL EXTRACTION
1229. SMOKE LESS CANDLE
1230. SPICE OIL & OLEORESINS
1231. SOLVENT EXTRACTION PLANT (OIL CAKE BASED)
1232. SYNTHETIC ALMOND OIL
1233. SYNTHETIC TALLOW
1234. SYNTHETIC GHEE
1235. VEGETABLE OIL EXTRACTION & REFINING
1236. WADDING OIL (100%) FOR WADDING OF COTTON HOSIERY CLOTH IN DYEING PROCESS
1237. WAX EMULSION FOR TEXTILE
1238. WAX FLOOR POLISH

PAINT, ENAMEL, SOLVENTS, THINNERS, INKS & VARNISH

1239. ACRYLIC EMULSION PAINTS
1240. ALUMINIUM PAINT
1241. AUTOMOBILE PAINTS
1242. BALL POINT PEN REFILL INK
1243. BITUMINIOUS ROAD EMULSION
1244. BITUMEN
1245. BITUMINIOUS FELTS FOR WATER & DAMP PROOFING
1246. BITUMINIOUS ROAD EMULSION RAPID MEDIUM & SLOW SETTING
1247. BUFFING & POLISHING
1248. CEMENT PAINT FOR WHITE & GREY CEMENT

1249. DISPERSANT
1250. DRY DISTEMPER
1251. DRY DISTEMPER & CEMENT PAINT
1252. DUPLICATING INK BLACK FOR GESTNER DUPLICATOR
1255. EMULSION PAINTS (WATER BASED)
1256. HAMMERTONE PAINT
1257. INSULATING VARNISH & WIRE ENAMEL
1258. IRON OXIDE PIGMENTS
1259. INSULATING VARNISH (POLY VINYL BUTYRAL BASED, FFC GRADE)
1260. LIME COLOUR (CEMENT COLOUR)
1261. SYNTHETIC RED OXIDE FOR FLOORINGS
1262. SOLVENT & THINNERS
1263. MARKING INKS (WATER PROOF)
1264. METAL NAPHTHANATE (AS DRIER FOR PAINTS)
1265. N.C.PUTTY
1266. OFFSET PRINTING INK
1267. OIL BOUND DISTEMPER PAINT
1268. PAINT BRUSHES
1269. PAINT REMOVERS
1270. PAINT INDUSTRY
1271. PAINT & VARNISH
1272. PICTURE VARNISH
1273. POWDER COATING PAINT
1274. PRINTING INKS (OFFSET, FLEXO & ROTO GRAVURE)
1275. PRIMER PAINT & ENAMEL PAINT
1276. PUTTY & WATER PROOFING PAINT
1277. PRINTING INKS (FLEXO-GRAPHIC INK)
1278. PUTTY (METAL CASEMENT)
1279. RED OXIDE PRIMER (ANTI CORROSIVE)
1280. REFRECTORY PAINT (GRAPHITE BASED)
1281. SCREEN PRINTING INKS
1282. SILK SCREEN PRINTING INK FORMULATION FOR PLASTIC, PAPER, CLOTH
1283. STAMP & PAD INK
1284. STOVING PAINT
1285. SPIRIT SOLUBLE MALEIC RESIN
1286. TEXTURE PAINT
1287. THINNERS AND ITS ALLIED PRODUCTS
1288. TONER INK
1289. VARNISH THINNER (SOLVENT)
1290. VACUUM METALLIZING LACQUERS
1291. WOOD PRIMER

PHARMACEUTICAL, DRUGS, AYURVEDIC/HERBAL COSMETICS & MEDICINES, HOMOEOPATHIC MEDICINES, DISPOSABLE SYRINGE, DENTAL COLLEGE & FINE CHEMICALS ETC.

1292. AROMATIC PILLS
1293. ASPIRIN
1294. AYURVEDIC PAIN BALM OINTMENTS
1295. AYURVEDIC CHURAN AND TABLETS
1296. AYURVEDIC TABLETS (HAJMOLA TYPE)
1297. AYURVEDIC/HERBAL PHARMACY
1298. AYURVEDIC SHERBATS
1299. AYURVEDIC PRODUCTS
1300. BULK DRUGS (E.O.U)
1301. BLOOD BAGS
1302. CALCIUM GLUCONATE
1303. CAPSULE, TABLET & INJECTION WITH MODERN INSTRUMENTS
1304. CASHEW FENI
1305. CHLOROQUINONE PHOSPHATE (BULK DRUGS)
1306. CLINICAL THERMOMETER
1307. DENTAL CLINIC

1308. DENTAL COLLEGE
1309. DENTAL GRADE EUGENOL
1310. DEXTROSE MONOHYDRATE, LIQUID GLUCOSE
1311. DEHYDRATED ONION & ONION POWDER
1312. DEXTROSE POWDER (ANHYDROUS FROM STARCH)
1314. DEXTROSE SALINE SOLUTION
1315. DISTILLERY (I.M.F.L)
1316. DISPOSABLE NEEDLES FOR SYRINGES
1317. DISPRIN
1318. DISTILLED WATER
1319. EMPTY HARD GELATINE CAPSULES
1320. FILLING & PACKING OF CAPSULES
1321. GLUCOSE - D - POWDER
1322. GLYCERINE
1323. HERBAL COSMETICS
1324. HERBAL SHAMPOO
1325. HERBAL HAIR OILS (AYURVEDIC)
1326. HOMOE & BIO-MEDICINES WITH MOTHER TINCTURE
1327. HOMOEPATHIC MEDICINES
1328. HYPODERMIC NEEDLES
1329. I.V. FLUIDS
1330. IBUPROFEN
1331. INFUSION & TRANSFUSION SETS (I.V. SET)
1332. INJECTABLE FOR PHARMACEUTICALS
1333. INJECTION AMPOULES PACKAGING BOX
1334. INTEGERATED SURGICAL COTTON
1335. ICE MAKING PLANT
1336. ICE & COLD STORAGE
1337. LACTOSE & BY PRODUCTS PROCESSING FROM MILK
1338. LICHEN (JATAMANSI CHARILA)
1339. LIQUID GLUCOSE AND ITS BY-PRODUCTS
1340. L-LYSINE MONOHYDRO CHLORIDE
1341. LIQUID GLUCOSE FROM POTATOES
1342. MEDICAL COLLEGE
1343. NICOTINE FROM TOBACCO WASTE
1344. OINTMENT-AYURVEDIC (YELLOW & WHITE)
1345. PHARMACEUTICAL AND FOOD GRADE GELATINE
1346. PHARMACEUTICAL INDUSTRY (TABLETS, CAPSULES, LIQUID, GEL, OINTMENT POWDER INJECTABLE)
1347. PHARMACEUTICAL UNIT (EOU) WITH FORMULA TIONS, INJECTABLES, ETC. PYRIDINE & DERIVATIVES
1348. SALT (IODIZED SALT)
1349. SALINE & INJECTION WATER
1350. SALINE WATER & DEXTROSE SOLUTION (I.V.FLUID IN PLASTIC BOTTLES)
1351. SORBITOL
1352. STARCH (MAIZE)
1353. SURGICAL ADHESIVE PLASTER
1354. SURGICAL BANDAGES
1355. SURGICAL GLOVES
1357. SURGICAL COTTON
1358. SURGICAL COTTON AND BANDAGE
1359. SYNTHETIC CAMPHOR POWDER
1360. TABLETS & CAPSULES
1361. TISSUE CULTURE
1362. TINCTURE FROM RECTIFIED SPIRIT
1363. TRIMETHOPIME
1364. VETERENARY MEDICINES (ONLY FORMULATIONS)
1365. VITAMIN 'C', SORBITOL' ANHYDROUS DEXTROSE, STARCH

PULP, PAPER, STRAW/GREY BOARD, KRAFT PAPER, PACKAGING, PAPER CARRY BAGE, PAPER FROM AGRO WASTE & STATIONERY ETC.

1366. AMMONIA PAPER
1367. AUTOMATIC BOOK BINDING
1368. ADHESIVE (FEVICOL TYPE)
1369. ALL PIN & GEM CLIPS
1370. CARBON PAPER
1371. CARD BOARD
1372. CARBON LESS PAPER
1373. CELLPHANE PAPER
1374. COMPUTER FORMS & SECURITY PRINTING PRESS
1375. CORRUGATED BOARD & BOX (PRINTED & LAMINATED)
1376. CORRUGATED BOARD AND BOXES FROM FROM CARD BOARDS
1377. CORRUGATED CARTONS FROM PLAIN PAPERS
1378. CORRUGATRED PACKING & MATERIAL (BULB & TUBES PACKING)
1379. DESK TOP PUBLISHING
1380. DEFOAMING AGENT FOR PAPER PLANT
1381. DRINKING STRAW PAPER
1382. D.T.P CUM OFFSET PRESS
1383. EGG TRAYS
1384. EXERCISE NOTE BOOK, REGISTER AND PAD
1385. FLEXOGRAPHIC INK
1386. GREETING CARD BY OFFSET PRESS
1387. HAND MADE PAPER FILTER PAPER
1388. HARD BOARD
1389. INJECTION AMPOULES PACKAGING BOXES
1390. INSULATIING PAPER
1391. KRAFT PAPER
1392. KRAFT PAPER FROM BAGASSE
1393. LAMINATED PACKAGING PAPER WITH PRINTING
1394. LAMINATION & COATING ON PAPER
1395. M.G. PAPER FROM WASTE PAPER
1396. MILL PAPER FROM WASTE PAPER
1397. MILL BOARD FROM RICE & WHEAT STRAWS
1398. MILL BOARD FROM WASTE PAPER
1399. MINI PAPER PLANT FROM SISAL
1400. MINI PAPER PLANT
1401. MULTI WALL PAPER SACKS
1402. NEWS PAPER FOR CHILDREN
1403. NEWS PRINT PAPER FROM RICE STRAW BAGASSE
1404. NEWS PAPER CHILDRENS
1405. NEWS PRINT PAPER
1406. OFFSET AND TREADLE TYPE PRINTING PRESS
1407. MILL BOARD BASED ON RICE STRAW
1408. PAPER AND BOARD FROM STRAW
1409. PAPER & PAPER PRODUCTS
1410. PAPER ENVELOPES
1411. PAPER CARRY BAGS
1412. PAPER BOARD CARTON
1413. PAPER CONES FOR LOUD SPEAKERS
1414. PAPER FROM AKRA
1415. PAPER FROM BAGASSE WITH CORRUGATED BOARD & BOXES
1416. PAPER FROM BAMBOO
1417. PAPER GLASSES FOR BEVERAGES
1418. PAPER FROM RICE HUSK & WHEAT HUSK
1419. PAPER FROM TREE BARK, EUCALYPRUS WOOD
1420. PAPER PRODUCTS
1421. PAPER PLANT (WHITE WRITING & NEWS PAPER FOR PULP & WASTE PAPER)
1422. PAPER PLATES, PAPER GLASS
1423. PAPER CONES & TUBES
1425. PAPER PLANT WITH DTP & PRINTING & PUBLISHING UNIT
1426. PAPER BASED PHENOLIC SHEET
1427. PAPER CUP FOR ICE CREAM
1428. PAPER TUBES SPIRAL WINDING COMPOSIT CONTAINER
1429. PAPER LABLE FOR BEER BOTTLES
1430. PARTICLE BOARD & BLACK BOARD WITH SANDING & LAMINATION OF PARTICLE BOARD
1431. PARTICLE BOARD FROM RICE HUSK
1432. POUCH FILLING & MAKING FOR TOMATO SAUCE
1433. POUCH MAKING &

GRAVURE PRINTING
1434. PROCESSING OF PAPER FOR FEEDING IN COMPUTER
1435. PULP FROM BAMBOO & WOOD
1436. PAPER FILES
1437. PLAYING CARDS
1438. ROSIN SIZING AGENT (FOR PAPER PLANT)
1439. SAND PAPER
1440. SANITRY NAPKINS
1441. SILICON COATED PAPER
1442. STENCIL PAPER
1443. STRAW BOARD AND GREY BOARD
1444. STRAW BOARD & MILL BOARD
1445. STRAW BOARD AND PAPER BOARD
1446. TISSUE PAPER FACIAL
1447. TISSUE MOIST TOILETERY CLEANSING TISSUE AND RELATED PRODUCTS
1448. TISSUE PAPER ROLLS
1449. TETRA PACK FOR MILK PACKAGING, GHEE & OTHER LIQUIDS
1450. TOILET PAPER ROLLS
1451. TOILET PAPER & NAPKINS
1452. WAX COATED PRINTED PAPER
1453. WET FACE FRESHNER TISSUE
1454. WHITE WRITING & PRINTING PAPER
1455. WRITING & PRINTING PAPER (PAPER MILLS)

PLASTIC, B.O.P.P, ACRYLIC, DISPOSABLE PLASTIC PRODUCTS, PET PRODUCTS, P.V.C, H.D.P.E, P.P, L.D.P.E., P.U, A.B.S, THERMOFOARMING, MASTER BATCHES, & POLYMER AND RUBBER PRODUCTS, TYRE, TUBE, ADHESIVE, SHEET, COIR & MANY OTHERS

1456. ABS GRANULES FROM ABS SCRAPS FROM OLD T.V. CABINETS, WHITE GOODS ETC.
1457. ACRYLIC BEADS
1458. ACRYLIC COPOLYMER EMULSION
1459 ACRYLIC LATEX
1460. ACRYLIC SHEET
1461. ACRYLIC SHEET & MOULDED PRODUCTS
1462. ACRYLIC TEETH
1463. AUTO TUBES
1464. AUTO FLAPS FOR TRUCKS & BUSES
1465. AUTO TYRES & TUBES
1466. BABY BOTTLES (PLASTIC) WITH WHITESILICON RUBBER NIPPLES
1467. B.O.P.P. FILM
1468. B.O.P.P. PRESSURE SENSITIVE SELF ADHESIVE TAPE
1469. BABY NIPPLE (SILICON)
1470. BABY NIPPLE (BIG SIZE)
1471. BALLOON PLASTIC ADVERTISING
1472. BLISTER FILM PVC
1473. BLISTER PACKAGING & POUCH PAKAGING
1474. BLOW MOULDING PLASTIC CONTAINER
1475. COATING ON METALIZED POLYESTER FILM/METALISED PAPER/ ALIMINIUM FOIL
1476. COATING ON PLASTIC (ELECTROLYSIS) & GLASS
1477. COIR FOAM (RUBBERISED)
1478. COLOUR COATING ON PLASTICS
1479. COLOUR MASTER BATCHES FOR VARIOUS PLASTICS
1480. CYCLE TYRES AND TUBES
1481. DISPOSABLE PLASTIC CUPS GLASSES, ETC.
1482. DISPOSABLE PLASTIC SYRINGES & NEEDLES
1483. DISPOSABLE PLASTIC SYRINGES
1484. DOUGH MOULDING COMPOUND (D.M.C)
1485. EPOXY RESIN
1486. EXPANDED POLYESTRENE MOULDING (THERMOCOLE)
1487. F.R.P AUTO,SCOOTER ROOFS & CEILINGS
1488. F.R.P PRODUCTS (HELMET, WASHBASIN SHEETS, ROOFING SHEETS)
1489. FIBRE REINFORCED PLASTIC (HIGH PRESSURE MOULDING WITH SMC BMC AND DMC)
1490. FIELD RUBBER CONVERTED TO THE 60% LATEX RUBBER
1491. FLEXIBLE P.U. FOAM
1492. FORMALDEHYDE CROCKERY & OTHER ITEMS
1493. FORMALDEHYDE RESIN (UREA, PHENOL,MELEMINE)
1494. GASKET SHEET
1495. GUM BOTTLE (PVC)
1496. GLASS BEADS
1497. HDPE COATED PAPER SACK
1498. H.D.P.E. BAGS
1499. H.D.P.E. CONTAINERS (BLOW MOULDING)
1500. H.D.P.E. CONTAINER, POLY JARS BY INJECTION MOULDING (FOOD GRADE)
1501. H.D.P.E. JERRY CANS
1502. HDPE MANUFACTURING FROM ETHYLALCOHOL
1503. H.D.P.E PIPE AND FITTINGS
1504. H.D.P.E. PIPES
1505. H.D.P.E PRINTED BAGS
1506. H.D.P.E TWINES AND ROPES
1507. H.D.P.E. & L.D.P.E PIPES AND FITTINGS
1508. H.D.P.E/PP BOX STRAPPING
1509. H.D.P.E/PP WOVEN SACKS USING PLAIN LOOMS
1510. HOLOGRAM STICKERS-3D
1511. H.M BAG PLANT WITH PRINTING UNIT
1512. HAWAI CHAPPALS (RUBBER)
1513. I.V PLASTIC BOTTLE
1514. ICE CREAM CUP (PLASTIC)
1515. INJECTION MOULDED AUTO COMPONENTS
1516. INJECTION & BLOW MOULDED PLASTIC PRODUCTS
1517. INJECTION MOULDED PLASTIC PRODUCTS
1518. INTEGERATED COMPLEX ESTER'S & ALLIED PRODUCTS (D.O.P,D.B.P, & ETHYL ACETATE, BUYTL ACETATE, WIRE ENAMELS, JELLY CABLE COMPOUND)
1519. L.D.P.E. (LOW DENSITY POLY ETHYLENE) GRANULES FROM VIRGIN (L.D.P.E. RESIN)
1520. INTEGERATED SURGICAL RUBBER GOODS INDUSTRY
1521. INJECTION MOULDED PLASTIC BALLS
1522. L.D.P.E FROM ETHYL ALCOHOL
1523. LDPE MOULDED PRODUCTS
1524. LAMINATION OF COEXTRUSION MULTILAYER FILM IN ROLL FORM
1525. LATEX RUBBER
1526. LATEX RUBBER CONDOM
1527. MASTER BATCHES (COLOURED, P.V.C, L.D.P.E, H.D.P.E, ETC.)
1528. MELAMINE FORMALHYDE RESIN
1529. MOULDED LUGGAGE
1530. MULTI-LAYER (3 LAYER BAGS)
1531. MULTI-LAYER (3 LAYER) FILM WITH LAMINATION & PRINTING
1532. OIL SEAL
1533. PET BOTTLE/CONTAINERS
1534. PET BOTTLES FROM PRE FORM
1535. PET BOTTLE & MINERAL WATER
1536. PET PRE-FORM FROM PET RESIN
1537. PET PRE-FORM CUM PET BOTTLES
1538. PET PRE-FORM PET BOTTLES CUM MINERAL WATERS
1539. POLY CARBONATE RESIN
1540. PTFE COMPONENTS
1541. PU/PVC SOLE FOR SPORT SHOE BY IMPORTED M/C.
1542. PVC BATTERY SEPARATOR
1543. P.V.C COMPOUNDS (FRESH)
1544. P.V.C COMPOUNDS (SCRAP)
1545. P.V.C ELECTRICAL INSULATING TAPE
1546. P.V.C. EXTRUSION PROFILES
1547. P.V.C FITTINGS
1548. P.V.C FLEXIBLE FUSIBLE POWDER HEAT FUSIBLE POWDER
1549. P.V.C GRANULES (FOR

INSULATION & SHEETS GRADES)
1550. P.V.C GRANULES FROM PVC SCRAPS (WITH POLLUTION CONTROL)
1551. P.V.C HOSES
1552. P.V.C LEATHER CLOTH
1553. P.V.C FLEXIBLE PIPES
1554. P.V.C PIPES AND FITTINGS
1555. POLYTHENE BAGS (PRINTED)
1556. PVC PLASTICS FILM SHEET SOFT/RIGID
1557. PVC RESIN AND COMPOUND
1558. PVC RULAR
1559. PVC STABLIZERS (SINGLE PACK SYSTEM)
1560. PVC WIRE AND CABLES
1561. PAPER BASED PHENOLIC SHEET FOR ELECTRICAL
1562. PHENOL FORMALDEHYDE RESIN
1563. PHENOLIC RESIN
1564. PLASTIC BEADS FROM PLASTIC SCRAPS
1565. PLASTIC BUTTONS
1566. PLASTIC CANS
1567. PLASTIC COLLAPSIBLE TUBE
1568. PLASTIC CORRUGATED SHEET & BOXES
1569. PLASTIC FILM AND SHEETS WITH PRINTING FLEXO & ROTO/LDPE/HDPE/PP/HM/PVC
1570. PLASTIC FILTER MASTER BATCH & OTHER MASTER BATCHES FOR VARIOUS PLASTICS
1571. PLASTIC JERRY CANS
1572. PLASTIC GRANULES OR POWDER FROM PLASTIC SCRAP
1573. PLASTIC INJECTION MOULDED T.V. CABINETS
1574. PLASTIC ITEMS MANUFAC TURE FROM POWDER MELAMINE
1575. PLASTIC GOODS
1576. PLASTIC PIPES & TARPAULINES
1577. PLASTIC SHEET FROM SCRAP
1578. PLASTIC PLANT (BLOW MOULDING & INJECTION MOULDING)
1579. PLASTIC PRODUCTS (GOLD, SILVER, NICKEL)
1580. PLASTIC TOYS
1581. POLYESTER BEADING
1582. POLYESTER FILM
1583. POLYTHENE BAGS & AUTOMATIC PRINTING
1584. POLYTHENE PRINTED BAGS
1585. POLYURETHANE FOAM AND ITS PRODUCTS
1586. PROPYLENE FILM (PRINTED) & BAG MANUFACTURING
1587. PLASTIC MATS
1588. RAINBOW COLOUR ON PVC FILM & SHEET
1589. RED MUD PVC PIPES AND FITTINGS
1590. RE-RUBBERISED OF SOLID TYPE
1591. RESIN COATED SAND REXINE
1592. REXINE CLOTH & ALLIED PRODUCTS
1593. RUBBER ADHESIVE
1594. RUBBER AUTO PARTS
1595. RUBBER BELTING
1596. RUBBER MOULDING UNIT INCLUDING LINING RUBBER SHEETING
1597. RUBBER RECLAIMING
1598. RUBBER ROLLERS FOR TEXTILE MILLS & PAPER INDUSTRIES
1599. RUBBER & PLASTIC SHEETS, MATS & FLAPS
1600. RUBBER SHEET AND ALLIED HOSPITAL RUBBER GOODS
1601. RUBBERIZED PVC GASKET
1602. RUBBERISED COIR
1603. RUBBER COMPOUND FOR AUTOMOBILES
1604. SAFETY BELTS
1605. SILVER AND GOLD PLATING ON PVC AND NYLON-6
1606. SILICONE RUBBER NIPPLES/ TEATS
1607. SPECTACLE FRAMES (PLASTIC)
1608. SPUNGE RUBBER
1609. SURGICAL EXAMINATION GLOVES
1610. SYNTHETIC PEARL COATING ON POLYSTYRENE BEADS
1611. SYNTHETIC RUBBER ADHESIVE
1612. TEFLON MANUFACTURING
1613. TEFLON TAPE
1614. TEFLON TAPES & CABLES
1615. THERMOCOLE SHEET AND MOULDED PRODUCTS EXPANDED POLYESTERENE EXTRUSION PROFILES
1616. THERMOFORMED PACKAGING (BLISTER PACKAGING & POUCH PACKAGING)
1617. THERMOPLASTIC POLYURETHANE
1618. THERMOFORMED CUPS, PLATES & GLASS WITH HIPS SHEET
1619. THERMOCOLE
1620. THERMOCOLE BASED DISPOSABLE GLASS, CUPS & PLATES
1621. TOOTH BRUSHES
1622. TOY BALLOON, DECORA TIVE & INDUSTRIAL BALLOONS
1623. TREAD RUBBER
1624. TYRE RETREADING (HOT)
1625. TYRE RETREADING BY COLD PROCESS
1626. TYRE TUBES & FLAPS
1627. TYRE & TUBES
1628. UNSATURATED POLYESTER FOR REXINE
1629. V-BELT AND FAN BELT
1630. VINYL ASBESTOS AND PVC WALL PAPER
1631. VITON (FLUORO ELASTOMER)

SOAP, COSMETICS & PERFUMS

1632. ACID SLURRY, SYNTHETIC DETERGENT POWDER
1632. ACID SLURRY
1633. AGARBATTI SYNTHETIC, PERFUMERY COMPOUND
1634. AFTER SHAVE LOTION
1635. ANTISEPTIC CREAM
1636. BETA IONONE
1637. BLEACHING POWDER
1638. BLUE DETERGENT POWDER
1639. CLEANING POWDER (VIMTYPE)
1640. COLD CREAM
1641. COLOURED FLAME & PERFUMED CANDLES (RED, BLUE, GREEN FLAME)
1642. COSMETIC INDUSTRY (MODERN)
1643. COSMETIC INDUSTRY (SHAMPOO, SPRAY PERFUME, TALCUM POWDER
1644. DETERGENT POWDER (ARIEL TYPE)
1645. DETERGENT POWDER (NIRMA TYPE) FULLY AUTOMATIC PLANT
1646. DETERGENT WASHING POWDER
1647. FISH OIL SOAP
1648. GLYCERINE TRANSPARENT SOAP
1649. HAIR REMOVING CREAM
1650. HERBAL COSMETICS
1651. HERBAL SHAMPO & CREAM
1652. HERBAL/AYURVEDIC COSMETICS
1653. INCENSE POWDER, INCENSE STICKS & INCENSE CAKE
1654. OPTICAL WHITENERS
1655. ROSE OIL EXTRACTION
1656. SHAMPOOS (COCONUT OIL BASED COLD PROCESS)
1657. SHAVING CREAM
1658. SINDUR (KUMKUM)
1659. SOAP COATED PAPER
1660. SPRAY DRIED DETERGENT POWDER
1661. STAIN REMOVER
1662. TALCUM POWDER (FACE & TOILET POWDER)
1663. TOILET AND HERBAL SOAP
1664. TOOTH PASTE & POWDER
1665. WASHING DETERGENT POWDER AND WASHING SOAP
1666. WASHING POWDER LIQUID DETERGENTS, LOTION & SHAMPOO

TEXTILE INDUSTRIES, READYMADE GARMENTS, COTTON, DYEING, BLEACHING, CLOTH, HOSIERY, POWER LOOM, HAND LOOM, WOOLLEN, SILK, SOCKS, SURGICAL COTTON & MANY OTHERS

1667. ANGORA RABBIT WOOL
1668. BUCKRAM
1669. CANVAS SHOES, JUNGLE BOOT, BOOT RUBBER KNEES & BOOT COMBAT
1670. CARPET FROM COTTON WASTE
1671. CERAMIC THREAD GUIDE
1672. COTTON BUDS/SWABS
1673. COTTON FROM WASTE YARN
1674. COTTON ROLLS
1675. COTTON SPIDERS FOR LOUD SPEAKERS
1676. DENIM CLOTH
1677. DENIM CLOTH (INTEGERATED UNIT WITH BLEACHING, DYEING AND PRINTING)
1678. DISPERSENT FOR TEXTILE
1679. DYEING & BLEACHING
1680. DYEING OF HANK YARN
1681. EMULSIFIER FOR WOOL BATCHING OIL
1682. EMBROIDERY ON FABRICS
1683. GARMENT DYEING, WASHING & STITCHING (JEANS, JACKETS, SKIRTS & SHIRTS)
1684. GOVES KNITTING
1685. GUNNY BAGS
1687. HDPE WOVEN SACKS
1688. HDPE TARPAULINS USING PLAIN LOOM WITH LAMINATION
1689. HDPE/PP WOVEN SACKS USING CIRCULAR LOOMS
1690. HOSIERY CLOTH (COTTON) PROCESSING (BLEACHING, DYEING, FINISHING OF CLOTH)
1691. HOSIERY INDUSTRY
1692. HOSIERY MERCERISING
1693. HOSIERY PRODUCTS LIKE VEST, BRIEF, T-SHIRTS & SOCKS
1694. JACQUARD FABRICS
1695. JUTE COIR, GRASS ROPE/ SUTLI MAKING
1696. JUTE FELT
1697. JUTE TWINFS
1698. KNITTED FABRICS
1699. LAMINATED JUTE BAGS
1700. LAMINATION OF HDPE WOVEN CLOTH (JUTE,COTTON, PAPER)
1701. NYLON YARN CRIMPING, DOUBLING AND BLEACHING
1702. PIGMENT BINDER FOR TEXTILE PRINTING
1704. POLYESTER RESIN FOR WIRE ENAMEL
1705. POLYESTER RESIN
1706. POLYESTER YARN FROM WASTE POLYESTER ZIP FASTENERS
1707. POWER LOOM
1708. READYMADE GARMENTS & HOSIERY
1709. READYMADE GARMENTS MERCHANDISE
1710. READYMADE GARMENTS & COVERS
1711. READYMADE GARMENTS & EMBROIDERY OF GOWNS, SHIRTS, BLOUSES, T-SHIRTS ETC. (ONLY LADIES)
1712. READYMADE SALWAR SUIT
1713. RECOVERY OF NYLON FROM NYLON WASTE
1714. ROTARY PRINTING AND DYEING ON COTTON, SYNTHETIC TEXTILE
1715. SANITARY NAPKINS
1716. SCREEN PRINTING ON COTTON CLOTH
1717. SEWING THREAD REELS & BALLS MAKING INDUSTRIES
1718. SCREEN PRINTING ON COTTON, POLYESTER & ACRYLIC
1719. SHAWLS (WOOLLEN)
1720. SHOE LACES
1721. SILK FABRICS ON HANDLOOM
1722. SOCKS KNITTING
1723. SPINNING, DOUBLING DYEING MERCERISING & BLEACHING OF COTTON YARN
1724. SPINNING & CARDING OF WOOL INTO YARNS
1725. STARCH BOOK BINDING CLOTH
1726. SURAT JARI
1727. SURGICAL COTTON & BANDAGE
1728. SYNTHETIC TEXTILE INDUSTRY(SUITING, SHIRTING, SAREES) TERRY CLOTH
1729. T-SHIRTS
1730. TOWELS, BED SHEET COVERS
1731. TERRY TOWEL
1732. TERRY FABRICS WEAVING UNIT
1733. TEXTILE AUXILLIARIES & CHEMICALS
1734. TEXTILE BLEACHING, DYEING & FINISHING & PRINTING OF COTTON FABRICS
1735. TEXTILE (HOSIERY)
1736. TEXTILE MILL
1737. TEXTILE DYEING & PRINTING
1738. TEXTILE PRINTING (JOB WORK)
1739. TEXTILE PIGMENT PRINTING BINDER
1740. TOWEL (TERRY)
1741. VELVET CLOTH BY FLOCKING PROCESS
1742. VISCOSE STAPLE FIBRE
1743. WADDING OIL (100%) FOR WADDING OF COTTON HOSIERY CLOTH IN THE DYEING PROCESS
1744. WEAVING OF DASUTI CLOTH WITH PRINTING, DYEING, EMBROIDERY & FINISHING
1745. WASHING OF JEANS & OTHER GARMENTS
1746. WORSTED WOOLLEN YARN CLOTH
1747. ZARI GLITTER SALMA SITARA OF PLASTIC FILM

INFOTECH/IT, HOSPITALITY, HOSPITAL, COLLEGE, SCHOOL, MEDICAL, ENTERTAINMENT CLUB, WARE HOUSING & REAL ESTATE, PROJECTS

1748. AMUSEMENT PARK
1749. AMUSEMENT PARK CUM WATER PARK
1750. BANQUET HALL
1751. CALL CENTER (DOMESTIC)
1752. CALL CENTER (INTERNATIONAL)
1753. CHILDREN RECREATION CENTRE
1754. COLD STORAGE
1755. COMMUNITY HALL
1756. COMPUTER EDUCATION INSTITUTE
1757. COMPUTER SOFTWARE
1758. COLLEGE
1759. CYBER CAFE
1760. DENTAL CLINIC
1761. DENTAL COLLEGE
1762. DIAGONOSTIC CENTRE
1763. E-COMMERCE/BUSINESS
1764. E-SCHOOL (Rs. 5000/-)
1765. ENGINEERING COLLEGE
1766. ENTERTAINMENT CLUB
1767. ENTERTAINMENT CLUB, HOLIDAY RESORT, 4 STAR HOTEL, AMUSEMENT PARK CUM WATER PARK, MUSHROOM & ITS PRODUCTS, FISH FARMING, LAKE FOR BOATING, DEER PARK
1768. FASHION TECHNOLOGY INSTITUTE
1769. FAST FOOD PARLOUR
1770. FIVE STAR HOTEL
1771. FOOD PARLOUR
1772. FRANCHISE TRAINING PROGRAMME FOR IIT & ENGINEERING ENTRANCE EXAMS.
1773. GOLF COURSE
1774. HEALTH CLUB, BEAUTY PARLOUR
1775. HEALTH CLUB AND FITNESS CENTER
1776. HEALTH RESORTS
1777. HOLIDAY RESORTS
1778. HOLIDAY RESORT CUM

Above all the Detailed Project Report are available at *"ENGINEERS INDIA RESEARCH INSTITUTE"*. 4449, Nai Sarak (D), Main Road Delhi - 110 006

● Ph : 91-11-23918117, 2391 6431, 2392 0361, 31082370 ● Fax : 91-11- 2391 6431

● E-Mail : eirisidi@bol.net.in

ENTERTAINMENT CLUB WITH 4 STAR HOTEL
1779. HOSPITALS
1780. ICE CREAM PARLOUR
1781. INTERNET SERVICE PROVIDER (I.S.P.)
1782. MEDICAL COLLEGE
1783. MEDICAL COLLEGE, HOSPITAL & RESEARCH INSTITUTE
1784. MEDICAL TRANSCRIPTION CENTRE
1785. MENTAL RETARDATION HOSPITAL & CEREBRAL PALSY
1786. MOTEL/SMALL HOTEL
1787. MULTISTOREY COMMERCIAL COMPLEX
1788. MULTISTOREY RESIDENTIAL COMPLEX
1789. NURSERY SCHOOL
1790. NATURE CARE CENTRE
1791. NURSING HOME
1792. ONLINE SHOPPING MALL (RS. 5000/- REPORT)
1793. PORTAL
1794. REHABILITATION CENTRE FOR AGED & NEEDY PERSONS
1795. RESIDENTIAL CUM COMMERCIAL COMPLEX
1796. RESTAURANT
1797. RESTAURANT WITH PUB
1798. SCHOOL (PRIMARY)
1799. SCHOOL (HIGHER SECONDARY)
1800. THREE STAR HOTEL
1801. TOURIST CLUB
1802. TRAINING INSTITUTE FOR MEDICAL TRANSCRIPTION
1803. VIDEO FILM STUDIO
1804. WARE HOUSE
1805. WEBSITE DESIGN & E-MAIL REGISTERING

AGRO BASED INDUSTRIES

1806. COAL BRIQUETTES FROM AGROWASTE
1807. FURFURALFROM RICEHULL
1808. MUSHROOM CULTIVATION & PROCESSING (BUTTON)
1809. MUSHROOM GROWING & PROCESSING WITH AIR CONDITIONING
1810. MUSHROOM CULTIVATION & PROCESSING UNIT DEHYDRATION & PACKAGING OF OYSTER & PADDY STRAW MUSHROOMS
1811. ORGANIC MANURE
1812. PAPAYA CULTIVATION
1813. PAPAYA & TOMATO CULTIVATION
1814. PROCESSING & UTILISATION OF COCONUT
1815. PROCESSING OF SHEEP HAIR TO PRODUCE WOOL

BAKERY, CONFECTIONERY & FOOD PRODUCTS

1816. AGROLACTOR SOYA MILK
1817. APPLE FRUIT JUICE WITH CANNING BOTTLING
1818. AYURVEDIC SHARBAT
1819. BAKERY UNIT (PASTRIES, BREAD, BUNS, CAKE, TOFFEE ETC.)
1820. BAKING POWDER
1821. BANANA & ITS BY PRODUCTS
1822. BANANA POWDER
1823. BANANA WAFERS
1824. BANANA CULTIVATION
1825. BEER INDUSTRY
1826. DEHULLING OF JAUN FOR BEER
1827. BEER & WINE
1828. BEER, ALCOHOL, IMFL
1829. BESEN PLANT
1830. BISCUIT PLANT
1831. BREAD & BISCUIT PLANT
1832. BOTTLING PLANT COUNTRY LIQUOR FROM RECTIFIED SPIRIT
1833. BRANDY
1834. BREAD RUSKS
1835. CANNED FRUITS & VEGETABLES
1836. CANNING & PRESERVATION OF MEAT
1837. CANNING & PRESERVATION OF VEGETABLES
1838. CANNING OF MANGO PULP & MANGO SLICES
1839. CARBONATED BEVERAGS
1840. CASHEW FENI
1841. CASHEW NUT (DRIED & FRIED)
1842. CATTLE BREEDING
1843. CATTLE BREEDING & DAIRY FARM TO PRODUCE MILK
1844. CATTLE FEED FROM TAPIOCA
1845. CHEWING GINGER & AMLOKI
1846. CHEWING GUM
1847. CHILLI SAUCE
1848. CHILLI POWDER
1849. CHOCOLATE
1850. CIDER PLANT
1851. COCOA POWDER
1852. COCOA BUTTER & COCOA POWDER
1853. COCONUT SHELL POWDER
1854. COCONUT WATER
1855. COCONUT SWEET (WATERY)
1856. COCONUT MILK POWDER (DEHYDRATED)
1857. COCONUT PRODUCTS & BY PRODUCTS (INTEGRATED PLANT)
1858. COLD DRINK
1859. CURRY POWDER
1860. DAIRY FOR MILK PROCESSING (GHEE, BUTTER & PANEER)
1861. DAIRY PRODUCTS
1862. DAIRY PRODUCTS MILK PACKAGING IN POUCH (GHEE, BUTTER, ETC.
1863. DAIRY FARM TO PRDUCE MILK WITH PACKAGING (COW)
1864. DAIRY FARM TO PRDUCE MILK WITH PACKAGING (BUFALLOE)
1865. DAIRY FARM & MILK PRODUCTS
1866. DAL MOTH, CHANACHUR & BHUJIYA
1867. DEHYDRATION OF FRUITS & VEGETABLE
1868. DESICCATED COCONUT POWDER FROM COCONUTS
1869. DEHYDRATION & CANNINGOF FRUITS & VEGETABLES
1870. DRY FRUIT ROASTING & PACKAGING
1871. DRYING OF RED CHILLIES, HALDI, DHANIYA, PEAS & GROUND NUT
1872. EGG POWDER
1873. FISH CANNING IN TIN & POUCHES
1874. FISH DEHYRATION (DRYING OF FISH)
1875. FISH MEAL
1876. FISH PROCESSING (BEAST FREEZING PROCESSES)
1877. FLAVOURS FOR FOOD INDUSTRIES
1878. FLOUR MILL (ROLLER)
1879. FROZEN MEAT
1880. FOOD DEHYDRATION (FRUITS & VEGETABLES)
1881. FRIED & ROASTED GROUND NUT, GRAMS, PEAR ETC.
1882. FRUIT JUICE MAKING & PACKAGING IN PLASTIC CONTAINER
1883. FRUIT JUICE IN TETRA PACK (DRINKS)
1884. FRUIT JUICE, SQUASHES, SAUCE & KETCHUP, JAM, JELLY, VINEGAR ETC.
1885. GARLIC FLAKES
1886. GARLIC POWDER
1887. GHEE & BUTTER
1888. GINGER (PULVERISED)
1889. GINGER GLAZING & PRESERVATION
1890. GINGER STORAGE
1891. GINGER PROCESSING
1892. GINGER OIL & GINGER DUST
1893. GINGER POWDER (DRY) & OLEORESIN
1894. GRAPE DEHYDRATION
1895. GRAPE CULTIVATION
1896. GRAPE JUICE
1897. HONEY PROCESSING & PACKAGING
1898. ICE CREAM & ICE CANDY
1899. ICE CUBE
1900. INVERT SUGAR
1901. IDLI MIX, DOSA MIX SAMBHAR MIX, VADA MIX, GULAB JAMUN MIX
1902. INSTANT COFFEE & INSTANT TEA

1903. INSTANT NOODLES
1904. INSTANT SOUPS
1905. IODIZED SALT FROM CRUDE SALT
1906. JAM CHUTNEY PICKLES & SQUASHES
1907. KATHA MANUFACTURING
1908. LECITHIN (SOYA BASED)
1909. LEMON & ITS PRODUCTS
1910. MACARONI MANUFACTURING
1911. MACARONI, SPAGHETTI, VERMICELLI & NOODLES
1912. MAIZE & ITS BY PRODUCTS MALTING PLANT
1913. MANGO PAPPAD (AAM PAPPAD)
1914. MANGO POWDER RIPE
1915. MANGO POWDER
1916. MANGO PROCESSING & CANNING (MANGO PULP)
1917. MEAT PROCESSING (CHICKEN MUTTON)
1918. MEAT PROCESSING (BUFFALO)
1919. MENTHOL BOLD FROM MENTHOL FLAKES
1020. MILK POWDER
1921. MILK POWDER & GHEE
1922. MILK POWDER, GHEE & SPICES
1923. MILK PRESERVATION & MARKETING TO WHOLE SELLERS
1924. MILK PRESERVATION & MARKETING TO WHOLE SELLERS (IN POUCHES)
1925. MILK TOFFEE MANUFACTURES
1926. MINERAL WATER
1927. MINERAL WATER IN POUCHES
1928. MINI FLOUR MILL ATTA MAIDA, SUJI & WHEAT BRAN
1929. MITHAI/HALWAI (SWEET & NAMKEEN)
1930. MUTTON PROCESSING
1931. PAN MASALA (MEETHA, SADA, ZARDA) MAKING & PACKING
1932. PAN MASALA AND POUCH MAKING
1933. PANEER (CHEESE)
1934. PAPAD & BARIYAN
1935. PAPAD PLANT
1936. PEPSICOLA IN POLYTUBES
1937. PETHA PACKAGING
1938. PICKLES
1939. PIGGERY/MEAT/CHICKEN PROCESSING
1940. PINE APPLE JUICE CANNING
1941. POTATO & ONION POWDER
1942. POTATO & ONION FLAKES
1943. POTATO CHIPS
1944. POTATO GRANULES
1945. POUCH FILLING FOR SAUNF SUPARI ILAICHI ETC.
1946. PRESERVATION OF RAWS MANGO JUICE
1947. PROCESSED CHEESE & MARINE PDTS.
1948. PULP FROM TARMARIND
1949. READYMATE PROCESSED FOOD
1950. RICE & CORN FLAKES
1951. RICE BASMATI (TRADING)
1952. RICE POLISHING & PACKAGING IN POUCH
1953. ROASTED/SALTED/MASALA/ CASHEW NUTS ALMONDS & PEA NUT
1954. ROLLER FLOUR MILL

INFOTECH/IT PROJECTS

1955. MEDICAL TRANSCRIPTION
1956. E-COMMERCE
1957. CYBERCAFE
1958. INTERNET SERVICE PROVIDER (ISP)
1959. COMPUTER EDUCATION CENTRE
1960. PORTAL (WEBSITE DESIGN)
1961. CALL CENTRE

TERMS AND CONDITIONS

FOR INDIA

1. Please ask for Quotations of Each ***Market Survey Cum Detailed Techno Economic Feasibility Report.*** **Payable in advance through Draft/M.O./Cash in favour of 'ENGINEERS INDIA RESEARCH INSTITUTE', Delhi. Delivery by Regd.post within 2 Days. (Postage Free)**

2. Ask for the Hi-Tech Projects Monthly magazine. Each Magazine covers many Project Profiles for selection of Industry.

FOR OVERSEAS

1. Please ask for Quotations in US $ of Each ***Market Survey Cum Detailed Techno Economic Feasibility Report.*** **Payable in advance through Draft/M.O./Cash in favour of 'ENGINEERS INDIA RESEARCH INSTITUTE', Delhi. (Payable in India) Delivery by Regd.post within 4 Days.**

2. Ask for the Hi-Tech Projects Monthly magazine. Each Magazine covers many Project Profiles for selection of Industry.

ENGINEERS INDIA RESEARCH INSTITUTE

4449, Nai Sarak (D), Main Road, Delhi - 110 006 (India)
Ph:. 91-11-23918117, 23916431, 23840361, 31082370
Fax: 91-11-23916431 E-Mail : eirisidi@bol.net.in
Website:www.startindustry.com
Also at : 4/27, Roop Nagar, Near Roop Nagar No. 1 School, Delhi - 110 007 (India) Ph:. 23840361